CW00407258

The
Olduvai
Imperative

Selected titles from the YOURDON PRESS COMPUTING SERIES
Ed Yourdon, *Advisor*

ANDREWS AND LEVENTHAL   Fusion: Integrating IE, CASE, and JAD
AUGUST   Joint Application Design
BAUDIN   Manufacturing Systems Analysis with Application to Production Scheduling
BELLIN AND SUCHMAN   Structured Systems Development Manual
BLOCK   The Politics of Projects
BODDIE   Crunch Mode: Building Effective Systems on a Tight Schedule
BODDIE   The Information Asset: Rational DP Funding and Other Radical Notions
BOULDIN   Agents of Change: Managing the Introduction of Automated Tools
BRILL   Building Controls into Structured Systems
CHANG   Principles of Visual Programming Systems
COAD AND NICOLA   Object-Oriented Programming
COAD AND YOURDON   Object-Oriented Analysis, 2/E
COAD AND YOURDON   Object-Oriented Design
CONNELL AND SHAFER   Structured Rapid Prototyping
CONSTANTINE AND YOURDON   Structured Design
DeGRACE AND STAHL   Wicked Problems, Righteous Solutions
DeMARCO   Controlling Software Projects
DeMARCO   Structured Analysis and System Specification
EMBLEY, KURTZ, AND WOODFIELD   Object-Oriented Systems Analysis
FLAVIN   Fundamental Concepts in Information Modeling
FOLLMAN   Business Applications with Microcomputers
FOURNIER   Practical Guide to Structured System Development and Maintenance
GLASS   Software Conflict: Essays on the Art and Science of Software Engineering
GROCHOW   SAA: A Guide to Implementing IBM's Systems Application Architecture
KING   Current Practices in Software Development: A Guide to Successful Systems
KING   Project Management Made Simple
LARSON   Interactive Software: Tools for Building Interactive User Interfaces
MARTIN   Transaction Processing Facility: A Guide for Application Programmers
McMENAMIN AND PALMER   Essential System Design
MOSLEY   The Handbook of MIS Application Software Testing
PAGE-JONES   Practical Guide to Structured Systems Design, 2/E
PINSON   Designing Screen Interfaces in C
PUTNAM AND MYERS   Measures for Excellence: Reliable Software on Time, within Budget
RIPPS   An Implementation Guide to Real-Time Programming
RODGERS   ORACLE®: A Database Developer's Guide
RODGERS   UNIX®: Database Management Systems
SERBANATI   Integrating Tools for Software Development
SHLAER AND MELLOR   Object Lifecycles: Modeling the World in States
SHLAER AND MELLOR   Object-Oriented Systems Analysis: Modeling the World in Data
SHILLER   Software Excellence
THOMSETT   Third Wave Project Management
TOIGO   Disaster Recovery Planning: Managing Risk and Catastrophe in Information Systems
VESELY   Strategic Data Management: The Key to Corporate Competitiveness
WANG (ed.)   Information Technology in Action
WARD   System Development Without Pain
WARD AND MELLOR   Structured Development for Real-Time Systems
YOURDON   Decline and Fall of the American Programmer
YOURDON   Managing the Structured Techniques, 4/E
YOURDON   Managing the System Life Cycle, 2/E
YOURDON   Modern Structured Analysis
YOURDON   Structured Walkthroughs, 4/E
YOURDON   Techniques of Program Structure and Design
YOURDON INC.   YOURDON™ Systems Method: Model-Driven Systems Development

The
Olduvai
Imperative

CASE and the State of Software Engineering Practice

Peter DeGrace
and
Leslie Hulet Stahl

Prentice-Hall International, Inc.

This edition may be sold only in those countries to which
it is consigned by Prentice-Hall International. It is not to
be re-exported and it is not for sale in the U.S.A., Mexico,
or Canada.

Adobe Illustrator is a trademark of Adobe Systems Inc.; *Aide-de-Camp* is a trademark of Software Maintenance and Development Systems, Inc.; *Apple*, *HyperCard*, and *Macintosh* are registered trademarks of Apple Computer, Inc.; *ClickArt* is a registered trademark of T/Maker Co.; *ConvertIt!* is a trademark of Heizer Software; *Correct Grammar* and *Lifetree* are trademarks of Lifetree Software, Inc. (by Working Software Inc.); *Grammarik Mac* is a trademark of Reference Software International; *Guide* is a trademark of OWL International; *Helvetica*, *Times*, and *Palantino* are trademarks of Linotype AG and/or its subsidaries; *ITC Franklin Gothic* is a registered trademark of International Typeface Corporation; *ithink* is a trademark of High Performance Systems; *Medusa* is a trademark of Lorvad; *Microsoft* is a registered trademark of Microsoft Corporation; *More II* is a trademark of Symantec Corporation; *PageMaker* is a registered trademark of Aldus Corporation; *PowerTools*, *FastTask*, *FreeFlow*, *DataModeler*, *QuickChart*, and *ObjectMaker* are trademarks of Iconix Software Engineering, Inc.; *RightWriter* is a registerd trademark of Que Software; *SuperPaint 2.0* is a trademark of Silicon Beach Software; *ToolBook* and *Asymetrix* are registered trademarks of Asymetrix Corporation.

The names of other products and companies mentioned in this book may be trademarks, trade names, registered trademarks, service marks, or service names.

© 1993 by Prentice-Hall, Inc.
A Division of Simon & Schuster
Englewood Cliffs, New Jersey 07632

All rights reserved. No part of this book may be
reproduced, in any form or by any means,
without permission in writing from the publisher.

Printed in the United States of America

10 9 8 7 6 5 4 3 2 1

ISBN 0-13-220104-6

Prentice-Hall International (UK) Limited, *London*
Prentice-Hall of Australia Pty. Limited, *Sydney*
Prentice-Hall Canada Inc., *Toronto*
Prentice-Hall Hispanoamericana, S.A., *Mexico*
Prentice-Hall of India Private Limited, *New Delhi*
Prentice-Hall of Japan, Inc., *Tokyo*
Simon & Schuster of Southeast Asia Pte. Ltd., *Singapore*
Editora Prentice-Hall do Brasil, Ltda., *Rio de Janeiro*

Contents

PART III.
POMP AND CIRCUMSTANCE

Figures

Tables

Preface

This is a book about Computer-Aided Software Engineering (CASE), about tools in general, and about a clash of cultures in our field that prevents tools from being used effectively. It is not simply about how to use or select a specific tool (although we *do* offer many pointers and recommendations on specific tools), because we believe there is enough of that kind of information available for you already. After all, we have CASE all over the place! We have the CASE products themselves and tons of literature about them. We have hordes of CASE vendors and their representatives, with their product literature. We have the CASE gurus and book writers (like us) producing a continuous stream of exhortations and "wise" counsel about CASE, its benefits, and its problems, and the CASE conferences with the attendant literature, briefings, and handouts.

There are many people who make decisions about programming and how it should be done. Their decisions will affect many aspects of our field, including the tools available to you, the training you will be expected to undergo, the languages you may use, and even the way you are expected to think.

There is so much *stuff* about CASE, but there is something wrong. Why haven't we taken to CASE the way we took to third-generation languages, to micro-computers, or to computing in general? Why do we find "users" with their CASE tools still in their desk drawers and not on their workstations? Why is it that many people do not know anything about CASE or, if they do, are apathetic toward it?

These are the types of questions this book addresses. It will help you identify and recognize the issues that are important to you, and it will help you deal with them. It describes the "state of practice" associated with using tools in software engineering, and we have tried to cover as much of the field as possible. Therefore, this book will give you a good general view of software engineering as we found it being practiced in many environments.

We've provided in-depth coverage of the following topics: systems engineering, software quality, two cultural views of software engineering, software maintenance, documentation, the differences between software and hardware, the differences between business and scientific programming, standards, metrics, and how to deploy CASE.

In the Introduction, we develop two themes: the apparently inherent human need to make and use tools, which we call the *Olduvai Imperative*, and the expression of this need in two contrasting cultural forms. We then use these themes through the book to clarify the muddy issues we found concerning software engineering.

We didn't originally intend to write this kind of book. We had originally planned on an exhaustive investigation of the current CASE products. If we had done so, we would have only been duplicating work that already exists, but with our own personal spin applied. Instead, during our investigation of the subject, we found some disturbing things and these are the areas we decided to address instead.

We asked one of our correspondents, who works in a major software enterprise, if he thought his company would like to market a low-end CASE tool set. He responded with something like: "CASE is a four-letter word around here. We don't use it, so why should we sell it?"

The inference here is that they will market only the stuff that they value and they do *not* value CASE.

Why does it so often seem that CASE is *inflicted* on programmers rather than made available to them? Why do we get comments like: "No [CASE] tool yet has demonstrated to me that it can improve my productivity in producing bullet-proofed programs."

That comment is from one of our correspondents who has a B.S. in Computer Science, is *very* savvy, and produces software in several languages. He is familiar with Structured techniques, but he uses the concepts informally. The CASE tool he uses is one of the Lightspeed™ products, which is composed of a compiler and a debugger. This is his only tool for his current project. The only time he uses CASE tool graphics is when he is working on team projects, and then he only uses them for communication and not for analysis and design.

Vaughan Merlyn, chairman of CASE Research Corporation, is a world-renowned expert on CASE and its deployment. He talked about the "Good News and Bad News" about CASE at the opening of his Second Annual CASE User's Conference. Here are some of his "bad news" comments:

CASE is still:

- "being approached experimentally [we believe skeptically]"

- "tactically [we believe at too low a level]"

- "[it] involves very long learning curves"

and:

- " 'Data People' [are] more receptive [to it] than programmers"

- "[end] users are more receptive [to it] than IS [information systems] professionals"

- "[it] offers greater leverage for new development [most of what we deal with is already written]"

- "[the] quality impact [is] more apparent than productivity [the old tradeoff between getting it done well or getting it done Tuesday]"

There is some good news, to be sure, because there *have* been successes and data management professionals *do* see CASE as valuable. But, there are many challenges. The difficulties and skepticism about which Merlyn is commenting are the same as what we have seen in our "lookout" on the subject.

It seems (to us anyway) that CASE is an industry in search of itself. For, although there is such hype about CASE (and make no mistake about it, this book adds to the general noise), there has not been the response to CASE that one would expect considering the public's overwhelming response to other aspects of the computer revolution.

We have come a long way, though. At first, only large organizations used computers because large, expensive machines were all that existed. Therefore, computers were rather remote from the general public. Even then, however, they were gobbled up as fast as they could be made.

Then, when microcomputers hit the market, all hell broke loose. It seemed that each year computer power (by this we mean memory and processing speed) increased by an order of magnitude and the cost decreased by an order of magnitude until computers were available to anyone and were bought by just about everyone.

The computing industry—hardware *and* software—has become one of the largest industries in the world. As this is being written, it may have reached the top position. Computers are used just about everywhere, and applications that were not even dreamed about just a few years ago are all over the place today. Computer games, once just a fad, have found what seems to be a permanent niche in our emerging world culture. Memory chips are the objects of incipient trade wars. We can even do our income taxes and transmit the information to the IRS on our PCs using modems. New technology is producing the pen-based and voice-recognizing computers, and all the predictors indicate hot markets for them.

And yet, CASE seems to be having trouble catching on. Less than 30% of the potential users actually use it. Those who *do* use CASE tend to use the simplest and most elementary functions. People just aren't stampeding to demand these products.

And, if you look at the world market, you will find an interesting fact: the Japanese, who are beating the pants off just about everybody in many marketplaces, are the most apathetic toward CASE. A smaller percentage of Japanese companies than other producers uses or plans to use CASE. And, a higher percentage has rejected or not considered what there is available in CASE [Grindley 1989]. Are they telling us something?

Japanese skepticism aside, there is a world market for CASE, to be sure, but it has hardly been penetrated. By *penetrated* we mean CASE tools being commonly and thoroughly used by software engineers to do their work.

Why is CASE not penetrating well? Why is CASE not welcomed loudly as labor-saving help? Why do large, data rich organizations seem to move to CASE in a big way and scientific application writers do not? Why is there so much resistance to CASE? Is there an education problem, are we just slow in catching on, are we excessively conservative, or is there something else going on?

We believe that something else *is* going on. We believe that there are some significant issues hindering the introduction and universal use of CASE. We think this book can help.

It is difficult to get a good angle on the issues, so we are going to first back up a little to show them clearly. We will draw some threads from a spindle and later we will weave them into a canvas that we will use to paint the picture of CASE. Also, we have collected information from many associates to whom we refer as our *correspondents*, and we have woven in many of their comments.

Throughout the book, you will notice little icons in the margins of some of the pages. These icons correspond to the icons that represent each chapter. Whenever we refer you to a discussion in another chapter, we have provided these icons as nagivational aids for those of you who prefer visual cues.

We hope you enjoy the trip.

Peter DeGrace and Leslie Hulet Stahl

Acknowledgments

A Very Special Team of People:
   Dennis Alger, Wayne Ingalls, Diane Jurgens, Christina Martin, and Ed Dryer.

Others who were very helpful:
   Jon Seward, Gary Shurtleff, Linda Phillips, Mary Warfield, Gene Hopp, Annette Langille, Larry Day, and, most especially, Gail Worthington.

Doug Rosenberg, Iconix Software Engineering, Inc., for all his useful comments and help in using the tools.

David Stahl, for financial, spiritual, and emotional support.

We would also like to thank our reviewers, Charles Martin and Robert Glass, and other reviewers whose names we do not know.

ABOUT THE AUTHORS:

Peter DeGrace is a former programmer trained in COBOL and FORTRAN who ended up in a software engineering reference library. There, he discovered many problems, questions, and answers about software development, software and systems engineering, and CASE.

Peter's education and experience includes data processing, COBOL and FORTRAN programming, systems analysis, software development, CASE tools, software methodologies, economics, and 20th century thought and expression.

Peter is a MENSAn, which might explain why he *enjoys* studying economics (especially labor theory), anything related to the computer field, living in the Pacific Northwest, music (which he discovered late in life), fine art (which he discovered early in life), and playing with his two dogs, Desdemona and Cleopatra.

Leslie Stahl is a technical writer, editor, illustrator, technical support specialist, and computer consultant. As the owner and editor-in-chief of Documents Unlimited Company, she has served many clients worldwide providing free-lance writing, editing, hypertext design and development, software testing, training, and electronic publishing services.

When she isn't working on books with Peter or hyperizing stuff, Leslie enjoys writing horror fiction, fishing, playing Scrabble or progressive Rummy, and her pets: Bruno (generic dog), Grunt (purebred Great Dane), Chuckie and Arielle (basic Cockatiels), Bert and Ernie (Amazon parrots), Buster Batty (homely Conure), Louis-Louis (Goffin's Cockatoo) and, most of all, David (pedigreed husband).

CONTACTING THE AUTHORS:

Peter DeGrace and Leslie Stahl
c/o Yourdon Press
Simon & Schuster Education Group
113 Sylvan Avenue, Route 9W
Englewood Cliffs, NJ 07632

Peter DeGrace
America Online ID: DeGrace
Internet: degrace@aol.com

Leslie Stahl
America Online ID: LeslieDS
CompuServe ID: 72600,1762
Internet: leslieds@aol.com
    or   72600.1762@compuserve.com

PART I.
Form and Essence

Photo courtesy of NASA

Introduction

On the sun-blasted plains of equatorial Africa, in the Serengeti of northern Tanzania, is a steep-sided ravine about 30 miles long and 295 feet deep. Layer after layer of geological deposits describe a history of the area covering a time span from about 2,100,000 to 15,000 years ago. This is the gorge called *Olduvai* [Britannica, 8:912:3b]. (See Figure I-1.)

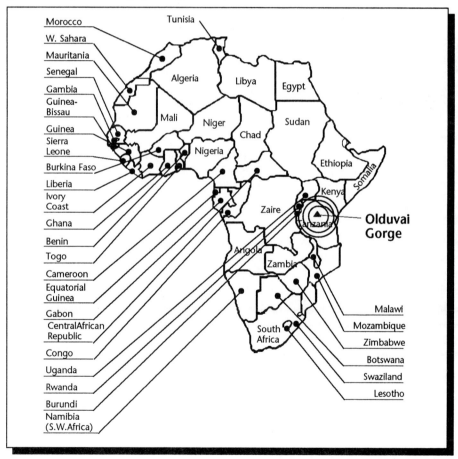

Figure I-1. The Location of Olduvai Gorge

The gorge once encompassed a 16-mile diameter volcanic basin containing a lake. It was surrounded by lush tropical forests, and was a riot of activity and life. Numerous volcanic eruptions and fluctuations in the level of the lake led to the rapid burial of deceased hominids—our early ancestors—and their associated remains. Over the millennia, layers of debris, volcanic ash, and the detritus of erosion collected on top of these deceased hominids.

Then, countless more millennia of erosion ate away at the layers of deposits, and rifting exposed and rotated the layers until they could be viewed by modern explorers [Britannica, 8:912:3b; 8:913:1a].

In 1931, L.S.B. (Louis Seymour Bazett) Leakey, the Kenyan archæologist and anthropologist, and Mary, his wife, began their research at Olduvai Gorge in Tanzania (also called Oldowai). Olduvai became the site of L.S.B.'s most famous discoveries. "The magnet that drew Louis and Mary Leakey back to Olduvai Gorge year after year was the existence there of large numbers of extremely primitive stone implements. Mary Leakey ... [even] published a splendid monograph on the stone [tool] culture at Olduvai." [Edey 1972]

Mary uncovered the fossilized remains of a hominid that was named Zinjanthropus (whom we will call *Z*; one source refers to *Z* as *1470 man*; see Figure I-2). This hominid was believed to be 1,750,000 years old [ibid; Reader's Digest History of Man 1973]. However, *Z* was probably not in a direct line with us. Another hominid found there by Louis, *Homo Habilis*, most probably was. *Homo Habilis* stands for *Handy Man*: a clever tool user. This *H. Habilis* beat out *Z* and two other hominids and evolved into *H. Erectus* who evolved into us, *H. Sapiens* (*Thinking Man*). As we shall see, Thinking Man has well and faithfully kept the tradition started by Handy Man: that of a clever tool user.

We humans come from a line of primates that had (or developed) stereoscopic vision, an upright posture and gait, an opposable thumb, a sophisticated social structure (judging by our other primate cousins) and, eventually, language. Along the way, our brain size and capacity grew to its modern form (see Figure I-2).

However, we are the only carnivorous animals that are not equipped with tearing claws or incisors long and sharp enough to serve as hunting weapons. Because of this lack, humans cannot easily cut into their prey and get at the meat inside. Early humans had to use *something* other than just their intelligence to help them kill and cut up their food. They found, used and, eventually, manufactured tools.

APE MAN The brain size of *Australopithecus,* who lived in Africa some 5 million years ago, was about 480 cc—little larger than that of the apes he resembled, and only one-third the size of modern man's. His jaws were powerful, to chew raw meat.

'1470 MAN' The most startling fact about the 2.5-million-year-old skull found by Richard Leakey in Kenya in 1972 is that its brain capacity is about 800 cc—double that of a chimpanzee, and well on the way toward modern man's 1450 cc.

UPRIGHT MAN The skull of *Homo erectus,* who lived half a million years ago, held a larger brain than that of his predecessors. Its capacity was about 1000 cc—more than twice that of an ape. His jaw was still prominent, but his teeth were getting smaller.

NEANDERTHAL MAN The skull of the Neanderthaler, who emerged about 70,000 years ago, was large, and he had a brain slightly larger than modern man's. His jaws jutted out, but were becoming less prominent in proportion to the face. His brows were overhanging.

HOMO SAPIENS SAPIENS The physical characteristics of modern man, with his well-proportioned face and fully developed chin, have finally evolved over the last 30,000 years. In this time, our species has divided into three main racial groups—the Caucasoids, the Mongoloids, and the Negroids.*

© 1973 *Reader's Digest History of Man: The Last Two Million Years*

Figure I-2. Man's Expanding Brain

*The Australian Aborigines are now commonly considered to also be a distinct racial group.

The true original tools were made by nature, handed up from the ground to be used by anyone intelligent enough to recognize their value. Many stones with sharp fractures were once assumed to be man-made artifacts. Because of some characteristic details, these rocks, which were fractured by glacier pressure, wave action, or temperature changes, have now been recognized as nature-made rather than man-made. However, some early humans were intelligent enough to pick them up and use them as tools.

The first humans were casual tool users, employing these naturally formed stones and whatever sticks or tree branches were at hand. They could use a piece of sharp-edged stone to cut through animal hides. However, these early forms of tools were not all that unique, and other animals have used tools in a similar way. For example, chimpanzees often use a sharpened stick to extract termites from mounds, and otters will crack clams open on a rock that they rest on their abdomens. We call this *opportunistic tool use*. What really set humans apart from animals was when we began to deliberately *manufacture* and *use* tools. It appears that *H. Habilis* was the first early hominid to do both.

Once *H. Habilis* broke the secret code of how to make tools, he became quite prolific at it. By this proficiency, *H. Habilis* obtained an advantage in his environment, either by mimicking the desirable characteristics of strength, speed, or killing power of other species, or by obtaining a unique advantage, as with projectiles.

The apparent need to make and use tools to gain an advantage is what we call the *Olduvai Imperative*.

Among the artifacts discovered at Olduvai were numerous examples of Paleolithic tools. The primitive Oldowan chopping tools are the oldest known manufactured tools. It is not very likely that they were made by Z, who was much too deficient in the brain-pan area. They were most likely made by our friend *H. Habilis*.

Early tools are classified by their *industry*, or type of workmanship. The tools are identified by the name derived from the site at which the type of tool first drew archæological attention. For example, the primitive chopping tools that persisted for nearly 2,000,000 years were first identified at Olduvai. (See Figure I-3.) Therefore, they constitute the so-called *Oldowan industry*, regardless of the part of the world in which other tools of similar design are found [Britannica 28:714].

However, this does not imply that there were abrupt transitions at certain times between one industry and another: there was no abrupt end to one type of tool with the development of a new tool. Rather, as new techniques were developed through experimentation and refinement, *the tool evolved to better fit the user*. This effect is integral to our concept of the Olduvai Imperative.

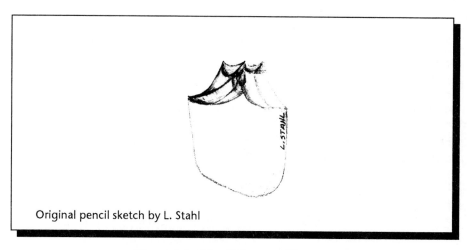

Original pencil sketch by L. Stahl

Figure I-3. The Oldowan Chopper

As time passed and the tool user's skills improved, the average size of the tools decreased. (You may notice a certain similarity between Paleolithic tools and computers, in this regard.) As an aside, this trend was reversed in the Neolithic period when people became less nomadic and settled in permanent colonies. Then, heavy woodsman's axes and adzes became essential for clearing forests. It was at this point that tool size became a *function* of the intended use rather than an *effect* of the level of craftsmanship or technology, another effect of the Olduvai Imperative.

Within a few hundred thousand years, a transition took place, from simply using tools to actually making tools. But, it took from 2,600,000 years ago until just 40,000 years ago before humans made the transition from simply chipping the flakes off the flint to actually developing a flake-tool industry in which pre-shaped flakes were purposefully detached from a core that was then discarded. Figure I-4 illustrates the process of creating these tools [Britannica 28:714].

Fully modern humans—*Cro-Magnon*—emerged within the period of the flake-tool industry. *Cro-Magnon* provided a variety of specialized tools. *C.M.* was the first to develop tools made of materials other than stone. They used slivers of bone for needles, pins, and awls, and they used larger pieces for barbed hooks. They carved sections of antler into divided wedges that formed the dart-like projectiles they needed for spear throwing. Sandstone polishers were added to the toolkit to sharpen and shape tips and needles and other articles [Britannica 28:715].

FASHIONING THE FIRST TOOLS

The tools and weapons used by early man are important clues in tracing his evolution, since his bones are usually only found by chance. The similarity between implements from widely separated periods shows that development was very slow. Although a pebble-tool and a hand-axe are similar implements, and produced by the same techniques, it took prehistoric man several hundred thousand years to move from one to the other.

PEBBLE CUTS PEBBLE To make his first tools, man merely struck one pebble, usually a flint, against another, aiming acute blows at the edge to detach flakes. The result was an implement that was crude, but effective enough for the simple tasks that faced early man, such as skinning and chopping up animals for meat.

SHARPER POINTS Stone hand-axes, which were much more versatile than simple pebble-tools, were developed by *Homo erectus,* or "Upright man," who first appeared about half a million years ago. Their sharp points and edges were achieved by patiently chipping away a succession of thin flakes with a piece of bone or hard wood.

© 1973 *Reader's Digest History of Man: The Last Two Million Years*

Figure I-4. Fashioning the First Tools

The *atlatl,* a dart-thrower, was developed by the end of the Paleolithic era. It was the first projectile weapon and one that conferred a unique advantage, these days called a *standoff capability*. It was a hand-held stick made of wood or antler that was notched at one end. It functioned as an extension of the arm, and added considerable force to a short spear or javelin tipped with flint or bone. (See Figure I-5.) The atlatl is another example of the Olduvai Imperative at work.

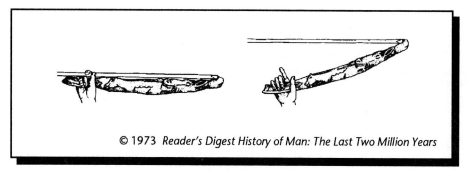

© 1973 *Reader's Digest History of Man: The Last Two Million Years*

Figure I-5. The Atlatl

The tipped projectile represented still another innovation, for it was the first *hafted* implement—the first evidence of fitting a handle to a tool point. This not only made both small and large cutting tools more useful by extending their reach and flexibility, but it also protected the user's hands from being damaged. Then, between 30,000 and 15,000 years ago, the bow was developed, which virtually catapulted humanity into an inventive frenzy. (See Figure I-6.)

During the Neolithic Period (or New Stone Age), which began around 7,000 B.C., there were many advances in tool development. During this era, ground tools were developed, where the basic tool was chipped to rough shape in the old manner and then rubbed with (or against) a coarse abrasive stone to remove the chip scars. Both the entire surface of the tool and its working edge could be worked in this way. Polishing was a last step. (See Figure I-7).

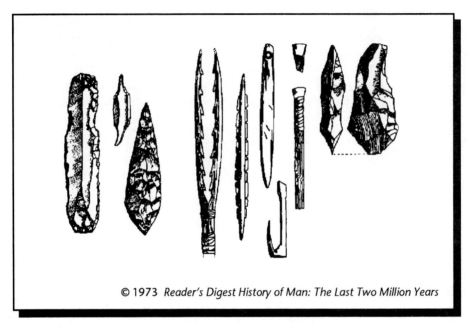

© 1973 *Reader's Digest History of Man: The Last Two Million Years*

Figure I-6. A Plethora of New Tools

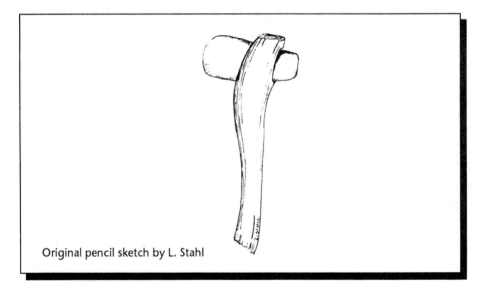

Original pencil sketch by L. Stahl

Figure I-7. A Neolithic Polished Tool

Also during this period, the ice sheets were receding from the area and humans moved from a hunting society into a herding and farming society. Life became much more sedentary. This led to even more rapid advances in tool development since the land needed to be cleared for agricultural use. This led to the mining of flint for creating heavy, polished axes. The invention of pottery led to the development of potters' kilns, which were, in turn, necessary steps to the smelting of metals and metalworking. Metalworking led to copper casting and smelting, which led to the development of bronze, which led to iron and steel tools, which led to metallic cutting, drilling, and abrading tools, which led to more highly specialized tools, and so on, and so on.

Throughout the history of tool development, we see the transition from natural to man-made; from rough to smooth; from large to small; from general to specific.

This, then, is the *Olduvai Imperative*: the inherent need to take the materials Nature has offered up and adapt them to gain an advantage in the user's environment, either by mimicry or invention. It is our hallmark. It is our most distinctive and easily recognizable characteristic. Ever since man began developing tools, no matter where he went and no matter what he did, he saw himself in relationship to his tools or what they helped him build. No monument, no church, no tomb, no hero or villain, in fact, no cultural artifact is complete without this relationship being portrayed somehow. Even the most intangible of artifacts, like literature or music, cannot be produced without tools. The use of tools is so universal, so pervasive, that it is often overlooked as being instrumental in our success as a species.

Humanity eventually spread throughout the world, created cultures everywhere, and channeled this imperative in special ways. Two of these cultures contain an essential contrast we need for talking about our world of software engineering. So, here we present a concise history of Greece and Rome.

The Beginnings of Ancient Greece

Ancient Greece began in the Ægean basin between 1900 and 1600 B.C. Its culture endured into 15th century A.D. The Ægean Basin was the site of the well-developed Minoan civilization, with cities and ornate palaces. The people who lived there used gold and bronze for jewelry and other ornaments, and made pottery and paintings. At that time, the Greeks (or *Hellenes*) were simple, nomadic sheepherders. They came from the grasslands east of the Caspian Sea, driving their flocks and herds before them, finally settling in the Ægean basin.

Practically as soon as they were settled, others started invading them [Compton's 1991; Grolier's 1992].

The *Achæans* were the first invaders. These are the people about whom Homer later wrote. The Dorians came three or four centuries later and conquered the Achæans. Other tribes, the Æolians and Ionians, settled on the islands in the Ægean Sea and on the coast of Asia Minor.

Many of the invaders were still in the barbarian stage. They plundered and destroyed the Ægean cities. However, as they settled and intermarried with the people they conquered, they gradually absorbed some of the Ægean culture. This formed the beginning of the classical age of Greece and the city-states [ibid].

The Greek City-States and Their Colonies

The Greek *city-states* were self-governing cities and their surrounding lands. (The Greek word *polis*, as in *metropolis*, literally means "city" and the area of countryside around it.) The Greek city-states operated completely independently, and never united to form a single nation. More like countries, they had their own lands, laws, taxes and, often, cultures.

The city-states were usually very small. Athens was probably the only Greek city-state with more than 20,000 citizens, and it was wealthier than any other Greek state. Its population increased dramatically as foreigners streamed in to share in the prosperity. The period in which Athens flourished was one of the most remarkable and brilliant in the world's history. Education and learning became fashionable. The arts advanced as never before in history. Painters and sculptors competed in beautifying Athens with the works of their genius. Even today, although they have been partially destroyed by time and vandalism, these art treasures remain among the greatest surviving achievements of human skill.

Similar city-states were located all over the Greek world, which had outposts throughout the Ægean Basin and beyond. There were Greeks in all the islands of the Ægean. The Greeks also settled the nearer-lying Cyclades (from the Greek word for *circle*), which encircled the sacred island of Delos, and the southern island of Crete.

But, most of the city-states were separated by the physical barriers of sea and mountain, and the social barriers of local pride and jealousy. Therefore, the various independent city-states never united into a single Greek-speaking political unit. Instead, they only formed alliances when one powerful city-state tried to conquer the remainder; ancient Greece never became a unified nation [ibid]. Later, in Chapter 1, you will see some parallels in our modern world.

The city-states shared many things: language, religion, literature, similar customs, religious leagues and festivals, and the Olympic games. Nonetheless, it was often hard to get the city-states to cooperate, even during times of foreign invasion. However, the *Iliad* tells how Greeks from many city-states—including Sparta, Athens, Thebes, and Argos—joined forces to fight Troy, their common foe in Asia Minor. The Greek city-states were again able to combine when they were threatened by the power of Persia [ibid].

The western shores of Asia Minor were fringed with Greek colonies, reaching out to the Black Sea. Greek colonies in Africa included the colony of Cyrene (now the site of a town in Libya) and the trading post of Naucratis in Egypt. The Greeks also colonized Sicily. There were so many colonies in Sicily and through southern Italy that the region became known as Magna Græcia (Great Greece).

However, the lack of unification among the city-states, combined with their physical isolation, made them easy prey for would-be conquerors. (Again, this becomes important in Chapter 1.) First Sparta was conquered, and then Thebes. Greece was weakened and became prey to Philip of Macedonia and his son Alexander. Eventually, the city-states came under the influence of and were dominated by Rome. The age of the Greek city-states was at an end.

The Greek Culture

It is not this tale of conquest, though, that interests us; it is the Greek culture. The roots of the Greek culture were formed before the city-states existed.

There were many talented men whose work affected the Greek culture. They worked in many fields. There were the great architects, Ictinus and Callicrates, who designed the Parthenon, and the sculptor, Pheidias, who carved a 40-foot-high gold and ivory statue of Athena to adorn it. In literature, there were the epic writers, like Homer, and the lyric poets, Archilochus, Alcman, and Sappho. There were the dramatists and playwrights, Æschylus, Sophocles, and Euripides, and the historians, Herodotus and Xenophon. These men lived throughout the entire Greek world, in the colonies as well as on the Greek peninsula itself.

In the 5th century B.C., the center of Greek culture passed to Athens when it rose as a wealthy democratic state. It was there that the Greeks reached the peak of their extraordinary creative energy. This was the greatest period of Greek literature, architecture, and sculpture. Philosophers turned their thoughts from the study of matter to the study of mankind. Toward the end of the century, Socrates ushered in the most brilliant period of Greek philosophy. He passed his wisdom on to his pupil Plato, who in turn handed it on to "the master of those who know," the great Aristotle [ibid].

The Greek artists and philosophers were eagerly sought as teachers in other lands. What were the ideas for which the world reached out so eagerly? First, the Greeks were determined to be guided by reason and follow the truth wherever it led. Above all else, they were *reasonable*. This showed in all of their greatest art. Their central doctrine was "nothing to excess" (*meden agan*) [ibid]. The Roman poet Horace later interpreted this doctrine as "the golden mean."

They explored Nature, eventually preferring simpler and more natural explanations of phenomena in place of more sophisticated, supernatural ones. By doing so, they developed the principal of parsimony and, thus, invented Science.

This great culture burned brightly and then smouldered quietly until 1453 when it was finally extinguished by the astonished Turks when they occupied Constantinople.

Rome Enters the Picture

Beginning as a tiny settlement on the Tiber, Rome had been developing since the 10th century B.C. However, according to tradition, Rome was founded in 753 B.C. [Reader's Digest History of Man 1973].

The earliest Romans were peasant farmers who moved south into Italy from central Europe. One group of people, the *Latins*, settled on the south bank of the Tiber. They named the plain on which they settled *Latium*.

There was a point along the Tiber having an island in the middle. This made a good crossing point, and the Latins built a bridge there. A trading center was built at this point, forming the beginnings of Rome. Houses were built along the edges of the river and up into the seven surrounding hills. Capitol Hill was the highest of these hills. On its summit, the Latins built many religious shrines. They also built fortifications to which they could escape when they were in danger [ibid].

The early Romans were not wealthy or warlike. Their civilization was very primitive compared to the civilized Etruscans who existed in northern and central Italy from 800 to 200 B.C. However, the bridge over the Tiber made Rome an essential link in a valuable trade route. Goods passed between the Etruscans and the Greek trading colonies in southern Italy and Sicily. The bridge was so important that the high priest of the Roman religion was called the *Pontifex Maximus* or "chief bridge-builder." This exalted position retained its importance for so long that the pope in Rome, 2500 years later, is still called the *pontiff* [ibid].

However, the rich Etruscans exerted a powerful control over the early Romans. For nearly a century, Rome was governed by a series of cruel Etruscan chieftains who were called the "kings" of Rome.

In 509 B.C., the Romans finally revolted against the cruelty of the Etruscans and expelled them. The Etruscans mounted a counterattack on Rome. Despite the bravery of Horatius, the defender of Rome, the Etruscans conquered Rome again. However, the Etruscan system of monarchy was not restored. Instead, the Romans developed the republican government system. Under this system, no one man was allowed to become powerful enough to be a threat to the state [ibid].

There were three classes of people in Rome: patricians, plebeians, and slaves. The *patricians* were the city's aristocracy. Only the patricians were allowed to perform religious rituals and hold public office. The *plebeians* made up the majority of the citizens. They were barred from public office until they fought for and won the right to elect their own representatives in the 5th century B.C. Slaves formed the third class. Most of the slaves were prisoners of war. The slave class grew throughout the course of Roman history. The struggle between the three classes also grew throughout Rome's history [ibid].

Rome eventually absorbed the Etruscan empire by the 4th century B.C. Then, it had to confront the super-power of Carthage in North Africa. Carthage had colonies of its own and a large naval fleet. After centuries of war with Carthage, and the marauding of Hannibal with his elephants, Rome finally scored a number of major defeats against the Carthaginians. In 146 B.C., the Roman legions stormed Carthage and burned it to the ground. Then, its site was ploughed under and salt was thrown into the furrows so that the land would remain barren and unusable forever [ibid].

At about the same time, around 200 B.C., Rome became a decisive factor in Greek affairs. The Greek city-states became subject to Rome, but they enjoyed local autonomy. The upper classes controlled the local governments and Greek was retained as the official language. For a time, there was much prosperity. Many cities were patronized by the Roman emperors, and Athens flourished as a university town [ibid; Grolier's 1992].

When Rome conquered the Greeks, the Romans absorbed the best of Greek culture and passed its legacy of art, architecture, and philosophy on to the Western world. It was from the Greeks that the Romans learned about sculpture and literature. And, the Romans added to the Greek culture the typically Roman sense of discipline and respect for law and order.

Macedonia became a Roman province in 148, and the Achæan and Ætolian leagues were dissolved in 146. By the end of the 1st century B.C., Pompey the Great, Julius Cæsar, and Cæsar Augustus had settled the eastern provinces of the Roman Empire into their final form.

Our Greco-Roman Heritage

The essential root of Rome's greatness was her unsurpassed framework of a culture that was Greek in origin and Roman in application. "She was too engrossed in government to create as bountifully in the realms of the mind as Greece had done; but she absorbed with appreciation, and preserved with tenacity, the technical, intellectual, and artistic heritage that she had received from Egypt, Greece and the East. She made no advance in science, and no mechanical improvements in industry, but she enriched the world with a commerce moving over secure seas, and a network of enduring roads that became the arteries of a lusty life. Along those roads, and over a thousand handsome bridges, there passed to the medieval and modern worlds the ancient techniques of tillage, handicraft, and art, the science of monumental building, the processes of banking and investment, the organization of medicine and military hospitals, the sanitation of cities, and many varieties of fruit and nut trees, of agricultural or ornamental plants, brought from the East to take new root in the West. Even the secret of central heating came from the warm south to the cold north. The south has created the civilizations, the north has conquered and destroyed or borrowed them.

"Rome did not invent education, but she developed it on a scale unknown before, gave it state support, and formed the curriculum that persisted till our harassed youth. She did not invent the arch, the vault, or the dome, but she used them with such audacity and magnificence that in some fields her architecture has remained unequaled; and all the elements of the medieval cathedral were prepared in her basilicas. She did not invent the sculptural portrait, but she gave it a realistic power rarely reached by the idealizing Greeks. ...

"Her language became, by a most admirable corruption, the speech of Italy, Rumania, France, Spain, Portugal, and Latin America; half the white man's world speaks a Latin tongue. Latin was, till the eighteenth century, the Esperanto of science, scholarship, and philosophy in the West; it gave a convenient international terminology to botany and zoology; ... it still writes medical prescriptions, and haunts the phraseology of the law. It entered by direct appropriation, and again through the Romance languages (*regalis, regal, royal; paganus, pagan, peasant*), to enhance the wealth and flexibility of English speech. Our Roman heritage works in our lives a thousand times a day." [Durant 1966, pp.671-672]

The Romans borrowed from the art and science of the Greeks and drew upon their religious philosophy of Stoicism. As Christianity grew and spread, it was profoundly influenced by Greek thought. Throughout the period of the barbarian invasions, Greek learning was preserved by Christians in Constantinople, by Muslims in Cairo, and across North Africa to Spain. The light of Greek culture shone again in the Middle Ages when the great universities were founded in Italy, France, and England, and the Muslim culture did the West the immense favor of transmitting much of our heritage back to us. This then became the foundation for the Renaissance.

During the Renaissance, the Greek culture provided an impetus for the rebirth of art and literature. Modern science rests on the Greek idea of humanity's capacity to solve problems by rational methods. You can see the influence of Greek thought in almost every phase of life. "Except the blind forces of nature, nothing moves in this world which is not Greek in its origin." [Commonly attributed to Sir Henry Maine.]

Rome's Decline

The ancient Roman Empire dominated the world for almost 500 years. At its widest extent, the Romans ruled or directly controlled an area that covered some two million square miles. Its western boundary was the Atlantic coast of Spain. It extended to the shores of the Caspian Sea in the east. From north to south, it ranged from Britain to Egypt.

The truly remarkable thing about the Roman Empire is that this amazing world power developed from the inhabitants of a single city. Sixteen hundred years after the collapse of this gigantic empire, we still see the marks of its existence. However, Rome's decline was as magnificent as its rise to prominence.

Will Durant, in *The Story of Civilization,* had this to say about Rome and its spectacular decline: "A great civilization is not conquered from without until it has destroyed itself within." [ibid, p.665]

Durant indicated that there were many reasons for the decline of Rome, but that the essential causes lay in her people: decaying morals; the class struggle; tremendous decreases in population; bureaucratic, social, and moral despotism; and consuming wars. Rome's decline is one of the most important problems in history.

Here are what we believe are some of the key reasons:

- The demands of the empire distracted it.

- Its cities became merely administrative centers and were no longer actual players in the economy.

- Barbarians incessantly encroached on the empire.

- The Roman culture was diluted by vibrant newcomers.

- The political structure deteriorated.

But, we believe the main reason for Rome's decline was that the inspiration of Greece was extinguished, and the Greek Idea faded. So, given the preceding discussion and our qualifications as armchair historians, we present here "The DeGrace and Stahl Condensed Theory of History": *Rome* fell because it ran out of *Greeks*. It no longer had the juice—the fuel—to continue in the West. In the East, however, it continued until 1453 when it finally succumbed to the Muslim invaders of Asia Minor. But, we believe that it was no accident that the capital of the Eastern Roman Empire was built on an ancient Greek city, Byzantium, and that it was 1000 miles closer to the heart of Greece itself, where the embers of ancient Greece still smouldered.

This Greek/Roman tension continues on. It is embedded in the clash of Romantic vs. Classic periods of culture, and of essence vs. form in design. This tension, properly balanced, accounts for the rise of great cultures and empires; almost all of them becoming stale and arid, with their cultures based on form as their empires died. ❧

Chapter 1.
CASE: Threads and Borders

In this chapter, we will discuss the threads and borders of the field of software engineering. We will then describe the landscape of software engineering tools.

Threads

Several threads ran through our research. The two most important are: (1) the Rome/Greece contrast that appears to split our field, and (2) how we gain an advantage from the tools we use.

Greece vs. Rome

We are very aware that the historical generalizations we've made in the introduction are exactly that, and they reveal, perhaps, only the *impressions* that Will Durant and our other sources had of the Greek and Roman cultures. Roman philosophy is very different from Greek philosophy, but they both have their equivalents in today's society: particularly in the American workplace. These equivalents have serious influences on our work. But, we are not writing a history here; we want to present highlights of these cultures in a distinctive and contrasting way, and then bend them to our purposes like any other tool material.

In ancient Greece, an individual would act as an agent in his own behalf, or combine with other people to act together as a team. In a Greek work environment, you bring your tools to work with you, you do your stuff, and then you pack up your tools and take them home. You are an individual ... an independent contractor. You are not owned body and mind. You are merely providing a service for compensation.

In Rome, one's first duty was to the group, clan, class, or faction upon which one depended for status. Known as *gravitas*, this meant sacrificing oneself for the good of the organization, and giving up one's individuality and identifying closely with the group. In a Roman environment, you go to work, the company hands you your tools, and then it holds you and your mind hostage until you sever your relationship with the organization. You are not an individual: you are owned by the organization body and mind, twenty-four hours a day. There are substantial rewards for this, however. The organization provides you with security, money, and power.

This issue of Greece vs. Rome has not yet been entirely resolved in our society; but, we have found it over and over again in our research. It affects who chooses tools, who makes them, and who uses them. In the chapters to come, we will point out this contrast. For now, we offer Table 1-1, which lists the important contrasts between the Greek and Roman perspectives in software engineering.

We have named these two groups so that we can easily refer to them in succeeding chapters. The first (informal) group we call *Greek* and the second (formal) group we call *Roman.* This is why we spent the time discussing the dynamics of these two civilizations in the previous chapter. As we discuss the main issues of tools, we will show you the implications for both types of groups.

We are not making any moral statements here; that is one reason we chose names that represent two very great civilizations. We are not suggesting that one group is superior or inferior to the other. However, we do stress the positive side of the Greek view in this book. That is because we see an imbalance in our field. This imbalance stresses the Roman view at the expense of the Greek view.

We accept the differences between the groups (at least, we *think* we do). And, we know that how well the tools and methods of our field are accepted varies according to where a person is on the Greek-Roman scale. For example, a Greek-type programmer will only reluctantly accept CASE tools (especially data-flow diagram editors) if he finds himself working in a group larger than he can handle. Conversely, a Roman-type developer expects always to be in such groups because he expects to work on very large projects and *expects* these kinds of tools to be available.

It seems to us that there is a negative aspect to the Roman view. It suggests that those who use informal methods (the Greeks) are somehow unfit to be programmers and must be expunged from programming groups. We know of software development projects where these so-called *eccentrics* were indeed expunged. The saying went: "We had the firing squad in the parking lot."

Table 1-1. Greece vs. Rome	
Greece (or the Greek way)	**Rome (or the Roman way)**
Organizes things	Organizes people
Informal	Formal
Writes the programs	Manages the projects
Motivated by the problem at hand	Motivated by group goals
Uses structured stuff (explained later in this chapter)	Uses STRUCTURED STUFF (explained later in this chapter)
Minimum documentation	Maximum documentation
Works on a human scale	Works beyond human scale
Works alone or in small groups	Works in large organizations
Uses *things* as tools	Uses *people* as tools
Democratic	Imperial
Empirical/inductive	Analytical/deductive
Intuitive	Logical
Class based on merit	Class based on function
Engineer/scientist	Manager
Substance	Form
Does things	Plans things or goes to meetings

To let you know where *we* fit on the Greek-Roman scale, we both see ourselves as Greek in temperament, although we would both place the *other* closer to the Roman end of the scale. We favor the Greek temperament because it provides creative juice. Unless there is some creative juice present, programming is dull, boring, and uninteresting. We don't want to work in such environments.

Of course, we must give Cæsar his due; but, when Cæsar's method takes all the creativity, visualization, passion, and magic out of our work, then we will object. And, to us, that is what often seems to be happening using Cæsar's methods. We find that the system is analyzed down to the most minute detail, to the point where the actual writing of the software becomes automatic.

This might be where the future is leading us, and some observers believe it to be. But, if it is, then it will be an uninteresting future and the next book we write will be about how to switch careers. We hope these observers are wrong, or wrong to a large extent.

We have no problem with code generators producing COBOL at prodigious rates; we need them. It is a blessing to have some help there. But, we hope that no one mistakes the organizational power of the Roman method with the necessary creativity of the Greek one. When the balance between the Roman and Greek ways are overwhelmed by the Roman, the human interfaces are multiplied, the programmers are not able to form an integrated view of the problem they are solving, any shared vision of the solution disintegrates, costs go up, and quality goes down.

Along this line, here is a convention that appeared earlier and will appear periodically throughout this book. When we are referring to the Roman view of some concept (for example, Structured Stuff[1]), we will use all uppercase letters: STRUCTURED STUFF. When we refer to the Greek view, we will use all lowercase: structured stuff. When we refer to the balance we urge, which allows each side an appropriate role, we capitalize the first letters: Structured Stuff. In our opinion, the appropriate roles are that the Romans provide a working context in which the Greeks get to do their stuff and express their results in formal terms for the Romans.

---

[1] Structured analysis, design, and programming together with the Waterfall model.

Greece vs. Rome in Different Kinds of Shops

As an example of the Greek-Roman contrast we ran across repeatedly, we present the following descriptions of two kinds of software development shops. One is large and either has an internal customer, such as Payroll, or it has a very large external customer, such as the government. The other is small and usually deals with individual outside customers.

We have noticed that when we are dealing with a programming shop that has as its main customer either another part of its enterprise or the government, it has certain characteristics:

- It tends to be very formal

- It produces larger programs than otherwise would be the case

- It over-manages software projects

- It has a fairly strict hierarchy

- It loves CASE and methods such as STRUCTURED STUFF

- It produces a great deal of documentation of rather poor quality

When the customer is *outside* the enterprise (but not the government) the characteristics change:

- The organization tends to be less formal

- Programs seem to be smaller and have less functionality than otherwise would be the case

- Projects are, if anything, under-managed

- The hierarchy is not rigid

- CASE is a four-letter word and programmers use structured stuff

- Documentation is minimal, but may be of the highest quality

We know of an excellent teacher of Structured Analysis and Design who cannot produce software very well when he practices STRUCTURED STUFF in the workplace.

We know of another practitioner who does very well producing software, but he does not use STRUCTURED STUFF. Instead, he uses structured stuff. What we mean by this is that he holds the *ideas* of structured stuff in his mind and uses them informally in his work.

The first practitioner *loves* CASE and METHODS; the second sees no use for either one in the formal sense.

We know of an even better teacher who was first a successful practitioner. He gave up teaching structured stuff because the officials where he worked complained that he didn't teach STRUCTURED STUFF.

We have written about the parable of two programmers [Rickert 1985, p.16] in our previous book [DeGrace and Stahl 1990]. In the parable, two enterprises have exactly the same problem. The problem is given to two programmers to solve.

The first programmer sees the problem as an opportunity to use orthodox methods and create a team to produce the solution. He shows a great deal of activity: meetings, reports, etc. The other programmer sees the problem as an opportunity to apply his skills to solve the problem and spends his time *thinking* with little apparent outside activity.

The first programmer had an overblown solution and schedules for repair and testing. The other programmer produced a simple solution with no known problems. The first programmer was rewarded and the second was chastised.

We cannot state categorically that this is the state of affairs in our field, but why were there so many knowing smiles when we showed the story around to our correspondents? Why did it seem to reflect the experience so many of us had? We believe that there was much truth in it. Some people depend on organization, thrive on formal processes, and use other people as tools. Other people depend on themselves, prefer informal processes, and use inanimate objects as tools.

The Tool-Giving Advantage

Here are some questions for you to keep in mind as you proceed through this book.

How well do tools help the person, the Greek in us, and how often do they help the Romans around us? To what degree do CASE tools help you solve your problems and to what degree do they interfere?

Do we lose the advantage we originally gained? CASE tools might introduce a method of analysis (for example, entity relationship analysis) by making it possible to create the diagrams quickly and neatly. But, after that, do they (and the method that rides on them) get in the way?

Do we become infatuated with the method and forget the problem? Do CASE tools help solve new problems, or do they just allow us to understand the solutions to problems that we've already solved? Does the tool fit the user's "hand" or is the user's hand forced to fit the tool? Is the purpose of the tool distorted in order to use it? Is only a small part of the tool used?

These are important questions. Their answers have to do with issues such as productivity, profit, careers, ambitions, "getting along by going along," ability to compete, psychological pain, and a host of other issues.

We have discovered that there is precious little going on that directly relates to how problems are *actually* solved, how computer programs *really* are produced, and how programmers *really* work. But, there is no end to the lists of how problems *should* be solved, how programs *should* be produced, and how programmers *should* work. These "shoulds" are in the hands of the Romans in our world, and *they* make the decisions about the tools we use. It is only by luck that programmers end up with useful tools selected by the "technology staffs" that are supposed to support them; some of the most effective and used tools we've seen are those made by programmers themselves.

In the following chapters, we will point out these *shoulds*, and we will indicate other problems in obtaining the appropriate tools for programmers. And, we will ask the question: "Where is the advantage of using the tool?"

Other Threads

Another thread that appears in several chapters involves a group of words that describe the internal characteristics of software: the "... ilities." We present them early on to provide a basis for discussion in later chapters.

And, finally, we reexamine some ideas from some of the best and most respected among us. This thread occurs several times and we use it to support the central theme of this book; namely, that there is a Roman-Greek split in our ranks.

Borders

The borders of our field are determined in part by the definitions used in describing our field. So, we need to settle on some definitions. Consider the following ones:

Computer-Aided . . .

Computer-aided is the "CA" portion of *CASE*. However, nobody is quite sure what exactly *computer-aided* anything includes. What kind of aid is being provided and for whom? We have an image of the computer as an aide; a reliable companion helping us with our tasks. However, the reports we often get show a machine that is inflicted on people, requiring them to feed it regularly and in very special ways, and requiring them to conform to it rather than the other way around. The former is an example of the Greek approach while the latter is an example of the Roman. It is particularly grating to Greek-type software engineers when they discover that machines are being inflicted on them, since they know better.

Another aspect of this is the question: "What is the subject and what is the object of the computer aid?" In many organizations, CASE and other computer-aided tools aid the managers of the enterprise and not the people who are actually trying to produce the product.

We know of one "tools" organization that worked mightily to provide a comprehensive software engineering environment. But, the first tools they produced aided the managers and actually burdened the software engineers and made for many complaints.

This system was described at many presentations and seemed to be very high-tech. But, when people asked questions about how the tools were being accepted by the users, there was some hesitation. Then, there was an admission of some difficulty convincing users that the system was really there to help them. Finally, this software engineering environment became a victim of the *crock-pot effect*: when formerly fashionable kitchen appliances are pushed further and further back on the counter top to finally become merely storage places for food or truly useful tools.

This system was an example of something produced for an internal market that also served the government market. A great deal of money and effort was spent on it, but it was always difficult getting people to use it voluntarily. It probably found a small niche somewhere but, for the most part, it has disappeared from view.

It was clear that this high-tech solution wasn't really all that high-tech, at least from the workers' perspective. The concept was Roman even though the original developers were probably Greek and the tools would be used by Greeks. No wonder the developers missed the mark so widely!

Software Engineering

Webster's New World Dictionary of Computer Terms [1988] defines *software engineering* as follows: "A term coined in 1967 by the Study Group on Computer Science of the NATO Science Committee to imply the need for software manufacture based on the types of theoretical foundations and practical disciplines traditional in established branches of engineering. Software engineering is concerned with the development and implementation of large-scale software systems on production-model computers. Encompasses a broad range of topics related to the controlled design and development of high-quality computer software, including programming methodology (structured programming, ego-less programming, software quality assurance, programming productivity aids) and management of software projects (structured walkthroughs, chief programmer teams, program support library, HIPO Technique)."

Do we really *engineer* programs, or is it a fervent hope that someday we will understand enough about programming to draw some conclusions about it that reflect on Nature? And, can those reflections be observed and commented upon by scientists and then applied to practical purposes?

We believe that the elements are there, perhaps just below the surface, and that we can employ them to produce software. We believe the kernel of structured stuff is one of these elements. Our position is that *software engineering* means just that: the engineering of software, although current engineering practices today might be more of a craft than a science. Someday, we are sure we will have an engineering field and science of our own.

When we talk about software engineering, we run into the Rome vs. Greece issue again. The Waterfall model is used in the Roman sense, and the All-at-Once model is used in the Grecian sense. But, when the Romans try to foist their preferred method on the Greek workers, trouble happens as we previously discussed. The folks who want us to use their methods seldom try out these methods in the real world.

One of the hallmarks of the Greek civilization was the invention of Science: the orderly way of investigating the world around us and getting answers from Nature. We have institutions to do this: for example, the

Software Engineering Institute, the Software Productivity Consortium, the Microelectronics and Computer Technology Corporation, and many universities around the country. But, there is very little work done on how programs *are* written and very much on how they *should* be written without investigating the validity of the *shoulds*. This is very Roman, and is not very good science.

Another problem confusing things in our field at this time is corporate data management. It is seen as a *software engineering* issue, and it isn't. It is a *systems engineering* issue. It takes on characteristics of systems engineering. It does planning, allocating, organizing, coordinating, administrating, and conserving, which are much different from the characteristics of software engineering. Software engineers certainly can help with data management; but, it is possible to have data management without software engineers.

Once you begin to mingle systems engineering ideas with software engineering ideas, you end up with gigantic software engineering projects that are doomed to failure.

CASE

CASE is not only a combination of the above two problems, but has problems of its own. We do not yet know (and we may never know) what the limits of CASE are. Some want the "SE" part of CASE to mean *software engineering* and others want it to mean *systems engineering*. We take it to mean *software engineering*, but we have great sympathy for the other position.

So, when we use the term *computer-aided,* we are referring to a continuum. At one end of the continuum is the computer aiding the person using it. At the other end of the continuum is the computer aiding the project managers and the supervisors of the person who is actually using the computer.

When we use the term *software engineering,* we mean the current practices for analyzing problems, determining whether they can and should be solved by a computer, and then devising the instructions to do so.

When we use the term *CASE,* we mean *computer-aided software engineering,* although we will discuss with some sympathy another understanding of the term in the next chapter.

CASE tools are software that is used by programmers to do their jobs and are not ordinarily not used by other folks. A data-flow diagram editor and a code debugger are CASE tools, while word processors and Space Invaders are not (useful though they may be).

General-purpose software used by other folks set the side borders of CASE. But, these borders are pretty porous; many of us use tools that other workers use and we depend on them to help us do our jobs. Usually, these are the general tasks that are similar to those everywhere; but there are some exceptions.

Spreadsheet applications seem to be very popular with programmers. They find many interesting and unanticipated uses for them. We know of one programmer who uses a spreadsheet as a reformatter, and another who used one as a prototyper and finally as a delivery system. Then again, programmers have found a whole host of applications for some popular end-user applications such as HyperCard and ToolBook. General-purpose graphics editors are another example, as are outliners. One of the authors of this book uses an outliner called MORE from Symantic Corporation to produce action diagrams in a prototyping mode.

Finally, there are the modeler or simulation software. One good example is i**think**™.[2] We would describe it as a combination of a data-flow diagrammer and a spreadsheet.

CASE usually does not include "system" software, where *system* refers to the operating system of the computer being used by the programmer. Such software includes the lower level input and output, user interface, and memory and window management routines, although programmers must deal with these as part of their job in programming.

Compilers and linkers (loaders) are on the lower border, close to system software, because they usually come with the hardware you buy. But, compilers and linkers are, indeed, included in CASE because they (along with symbolic debuggers) usually comprise a tool known as a *language processor*. This type of tool is the most popular tool used by Greeks.

Also, compilers and linkers deal not only with what *we* can read but with what the *computer* is sensitive to. Compilers can provide sophisticated cross reference and code analysis information on the modules being compiled, and are therefore very *useful* to programmers. Some provide checks on typographical errors and language ambiguities by providing "stray" name lists. They provide information on all the external code that the routine being compiled will attempt to access. They can tell which variables have been created but not used, and which have been created and used but have not been initialized. They can identify "mixed mode" operations: variables of different types being

---

[2]Previously called *Stella* and described in "Playing with Stella," by John Palmer, *American Programmer*, Vol. 3, No. 9, September 1990, p.29.

used in the same computation. These are flagged as errors or warnings, especially in older languages like FORTRAN, which is not known for its rigor.

Compilers can give you statistics like the size of the module, the number of unique tokens, the total number of tokens and other code analysis data, and they usually reformat the source code to make it easier to read. Many folks write programs that analyze compiler output to produce graphics and other useful information.

Linkers connect programs or modules, making them into one executable unit. Loaders read this executable unit into computer storage making it ready for execution. Linkers are sometimes associated with loaders to become linkerloaders. This service software can also provide much useful information. Whereas compilers can tell which routines are called by the module being compiled, linkers can tell which routines call the one being linked to the system. This is very useful information in rat-killing, risk analysis, analyzing change effects, and in making "call trees" to help in understanding the program. Linkers tell you other useful stuff like any routines that were called but weren't found anywhere in the system.

Systems engineering lies at the upper border of our field. Many types of software tools are used here, such as:

- Corporate and project planning tools

- Strategic planning tools

- Market research tools

Other kinds of software used here are:

- Modeling tools, such as the IDEF series of diagramming and analysis aids

- Executive information systems

- Alternatives/options-analysis tools

- Knowledge-based systems specially designed for project managers

- Data analysis tools used by data resource management for estimating database size, and

- Other aids used specifically for getting a handle on data volumes

This upper border of our field is not as clear as the lower one because the techniques of systems engineering and corporate management frequently involve analysis and the diagrams with which we are familiar.

The territory enclosed by these borders is the subject of this book. (See Figure 1-1.)

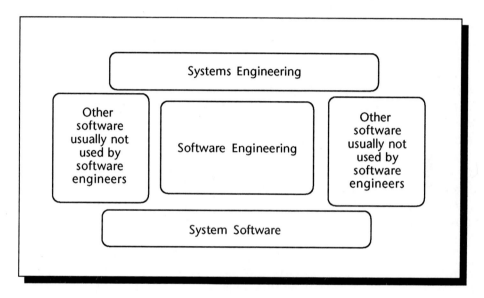

Figure 1-1. Borders

Now that the borders are set, here is a list of the tools that are included in CASE:

A normal basic set would contain editors, compilers, linkage editors/ loaders, and symbolic debuggers. Among the editors are:

- General text

- Language and language-sensitive

- Data dictionary

- Documentation (user, maintenance, customer, etc.)

Also included would be language processors, "products and services that work with code for comprehension, modification and testing." [Zvegintzov][3]

Then, there are graphics tools, such as those for producing data-flow diagrams, entity-relationship diagrams, structure charts, context diagrams, state transition diagrams, decision trees, and decision tables. Frequently, these tools save information about the contents of the diagrams and store it in data dictionaries. There was a time when data dictionaries simply listed the data used and created by programs. But, now they store all kinds of stuff, even the relationships among the stuff.

Then, there are analyzer tools, such as for debugging programs, measuring their complexity, and describing how they use variables. Other tools produce call trees of the interrelationships among modules, and others diagram control structures, which show the relationships among control statements inside modules.

There are tools for configuration management, code management, executable file "build" programs, and file management systems that manage various forms of the same module and various configurations of the same program.

Other types of tools are the "after market" tools, used especially in business programming to assist programmers in dealing with incomprehensible error messages and other complexities of large hardware and DBMS environments.

Then, there are the documentation tools. These build the documentation required by so many folks in large projects. They include tools for doing requirements tracing: editors that use templates to produce the many different types of documentation needed.

After the documentation tools are the maintenance tools. These include some of the analyzers listed previously, but they also include aids to understanding code since that is one of the fundamental processes in software maintenance. Here, tools include pretty-printers, which improve the format of code, and restructurers, which improve the code itself by removing old structures such as GO TO statements and replacing them with IF THEN ELSE statements. Finally there are the testing tools, such as test data generators, test analyzers, path coverage analyzers, static analyzers, and test coverage tools.

Another way of looking at tools is to organize them into Upper CASE, Lower CASE, and ICASE.

The first tools actually *called* CASE were the Upper CASE types. They supported the work involved in the initial stages of projects, such as systems analysis and options analysis; but, they usually were not sophisticated enough

---

[3] This is one of the best cataloging schemes for software we've ever seen.

to perform risk analysis, which was a very large shortcoming. These tools were essentially data-flow diagram editors, which soon were connected to a data dictionary and expanded from there. Excelerator, Teamwork, and CASE 2000 are examples of early entries into this market. Other types include data modelers, structure chart makers, and documentation aids for functional specifications, requirements documents, alternatives and options analyses, etc.

The James Martin Productivity Series, Volume 6, evaluates the main Upper CASE tools. They have done a very good job, and we don't propose to duplicate their work here. During the preparation of this book, however, we heard about a product that you might find useful. It's a tool for selecting tools, from CASE Consulting Group.[4] Also, see Appendix A for our own early attempt at mapping the types of tools into applications. As an aside, if we were going to do a book based only on James Martin, or on the information in Appendix A, or on the CASE Consulting Group's tool, it would simply be another detailed duplication of work that already exists. However, during our research for this book, we discovered all of these other *issues* that greatly affect CASE. That is why we've ended up with the book that we've written.

X/A

Upper CASE tools usually support the paradigm know as the *Waterfall*. They are sometimes called methodology *companions* (not our term; we would use the term *dictators* because they enforce a methodology). They tend to be weighted in favor of the organizational type—the Roman way—and not enough for the individual type—the Greek way. The idea is that they will be used for massive software projects designed and built by very large teams. These tools have networking capabilities with check-in and check-out facilities, access to project databases (folks now call them *repositories*), and they are tied into project management facilities, sometimes in sinister ways.

One of the authors of this book knows of a set of requirements for a so-called *workbench* where the project management personnel could "monitor" the activity of anyone on the project in such a way that those being monitored wouldn't be aware that they were being watched. That's pretty scary.

However, there are other software development paradigms, such as prototyping, hacking, handcuffing, and incremental development, and only a few tools support them. Prototyping tools—such as Prototyper from Smithers and Barnes—and some modelers—such as i**think**—are being more widely used. However, programmers working with the other methods still mostly rely on back-end, or Lower CASE, tools.

---

[4]Toolfinder, from CASE Consulting Group, 11830 Kerr Parkway, Suite 315, Lake Oswego, OR, 97035; (503) 245-6880; FAX (503) 245-6935.

Lower CASE tools come into play during the latter stages of Roman-type projects, and during all the stages of Greek-type projects. They include the more traditional tools: editors, compilers, linker/loaders, debuggers, restructurers, and programmer aids. They tend to be Greek in nature, used by individuals to aid them in their work, which is the classical use of a tool.

ICASE, which stands for Integrated Computer-Aided Software Engineering, tries to integrate all the tools required for development (and sometimes maintenance) into a seamless whole. It hasn't had much success yet.

Another aspect of ICASE and Upper CASE tools is their usefulness in doing systems engineering work. They help to illustrate and save the context within which the business operates: the enterprise model where the main players are described, the business rules set down and made explicit, the competitors listed, the markets described, the suppliers listed, and the goals of the business made known. This is becoming increasingly important in business systems work. These tasks haven't been done as often or as thoroughly before the advent of CASE because of the vast amounts of data that must be managed.

Associated with ICASE are the *mega-models*. These purport to provide a framework within which all development and, sometimes, maintenance can be done. These usually expect tools to be used. Here is a list of those we know about:

- *METHOD/1* from Andersen Consulting

- *Summit* from Coopers and Lybrand

- *Productivity+* from DMR of Canada

- *4FRONT* from Deloitte & Touche

- *Pride* from M. Bryce and Associates, Inc.

- *Stradis* from McDonnell Douglas

- *Information Engineering Facility (IEF)* from Texas Instruments

- *Rapid Application Development* from James Martin Associates

- *Productivity Breakthrough Projects* from JMW Consultants, Inc.

Some tools are tightly bound to the methodology they support. For example, IEF from Texas Instruments is bound to the information engineering methodology. Some are loosely bound and can support many methods. Among these are Excelerator from Intersolv and the PowerTools™ tool set from Iconix Software Engineering, Inc.

So, this is what our canvas looks like. It has some interesting threads running through it, about Greece and Rome and about the advantage of using tools. It has borders: it usually doesn't include common consumer or end-user software, only software used by software engineers. At the lower border, it interfaces with system software; at the upper border, it interfaces with systems engineering. In the next chapter, we will take a long look at systems engineering. So, let's render unto Cæsar. ...

Chapter 2.
Systems Engineering:
Render Unto Cæsar

At the top of our world sits systems engineering. It is the most Roman of activities. Producing nothing itself, it makes it possible to produce the largest and most ambitious efforts. It is the middleman, the fiduciary function, and the facilitator of large projects. It attempts to manage size and complexity. Whenever large projects are attempted, systems engineering is done, one way or another.

By *large*, we mean projects of more than at least one person's effort per year; probably larger than a small team effort (seven people or less). By *systems engineering*, we mean the planning, resource allocation, functional subdivision, management, integration, and evaluation needed to produce a large, complex thing or process. The complexity could arise because the system's components are produced from disparate technical domains, or because the project is so large that its sheer size makes it complex.

Some examples of systems engineering are bridge building, city traffic control, air traffic control, and the construction of skyscrapers, aircraft carriers, weapons, space ports, and distribution systems.

NASA produces its products by means of systems engineering; so does the Department of Defense. In fact, so do hospitals, banks, insurance companies, and many other enterprises even though they usually don't use the term *systems engineering*.

Vaughan Merlyn thinks that CASE should mean Computer-Aided *Systems Engineering* [Merlyn 1989, p.4].[5] We have great sympathy for his point of view. One of the reasons why the Waterfall model (the traditional way of producing software) frequently fails is that systems engineering wasn't done or was done as part of software development. Very often the projects on which we work are large enough that they require a systems engineering approach.

Fred Brooks in *The Mythical Man-Month* describes an excellent example of a project manager in a systems engineering position. This manager is trying to make some sense out of enormous complexity by using budgets of various

---

[5] **Author's note:** This is probably no longer in print, but you can call CASE Research at (206) 453-9900. Vaughan has stated the same theme in several talks he has given around the world.

types, such as core (memory) and machine cycles, besides the bean counter's usual cost and time figures [Brooks 1982].

Nevertheless, we believe that there are significant differences between *systems* engineering and *software* engineering; and, this *book* is about computer-aided *software* engineering. However systems engineering has implications for software engineering; so, this *chapter* is about the differences and the implications.

We will first look at systems engineering from a business view, and then from the view of a major practitioner, the Department of Defense. Next, we will examine three system errors that affect us. Finally, we will explore the implications of systems engineering for us software engineers and for the tools we use.

Systems Engineering: A Business View

Businesses are themselves systems. They are of interest to us because they frequently produce large software systems and have trouble doing it. *Systems analysts* are systems engineers who look at businesses as systems in order to understand the software systems they need. One reason businesses have trouble producing large software systems is that they don't do the analysis up front.

In the following example, both a business as a system and the system it wishes to produce are discussed.

Daniel Appleton describes one very large project as a *system* because of its size [Appleton 1986, pp.62-64]. "A company started out by wanting to replace its cost and scheduling systems. A first glance showed that they needed to be replaced, and it looked like a 5-megabuck deal.

"The new system was further subdivided into 13 major functions and the cost went to 10 megabucks. Teams were created to evaluate 11 of the 13 functions. Each team was composed of 5 people who were mainly users. The teams decomposed the functions into 700 requirements and gave a new cost estimate of 20 megabucks.

"Constraints were now added: no more than 50 developers and 20 megabucks! By the time the disaster happened, there had been 4 different project managers, and 2 different user team leaders. 'It began to dawn on people that this was no longer a project, or even a system. No one was sure what it was.'

"He goes on: 'Once again the original project was not a project at all. It was a dream. This dream, when stuffed into the big end of a structured, functional decomposition system development methodology, not only got stuck, it turned into a nightmare. Managers then had to face the problem of how to divide the nightmare into some doable projects [do the project breakdown part of systems engineering], each of which had the potential of becoming a nightmare itself. The only algorithm known to successfully decompose very large projects into doable projects was practiced in secret by the Druids. Most IS managers depend on miracles.'

"He offers help in two ways.

"First, assess the project based on 11 criteria. Then, rate the project on a scale of 1-10 for each criteria. Add up the total score and, if it is higher than 90, the project is doable. If it is lower, then 'you have an incipient very large project on your hands.' Here are the criteria:

"1. Does the proposed project automate a known static process? [*yes* rates high]

2. How *tight* is its scope; how many interfaces are there with existing systems? [*tight* and *very few* rate high]

3. Does it replace more than one existing system? [*one system* rates high; *more than one system* rates lower]

4. How few and fixed are the requirements? [the fewer and more fixed the better]

5. How complex are the requirements? [the simpler the better]

6. Is the estimated total development no more than 12 months? [*yes* is good]

7. Is there a dedicated development environment? [*yes* is good]

8. Is there an established software database architecture? [*yes* is good]

9. Does a single individual have responsibility and authority for project success? [*yes* is good]

10. Is a formal system development methodology strictly enforced? [*yes* is good]

11. Are knowledgeable users committed to the project? [*yes* is good]"
[DeGrace and Stahl 1990, pp.192-193]

Look at his criteria; the questions are among those a systems engineer
would ask in assessing the risks and feasibility of some project. You might have
to live with low scores on a point or two. Perhaps the requirements are neither
few nor fixed. But, once you know that, you can take measures to mitigate the
effect. For example, you can prototype the system to elicit the requirements
from the customer and users.

The lesson here is that if the project managers do systems engineering up
front instead of backing into it, they stand a better chance of succeeding.

Appleton then offers the asset-based life cycle shown in Figure 2-1. Here is
another aspect of systems engineering: *management*.

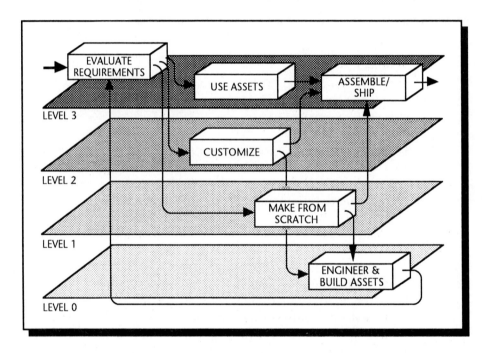

Figure 2-1. An Asset-Management Model

This model is a way to create and manage assets that can be reused to do other work. It starts with a requirements evaluation. Then, a decision is made on how to create and assemble them into the system to be shipped: use assets directly from the asset inventory, customize assets that are already there, or make some from scratch. If you customize an asset or make one from scratch, the developers go through a process of converting it into a new asset. Appleton does not specify what would go on, but it is reasonable that the new asset needs to be cataloged and, perhaps, made portable, robust, and able to be modified. (See Chapter 3, *Software Quality: An Odyssey Through the Ilities*, for some ideas on how to do this.) Then, it is entered into the inventory.

In addition, Appleton describes the environment in which this management takes place. It has three parts:

1. An information architecture that deals with requirements.

2. A computer systems architecture that manages the hardware and operating system software.

3. A control architecture that contains planning, system development, and project-management procedures, as well as technical and data standards and quality assurance.

What he describes is a systems engineering organization where project evaluation ratings and asset management would be done routinely as a part of the initial planning; where evaluations help define which assets to acquire; and where acquiring assets helps the scores of evaluations by creating reusable components. This helps to make projects doable.

Appleton's model does not show a make or buy process, and that is certainly a part of the deliberations. But, his three-part architecture is right on. We have noticed time and again that when systems engineering is missing from projects, they are difficult to contain and they evolve into the monsters that managers have nightmares about [ibid, p.195].

Here is another look from the book *Wicked Problems, Righteous Solutions*. It is a description of the Initiation Phase of a project that follows a method of development called the Waterfall [ibid, pp.28-30]:

The Initiation phase often originates at the senior management level, either as a result of strategic planning or arising from the operations of the business. (See Figure 2-2.)

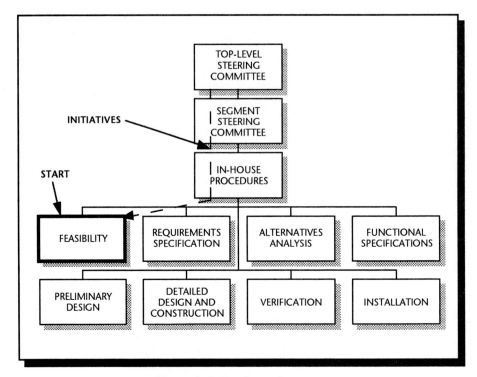

Figure 2-2. Business Systems

"The problem to be solved is stated in a general way, often as only an objective. Sometimes, management applies initial priorities and limitations, such as: 'This project is of strategic importance, but it must be done for under five million dollars.' My correspondents tell me that applying these initial priorities and limitations is useful later on when they are attempting to limit the project to a manageable size or keep it on track.

"A team of people with the appropriate knowledge and skills is formed to evaluate the problem and propose solutions. Some interpreters of the theory conclude that there is no need here for assistance from computing experts. The bulk of the analysis is performed by the users, since they are most familiar with the problems they want to solve. However, as we shall see, this leads to problems.

"The team uses the original problem statement, often in the form of a memorandum, an authorization to spend resources, and whatever documentation exists for the present system if there is one. The team then sets about expanding and clarifying the original statement, refining it for evaluation, and describing the problem in terms of the present system and *its* problems and limitations. This 'present' system used to be a manual one, such as a system for making out paychecks, where you would fill out a timecard and take it to a bookkeeper who would write out a check for you. However, these days, this type of paycheck system is likely to be a first- or even second-generation computer system.

"Sometimes, a business system contains flaws that cannot be solved by automation, such as turf, cultural, and political issues. These must be identified and dealt with either by fixing the current system or by declaring these other issues as limiting factors in the new system.

"Turf issues are problems of conflicting charters and feelings of ownership. For example, during a period of decentralizing their computing services, a data-center technology staff may feel that they should set the standards for workstations, while newer organizations, mainly originating from using groups, may feel that it is *their* charter to do that activity.

"Cultural issues involve the terminology being used, the environment in which the system will operate, issues about what to produce and how to produce it, and the organization's place in the enterprise. There is a business culture, an engineering culture, and a data-center culture, all of which have different terminology and environments, produce different things, and make competing claims on the enterprises' resources.

"Political issues involve decisions that affect more than one organization, such as who decides what hardware and software will be 'standard' throughout the entire enterprise. Political issues also involve decisions about which organization will have the ultimate responsibility for the project being considered.

"All of these issues should be discovered and expressed so they can be accounted for in the development cycle. Otherwise, there is a risk of encoding these flaws into software that will later seem to be harder even than concrete. ..."

"The next activity, which is sometimes a separate phase, is called the Options Study or Feasibility Analysis. During this activity, the developers imagine a range of solutions, perform a cost-benefit analysis on each, apply any 'spin' required by their own organization, pick the best candidate, and take it to their management for review and the authorization to continue. If approved, the information (a clarified, expanded problem statement, an Options Study, and a Cost-Benefit Analysis) is passed to the next phase for further analysis and refinement.

"The Options Study provides management with a set of solutions to the problem they want solved. One of these options should always be: 'Do nothing!' This allows management an 'out': a cooling off period for the times when the 'snake oil' salesmen come to town hyping the latest stuff your company should have.

"Another reason to include a 'do nothing' option is the 'Abilene Paradox' first observed by Jerry Harvey [Harvey 1988, pp. 16-43]. It goes something like this: One decision maker suggests a project, but has no good reason for it except to see what others will say about it. Well, as it often happens, the others have no real reason to object and they assume the suggester is highly motivated, so they go along with the suggested project. As a result, the project gets started and nobody really wants it.

"A 'Do nothing!' option allows decision makers a chance to reconsider and to escape the paradox early on, before a lot of money is spent on it. If you think this is hooey, please read Jerry B. Harvey, *The Abilene Paradox: The Management of Agreement,* Organizational Dynamics, Vol. 17, No. 1, Summer, 1988, pp.16-43." [DeGrace and Stahl 1990, pp.34-36]

Notice how much other stuff is done here. But, it is precisely this other stuff that causes so much trouble in projects using the Waterfall. That is because the other stuff is, to a large extent, *systems engineering,* and software engineers aren't naturally systems engineers, although systems analysts come close to it. At the end of this chapter, we will offer some advice on how to survive in a systems engineering world.

Another view of systems engineering from the business community is that of managing data as a resource and the activities of a data administrator (DA). Here is what James Martin has to say about some of the data administrator's tasks:

"In order to computerize the activities of a corporation, the data items it uses must be defined, cataloged, and organized. This is often difficult and time consuming because data have been treated rather sloppily in the past. What is essentially the same data item type has been defined differently in different places, represented differently in different computers, and given different names. Data item types which were casually thought to be the same are found to be not quite the same.

"The data administrator has the job of cleaning up this confusion. Definitions of data item types must be agreed upon and documented. Much help from end users is often needed in this process." [Martin and McClure 1985, p.232]

Here, systems engineering and software engineering are close. Software engineers design and build databases for the data resource manager. In those rare times when an actual architecture is created and put into place, software engineers do it. But, they do this at the behest of someone who is trying to bring some order to the extremely complex world of business data.

The data resource manager, the facilities folks, and the manufacturing folks all make up the systems engineering staff of the enterprise.

However, this organization can have a secret life of its own. "Anyone who works for a large organization is aware of a disparity between the way things work 'on paper' and the way they work in reality. There is the way the manual says to do the job—and then there's the way you really do it. There is the "org" chart—and then there are the people who really make things happen. There are the formal meetings—and then there are the encounters in the hallway where who does what really gets decided." [Feinstein 1989] It is this *secret life* that often drives the turf, cultural, and political issues we discussed earlier, and that can actually control the enterprise.

Systems Engineering: A Government View

Another view of systems engineering comes from the System Engineering Management Guide, produced by Defense Systems Management College, Fort Belvoir, Virginia. It presents the Department of Defense's (DoD) view of the subject.

"System Engineering is most active in the planning period and in conceiving the system concept and defining the requirements for the system. As the detailed design is being finalized, system engineers resolve the interface problems, do tradeoff analyses, and assist in verifying performance. During the production phase, System Engineering is primarily concerned with verifying system capability and maintaining the baseline system. During the operations period [it] evaluates changes to the system, establishes their effectiveness and facilitates the effective incorporation of changes, modifications and updates." [System Engineering Management Guide 1986]

Figure 2-3 shows the main elements of systems engineering from the DoD's point of view, followed by a description of each element.

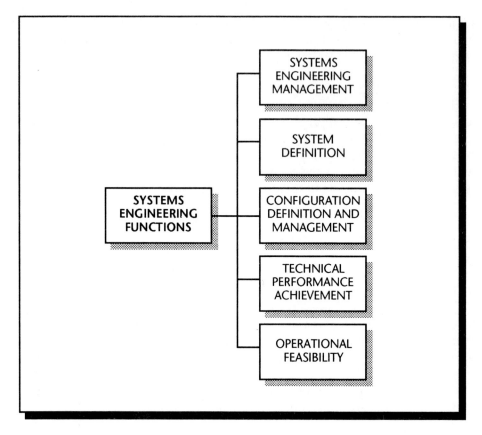

Figure 2-3. Systems Engineering From the DoD's Point of View

Systems engineering management is concerned with the process of mediating between the source of some need and the source of a means to satisfy the need. It is composed of four main topics:

- Organization
- System hierarchy
- System integration
- Work breakdown structures

In a corporation, this management function would be vested in some organization reporting to an executive committee that has considered and prioritized the needs of the corporation. This systems engineering management organization is often called a *project office*, a *program*, or, these days, an *architecture office*. It often performs the initiation phase of the project, and then spins off a separate and temporary organization to finish the work.

Figure 2-4 shows what a program office looks like in the DoD.

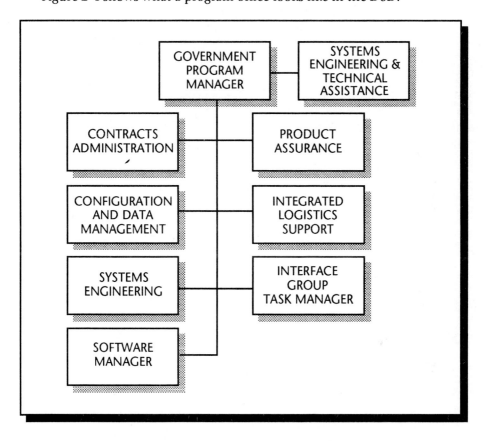

Figure 2-4. A DoD Program Office

It isn't very large considering the resources and enterprises it controls, yet offices such as this have produced and maintained our defense establishment. Notice how software and systems are separated here. NASA has somewhat larger staffs for their program offices, but they do more of the engineering than do the DoD offices. Nevertheless, their organizations look much the same.

Systems engineering management also does the first simplification of the new product or process by breaking it down into a hierarchy of main components. These, in turn, will be further decomposed into lower processes until there are doable projects.

System integration puts all the pieces together and oversees their testing as a complete unit. And, it compares the results with the original goals. Theoretically, what gets produced should match exactly what was originally asked for. However, this rarely happens.

The system integration folks have to decide whether what got produced is good enough. This, of course, causes all kinds of problems, especially political ones, and especially from folks who think we can specify things exactly or produce exactly what we specify.

Integration also manages all the plans needed for the project. Here is a list:

- Reliability

- Maintainability

- Quality assurance

- Human engineering

- Safety

- Logistics support analysis (figuring out how to buy and stock spare parts or how to repair irreplaceable items)

- Contamination and corrosion control

- Parts, materials, and processes control

- Electromagnetic control

- Vulnerability/survivability

- Mass properties control

- Packaging, handling, storage, and transportation

(Whew! That is a lot of plans!)

The system integration folks also start the master and working schedules. The master schedule identifies all the hardware and software contractual deliverables, test articles, major elements of work, and significant milestones. It can have various forms, Gantt charts suitable for presentation, and milestone or network charts. Program Evaluation and Review Technique (PERT) and Critical Path Analysis are tools that the financial folks (bean counters) use to keep things organized and working effectively toward the project's goals.

Integration also manages the interfaces among the components of the system. It uses Interface Control Working Groups (ICWGs) and Interface Control Documents (ICDs) for these purposes. Making sure that disparate things fit together is one of the main functions of systems engineering.

Finally, systems engineering management establishes Work Breakdown Structures (WBSs). These are financial control tools for disbursing, adjusting, or withholding money to projects. There are several types:[6]

- The Summary WBS is for the entire project and describes the work down to three levels.

- The Project Summary WBS does the same thing for a major part of the system being developed.

- The Project WBS shows all the work for the entire project.

- Finally, the Contract WBS shows all the work to be done on a contract.

The next major function is *system definition*, which translates the users' needs into a set of requirements that can satisfy those needs. It also does concept exploration to determine if the requirements are feasible. This could involve actually building prototypes. The systems engineer is trying to get a clear idea about the problem and which solutions make sense.

System definition decomposes the system *idea* into system *requirements* and down further into doable projects. Here is where complexity control is really exercised, and where the doable things are teased out of the complexity. During system definition, trade studies are done to establish the overall shape of the system and the most cost-effective way of composing and producing it.

---

[6]MIL-STD-881A is the Government document that describes in detail all these WBSs.

The main topics of *system definition* are:

- System definition and mission requirements analysis
- Functional analysis
- Requirements flowdown and allocation
- Trade studies
- System synthesis

The next function on the list is *configuration definition and management.* Here, the system specifications are generated and the configuration management processes are put into place.

As the size of systems grows, the opportunity for communications errors increases. This is where detailed system specifications are particularly needed so the communication problems inherent in large projects are not compounded. As Fred Brooks described in his classic *The Mythical Man Month* [1982], the more people there are involved in a project, the more time is spent on communication and *not* on producing the product. (This is a particularly Roman characteristic of large systems.)

On a three-person team, there are only three communication channels among the three people. However, on a four-person team, there are six channels. (See Figure 2-5.) As the size of a group grows from three members to ten, the number of possible communication paths is: 3, 6, 10, 15, 21, 28, 36, 45.

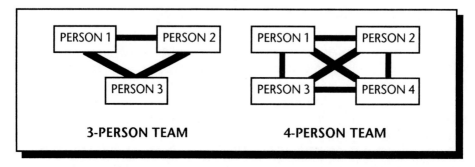

Figure 2-5. Communication Channels on Three- and Four-Person Teams

Detailed system specifications will help to keep everyone involved in the project working on the same system. Configuration management activities will coordinate the elements of the system to minimize confusion and reduce further communications errors.

When you manage *configurations*, you identify, organize, coordinate, and control any changes to the system. The controls are put into place to monitor the software versions, platform ports, and version schedules. *System configurations* can describe:

- The *components* of the system
- The *interconnections* between the components
- The *processes* used to create the components

The next function after configuration definition and management is *technical performance achievement*. It looks at:

- Risk analysis and management
- Technical performance measurement
- Performance verification

The last function is *operational feasibility*, which is concerned with:

- Engineering specialty integration
- System effectiveness
- Life cycle cost and design to cost
- Logistics and the logistics support analysis process
- Modification management
- Manufacturing and producibility

A typical contractor's systems engineering organization would look like Figure 2-6. The activities performed by each component of the organization are shown in Figures 2-6a through 2-6g. We have modified the structure somewhat from that shown in the System Engineering Management Guide to make it applicable to general technical and business organizations.

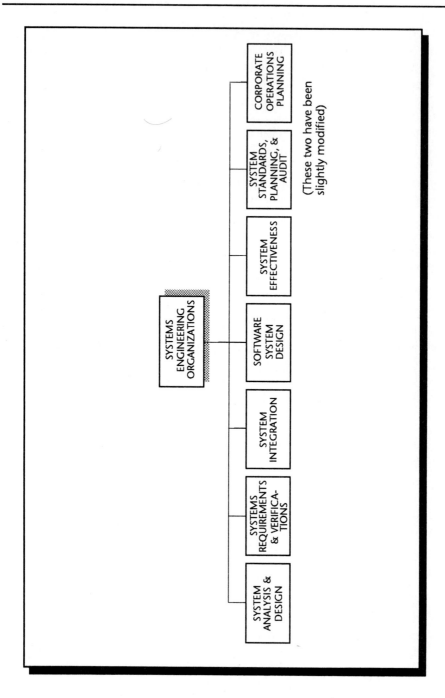

Figure 2-6. Systems Engineering Organizations

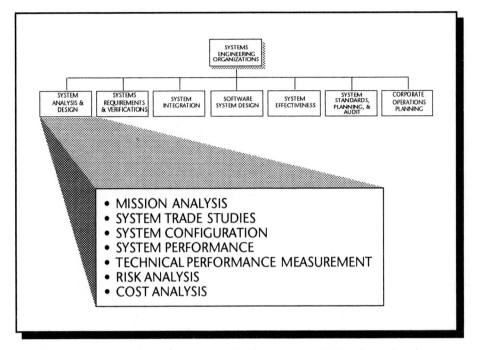

Figure 2-6a. The SYSTEM ANALYSIS AND DESIGN Organization

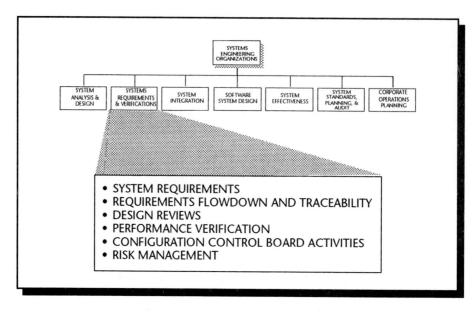

Figure 2-6b. The SYSTEM REQUIREMENTS AND VERIFICATIONS Organization

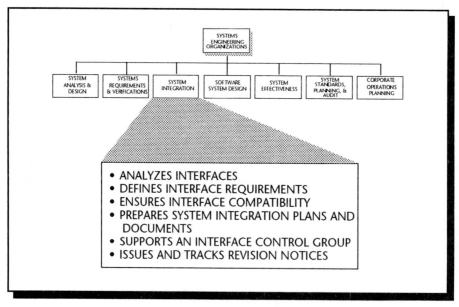

Figure 2-6c. The SYSTEM INTEGRATION Organization

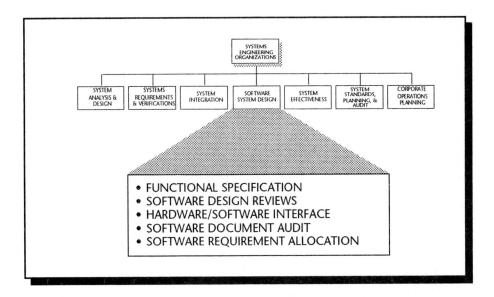

Figure 2-6d. The SOFTWARE SYSTEM DESIGN Organization

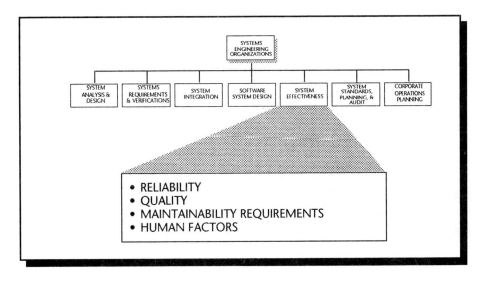

Figure 2-6e. The SYSTEM EFFECTIVENESS Organization

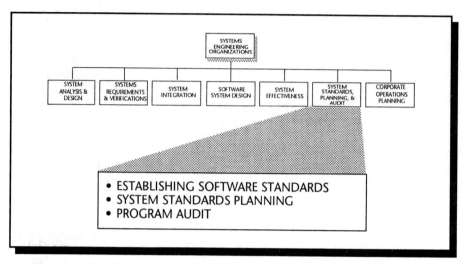

Figure 2-6f. The SYSTEM STANDARDS, PLANNING, AND AUDIT Organization

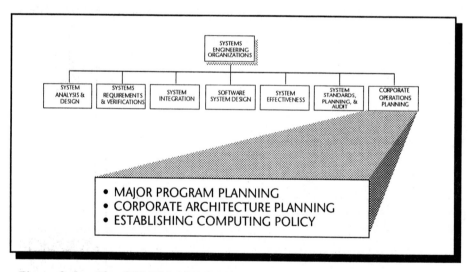

Figure 2-6g. The CORPORATE OPERATIONS PLANNING Organization

As you can see, this is a very extensive list of activities and will be expensive to do. Only very large organizations motivated by other large organizations like the Department of Defense can do them. But, the idea is that whether the system is a product or the business enterprise that wants it produced, certain considerations similar to the ones Appleton suggests ought to be done before giving projects their marching orders.

Underlying these issues is a consensus about managing the complexity of the systems with which we have to deal today. Deciding to pay attention to the list helps bring to the surface most of the important issues. Yes, it is expensive, but we suppose it's a case of "pay me now or pay me later."

Systems engineering is an umbrella activity—a Roman activity—under which software development and other Greek-like business activities take place. And yet, Systems Engineering still isn't much thought of explicitly as a separate field of study. Engineers from various disciplines arrive at Systems Engineering from their native disciplines. For example, a traffic-control engineer becomes a Systems Engineer when he analyzes and designs for traffic patterns.

There are indications, however, that the kinds of activities that go on in Systems Engineering are now being given more weight. Enterprise models, corporate data dictionaries, data-naming standards, and the Jackson System Design view of development (as a mapping of business activities to the eventual software system) all indicate that there is a growing awareness of the value of the bigger picture that Systems Engineering can provide.

Do the things we have described about Systems Engineering still match your ideas about what software engineering is?

Three *System* Errors

Lots of things go wrong with systems. Many problems occur because of poor workmanship, and would occur even with a simple system or where systems aren't involved. But, there are some errors that are essentially system-oriented, and are usually independent of workmanship. Indeed, good workmanship can actually make these errors worse. We will talk about three of them:

- *Goal displacement*—the case of the pepper shakers.

- *Functional distortion*—the case of the vendor-enhanced hospital system.

- *Functional distraction*—the shuttle disaster.

Goal Displacement

There is a national restaurant chain that suffers from the error of goal displacement. The evidence of this is that its pepper shakers are too full to let out very much pepper. It doesn't happen just once in a while at a few of the restaurants. It doesn't just happen very often. It *always* happens. The reason it always happens is because the pepper shakers are *completely filled*.

This particular restaurant chain uses the type of containers where the holes in both the salt and the pepper shakers are the same size. However, pepper has a slightly larger cross-sectional shape than salt. Pepper is also much less *massive* than salt. Therefore, to generate the force necessary to escape the shaker, it needs to accelerate a longer distance. When the shakers are completely filled, the pepper cannot gain the force needed to escape the container since there is not enough room to accelerate. If you want a generous serving of pepper on your pasta, you must completely remove the top of the container to sprinkle out what you want.

The reason why the shakers are so completely filled is that the managers instruct the staff to fill all the condiment containers to the top. This is to ensure that all the containers will be ready for the customers.

The goal is to be ready for customers; but, rather than giving *that* instruction, the managers of these restaurants tell their staffs to fill all the containers to the top. This instruction *displaces* the original goal.

This might seem to be a silly example and, more than once, one of the authors of this book (Peter DeGrace) was thought of as weird as he investigated the pepper shakers in these restaurants. There was a frightened waitress who thought that he was from the Department of Health, and there was a very testy manager who insisted on knowing *why* Peter was asking all these questions.

What this manager thought about the questions (or Peter for that matter) we can only guess at. But, here is what we are getting at: If the goal is A and you argue that B equals A, then you can replace A with B. However, if the argument is wrong, then you have goal displacement.

What does this have to do with systems engineering? Well, suppose your goal is to produce a better system. Suppose also that someone argues that imposing a rigorous development procedure is the way to accomplish that. Suppose that you impose this procedure and things go from bad to worse. Does this sound familiar?

Goal displacement occurred in two cases we know about where rigorous procedures were imposed. In both cases, the error was caused by not checking the argument.

In the first case, the predominant activity was software maintenance. The rigorous procedure caused delays, it destroyed the trust between the maintainers and their customers, and it inhibited a fundamental maintenance process: namely, learning the software.

The second case involved software development. The error was in not understanding what really goes on when software is produced. The rigorous procedure impeded the staff's creativity, the project "dried" up, and much of the staff said their good-byes.

Don't get us wrong; careful, precise work produced for people as well as for machines is extremely important. However, the procedures must be applicable. Maintenance procedures are *not* development procedures, and they must conform to the way human beings *actually* work, not to how they *should* work.

By not checking the argument that a rigorous development procedure would improve the software, the managers who imposed the rigorous procedure *displaced* the goal of producing good software with that of imposing rigor. This has caused a lot of rigor as far as we can tell: *rigor mortis* on some projects.

Functional Distortion

There is a common mischief done by the "finance" folks (bean counters) in many businesses. When they are discussing the process of the business, they frequently say something like: "Finance is what it's all about." And, who can argue with them? After all, even non-profit activities have to have financial functions. So, these folks often have the main say (and sometimes the *only* say) about what kind of record-keeping system will be used for financial activities. But, while these guys know a lot about *business*, they seldom know enough about the business they're *in* to make wise choices.

Consider, for example, a hospital system we know about. The finance folks bought a record-keeping system without consulting (or even thinking that they ought to consult) with the other parts of the hospital staff. Another part of the hospital staff actually does the record-keeping, and it is an important function, even for finance. The record-keeping involves maintaining a coded history of all the hospital's patients and the treatment they received (see Figure 2-7).

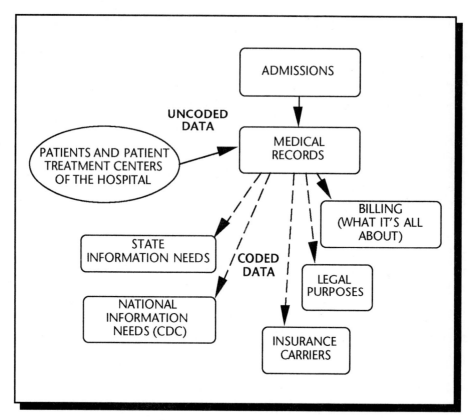

Figure 2-7. The Hospital's Information Needs

In this view, information passes from the treatment centers to the medical records specialists, who code it according to a scheme known as the International Classification of Disease (ICD, ninth year, clinically modified, or ICD-9-CM). The records staff receives reports from doctors and other health-care professionals, encodes it, and sends it on its way to functions inside and outside the hospital.

To do their work, the record keepers must be familiar with the disease process, medical terminology, medical phraseology, and the precision required by the coding scheme. For example, if a doctor uses the word *anomaly* in his diagnosis but really meant *atrophy*, the record keepers must detect and interpret the remark for the record. (*Anomaly* refers to a congenital condition, *atrophy* to one that occurs after birth.) The medical field requires that kind of precision.

Our correspondent describes the system that was purchased by the finance folks as one where:

- The records staff cannot always take the screens at face value and must interpret them in much the same way that they must interpret the doctors' statements: for precision and accuracy. They sometimes have to find work-arounds in order to get the correct information into the record system because the system does not implement the coding system consistently, thoroughly, or correctly.

- The system assigns codes that are no longer used by the medical facility; the staff must repeatedly delete them.

- The system does not allow the correct birth dates to be shown for patients born in the 19th century; it identifies a patient born in 1896 as being four years old. (The Lord only knows what will happen on January 1, 2000.)

- The system does not allow records to be posted in military time, which is used throughout the medical world. For example 20:47 should always mean 8:47 P.M.; but, the computer displays 08:47 p, which is its very own code and is not used by medical folks anywhere.

- Medical records are seen as *billing information gathering* rather than as part of the historical process of treatment. Record keepers are considered to be mere clerks rather than the highly trained staff they are, with hard-won expertise in the disease and treatment process.

Figure 2-8 shows a normal *context view* of a hospital system. We believe that this view is wrong for systems engineering. What should be used is the *mission view,* shown in Figure 2-9.

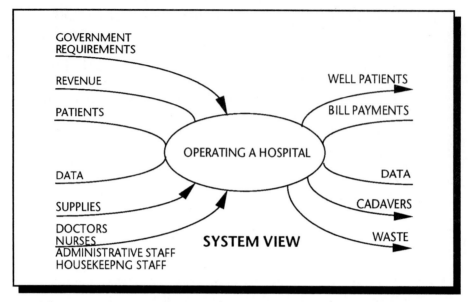

Figure 2-8. The Roman—Finance—System View of a Hospital System

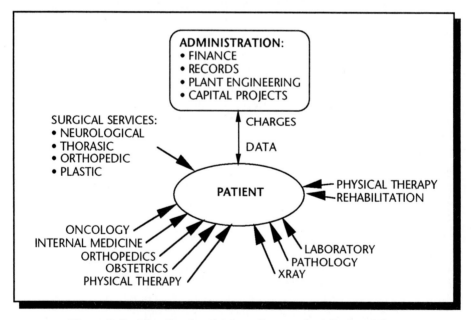

Figure 2-9. The Greek—Patient-Centered—Mission View

With the mission view in mind, the patient is "what it's all about," and the importance of the patient's treatment is paramount. Now, with this view in mind, it is more likely that when the vendor comes to visit, more of the players in the process will be consulted and will have a say in acquiring and enhancing their system.

But, with the old way, Finance saw itself as the center of the known world and attempted to impose on the whole hospital *its* needs for information and data processing; the functions of the other parts of the hospital were distorted by Finance.

To the doctors and nurses, the patients are "what it's all about." There are easier ways of making a living, such as being a Finance person. But, doctors and nurses usually have something else in mind.

Functional Distraction

Functional distraction occurs when members of an organization find themselves distracted by one (usually new) part of their assignment, and do not keep up with what is happening in the other parts of their assignment. The changes in NASA over the last fifteen years is one example.

NASA's been having a hell of a time since the moon landing. It is a characteristic of organizations that the folks who compose them want their organizations to continue. The folks at NASA had similar goals, but NASA no longer had an automatic source of funds and had to compete in Congress for funding. So, technical managers, who were used to fighting Nature and not politics, found themselves in deep political waters.

The Challenger disaster illustrates what functional distraction is. We're not saying that NASA management bent to political needs and decided to launch against good advice. (Even if that *did* happen, that's not what functional distraction is about.)

What we *are* talking about is that NASA management kept itself in the decision loop when it shouldn't have been. The best evidence of this is that management believed that the chances of a launch failure were 10,000 to 1. Actually, the chances were more like 100 to 1, which is *much* more likely.

In being distracted by the need to fight for money, NASA management lost contact with the technical staff. As a result, they used spurious arguments to counter the concerns of the rocket scientists and always fell back to the idea that the chance of anything happening was much smaller than it really was.

Incidentally, Richard Feynman, who made the calculation of the much higher probabilities of a Shuttle disaster, describes his work on the Challenger

Commission in his book *What Do You Care What Other People Think*, especially in the appendix [Feynman 1988].[4] Feynman is what we've been referring to as a *Greek*. He found himself in the *very* Roman environment of a Presidential Commission. His story, starting on page 113 of that book and continuing to the end, is an excellent and humorous illustration of the thread that winds its way all through *this* book.

The error NASA management made was in not knowing that they had other jobs to do that were essentially political. They should have excused themselves from the essentially technical decision-making process.

So, what does NASA's misfortune have to do with us? Well, have you ever ended up with tools you couldn't use because they were purchased by a big shot who was promoted from the data center who is solving ten-year-old problems but who thinks he is right on top of things? Have you ever discovered that there is a great void between what management thinks and what actually is the case?

These system errors all have some things in common. They all have to do with a person affecting other people; they all have to do with the Roman management hierarchy; they all have to do with the exercise of power over people; they all have to do with not checking or testing things in the real world; and, they all seem to have a big effect on CASE, as shown in the next examples.

CASE and System Errors

We've described system errors here because they affect us and our tools. Those who select tools for us commit *goal displacement* when they become enamored by the functions of the tools and forget that people must actually use them to get work done. They select the tools with the most functions; some of these functions are only partially operational. They look for the most power and the most capacity. Their goal of helping people is displaced by the goal of supplying the *most* functions in tools, not the *right* ones. Like the pepper in the shaker, some of our tools, especially the front-end CASE tools, are crammed so full they can't be used very well at all.

Functional distortion takes place when tools are selected by people with one limited point of view but who expect *everyone* to use the tools. For example, someone might have selected tools because they work on Sun workstations and IBM PCs, while the people for whom they made the selection use HP

---

[7]See especially p.214 and the Appendix starting on p.221.

Apollo workstations and Macintoshes. Or, tools that work well in a COBOL environment might be pushed down on scientific programmers.

Finally, we find that *functional distraction* takes place when tools are selected by people who are interested in achieving some other purpose. We know of an organization that was very interested in standards for political reasons. It wanted to make some CASE tool a standard as soon as possible. This organization simply picked a tool (a very expensive one) so it could announce that it indeed had a CASE standard.

The organization now has hundreds of copies of this tool. When the tool is used at all, it is used as a simple drawing tool, and much of the resources that were spent on purchasing it are wasted.

Those who do the work have to live with these systems errors; those who commit the errors go on with their careers oblivious to the mischief they caused.

Systems Engineering for Software Engineers

If you are going to be involved in systems engineering—either as a systems engineer or as a software engineer employed by systems engineers—here are some ideas that might help keep you from floundering, as we promised earlier in this chapter.

First, it is best to become familiar with the technical domains of the work being done. However, the chances are pretty good that you will first be a tool jockey, operating some diagramming tool and recording data in it for domain experts. If you find yourself in that position, here is what we recommend:

- Practice with the tool and become as fast and accurate as you can. The people you support will probably need fast, accurate feedback from you to review their analyses. This will help you to free up some time so that you can become knowledgeable in the domains at hand.

- Get up to speed on the vocabulary and jargon being used in your environment to prevent delays and miscommunications.

Second, groupware is one approach that might help, especially in clarifying systems features. GIBIS (group issue-based information system) from the Microelectronics and Computer Consortium in Austin, Texas, is an example. GIBIS is a hypermedia, networked, database information system that allows discussions over an extended period and various locations. It enables many folks to state problems in terms of issues that can be argued over a network.

The tool saves the issues and arguments, and can display any that the participants may want to explore. It appears to be a nifty way of gaining information for clarifying system features and examining risks [Conklin and Bergman 1988]. This could be an excellent preliminary to decomposing a system into its elements. But, be careful; Groupware is seen more as a Roman tool than a Greek one, and there is a danger of impeding rather than aiding the initial work of conceiving and clarifying system requirements.

There are systems engineering tools on the market. One that we looked at recently, called RDD-100 (Requirements Driven Development), from Ascent Logic Corporation, is one you should look at if you are going to get involved with this stuff. It has been in development for 15 years at TRW, it has a good user interface, it has a central database, and it offers several views of the system under design.

Finally, here are some diagramming techniques that might be especially useful: Gane and Sarson structured analysis, which allows for diagramming more than data flows; the IDEF series ($IDEF_0$, $IDEF_1$, $IDEF_{1x}$, and $IDEF_2$); real-time DFDs (ESML); decision trees and tables; data models; and data navigation diagrams. (See also *Diagramming Techniques for Programmers and Analysts,* by James Martin and Carma McClure [1985].)

Also, it would be valuable for you to develop an assortment of other skills. Some communication skills are effective speaking and listening, and effective presentations and meetings. Some useful skills with personal tools are word processing, scheduling, and creating and manipulating spreadsheets.

In distributed projects, you might consider portable, "luggable," or notebook computers as a way of taking your office with you. Also consider having a kit with the following items: templates for documents and figures, pens, chalk, spare lamps for overhead projectors, and perhaps rubber stamps to use for creating instant forms for data models and processes during those times when folks are just chatting and sketching is more appropriate than formal stuff.

In business planning, it is often necessary to decompose an existing system into its constituent parts to better understand how the system works as a whole. This is often done by the people who operate the system with the help of a software systems analyst (SSA). The SSA has the expertise with tools and diagramming similar to the situation of the tool jockey we described earlier.

The problem is that the work often gets hung up with definitions of the processes at the top or highest level. This happens for a number of reasons: the system operators are trying to help the analyst get an initial understanding of their system, or they have slightly different views of their system at a high level and argue about it, or they never even thought about it before and are struggling with unfamiliar views of their environment. This delay causes the analysis to stall. The hint here is to drive through this high level, known as the *context level*, by postponing discussions of controversial items until the lower levels are fleshed out. Then, work back up the levels resolving all unresolved definitional issues.

Breaking projects down into appropriate chunks is a tough problem. When decomposing software, if systems engineers don't decompose properly, software engineers have trouble. If they stop too soon, then software engineers have to finish the job or suffer incoherent code. If they stop too late, then software engineers have tightly coupled code with much redundancy because they are unable to spot common processing threads.

We recommend that new systems be decomposed down to human-sized functional chunks, with clean interfaces and clear budgets (memory usage, cycle time, etc.). For example, rather than specifying every part of a group of related software components, simply specify a library and its contents. Let the software engineers work out the details. We frequently hear of software being specified with no "look-around," no chance to determine more economical chunks, such as libraries that can be reused or might already be around.

Barring that, we recommend decomposing systems down to interdisciplinary teams. This seems, at first, to contradict our earlier message that systems complexity increases with the number of different domains. Wouldn't a team composed of a number of domains also be complex? There is some truth to that, to be sure; but, here are our arguments:

First, in spite of the increased complexity, these teams have a record of forming highly intense and focused teams, maybe because nobody is stepping on anyone else's toes.

Second, an interdisciplinary team's mission could very likely be constructed as a set of one-person jobs, but with the added benefit of being close to the people who produced the other parts of the system.

A Closing Thought on Systems Engineering

There is a story about the "CIA method" of software development. We are including it here because we think it illustrates something important about the differences between systems engineering and software engineering.

The CIA announces that it is going to build a very large system that it needs for a top secret, "black box" program. It rents a huge facility in Silicon Valley with all of the modern appurtenances. They stuff the facility with expensive equipment and analysts. This traditional, huge project attracts all of the spies in the world to find out what is going on. That's okay, though, because the project is actually a diversion. The real system is being designed by two Cal Tech students in their garage. &

Chapter 3.
Software Quality: An Odyssey
Through the "Ilities"

J.A.'s Code

Have you ever run across source code that could only be described as beautiful? One of the authors of this book (Peter DeGrace) has found code like this. He found it in an unlikely place. It was in a particularly cranky application that "never gave an inch." Here is Peter's story.

"At that time, I was a 'paleo-programmer'; you know, someone whose job was to maintain and enhance very, *very* old programs.

"One of the most challenging problems with this particular program was getting the input data correct. The data was composed mostly of numbers describing a mechanical structure and the various forces acting upon it. The program's output was a table containing numbers showing how each part of the structure behaved as forces were applied in different combinations and intensities.

"It was very common to have errors in the input data and very difficult to find them; there was always a problem whenever an engineer executed the program for the first time or used a new structure or tried a new feature. I'd get a phone call: 'The program has crashed! Fix it!' So, I'd haul out the listing and get set for a very long and frustrating day.

"It was very old FORTRAN. It had been worked, reworked, and overworked. After a while I could see the hands of the many people who were there before me, rat-killing, making it work with new data, new features, different forces, different material, under new operating systems, on a new computer, and with 'newer' FORTRAN. It was like being in a boisterous city on a day when everybody was outside shouting at and jostling each other on the streets.

"I'd get the new test case or version of the program and the error information from the job that crashed, and begin to track down the problem.

"In the program, data came roaring in like a plane at the airport. Then it was distributed, like the passengers in taxis and buses, to various parts of the program; the bulge of the onion that Plauger described as the shape of a typical program.

"After a while, some of the neighborhoods became familiar: a dilapidated data structure like an old building here, a seldom-used routine like an empty lot there, and noisy loops like open vendor stands all over.

"The data would enter these neighborhoods, get tossed around, squeezed, rattled, smeared, and changed in many ways. They would find themselves on dead-end streets, taking the wrong subway, being held up in rush-hour traffic, inching along, and finally emerging at the array where they were stored, like travelers finally reaching their hotel.

"My job was to find out who got lost, or mugged, or had their luggage stolen, or had somebody else's stuff, or were in the wrong place altogether (which was the most common problem).

"So, I'd begin by escorting some tourist data to their hotel. We usually could get out of the airport all right, but once we were in the city, we would invariably detour onto one of those noisy streets. I would let the data go on a little, getting bumped here and thudded there as they traveled down the street. There would be clanks and squeals and shouts and epithets (I imagined) with the poor data being jostled here and there, but usually making it to the street's end only to find themselves on another street with another hard time in store.

"However, certain data were very lucky. They were scheduled to go through J.A.'s neighborhood.

"This neighborhood was more like a fashionable residential area. There were no potholes in the streets, and all the houses were well cared for with manicured lawns, no litter, and an unobstructed view. They were quiet streets with majestic curves leading directly down to the hotel.

"I first ran into J.A.'s code after painfully tracing some data down to the statement that called it and passed the data to it.

"As I flipped to it in the listing, I immediately saw that something was different. There was J.A.'s main routine with several more routines leading gracefully from it, and one or two others leading from those.

"Here was code I could read as easily as I could read English! It seemed to leap up at me. It was clear, precise, powerful, and explicit. Here was the expression of an *extraordinary* mind! Everything was logically set out, and it was where you would expect to find it. The data were prepared in advance and were sent to the algorithm, which was set off beautifully. All the exceptions slipped easily around the main algorithm, falling on efficient error-handling procedures.

"There were no comments in the code (and none were needed), just some judicious indentation and 'white space.' And, above the code, in every routine, a preamble stated exactly what it expected, what it would do with good data, and what it would do with bad data. A couple of the routines contained historical notes describing enhancements to the code. Each preamble was signed by the initials *J.A.*

"Here, the data were at home. They knew what to do and, if they were in the wrong place, they would bounce happily down to the error code and 'return to the streets.' There they would emerge again to the cacophony:

"'*Watch out you ...*'

"'*Oh no!!*'

"'*What the ...*'

"'*Where the ... did you come from!*'

"Honk honk, crash, thud, *screech.*

"When I found J.A.'s code, I had the sense of finding a beautiful artifact. It was well designed, and the form of the code suggested its function. It had a certain *feel* to it—like something well polished—it had a finish on it that reflected the designer's mind. And, it never broke. It never did. It always took what you gave it, did what it could, and handed back the results, good or bad.

"I asked around trying to find out who J.A. was. I was told that he was an old hand who had worked on some of the programs. He was remembered as a quiet guy who, after a while, got promoted and then disappeared into management somewhere. They didn't think he was with the company any longer. I never did find him; but I will always remember his code."

It seems that not many of us can write code like J.A. But, there are some things we can learn and some things we can require of our tools, which can greatly improve the quality of our software. That's what this chapter is about.

Software Requirements

Whatever we do, we must ultimately satisfy our customer, who has three basic requirements for software:

- "Get my programs up and running!"

- "Keep 'em running and change 'em."

- "Move 'em to new platforms."

These requirements apply mainly to internal programming shops. If you're writing for the open market, the requirements might be something more like the following:

- "What do you have for me now?"

- "Keep it updated with fixes and new features."

- "Make sure I can use it with new operating systems!"

The "Up and Running" Syndrome

So, you have written the code. It now compiles and you have run some test cases. Are you finished? Well, most users and many managers seem to think so. But, most of the time, you have only produced what amounts to a rough draft. The best of us, like, perhaps, J.A., produce rough drafts that are as good as a final product. However, most of us still need to clean up the code and write the documentation for the user and the maintainer, and we seldom get the chance to do it. One of the most common failings we have found in our field is that we (or our bosses or users) think we are finished once we get something "up and running."

But, the real world is different from that. We believe that there is a *lot* more left to do. Here are some of the things that we think are important:

- Improve the modularity of the software; do any decomposition that is now indicated.

- Redraw (or make) the context diagrams when they were affected by the work, and make sure all the files are named.

- Describe all the data structures.

- Draw the call tree.

- Simplify the code and its "look."

- Remove the old "commented out" code.

- Edit all the commentary to make sure that it is accurate and current.

- "Prettify" the code, put in white space, make sure all the preambles are consistent, and do any necessary indentation.

- Run many more test cases, especially checking the ranges of input data to see that they are adequate. Also check any new portions of the program to see if there are any unwanted side effects.

- Do the required version control and configuration management.

- Produce the necessary documentation, such as users' and maintainers' guides.

As you can see, it's a long list. We estimate that after you have something up and running, you are perhaps only 50% through producing the program. However, there are usually not enough resources available to finish the job.

One reason for this is because our product is essentially invisible. You cannot see (and, therefore, neither can your boss or the customer) the long, hard-to-understand routines, the bugs lying close to the surface, the warnings that are *not* in the compiler listing because you turned them off when they got in your way, the problems that are caused by dangerous coupling that you might have thought would just be temporary and that you would fix later, the interesting but arcane algorithm you tried out but for which you didn't keep the comments current when you had to tinker with it, and so on and so on.

Another reason for the shortage of resources is that even if we *did* know about all these things, there often isn't enough *time* left in the project to make the programs robust and maintainable. And, that type of work is expensive; "productizing" software costs nine times what it took to build it the way we previously described [Brooks 1982, p.5].

Finally, while it might be the current fad in your establishment to pay attention to quality, we often hear: *"Quality is King but the Schedule is GOD!"*

The "Keep 'em Running and Change 'em" Syndrome

In maintenance, you are faced with problems resulting from the "up and running" syndrome. To the extent possible that it is possible to do so, you must correct these problems. But, at the same time, you are rat-killing and adding new features. The new features usually come from new requirements that were discovered by the customers as they used the product. It is quite common and should not be discouraged, only understood.

But, the results are that troubles are only compounded. If you weren't able to put quality into the code initially, what makes you think you will be able to do it during maintenance? Unless, of course, you steal the time.

What we usually find is that the code is "patched" over a period of time. It gets so bad that, after a while, no new features are added. This is not because there are no new requirements, but because there is too much risk involved in adding them. Too many side effects occur and it takes too long. It is better to throw the software away and start over. So, in practice, there is a measure of software maturity: software is mature when adding new features causes the mean time between failures to fall toward zero.

The "Move 'em to New Platforms" Syndrome

Programs have three parts:

- *Active code*, which is executed and involved in rat-killing and "enhancements."

- *Inactive code*, which is executed, but is not usually "visited" during rat-killing or enhancements. This is the "solid" stuff; it is either well designed and doesn't break or it isn't used much.

- *Vestigial code*, which is not actually executed but, nevertheless, its image appears in the object module. (See Figure 3-1.)

Inactive and vestigial code are affected by porting and conversions about as much as the active code, but the programmer is far less familiar with the former than with the latter. Even though programmers might want to use the conversion as an opportunity to "improve" the code, the unanticipated problems with inactive and vestigial code usually foul things up.

So, the work of adding quality seldom gets done even if programmers *want* to do it. In the short run, this seems very often cost-effective or expedient. But, you end up with "fragile" code that breaks a lot, can't be maintained, or can't be moved around easily.

Yet, when programmers want to put quality into their code, they must take some time to do so. This is often seen by managers and customers as unnecessary delay; the inexplicable delay they sometimes call *padding*. One solution to the delays caused by wanting to finish the job is to purchase the software from more "efficient" outside sources.

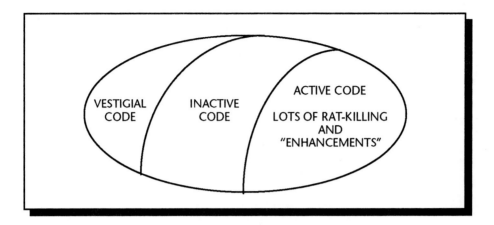

*Figure 3-1. The Parts of Code from the Point of View
of a Programmer's Familiarity*

However, these efficient outside sources are actually in the same boat as you. When *they* meet *your* schedule, have *they* done it with fragile code? And, were *they* qualified to produce good quality code in the first place?

One of our correspondents reported one such case, where a firm had the object code form of a program around for a while. The program worked well, but the users wanted to port it to a new super computer. So, they bought the source code, sight unseen.

It turned out to be 9,000 lines of FORTRAN B.C. code (code older than anyone remembers), all one routine, with few comments, a complex design, and subroutines simulated by means of assigned GOTOs. Our correspondent said he could not maintain it even if he could get it running on the super computer. His firm had no incoming receiving inspection; even if they had such a function, they would be hard put to define what was meant by "acceptable" code.

So, before we continue, we need to correct the perceptions some people have of the *composition* of programs. Some folks think that a program "contains" only the material that is relevant to the application domain of the problem being solved: for example, accounting or mechanical engineering. Some folks think that there is "software engineering" involved, but they're not quite sure exactly what that means. We think there are equal amounts of software engineering and application domain material in programs. (See Figure 3-2.)

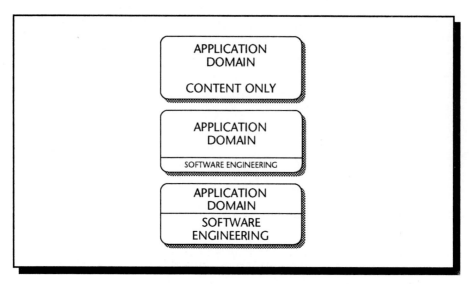

Figure 3-2. Three Views of "Program Content"

Our View of "Program Content"

Our view is that programs are composed of information and expertise from both the *application* and *software engineering* domains, in about a fifty-fifty mix. Programmers must know about the application domain but, when they do not know about the software engineering domain, they run afoul of the standards set by J.A.

In the rest of this chapter, we will discuss the quality of *software engineering* that goes into programs. First, we will take a Roman view of the issues. We will use a model of software quality produced by the Rome Air Defense Laboratory [McCall and Matsumoto 1979]. It is the best and most comprehensive we've found. This model has within it the essentials of most of the things we think of when we talk about the quality of *software*.

However, we've reorganized it and added more information. And, we connected the model to the three basic requirements of users:

- "Get my programs up and running!"
- "Keep 'em running and change 'em."
- "Move 'em to new platforms."

These three requirements are connected up with 11 characteristics of good software ("ilities") found in the model. They are:

- Correctness
- Reliability
- Efficiency
- Integrity
- Usability
- Rat-killing
- Flexibility
- Testability
- Portability
- Reusability
- Interoperability

These 11 characteristics are mapped to our customers' requirements. Then, a number of software engineering practices are mapped into these 11 characteristics (see Figures 3-3a through 3-3c). See Figure 3-4 for a list of software engineering practices. Later, we will take a Greek view by showing how coding techniques are mapped into each software engineering practice and, finally, how coding techniques support our customers' requirements.

Notice in Figures 3-3a through 3-3c how the characteristics group together to support customer requirements. We're not indicating that you ought to *develop* software considering only correctness, reliability, efficiency, integrity, and usability, expecting that the other characteristics will be optimized during maintenance or conversions. We *are* suggesting that the characteristics for which we optimize our code tend to satisfy more of *one* of the customer's requirements than the others.

If you see the software life cycle as consisting of development and maintenance punctuated by conversions, then all the characteristics are important. As this view contracts because of schedule and cost pressures, more and more of the characteristics of good software are sacrificed, even if they were known by the developers at the time the development, maintenance, and conversions were done.

The groupings offer an opportunity to do some tradeoffs early. We can actually sit back and ask question like: "Am I going to optimize my code for efficiency and give up some maintainability and portability? Or, will I do the reverse, judging that recent advances in hardware have so improved the speed of the platform for which I'm developing that I can afford to give up some processing efficiency for better maintainability and portability?"

If we didn't know better, those previous questions would be excellent examples of engineering tradeoffs.

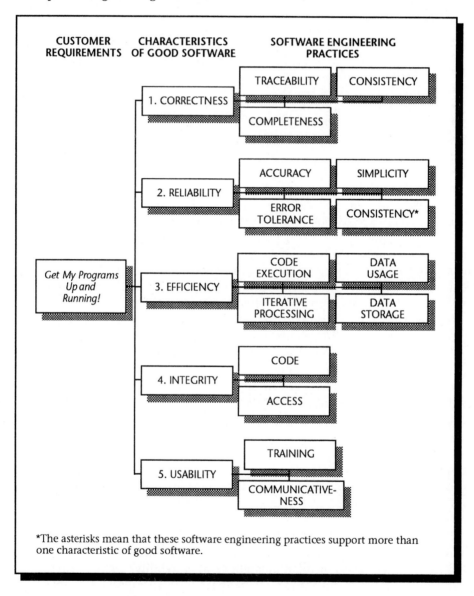

*Figure 3-3a. Characteristics of Good Software
Mapped to Customer Requirements*

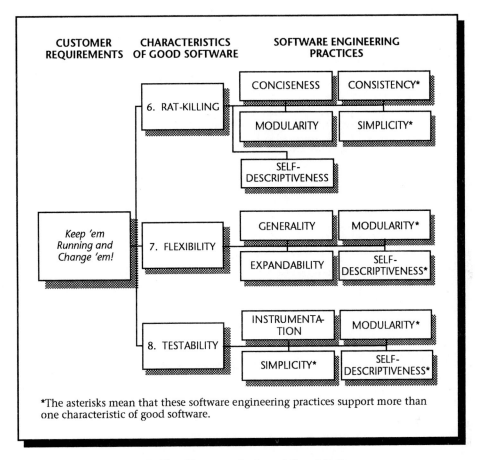

*The asterisks mean that these software engineering practices support more than one characteristic of good software.

Figure 3-3b. Characteristics of Good Software
Mapped to Customer Requirements (cont.)

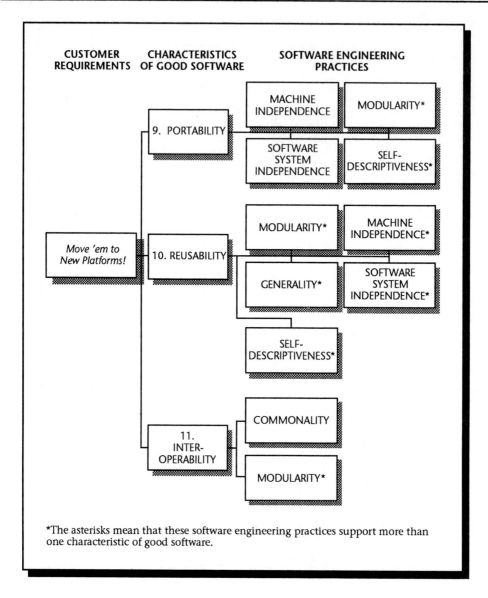

*Figure 3-3c. Characteristics of Good Software
Mapped to Customer Requirements (cont.)*

Access
   • Audit
   • Control
	Error Tolerance

	Generality

Accuracy	Instrumentation
	   • Module Test
	   • Integration Test
	   • System Test

Code Integrity	

Commonality
   • Communications
   • Data
	Machine Independence

	Modularity

Communicativeness
   • User Input Interface
   • User Output Interface
   • Operability
	Self-descriptiveness
	   • Implementation Language
	   • Effectiveness and Quantity
	     of Comments

Completeness	Simplicity
	   • Design Structure
	   • Data
	   • Control Flow
	   • Coding Techniques

Conciseness	
Consistency	

Expandability
   • Data Storage
   • Extensibility
	Software System Independence

	System Protection

Efficiency
   • Execution
   • Iterative Processing
   • Data Usage
   • Data Storage
	Traceability

	Training

Figure 3-4. Software Engineering Practices

We will now discuss the techniques by which this stuff is really accomplished. We've arranged the material by the characteristics of good software, then by the software engineering practices that apply, and then by the coding techniques of each practice to consider.

The material on specific coding techniques is fairly general. However, thanks to the contributions and suggestions of a gracious correspondent, we've added a special paragraph wherever there is a unique connection with COBOL. Nevertheless, the discussion and the illustrations that follow tie all the upper level stuff together with software engineering practice. We hope this will lead you to something you can actually *do* to improve software. We suggest that if, for example, you are a COBOL user, you might substitute the coding techniques that apply to commercial applications.

The material that follows tells you what the benefits are of applying these things to your software. If your boss wants to know why you need time to "finish" the code, show him these illustrations.

1. Correctness

Correctness (see Figure 3-5) is the extent to which a program satisfies its specifications (which is called *verification*) and fulfills the user's mission objectives (which is called *validation*). "Did we build the system right? Did we build the right system?" It exhibits the state of showing the absence of errors.

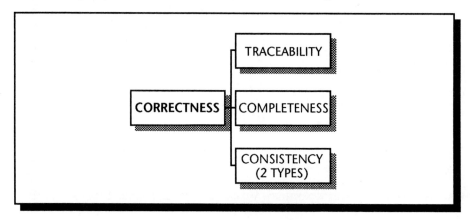

Figure 3-5. Correctness

Traceability

If you're doing a Waterfall or some formal method, then a great deal of effort was put into identifying and writing down requirements. It then becomes important, and sometimes it is a contractual requirement, to show how each requirement was satisfied.

You do this by tracing the requirements to the code that satisfies them. Frequently, several modules are involved in satisfying a single requirement and, sometimes, several requirements may be satisfied, at least partially, by a single module.

A requirements-tracing matrix is a common tool for showing the relationships between requirements and the modules that satisfy them. It is simply a box with columns and rows, with the requirements listed at the columns headings and the satisfying modules listed along the left-hand side. A common item that makes up the modules' prologues, in these cases, is an indication of *which* requirements the module is satisfying. Where a module intersects the column of the requirement it satisfies, draw an *X*. There should be at least one *X* somewhere in every column. Figure 3-6 is an example of a requirements matrix.

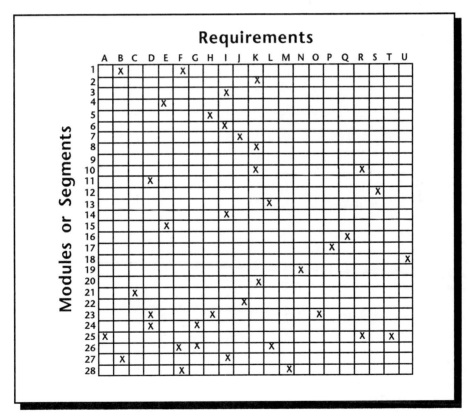

Figure 3-6. Requirements Matrix

Completeness

Completeness is that quality when the code lacks nothing, when it can be used as intended, and when it has no loose ends. Above that, complete code has the sense of being *consummate* and of being skillfully finished, like J.A.'s code.

For completeness:

- Check that each data element has a specific origin.

- Make sure that each data element is defined or computed in the program or obtained from an external source.

- Check that all the references to data and program names are unique, unambiguous, and have the same name throughout the program.

- Check that all referenced functions and data have been defined, and that all defined functions and data are used.

- For each decision point, check that all conditions and processes are defined.

- For transfers of control out of the module, check that the calling and called parameters agree.

- Check for dead code—code that cannot be reached by any path in the module—and mark or eliminate it.

- Finally, check that all problem reports are resolved.

Consistency

Consistency is a quality of code that permeates it and appears to hold it together. Things are in agreement among themselves, appear where expected and in the form expected, and exist in a harmony with other parts of the code. Such code gives a new maintainer the subtle feeling that s/he can indeed navigate through and maintain it.

There are two types of consistency: *procedure* and *data*. For *procedure consistency*, check that there is a standard or consistent method for calling sequences, input/output operations, and error-handling processes.

For *data consistency*, check that there is a standard or consistent method for representing local and global data. Check that there is a naming convention applied to all the program elements that can be given names. In many languages, but especially in COBOL, there is an old conflict in naming variables. Are you naming the bucket or what's *in* the bucket (for example, the water)? Do you prefer:

```
ADD TRAN-DOLLARS-AND-CENTS TO TOTAL-ACCUM
```

or

```
ADD TRAN-AMT TO TOTAL-AMT
```

In a commercial environment, where many programs might be communicating with one another across multiple data paths, consistency across programs improves the quality of the system as a whole. This includes program structure (paragraph names and the like) and data references: the same data element should have the same name across all the programs in the system and, equally important, dissimilar data elements should *not* have similar names.

Creating and assiduously using a data dictionary can be of great help here. A data dictionary lists all the data elements used in the system, and all the files, fields, and variables. A good data dictionary also shows where data elements are used.

2. Reliability

Reliability (see Figure 3-7) is the extent to which a program can be expected to perform its intended function with the precision the user requires and when the user needs it.

Accuracy

Accuracy is the extent to which the results of calculations approach the true value of the calculations and are free from error. Accuracy also involves the precision—the number of places—of the results. Where *correctness* is the passive state of showing the absence of errors, *accuracy* implies a positive exercise of care to give the right, informative answers.

In advance of design, analyze the accuracy requirements of the system. Then, in design, allocate accuracy to the modules of the system while considering the accuracy requirements for inputs, outputs, processing, and constants for each. Make sure that the math library you use is at least as accurate as the code must be, and that the numerical methods you use are as accurate as necessary. In testing, check to make sure that the outputs have the required accuracy.

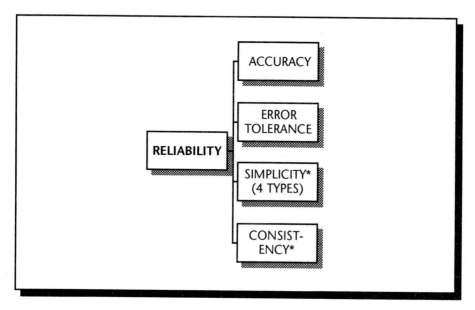

Figure 3-7. Reliability

Generally speaking, the operating systems, the constants provided by them, and the math libraries have the required accuracy; however, the precision with which the results are to be stated is usually left up to the programmer. Lack of or changed precision is a common headache in conversions; so, this characteristic should also apply to the "Move 'em to new platforms!" requirement of users.

In commercial programs, accuracy is not generally regarded as a problem. With a few notorious exceptions (factorial calculations required for pension or annuity computations) modern computers will produce programs that meet the user's accuracy requirements with little or no special attention by the programmer.

Error Tolerance

Error tolerance is the quality of software that deals gracefully with errors that occur because of incorrect inputs, unfamiliar paths, unexpected limits, or discontinuities of computations. Error-tolerant software informs the user that such an error has occurred, gives her an opportunity (if possible) to recover, and exits in as harmless a manner as possible, saving what needs to be saved and returning control to the appropriate agent.

The following practices about the software tolerating error conditions you can think about in advance. However, in practice, you cannot anticipate *all* errors in advance. By following the ideas here, you have a basis for handling those unanticipated error conditions rather easily and quickly in maintenance.

Error tolerance has five sub-criteria:

1. Functions that can be used concurrently should be controlled centrally to provide concurrency checking, read/write locks, checkout/checkin, etc. Some examples are: a database manager, I/O handling, error handling, etc.

2. When the software detects an error, it should be capable of correcting it online and then continuing processing. An example is an operator message stating that the wrong tape was mounted and processing will be suspended, but will continue when the correct tape is mounted.

3. Error conditions should always be passed back to the "called" routine and the decision made there about what to do with the error condition. This is especially true in libraries, the source images of which might be unavailable to the programmer. You should never, *ever* put a STOP or ABORT in a library routine.

4. You can cause the software to recover from improper input data by considering the following things: Define in advance the error tolerance of the input data, specifying the range of values for each item of data. Identify and resolve conflicting requests and illegal combinations. This last is very difficult sometimes, and new conditions pop up all the time. Some testers are still amazed when a new user casually walks up

to software in beta test and breaks it. Consider range test loops, multiple transfer parameters, and subscripts. Check output parameters for reasonableness during processing.

5. You should have a strategy for recovering from faults caused by the CPU, peripherals, and operating systems. Chances are that you are stuck here, but at least do the housekeeping and accounting tasks if possible and try to retire gracefully.

In a commercial environment, the degree of desired error tolerance is frequently (and perversely) directly related to how critical the application is. The most critical application—for example, an airline reservation system— must also be the most resilient and error-tolerant. The system simply must stay online come hell or high water. This makes for a rather sporty mainte-nance task.

Simplicity

Simple software is neither complex nor intricate. It is easy to understand. Such software has been written for human beings. As far as we can tell, machines don't complain about spaghetti code. Where *consistency* is the means by which you can determine correctness, similarly *simplicity* is the means by which you can demonstrate the positive care taken in providing accuracy.

There are four types of simplicity:

- Design structure simplicity
- Data simplicity
- Control flow simplicity
- Coding techniques simplicity

For *design structure simplicity*:

- Check that the design of a program is presented in a top-down fashion, usually accompanied by a call tree chart showing the program hierarchy. Modules should be independent; the processing in them should not be dependent on either the source of the input or the destination of the output. This is known as *loose coupling*.

- Module processing should not be dependent on prior processing. This type of code is often referred to as *reentrant*.

- Each module description should include I/O and processing limitations.

- Each module should have a single entrance and a single exit. Each module's processing should consist of computing a single function or transformation. This is known as *cohesion*.

For *data simplicity*:

- Check that record and storage structures, such as COMMON, are complete and unambiguous. An example of violating this guideline is a COMMON block defined two different ways among the modules that access it.

- Check that there is some means of determining where the data are used and set.

- Check for irrelevant data references in modules and remove them. An example of irrelevant data is a COMMON block reference, none of whose elements are set or used in the referencing module. Then, normalize the data. This means that each fact represented by a datum is stored in only one place.

Control flow simplicity is a measure of the number and types of paths that can be taken through the module. An example of control flow is an IF-THEN-ELSE block structure that divides the control flow into two paths: one beginning with THEN if the IF statement is true, and one beginning with ELSE if it is false.

You can calculate the number of paths by diagramming the module's paths, counting the number of areas enclosed by the various paths, and adding one. This is McCabe's Cyclomatic Measure. A good rule of thumb is to avoid having more than seven paths through the module's code.

There are two types of paths: one that causes the control flow to move downward toward the exit, and another that moves it upward toward the entry of the module. These latter are called *backward branching GOTOs* and should be minimized as much as possible.

For *simplicity of coding techniques*:

- Check that modules flow top to bottom and that no module modifies itself.

- Check that the following are minimized (and try to eradicate any that you find):

  - The use of negative or compound Boolean expressions
  - Jumping in and out of loops
  - Modifying loop indexes inside the loop

- Also, minimize the number of statement labels, nesting levels, branches, GOTOs, global variables (as opposed to local variables), and the number of unique variables used in a module.

In a commercial environment, you can improve source code simplicity by rigorously adhering to achieving a complete design before you begin coding. In this context, a "complete design" should include a complete block structure chart (flow chart) and associated pseudo-code. Sometimes, you might be dealing with a prototype or a problem that is not amenable to a complete design before coding begins. In such cases, you should reserve some resources for going back and making the resulting code simple.

In commercial programming, *flow charts* are often referred to as *structure charts*. Flow charts have fallen into disfavor as analysis tools, especially since data flow diagrams (DFDs) have taken over. However, they are still useful in design and construction because they show the logical paths through a portion of the code. As a result, they are also helpful in maintenance. Another type of flow chart is the *control graph*, which also shows the paths through source code. However, it is usually a simple diagram that does not show the source code or pseudo-code statements themselves. The flow charts are made before *or* after the code is written, and the control graphs almost always made after. We will say more about the usefulness of flow charts later.

Consistency is another element of reliability (marked with an asterisk in Figure 3-7). It has already been discussed.

3. Efficiency

Efficiency (see Figure 3-8) is the quality of software that uses the machine's resources economically, with a minimum of waste. All efficiencies are concerned with economy. Specifically, they are concerned with the efficiency of *code execution, iterative processing, data usage,* and *data storage.* These all have to do with conserving the machine's resources of time and space.

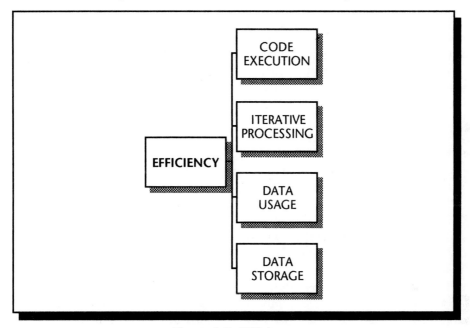

Figure 3-8. Efficiency

Code Execution

Code execution efficiency is the economy required by the customer, such as the run time, response time, and memory used. For code execution efficiency, check that the software performs according to the performance requirements of the solution (or the customer if performance is a last minute thing, as it so often is). To improve code execution efficiency, do the following:

- Use performance optimizing compilers or assemblers.

- Define compound expressions once.

- Minimize the number of overlays.

- Minimize module-to-module and module-to-operating system communication.

- If you are using a vector machine, make sure the code is optimized for vector computing.

Commercial programs often reflect the greatest conflict between maintainability and code execution efficiency. Many measures that are taken to improve execution efficiency can make the program "needlessly" complex for maintenance programmers. Conversely, other measures to "rationalize" or "neaten up" the source code can grossly degrade the program's execution time.

One good approach is to determine and make whatever concessions are necessary for program efficiency, but then document inline the technical *whys* and *hows* of the efficiency methods you selected. This a classic case of an engineering tradeoff.

Iterative Processing

Iterative processing efficiency is concerned with the economy with which the iterative constructs in the code perform their operations. For iterative processing efficiency, keep computations that do not depend on loop iterations out of the loops, and keep loops free of bit/byte packing.

In commercial programs, a complete structure chart is the best weapon for keeping only the necessary activities within loops and segregating non-loop activities to external logic.

Data Usage

Data usage and *data storage* have to do with the economy with which data is stored and processed. For *data usage efficiency*:

- Group data for efficient processing.

- Initialize variables when you declare them.

- Avoid mixed mode expressions (even though you might be clever with them).

- Choose common units and data types.

- Index or refer data for efficient processing.

If you are processing a series of operation codes, for example, arrange them in the order of frequency of use. Here, *efficiency* conflicts with *maintainability*, and alphabetical ordering might be easier for human beings to comprehend. A comment in the code explaining the ordering would be helpful.

Within commercial systems, an entirely new development methodology, data modeling, has come into existence to assist in analyzing and rationalizing data and data structures. Properly employed, this methodology can ensure correctly "normalized" data, without redundancies and with only logically correct dependencies.

In addition, data modeling prepares the way for unbinding the data from the process, and storing data in databases. Thus, data modeling makes things simpler for programmers and helps to do away with the need we find in commercial systems for so many data reformatters.

Data Storage

For *data storage efficiency*, use virtual storage facilities and be certain that common data are defined only once, that program segments are efficiently made, and that dynamic memory and data packing are used.

4. Integrity

Integrity (see Figure 3-9) is the extent to which the software is seen as being well-integrated and has a sense of wholeness. It also involves preventing access to software or data by unauthorized people, and the extent to which the software can be protected from viruses. The former is very important in banking and at the DoD; the latter is important in networks, especially PC networks such as electronic bulletin boards and commercial network services.

Code Integrity

Code integrity is the quality of the program that shows that all the modules fit together seamlessly; that they were designed by the same mind or according to the same set of standards; and that there was a system architect who gave the program its underlying wholeness. To optimize design integrity, make sure that the code is consistent and follows all appropriate standards and conventions. But, most important, make sure the overall look and design approach gives you the feeling of wholeness.

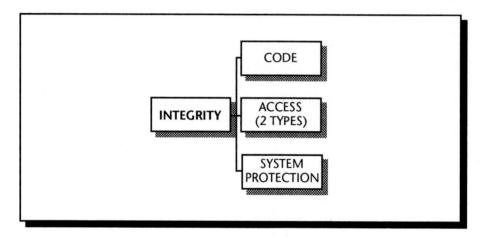

Figure 3-9. Integrity

In the commercial programming environment, a *program* is often referred to as a *module*. A system is frequently composed of many such modules/programs. Usually, each is individually developed. Only in the largest and most complex systems will more than one person develop one program. This means that, at the program level anyway, individual modules are initially one person's vision and reflect his or her world view.

Therefore, each program in a system is likely to have internal code integrity. Integrity among modules can be improved by assiduously using the data dictionary and by creating uniform interfaces among the modules of a system.

Access Integrity

Access integrity is concerned with keeping the program undamaged during operation and available to those authorized to use it. This form of integrity has to do with *access control,* and *access audit,* and *system protection.*

For *access control*, make sure that you provide user I/O and database access controls, and that you also provide memory protection across tasks.

For *access audit*, make sure there are provisions for recording and reporting accesses, and for immediately signaling access violations.

For *system protection*, make sure there are provisions for recording, reporting, and removing viruses.

In a commercial environment, access control and access audit are generally the responsibility of people outside the programming organization. Standards and procedures to regulate access and to record potential violations reside with production control organizations or with the dreaded DP auditors.

5. Usability

Usability (see Figure 3-10) is the quality of software that makes it easy or convenient to use and enables the user to be effective in the task for which the software is intended to help. It is a measure of the effort required to learn, operate, prepare the input to, and interpret the output of a program; the less effort, the better.

Training

Training involves developing lesson plans and other training materials for operators, end users, and maintainers; providing realistic exercises; and making available sufficient online help and diagnostic information.

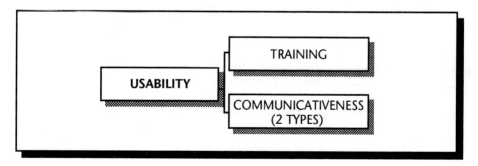

Figure 3-10. Usability

In a commercial development environment, this is usually outside the scope of the programmer's responsibility. Depending on the organizational structure, user training might be "contracted" out to a wholly separate organization, or be an itemized deliverable within a project work statement.

Communicativeness

In general, *communicativeness* should provide the user with adequate information concerning his interaction with the software. "By [simply] looking, [he should be able to] tell the state of the screen [or what have you] and the alternatives for action." [DeGrace and Stahl 1990, p.211, quoting Donald Norman from *The Psychology of Everyday Things*] The interface should provide the user with the means for creating a good conceptual model of the software. It should do this with "consistent presentations of operations and results and a coherent system image." [ibid] It should make it possible for the user "to determine the relationships between actions and results, between controls and their effects, and between system state and what is visible." [ibid]

There are three forms of communicativeness: user input interfaces, user output interfaces, and operability.

For *communicativeness of user input interfaces*:

- Define default values for input.

- Make sure that input formats are uniform.

- Make sure that each record is self-identifying.

- Make sure that the user can verify inputs prior to execution.

- Make sure that input is terminated by an explicitly defined end of input (for example, pressing RETURN).

- And, finally, make sure that you have made provisions for input from different media.

For *communicativeness of user output interfaces*:

- Make sure the user can selectively control the available output.

- Make sure that outputs have unique, descriptive, user-oriented labels and units of measure.

- Make sure that output groups of data are logically grouped in the user's context for easier examination.

- Make sure that the differences between error messages and outputs are unambiguous.

- Make sure that you have made provisions for redirecting output to different media.

When developing commercial applications, whether online or batch, the format, text, and meaning of the user interfaces will ordinarily be the subject of detailed specifications negotiated with the user. It is imperative that the actual "hands-on" user community be actively involved in developing and, if possible, testing these specifications.

Operability is the quality of software that makes it easy to operate. It has the sense of being practical and useful. For *operability*:

- Make sure that you have described all the steps of the operations.

- Make sure that all error conditions and responses are appropriately described to the user or operator.

- Make sure that provisions are made for the operator to interrupt, obtain the status of, save, modify, and continue processing.

- Make sure that the number of operator actions is reasonable.

- Make sure that you have described the job setup and teardown procedures.

- Make sure that you maintain hardcopy logs of interactions.

- Make sure that operator messages are consistent and responses are standard.

6. Rat-Killing

Rat-killing is the effort required to locate and fix an error in an operational program. (See Figure 3-11.)

Conciseness

Conciseness is that quality of the code where it and the comments describing it are brief and to the point, short and clear. Use the most powerful expressions of the language in which the software is being coded, leaving out all superfluous or unnecessarily expanded details. This gives the code a look of polished smoothness, *à la* J.A. However, avoid being laconic,[8] which suggests brevity to the point of curtness or ambiguity.

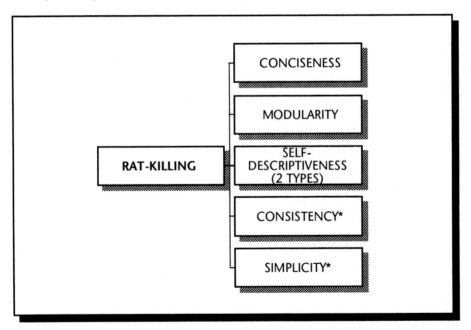

Figure 3-11. Rat-Killing

---

[8] Sometimes people use the word *terse* to describe their difficulty with C code; but, what they really mean is *laconic*.

The most popular commercial application language, COBOL, is burdened with a reputation for verbosity. But, if properly written, it can be concise and meaningful. As with any language, the line between concise-but-meaningful and laconic-and-obscure may be more a function of the reader's fluency in the language than some objective measure of conciseness. For the best results, always assume that the programmer who follows will be less expert with it than you.

Modularity

Modularity is extremely important to the production of high quality code. It refers to that characteristic of good software where code that performs a single function in a program is enclosed in a program unit such as a subroutine, function, or paragraph. This includes the notion of being able to be arranged or fitted together in a variety of ways.

In FORTRAN, a module is usually a subroutine that can communicate with other subroutines through global data or arguments passed to it by the calling routine when the called routine was invoked. For COBOL, modules are usually paragraphs that can communicate with all the other paragraphs of the program through the global data in the data division.

For *modularity*:

- Check that modules communicate only with modules of adjoining levels of the hierarchy.

- Check that standards for module size are in place and observed (approximately 50 lines per module, or about one page).

- Check that input data and controlling arguments are defined by the calling module.

- Check that output data and control are returned to the calling module.

- Check that modules do not share temporary data storage.

- Make sure that coupling is minimized and cohesion is maximized.

The new version of COBOL, ANSI COBOL 85, provides for nested programs using global and local data as necessary.

Modularity is so important that we offer here the best, most concise statement of it we've ever found [Shere 1988, pp.28-31]. You do not need to read it to get the idea of modularity we have presented here. Therefore, we have set it in a different typeface so you can skip to the next section if you prefer. However, if you are faced with optimizing modularity, then the following material will be a great help.

"The intent of modularity is to develop code that is easy to understand, maintain, and reuse. For these reasons, each module should perform a single function. As we consider the cohesiveness of each module and coupling among modules, the theme of performing an independent single function permeates the discussion.

"The notion of how big a single function can be is fuzzy. To place a bound on this definition, the average number of executable source lines of code (in a high-order language) of a system's modules should not exceed 100. [**Author's note:** We think 50 lines are more appropriate.] No individual module should have in excess of 200 executable lines of code.

"By using subroutines and nested CALLs, very complex functions can be programmed.

"Coupling is a measure of the dependence of one module on another module. It may be thought of as the relationship among modules. Cohesion is the substance of a single module. Cohesion relates to the nature of the structure within a module. These two concepts are discussed next.

"The five levels of coupling in decreasing order of preference are:

"• Data (preferred)
"• Common data (undesirable)
"• Control (undesirable)
"• External (forbidden)
"• Content (forbidden)

"Data coupling occurs when inputs are passed as explicit parameters. The 'CALL f(a,b)' in FORTRAN is an example of data coupling. This is the cleanest boundary and is preferred. When data coupling exists, a module can be thought of as a 'black box.' A black box consists of a process, input data, and output data. To the world outside the box, data can be inserted and output can be received without any knowledge of how the process is performed. Very complex functions, such as the stress on an aircraft as a function of altitude, speed, and load (weight), may be determined totally experimentally. The function may exist as a table of thousands or millions of points with no analytical description.

"Passing data from one module to another through common data is possible in many languages. Examples are labeled or global common in FORTRAN and compool tables in JOVIAL. This mechanism of passing data is undesirable. Depending on the sequencing of operations, data in common can be altered by a third module before the intended module reads the information. These errors are difficult to locate and can cause disastrous results. This approach should be forbidden for real-time systems.

"A control variable determines the type of processing to be performed. Two modules are control coupled if one of the modules passes or sends a control variable to the other module. The determination of whether or not data passed are control variables or external data depends solely on the perception of the sending module. If module A is control coupled to module B, then, from the viewpoint of module B, module A is not an independent function because module B knows something about the processing of module A; that is, module A is not a black box. If the control variable were passed by using common data, the problem is compounded. Because of possible erroneous changes in the common data, incorrect processing may occur. Errors of this nature are significantly more difficult to locate, or determine, than errors involving an incorrect calculation.

"External coupling is the interface level in which a module receives its input data by inspecting and using variables that are defined and reside in another module. This type of coupling is very bad because changes in one module cannot be made without inspecting other modules for unintentional effects. Maintenance becomes very expensive and difficult. External coupling should be forbidden from all programming practices.

"Content coupling is the worst of all types of coupling. Content coupling requires one module to understand the internal mechanics of another module. Examples of content coupling are sharing code (but not in a subroutine relationship), using a set of internal data (not externally declared) of another module, and knowing internal switch settings of another module. With content coupling, a change in code of one module can change the function of another module. Content coupling should also be forbidden in all programming practices.

"The second attribute of module design is cohesion, or binding. Cohesion is a measure of the association of the elements within a module. There are six types of cohesion. These are listed, roughly from best to worst:

"• Functional (required)
"• Sequential
"• Communicational
"• Temporal
"• Logical
"• Coincidental

"The premise of structured programming is that each module should perform a single function or logical transformation. Each statement within the module should contribute to this process. Generally, a module has functional cohesion if its purpose can be described in English using a simple declarative sentence. An example is 'REMOVE ADDRESSES WITHOUT ZIP CODES FROM THE FILE.'

"Functional cohesion is the strongest form of cohesion. Most company and government standards require functional cohesion. As long as a module exhibits functional cohesion, it is irrelevant whether it also exhibits other types of cohesion.

"Any module with multiple entry points or multiple exit points (except for exit points resulting from error conditions) either violates functional cohesion or possesses an unacceptable form of coupling with another module. Thus, these should be avoided. That is, each module should have a single entry point and a single exit point.

"A module is said to have sequential cohesion if it is based on the control structure organization. This typically results when a problem is flow charted and the modules are then specified from the flow chart. For example, the module whose description is 'SEARCH ADDRESS FILE. ELIMINATE DUPLICATES.' illustrates a simple sequence of two functions. Other clues of sequential cohesion are module descriptions that are either conditional or iterative. Examples are, respectively, 'ADD ADDRESS TO FILE UNLESS ZIP CODE IS ABSENT' and 'UPDATE TRAFFIC FILE UNTIL OPERATOR INTERRUPT.'

"Communicational cohesion has at least two definitions. One definition is modularization of a program based on grouping input and output activities in the same module. A module that performs all I/O operations on a database exemplifies this definition. Some people will argue that this type of cohesion is good. By isolating all DBMS I/O operations to a single module, it is possible to limit the effort required to change DBMS interfaces. Unless this approach is used, one is tied to a particular vendor for a long period of time.

"The other definition ... of communicational cohesion is a module with sequential cohesion and whose components communicate with each

other. The submodules either reference the same data or communicate among one another. An example of this type of cohesion is a module whose description is 'RETRIEVE COST DATA AND PLOT RESULTS.' Using this definition, communicational cohesion is fairly strong.

"A module whose basis is temporal is designed to handle time-oriented activities, such as initialization or termination. In this case, specific actions needed by a group of modules are grouped together and performed at one time by a single module. For example, a module whose description is 'RESET ALL FLAGS' or 'DOWNLOAD ALL FILES' has temporal cohesion.

"Modularizing a program by grouping logically similar activities is termed logical cohesion. An example is a module that prints error messages originating in various segments. This type of module typically induces control coupling of modules.

"Coincidental cohesion occurs when the elements of the module have little or no relationship to one another. Sometimes coincidental cohesion results when someone over-zealously limits the number of statements in a module. This can also result from attempts to eliminate duplicate code by creating modules of convenience."

Self-Descriptiveness

Self-descriptiveness is the quality of software where it reveals its makeup easily to anyone who reads it. There are two types of self-descriptiveness: the *effectiveness and quantity of comments* and the *self-descriptiveness of the implementation language*.

For the *effectiveness and quantity of comments*, check that standards for commenting are in place and observed. Especially check that comments do not just repeat the operation described in the code. Also, check that the quantity of comments per module meets the standard, that all the modules have prologue comments formatted in a standard way, and that the comments are set off from the code in a uniform manner.

Make sure that the following are commented:

* All transfers of control and destinations
* All machine-dependent code
* All non-standard high order language (HOL) statements
* The attributes of all declared variables
* All error conditions

For *self-descriptiveness of the implementation language,* check that:

- An HOL is used

- Variable names (mnemonics) describe the physical or functional property they represent

- Source code is logically blocked and indented

- There is one statement per line

Other elements of maintenance rat-killing that have already been discussed (marked with asterisks in Figure 3-11) are *consistency* and *simplicity.*

7. Flexibility

Flexibility is the quality of software that allows it to be easily and effectively changed and expanded. (See Figure 3-12.) It is a measure of the effort required to modify an operational program.

Generality

Generality is the quality of code when it can be used extensively by other modules, and when it can be reused in more than the first instance where it is executed. One example is a generic date routine that takes, for instance, a calendar date and converts it into a fiscal date, which is the form needed by accounting routines.

To optimize generality, maximize the degree of fan-in from other modules; do not mix input, processing, and output in a single function; and do not mix application and machine-dependent functions in the same module. Make sure the processing is neither data-volume limited nor data-value limited.

Expandability

There are two aspects to expandability: *data storage expandability* and *extensibility.* For *data storage expandability,* make sure that logical processing is independent of storage and array sizes and buffer space. Also, minimize the percentage of memory capacity committed in the current implementation. This allows room for expansion later.

For *extensibility*, make sure the accuracy, convergence, and timing attributes that control processing are parametric. Make sure that modules are table driven. Maximize the difference between the required speed of processing and the actual speed of the current system.

Within commercial systems, expandability and extensibility are functions of the availability of resources and are not generally of concern (or interest) to the application programmer. With the exception of internal tables, which, if data-driven, must include self-checking mechanisms to detect and avoid overflow, most commercial programs will simply request as many resources as they need. If that many aren't available, the operating system will close down the program (or compel it to wait) in response to imperatives that are outside the control of the application program or programmer.

Other elements of maintenance flexibility that have already been discussed (marked with asterisks in Figure 3-12) are *modularity* and *self-descriptiveness*.

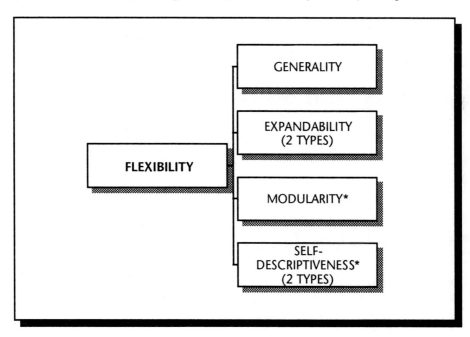

Figure 3-12. Flexibility

8. Testability

Testability is the effort required to test a program to ensure it performs its intended function. The more testing the better; the less work per test the better. (See Figure 3-13.)

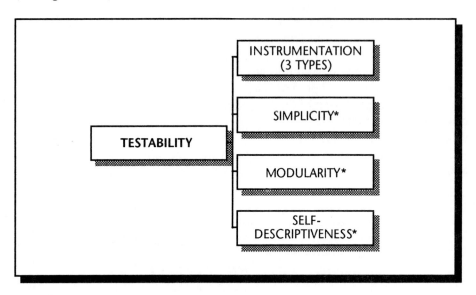

Figure 3-13. Testability

Instrumentation

In software testing, it is frequently necessary to add code, sometimes called *instrumentation*, to produce indications of how the system is performing. There are three types:

- module test
- integration test
- system test

In *module test*, this instrumentation is for processing path coverage inside a module. It should also aid in checking the boundaries of input parameters.

In *integration test*, instrumentation is used to test the interfaces among modules to see that they are regular and uniform. Instrumentation should also be prepared for the timing and storage performance requirements.

In *system test*, there should be instrumentation for module coverage, which is similar to path coverage described earlier. Also, test inputs and outputs used or produced by the instrumentation should be clearly identified and otherwise marked because of the large amount of data involved in system testing.

Sometimes this instrumentation is called a *test bed, test scaffold* or, more commonly, the *test version* of the software. It is often kept in separate directories and is part of the configuration of the software.

One of Djikstra's seminal requirements for a correct program is that it not only function correctly but it also demonstrates that it functions correctly. In a commercial environment, this can sometimes give rise to the existence of two versions of the same program: one is a "trace" version, which may produce volumes of output that would be unacceptable in a production environment, and one is a "production" version with the trace logic commented out or suppressed. Obviously, the possibility of discrepancies between the two versions gives rise to yet another opportunity for errors to creep in.

Other elements of maintenance testability that have already been discussed (marked with asterisks in Figure 3-13) are *simplicity, modularity*, and *self-descriptiveness*.

9. Portability

Portability is the effort required to transfer a program from one hardware configuration or software system environment to another. (See Figure 3-14.)

Machine Independence

Machine independence is that quality of code that is free from the unique, proprietary aspects of the machine on which it executes. For machine independence, do the following:

- Make sure that the programming language you use is available on other machines.

- Make sure that modules are free from I/O references that bind them to the current machine configuration.

- Make sure that the code is independent of word and character size.

- Make sure that the data representation is machine independent.

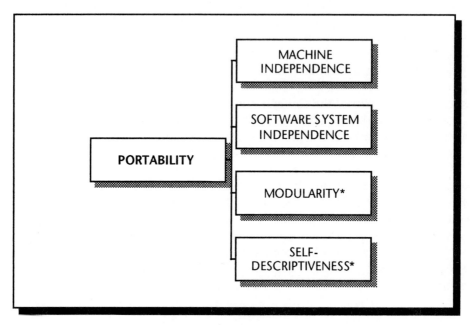

Figure 3-14. Portability

In commercial applications, particularly those developed and destined to run in mainframe environments, machine independence is low on the list of desirable attributes. Unless the customer is willing to specify it as a development criterion (and pay the concomitant price in development complexity and execution overhead), most programs are more-or-less tied to a particular machine or manufacturer and conversion to a different platform is a daunting and thankless task.

Software System Independence

Software system independence is that quality of the code that is free from the unique, proprietary aspects of the operating system under which it executes. For *software system independence*, minimize dependence in software system utility programs; make sure that a common, standard subset of the language is used; and minimize using vendor enhancements to the language.

For commercial programs, see our comments on machine independence.

Other elements of portable code that have already been discussed (marked with asterisks in Figure 3-14) are *modularity* and *self-descriptiveness*.

10. Reusability

Reusability is the extent to which a program can be used in other applications. (See Figure 3-15.) This also includes *parts* of programs such as, say, a set of nifty character string manipulation routines in FORTRAN and a set of all the date routines you could ever want in COBOL.

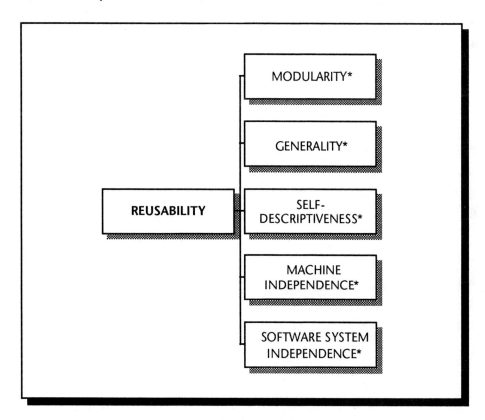

Figure 3-15. Reusability

The elements of reusability—*modularity, generality, self-descriptiveness, machine independence,* and *software system independence*—have already been described. But, there is one practice that can be added. The reusable quality of software would be improved if several indicators were added to the preambles of every module.

The first indicates that the module was reused in whole or in part. This indicator could provide information about the source of the original module. This would have the effect of tying all reused modules together. Having knowledge of the extent of reuse can thus give an indication of the processing types used in your shop. You might be able to tell, for example, that most FORTRAN programs use character string routines. This can provide you with information about FORTRAN language needs.

The other indicator ought to be one that suggests to a programmer the extent to which the module can be reused. If it has the five characteristics described above, it probably is a candidate for reuse. The function it performs, of course, must be needed elsewhere; but, at least someone can get an indication of the reusability of their inventory and can make decisions about what to do.

11. Interoperability

Interoperability is the quality of software that allows it to work easily and efficiently with other software. (See Figure 3-16.) It is a measure of the effort required to couple one system with another. This may occur at many levels, but it is usually accomplished through intermediate files.

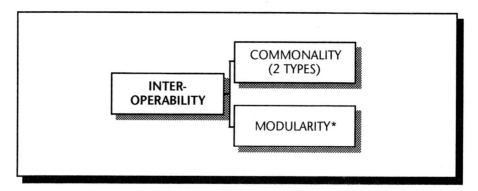

Figure 3-16. Interoperability

Commonality

There are two aspects of commonality: *communications* and *data*. *Communications commonality* refers to the ability of the program to pass messages and data to other programs in the system: the protocols. For communications commonality:

- Make sure that you know about and understand any requirements for communication with other systems.

- Make sure that protocol standards are established and followed.

- Make sure that there is a single module interface for input to and output from other systems.

Data commonality refers to the format and structure of data used by several programs. For data commonality, check that the data representations for communications with other systems are defined and agreed to. Also, if it is necessary to translate data, check that a standard is established and followed, and that a single module does each translation.

Another element of interoperability that has already been discussed (marked with an asterisk in Figure 3-16) is *modularity*.

Connecting Coding Techniques to Our Customer's Requirements

Now, let's take a Greek view of the issues by connecting the coding techniques to each software engineering practice and tracing these back to the user's requirements. This way, we can see how our coding affects our users.

Figure 3-17 is a series of illustrations that show how the coding techniques of each of the software engineering practices affects our customers' requirements. You might find them quite useful, which is why we included them. However, if you become bored with this type of diagram, you can simply skip over them. You can then refer to them later if you care to.

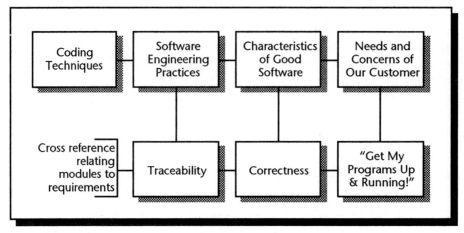

Figure 3-17. How Coding Techniques Affect Customer
Requirements

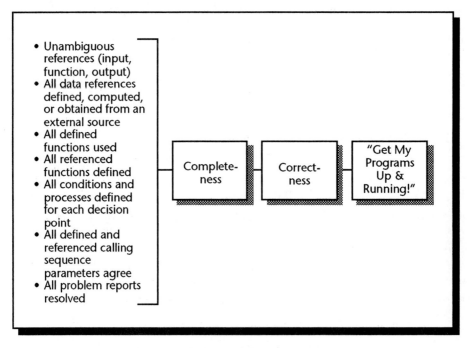

Figure 3-17a. How Coding Techniques Affect Customer
Requirements (cont.)

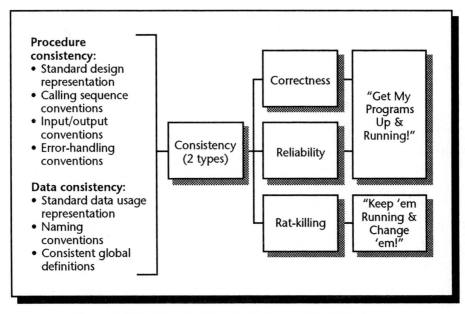

Figure 3-17b. How Coding Techniques Affect Customer Requirements (cont.)

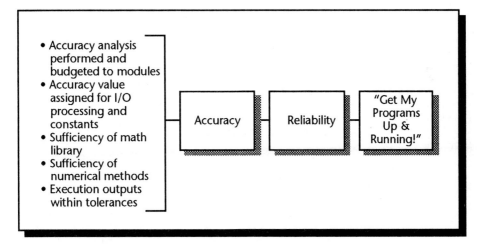

Figure 3-17c. How Coding Techniques Affect Customer Requirements (cont.)

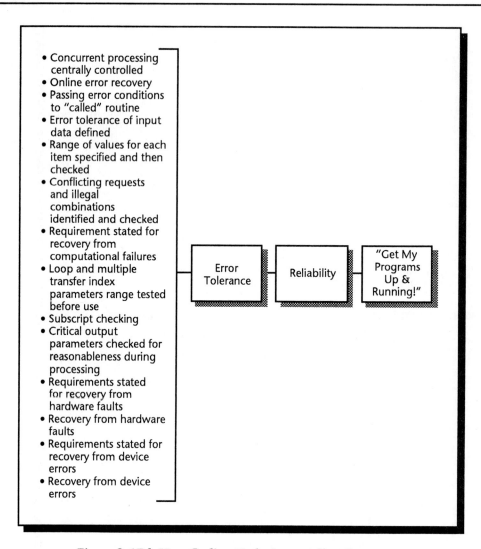

Figure 3-17d. How Coding Techniques Affect Customer Requirements (cont.)

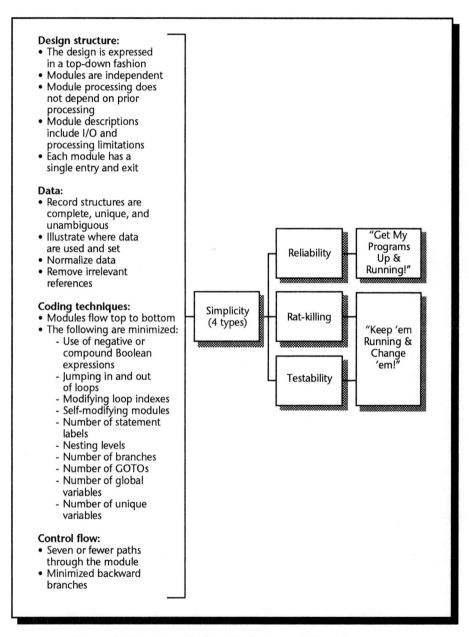

Design structure:
- The design is expressed in a top-down fashion
- Modules are independent
- Module processing does not depend on prior processing
- Module descriptions include I/O and processing limitations
- Each module has a single entry and exit

Data:
- Record structures are complete, unique, and unambiguous
- Illustrate where data are used and set
- Normalize data
- Remove irrelevant references

Coding techniques:
- Modules flow top to bottom
- The following are minimized:
    - Use of negative or compound Boolean expressions
    - Jumping in and out of loops
    - Modifying loop indexes
    - Self-modifying modules
    - Number of statement labels
    - Nesting levels
    - Number of branches
    - Number of GOTOs
    - Number of global variables
    - Number of unique variables

Control flow:
- Seven or fewer paths through the module
- Minimized backward branches

Simplicity (4 types)

Reliability

Rat-killing

Testability

"Get My Programs Up & Running!"

"Keep 'em Running & Change 'em!"

Figure 3-17e. How Coding Techniques Affect Customer Requirements (cont.)

113

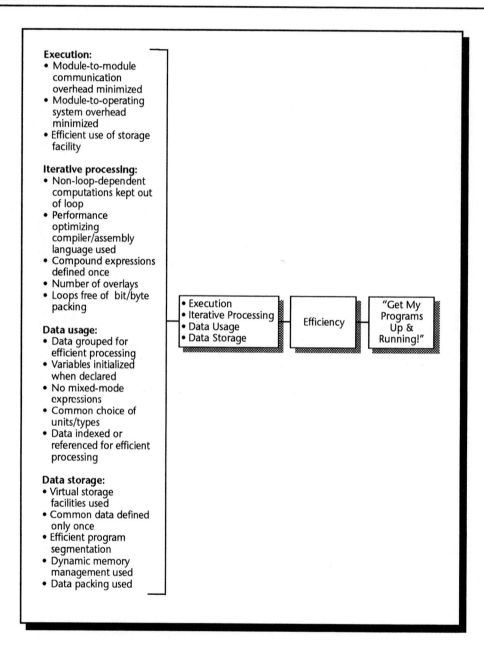

Execution:
- Module-to-module communication overhead minimized
- Module-to-operating system overhead minimized
- Efficient use of storage facility

Iterative processing:
- Non-loop-dependent computations kept out of loop
- Performance optimizing compiler/assembly language used
- Compound expressions defined once
- Number of overlays
- Loops free of bit/byte packing

Data usage:
- Data grouped for efficient processing
- Variables initialized when declared
- No mixed-mode expressions
- Common choice of units/types
- Data indexed or referenced for efficient processing

Data storage:
- Virtual storage facilities used
- Common data defined only once
- Efficient program segmentation
- Dynamic memory management used
- Data packing used

- Execution
- Iterative Processing
- Data Usage
- Data Storage

Efficiency

"Get My Programs Up & Running!"

Figure 3-17f. How Coding Techniques Affect Customer Requirements (cont.)

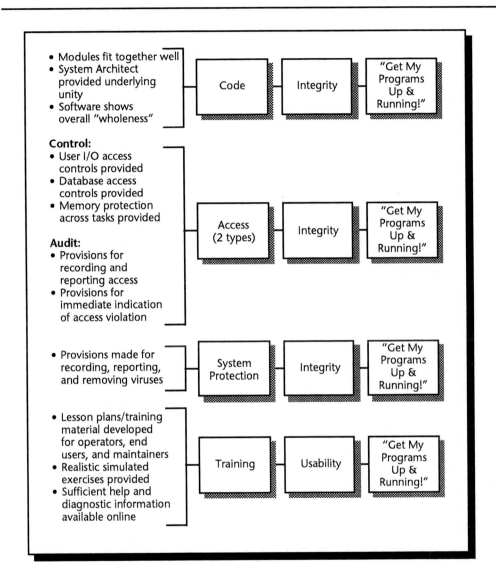

Figure 3-17g. How Coding Techniques Affect Customer Requirements (cont.)

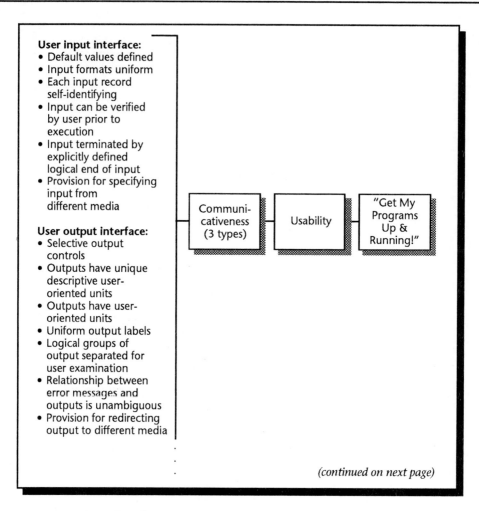

User input interface:
- Default values defined
- Input formats uniform
- Each input record self-identifying
- Input can be verified by user prior to execution
- Input terminated by explicitly defined logical end of input
- Provision for specifying input from different media

User output interface:
- Selective output controls
- Outputs have unique descriptive user-oriented units
- Outputs have user-oriented units
- Uniform output labels
- Logical groups of output separated for user examination
- Relationship between error messages and outputs is unambiguous
- Provision for redirecting output to different media

Communicativeness (3 types)

Usability

"Get My Programs Up & Running!"

(continued on next page)

Figure 3-17h. How Coding Techniques Affect Customer Requirements (cont.)

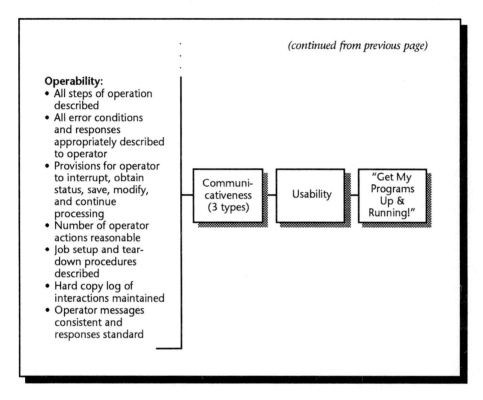

Operability:
- All steps of operation described
- All error conditions and responses appropriately described to operator
- Provisions for operator to interrupt, obtain status, save, modify, and continue processing
- Number of operator actions reasonable
- Job setup and tear-down procedures described
- Hard copy log of interactions maintained
- Operator messages consistent and responses standard

(continued from previous page)

Communicativeness (3 types) — Usability — "Get My Programs Up & Running!"

Figure 3-17i. How Coding Techniques Affect Customer Requirements (cont.)

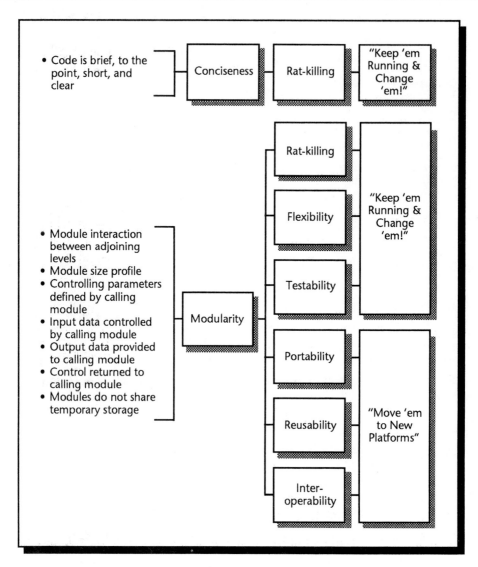

Figure 3-17j. How Coding Techniques Affect Customer
Requirements (cont.)

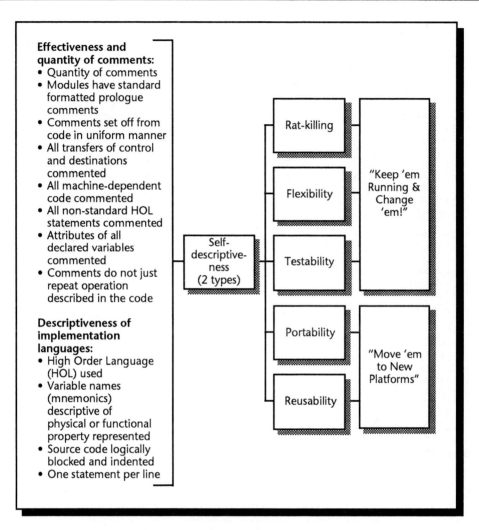

Effectiveness and quantity of comments:
- Quantity of comments
- Modules have standard formatted prologue comments
- Comments set off from code in uniform manner
- All transfers of control and destinations commented
- All machine-dependent code commented
- All non-standard HOL statements commented
- Attributes of all declared variables commented
- Comments do not just repeat operation described in the code

Descriptiveness of implementation languages:
- High Order Language (HOL) used
- Variable names (mnemonics) descriptive of physical or functional property represented
- Source code logically blocked and indented
- One statement per line

Self-descriptive-ness (2 types)

Rat-killing

Flexibility

Testability

Portability

Reusability

"Keep 'em Running & Change 'em!"

"Move 'em to New Platforms"

Figure 3-17k. How Coding Techniques Affect Customer Requirements (cont.)

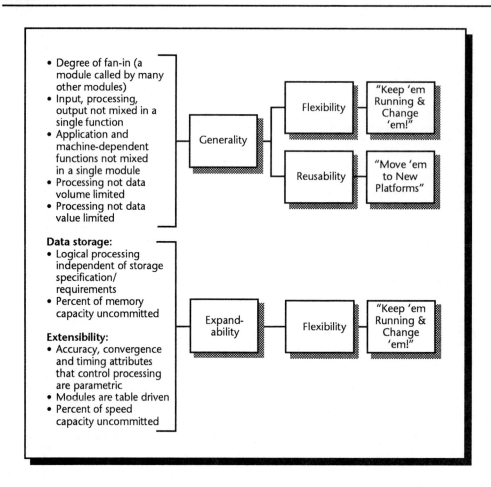

Figure 3-17l. How Coding Techniques Affect Customer Requirements (cont.)

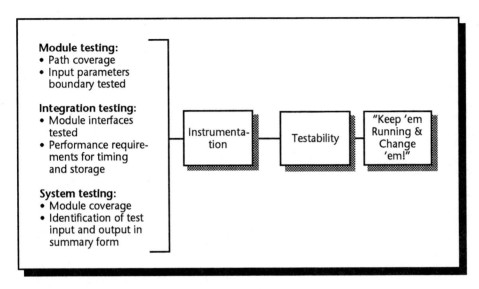

Figure 3-17m. How Coding Techniques Affect Customer Requirements (cont.)

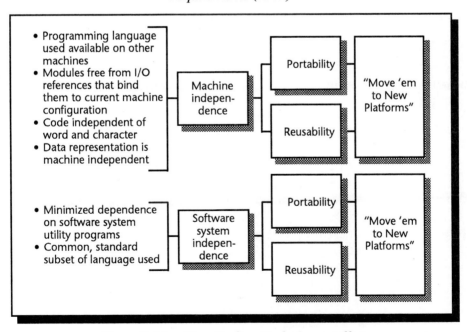

Figure 3-17n. How Coding Techniques Affect Customer Requirements (cont.)

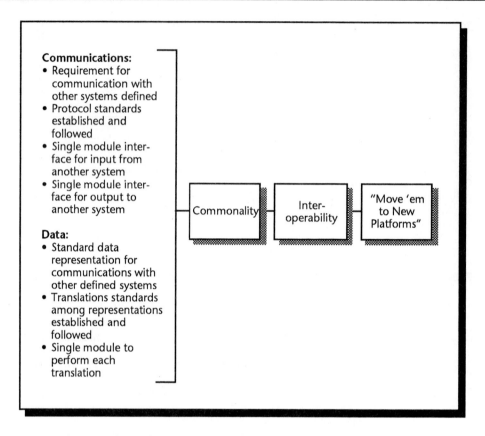

Figure 3-17o. How Coding Techniques Affect
Customer Requirements (cont.)

This model can be expanded. For example, we discovered that the programmers learn the software in maintenance. The characteristics of software that aid programmers in learning it are *completeness, consistency, simplicity, modularity,* and *self-descriptiveness.* Figure 3-18 shows what that part of the model would look like.

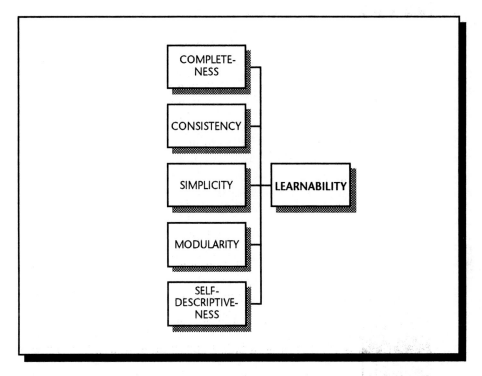

Figure 3-18. Characteristics that Aid in Learning Software

Some of the software engineering practices described in this chapter have more sensitivity than others. The top four are:

1. *Modularity*, which supports six of the eleven characteristics of high quality software

2. *Self-descriptiveness*, which supports five

3. *Simplicity*, which supports three

4. *Consistency*, which supports three

You might do well to regularly practice these four practices. J.A. did.

Implications for CASE

There are some tools that help you measure some of these characteristics. McCabe's ACT (A Complexity Tool) comes to mind as well as Logiscope from Verilog. But, generally speaking, the trends in tools have stayed away from the intrinsic quality of software.

These two tools produce graphs showing the paths that could be taken as the program that is being observed by these tools is being executed. These control graphs are very useful in spotting the complex code that needs to be improved and in "show and tell" sessions with managers who can allocate resources to do the job. (See Figure 3-19.) Logiscope, in addition, also produces many other metrics such as the Halstead measures (see the *Glossary*), lines of code, etc.

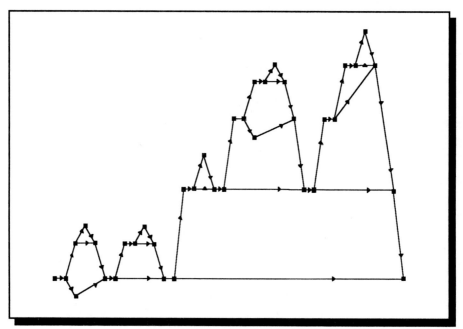

Figure 3-19. Control Graph from Verilog's Logiscope

If you're Roman, you're probably interested in *how many* defects occur with the software. If you're Greek, you're probably interested in *why* the defects occurred. The quality model that we've shown above provides you with some insight into the software engineering "whys" of defects. ❧

PART II.
Left Brain, Right Brain

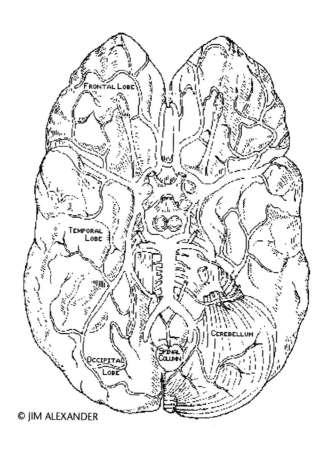

© JIM ALEXANDER

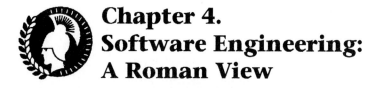

Chapter 4.
Software Engineering:
A Roman View

The Roman view of software engineering comes from the systems view of the organization described in Chapter 2. The Romans provide the structure necessary for a business to operate. In a Roman environment, things get done: supplies show up, there is an office in which to work, the office gets cleaned, and it is equipped for work. Your paycheck gets to you and, when you are ready to spend it, the shops are full of stuff to buy. And, you can get to the shops because you have a car, gas is easy to get, and the roads are there.

The Romans maintain the tension necessary to make things and to make them work: between form and function, between themselves and the Greeks, and between order and chaos.

The Roman view of software engineering concentrates more on the "what" of a problem: what the problem is, and what must be done to solve it. The Romans tend to be interested in *data* more than *process*; in *nouns* rather than *verbs*. The "what" of a problem can be anything from general goals and objectives to a fully analyzed and decomposed requirements document.

In this view, analysis, or the "what is to be done" is very important. The Romans frequently have options regarding the design or construction of the software, which is the "how it is to be done" of the project. For example, Romans might "out source" the development rather than perform it in-house. When it is done in-house, they also expect the implementation to be followed in an orderly, professional way, often supported by institutionalized procedures encountered first at university, or training school, and then in the organization itself.

Here is what software engineering looks like from the lofty aerie of the Roman [DeGrace and Stahl 1990, pp.34-53]. The Roman view is involved with the Waterfall method of software development, a top-down approach, and classic Structured Analysis, Design, and Programming (SADP).

It begins at some Initiation step, often originating at some senior management level as a result of strategic planning, arising from operation of the business, or in consideration of changing business conditions or opportunities. The problem to be solved is stated in a general way, often only as an objective. A team of specialists is called on to expand and clarify the problem and do a cost benefit analysis. Sometimes, especially if the initiative is from strategic planning, an Options Study is done.

Two documents are created during the Options Study, which are the deliverables for this phase: an *options analysis* and the *preliminary cost-benefit analysis*. Figure 4-1 contains sample outlines for these two documents.

A Requirements Gathering and Analysis Phase follows the Options Study. It uses the clarified problem statement, cost benefit analysis and, if there is one, the Options Study. In this phase, software engineers develop a complete set of requirements by analyzing the problem statement, the data to be used, and the processes required to transform the data. (See Figure 4-2.)

Here, Structured Analysis makes an appearance and diagrams come into play. First, there is a context diagram showing all the systems and the files used by each system. (See Figure 4-3.) This context diagram is then decomposed down to lower and lower processes using data-flow diagrams (DFDs). The DFDs describe what is currently going on and suggest what must go on in order to solve the problem. (See Figure 4-4.) DFDs show how data passes into an organization or a process within it, what transformations are made there, and how the data passes out of the organization or process.

File descriptions appear, where the information contained in each file is described. A data model is constructed using, say, entity-relationship diagrams (ERDs). (See Figure 4-5.) A data dictionary is started. The data dictionary contains entries for files, data structures, record structures, and the data elements in these, and elements in the programs that will make up the system. (See Figure 4-6.) Finally, when the processes of the DFDs are at the lowest level, mini-specs are written. (See Figure 4-7.)

By now, the problem has been well and thoroughly stated. The software engineers produce a complete set of requirements, which are a greatly enhanced and elaborated statement of the problem. They determine a basic architecture and sometimes conduct an Alternatives Study. (See Figure 4-8.) The Alternatives Study provides another set of options for management and the downstream software engineers.

Then, the software engineers hand off all this stuff to the designers and coders who design, construct, test, and install the solution starting with the preliminary design step.

The designers determine a basic structure for the software, they "map" the DFDs into it, and they establish control functions. (See Figure 4-9.) They refine the whole thing so that there is a top level set of functions, or a *driver* as it is sometimes called, which does nothing but traffic control. The driver systematically gives control to some mid-level routines that do some computing and control. These, in turn, hand over control to the low level functions that actually do the computing. They take input data and transform it into output data. Then, the coders code the thing up, test it, and install it.

If you are doing object-oriented development, then analysis and design proceed differently. First, you would differentiate the world of your problem into objects and their attributes, such as an employee and that employee's education and experience. Then, you would decompose each object into its component parts, such as a car and its engine. You would form the objects into classes of similar characteristics, such as the classes of *employees* and *vehicles*. You would create inheritance schemes and identify the object's methods (the functions or procedures inside the objects).

You would then design the methods of the objects as if each object were a program in itself. Here, DFDs, ERDs, state diagrams, and structure charts come into play. Finally, as in traditional development, you would code the objects.

The coders (who are often also the designers) write the code from the design. They maximize cohesion, minimize coupling, and optimize the code according to design specifications. (See Chapter 3 for more specifics on producing high quality code.)

They then test the system according to the test scenarios written during design. The tests also check the operation and performance of the software against the requirements and functional specifications. This is the verification portion of the test.

Next, they play the system in parallel with the existing system to see if it will do what it was intended to do: actually satisfy the customer. This is the validation portion of the test. Then, at the cutover date, the new system takes the place of the existing one.

This is an orderly, logical process. And, our correspondents tell us that it works. It works for well known problems and for automating well known processes.

Options Analysis Document—Contents

- Problem Definition
  - Problem statement (including a brief description of the enterprise)
  - Description of problems with current environment
  - Description of processes involved
  - Description of the organizations involved
  - Statement of the goals in solving the problem (if the problem goes away, what would things be like)
- Potential Solutions
  - Assumptions and constraints (turf issues, etc.)
  - Potential solutions (repeat as necessary)
    - Descriptions
    - Impact of this solution on the organization
    - How this solution maps into the goals
- Proposed System
  - Evaluations of all potential solutions
  - Recommendation and justification
  - Operational description of the proposed system

Preliminary Cost-Benefit Analysis Document

- Benefits
  - The goals that can be attained by this solution
  - Other benefits
    - Revenue improvements
    - Cost savings
    - Productivity improvements
    - Informational improvements
    - Other benefits
- Costs
  - Development (labor and material)
  - Maintenance per year
- Analysis
  - Net improvements
  - Net investment summary
  - Payback analysis
  - Cash-flow analysis

Figure 4-1. A Typical Options Study

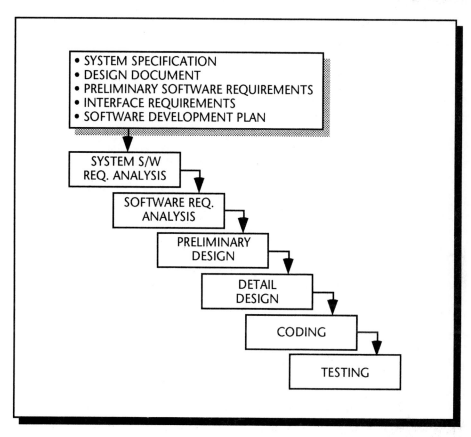

Figure 4-2. Requirements Gathering and Analysis

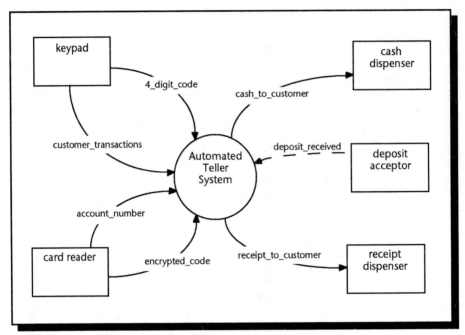

Figure 4-3. Example Context Diagram
(from Iconix FreeFlow™)

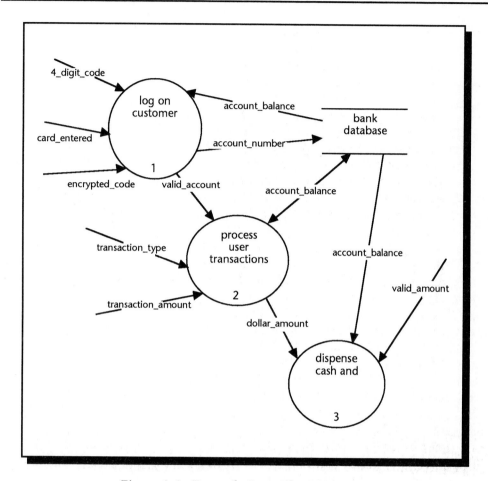

Figure 4-4. Example Data-Flow Diagram
(the child diagram of the context diagram shown in Figure 4-3)

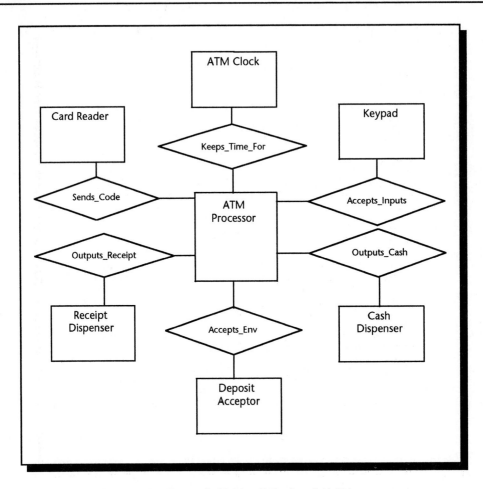

*Figure 4-5. Example Entity-Relationship Diagram
(from Iconix DataModeler™)*

```
• Relationship:
•
•
•
Authorizes =
    Assertions:   All ATM transactions must be authorized by
    the Bank.
    Attributes:   Transaction Identifier
    Time of Authorization
    Authorization Result
    References:   Systems Requirements Specification
Traceability:
    Description: An authorization permits the ATM to complete a
    requested transaction, based on the Bank having verified
    that the Customer is in good standing and the transaction is
    valid.
    Design Rationale: Each transaction must be individually
    authorized.
Banks_At =
    Assertions:   Only Customers with an open deposit account
    (checking, savings, money market) are able to bank at the
    Bank and operate the ATM.
    Attributes:   Account Number
    Account Type
    Account Status
    Account Balance
    References:   Systems Requirements Specification
Traceability:
    Description:   Customers who have opened deposit accounts
    may access those accounts directly at the bank or via the
    ATM.   One customer may have multiple accounts.
    Design Rationale:   Each account of each customer must be
    individually managed.
Dispenses_To =
    Attributes:   Item Dispensed     * Cash, Receipt*
    Customer
    Amount Dispensed
    Date Dispensed
    Time Dispensed
    Resulting Balance
    Transaction Identifier
    References:   Systems Requirements Specification
Traceability:
    Description:   The ATM may dispense cash and/or receipts to the
    customer in response to an authorization to complete a trans.
    Design Rationale:   Each dispensation must be individually
    executed.
Operates =
    Assertions:   Only logged in, validated customers are
    permitted to operate the ATM.
    Attributes:   Log In Time
    Four Digit Code
```

Figure 4-6. Example Data Dictionary Report
(from Iconix DataModeler™)

```
        Card Status
        Transaction History
        Log Out Time
        References:  Systems Requirements Specification
Traceability:
        Description:  As each customer logs in, operates the ATM,
        and logs out, the operation session data is recorded for
        later auditability.
        Design Rationale:  Each session must be individually
        recorded for auditability.

• Entity:
ATM Processor =
        Operations:  Check for Positive Account Balance
        Compare User Code to Card Code
        Compute Bills to Dispense
        Deposit Cash
        Dispense Cash and Receipts
        Log on Customer
        Process User Transactions
        Transfer Cash
        Update Account Balance
        Withdraw Cash
Automated Teller =
        Assertions:  All ATMs are serviced daily with money,
        receipt stock, deposit envelopes.  Communications between
        ATMs and Bank are over secure lines.
        Attributes:  Service Status
        Money Available
        Money Dispensed
        Operations:  Open
        Service
        Deposit
        Withdraw
        Check Balance
        States:  Open
        Closed
        References:  Systems Requirements Specification
Traceability:
        Alternate Names:  ATM
        Description:  The ATM allows customers to deposit,
        withdraw, and check balances of their accounts.
        Design Rationale:  Each ATM must operate independently,
        except for authorizations from the Bank.
Account Number =
ATM ID =
Auth Code =
Identifier =
Login =
Name =
PIN =
Service Date =
```

Figure 4-6. Example Data Dictionary Report (cont.)
(from Iconix DataModeler™)

```
%Subprogram compare user code to card code
.    (1.1)
.
%Inputs
 4_digit_code
 encrypted_code
.
%Outputs
 validated_code
.
.FUNCTION: compare the user's 4-digit code to the encrypted code on
the card.

BEGIN
 IF the user's code matches the encrypted code THEN
   set validated_code to TRUE
 ELSE
   set validated_code to FALSE
 ENDIF
END
```

Figure 4-7. Example Mini-Specs
(from Iconix FreeFlow™)

- Requirements Document

  - Boilerplate
  - Project scope
  - Project history to this point
  - Current system description (DFDs, ERDs, HIPO charts)
  - New system description (DFDs, ERDs, HIPO charts)
  - New system requirements (DFDs, ERDs, HIPO charts)

- Preliminary Program Plan

  - Statement of work
  - Work breakdown structure
  - Management plan
  - Documentation plan
  - Visibility and tracking plan
  - Schedules

- Alternatives Analysis Document

  - Objective
  - Scope
  - Operational approach
    — alternative 1
    — alternative 2
    — alternative n
  - Technical approach
    — approach 1
    — approach 2
    — approach n
  - Recommendation

Figure 4-8. Example Alternatives Study

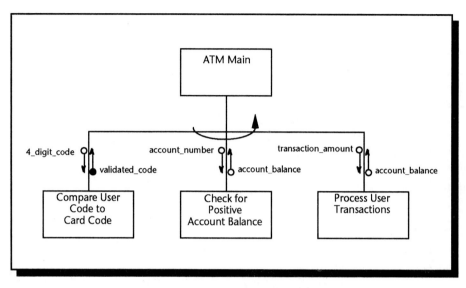

*Figure 4-9. An Example Structure Diagram
(from Iconix QuickChart™)*

The Overly Roman View

However, there is another view of software engineering: the *overly Roman* view, which we will now discuss. It involves an imbalance we see in our field and, to a larger extent, in the working world. Namely, in many organizations the Romans have completely taken over, especially in the larger, mature corporations. Organizations that are top-heavy, largely administrative and bureaucratic, that can't respond well to competition, and that drive the creative, innovative spirit out are what we call *overly Roman*.

The following examples describe two situations that actually occurred. The first situation deals with improving the market share for a software product. The second situation deals with developing a software system to solve a specific problem.

We will first present an ideal (or model) description of what *should have* happened. Next, we will describe what *actually did* happen. Then, we offer some suggestions about how things can be fixed.

Two Model Situations

In the first situation, the product was "buggy." That's why the market share was low. In the latter situation, there were too many systems that kept track of employee information, and these systems didn't work together. That's why overhead costs were high.

From these problem statements, initial decisions were made about how to proceed. In the former case, the problem was to make the software reliable and to make sure customers knew about it. In the latter case, the problem was to bring together into one integrated system all the systems that store and use employee information.

In the case of the "buggy" product, the corporation announced a new focus on quality and hired a Director of Quality who was given high status in the corporation. Plans were made, a Total Quality Management (TQM) program was announced, and testing was to be expanded. The solution was clearly in sight.

In the meantime, the case of the employee record system began to take on some form. A project was established with a manager and staff. Data were collected about what information was used and how it was used. The project's management decided to use the approach described above and developed a schedule for a new system to solve the problem.

There are some appealing things about these two models. They seem so "okay." The problems were challenges, to be sure, but they appeared to be very manageable, like the problems we had in school. These models are more like fairy tales: simple, straightforward, and orthodox. One gets a feeling of confidence in the organizations; that all is well in hand. One wants the heroes—the businesses—to succeed.

The organization with the "buggy" software problem had a good idea of what was causing it and a good idea of what had to be done to solve it, and then set about resolutely solving it.

And, the business with the employee information system followed good software engineering principles and used Structured Stuff in developing the system.

In addition, there was no dearth of information or help available. Many books have been written on these subjects, and gurus and seminars abound. Software Quality and Structured Stuff are popular topics.

Nevertheless, in real life both projects failed.

What Actually Happened

The reliability problem was never adequately solved. Soon after the new Director of Quality appeared, it became evident that the enterprise would have to change the way it did business. It turned out that the poor reliability was built into the way the enterprise managed its development.

Many of the managers operated on their own past experiences in software development. They insisted on slaying those old dragons and divorced themselves from what was really going on in the field and, unhappily, in their own company. One manager described his experience in programming as that of a naive programmer, inexperienced with Structured Stuff, with no training, and, who, in spite of all the resources available to him, simply didn't know what good programming practice was. Another manager exclaimed that nobody over thirty could even understand Structured Stuff.

This company also had a knack for underestimating difficulty. They operated under the faulty assumption that "all will go well." This optimism is common: "Computer programming ... creates with an exceedingly tractable medium. The programmer builds from pure thought stuff: concepts and very flexible representations thereof. Because the medium is tractable, we expect few difficulties in implementation; hence our pervasive optimism. Because our ideas are faulty, we have bugs; hence our optimism is unjustified." [Brooks 1982, pp.14-16]

The managers of this company still held to this misconception. They simply didn't see the difficulties ahead. Everything they tried became a terrible scramble at the end.

There wasn't a way to check the software against requirements since requirements weren't kept up to date, and the developers didn't talk to the users very much. The developers were also testers; as a result, the modules were well tested but not integrated well into the system. There was no sense of what good quality code looked like.

This was bad enough, but what really sank them was the way they went about trying to fix things. The managers of the enterprise thought they could simply *buy* high reliability. They had formed the habit of only talking with folks at their own level. So, they hired someone at their own level to talk with about reliable software.

The new Director of Quality knew what had to be done. However, he tried to institute the necessary changes without including the people who were responsible for the code in the first place. He set about writing his procedures, formalizing things, and putting his systems into place. He hired testers and inspectors, started an independent testing organization, and reported that things were ready.

The developers balked. They saw that they were being asked to do a lot of backtracking and found that people were now peering over their shoulders. They had to satisfy procedures written by people who didn't know what had been going on. But, we suspect, their *real* problem was a resistance to changes that were brought on without having any say in things.

The developers complained to their bosses, who themselves were having problems with these outsiders. Their overhead costs were going up and there was little to show for it. This set in motion the political collisions that brought the entire program to a halt.

The assumption that they could simply buy quality proved wrong. The organization never bought into the new way. All the commitment, announcements, added staff, and plans came to naught. The Director of Quality resigned, testing returned to the previous methods, the enterprise never did regain its market share, and it continues to stagger along servicing old technology with old technology.

Meanwhile, the employee information system stumbled into existence very late and way over budget. Few users liked it. Few developers liked it. Rather than assisting users with information, it made things worse. It never really did away with all the old systems. The users had to learn yet another system. And, although the developers attempted to design it well, it wasn't user friendly. The screens were inconsistent and hard to figure out.

The developers who produced those screens did them the way they did because there was no time to do them better. They had been working overtime for months to meet ever-tightening schedules. More and more meetings were held to plan "get well" efforts. More time was spent talking about things and not actually doing anything. The managers made solemn promises to one another to use an established, formal Waterfall method.

And, while management expected reports to be made in terms of the phases of the Waterfall, the developers were forced to use other methods. They couldn't hope to get good requirements without prototyping, yet they had to report that they collected the requirements according to the accepted interview methods. They had much of the system already prototyped, yet they had to write software development plans. In effect, they had to develop the software one way and report their work another way. This meant they were doing the better part of two developments. No wonder they couldn't do better!

Now, we don't claim that Roman projects are necessarily doomed to failure; but, the peculiar failure of these two projects attracted our attention to the organizations in which they operated. We examined these projects and some others, read the literature, talked with our correspondents, and arrived at a profile of what we call the *overly Roman* organization. The profile is divided into organizational characteristics, project orientation, type of software development and, finally, types of tools.

Characteristics of the Overly Roman Organization

We have discovered that overly Roman organizations have certain basic characteristics in common. They are:

- Formal
- Bureaucratic
- Detached
- Have high overhead costs

Formal

An overly Roman organization is very formal. Rank is extremely important. Communication is done by memoranda, meetings, and reports of meetings.

Work, value, commitment, and progress are reduced to elements on charts. Feelings, passion, and expressiveness are discouraged. Everything is reduced to logic. In this logical environment one would think that claims for new CASE tools (for example, their cost-effectiveness) are checked out pretty thoroughly, with charts and reports and such revealing the facts of the tool's usefulness.

But, ironically, in this environment claims are often accepted as *verified* when, in fact, they are only based on simple anecdotal evidence or vendor claims. On one project we know about, a vendor claimed that even though his CASE tools were expensive, and even though they made for more total work in the project, they would save money downstream in maintenance. Yet, the CASE tools were supposed to *help* the project and not make it more costly. And, there was simply no empirical evidence that downstream costs would be less or that the CASE tools would contribute to lower downstream costs even if there *were* such savings. Nevertheless, the project purchased these CASE tools based simply on the vendor's claims.

These formal organizations have their own language. It is a kind of bureaucratic code that grants these claims some high status. This status gave the managers confidence in their decision to buy the CASE tools for their project.

This formality results in the establishment of a highly bureaucratic structure, which we will discuss next.

Bureaucratic

Overly Roman organizations typically have many levels of management. In one of the enterprises we looked at, there were five levels of vice-presidents and thirteen levels of management in all. What could they possibly be useful for? The Catholic church conquered half the world with only four levels of management!

Several of the VPs in one organization we looked at were known by the regular folks before they were promoted. Every one of them had the reputation of being a bureaucrat; not one of them had a record of doing anything or being successful at anything other than talking about work. When one of them retired, the flyer announcing his retirement party listed all the projects on which he'd worked. He had seen none of them through to the end, and nobody familiar with the projects would call them successful (although extraordinary effort by unnamed heroes prevented some of them from being outright failures).

Overly Roman organizations are stratified by their many levels of management. Communication *between* the strata is more difficult than that *within* the strata. The folks at the top of the organization are shielded from what is going on. Workers frequently find that their customers are not the same as their boss's customers, or their boss's boss's customers, etc. The result is that management can't say for sure how those who report to them are doing. In one organization we studied, we knew someone who worked very hard to please his customer only to find that his work conflicted with his boss's efforts.

We found one project where programmers spent much of their time preparing for project meetings and then spent most of each meeting with nothing to do. They had to plan their work down to very low details even when they weren't sure about them. This gave rise to even more meetings and digressions.

The managers of these organizations are not fools; they're pretty smart folks who worked hard to earn their positions. They emulated the programs that made their competitors successful but things frequently didn't change. Projects weren't done any quicker or better, the error rates and costs didn't go down. They introduced quality improvement programs: Quality Circles, Total Quality Commitment, Continuous Quality Improvement, and so on.

And, of course, they found wonderful ways of defeating the basic purpose of these programs.

When they were first announced, these programs raised the expectations of the programmers. But, the programs were implemented from the top and were pushed down on the programmers with little effect. The programmers' expectations were dashed. Goals were set without consulting the programmers who must attain them. Here are some examples:

- A Continuous Quality Improvement (CQI) program is supposed to be an empowering activity. The workers who know the processes they use are empowered and, therefore, entrusted with improving them. The idea is to gradually and constantly improve the way they do work. Simply stated, this means that those who do the work describe the processes they use, determine if there are problems with the processes, and then set about trying to fix any problems they find.

    But, in the overly Roman organizations we looked at, the Romans put in place yet another new "methodology" and expected those who were going to use it to do CQI on it. The workers never had a chance to describe their current processes, and weren't even able to do CQI on the "approved" methodology because they really didn't know it. Any improvements might well have come simply from learning how to live with the new "methodology." When CQI was pushed down from the top the way the management staff pushed their favorite "methodology" down on the programmers, any empowering went out the window and the program failed. Management wrung its hands and had another excuse for failure.

- Sometimes, management decides to use metrics, selecting the ones to use, asking workers to report on them, and then expecting things to work. One commonly chosen metric is *defects*.

    Defects, especially changes in defect rates occurring in some process, are worthwhile reporting. But, when defects are related to people, they become threatening and reporting them is counterproductive and anti-Deming, the chief guru of quality!

    For example, one organization we studied instituted formal code reviews. The defects discovered during these reviews were to be reported to management. Since it was not difficult to know whose code

143

or design was being reviewed, it was easy to tell what an individual's defect rate was.

However, the purpose of code reviews is to reveal errors; the more errors discovered, the better. As soon as it became known that errors were to be reported *outside* the review, the participants became very defensive. The person whose code was being reviewed tried to find all the errors *before* the review. The reviewers were reluctant to report any errors, thinking that it was a form of snitching. Everybody grew to hate reviews, and so an opportunity to learn and develop in a secure collegiate atmosphere went away. This completely destroyed the value of the defect metric.

- Another organization we know about instituted *function points* as the basic software size metric. (Please see the chapter on metrics for an explanation.) Function points were never intended to measure the *programmer*, only the *software*. Yet, in every discussion of them we heard about, function points were always used as measures of programmer productivity. For example, programmers were given quotas of producing so many functions per month. As a result, programmers took to re-defining function points. One group defined a function point as any job step in the execution of a job. Another group defined one as a part of each person's day, with eight function points per day. So, again, a metric became irrelevant.

Metrics are useful, but they should:

- Be part of the work
- Arise from that work
- Be easy to get
- Be meaningful to the worker

Function points are none of these things.

In this type of an environment, tools salesmen sell mainly to managers or technical staff who are remote (to say the least) from the people who will have to use the tools. Purchasing decisions are made for "political" reasons at least as much as for technical reasons. Here are some examples:

- We know of a study that was done of database systems for workstations. Its results reflected poorly on the "preferred" system so the folks who did the evaluation were asked by their management to do it again, this time with a spin toward the "preferred" system.

- A CASE tool vendor we know of had a habit of only partially implementing new features. This made the tool more difficult to use and take longer to learn. This tool was going to be the "standard" in one group we studied. When the group questioned the vendor about this practice, the vendor explained that this was a "strategic" decision. This gave the questioners the impression that they shouldn't meddle. Those who persisted were treated poorly by their own management for challenging a "standard" vendor on his poor decisions. As a result, there are now many copies of this tool in the place. However, many of these copies are "shelfware," while most of the others are used as simple drawing tools. Considering that they cost 40 times as much as simple drawing tools, one would have supposed a different outcome.

Detached

In these overly Roman organizations, management is often detached and distant. When someone becomes a VP (or other big shot) in one of these organizations, they disappear into their offices and only reappear for the organization's rituals. It appears that they are trying to avoid working with or contacting those people who actually do the work. For example, they practically never talk directly to programmers, particularly one to one. When they do, the conversations usually become confrontations with no real information passed. Programmers have trouble voicing complaints and suggestions. Managers receive their information from their peers, gurus, vendors, competitors, and staff, and not from the programmers doing the work. Here are some examples:

- An overly Roman manager will turn even the smallest group into an elaborate hierarchy. One former high level manager we know recently acquired a very small group. Rather than use his new position as an opportunity to be close to programmers, he organized this small group into a hierarchy, with a separation between him and the programmers. There was an assistant, several lead programmers, and then the programmers themselves. The programmers were encouraged to contact their lead programmers about day-to-day matters and get their lead programmer's permission before talking to the boss's assistant. And the boss? Well, meeting with him was a rare event. One of the programmers told us that talking with the supervisor always gave him the feeling that he was delaying the supervisor from some really important meeting.

- We know of an organization that couldn't come up with a good set of requirements for their universal workstation. Therefore, they left it up to the vendors to specify it; but, no one ever talked with the programmers who were going to use the workstation. It became something programmers avoided because it didn't help them and it frequently got in the way.

- We know of another organization that, also without consulting the programmers, suddenly decided to reduce maintenance costs by 50% as part of a Continuous Quality Improvement program. Setting such a goal, especially one that stresses results rather than simply general improvement, is laudable. It provides a focus for everyone concerned, it suggests its own metrics, and it brings to bear only those improvements that lead toward the goal. But, this *particular* goal was unrealistic. For management to achieve real reductions in maintenance, short-term costs would have to go up to pay for making the inventory of software maintainable.

  Ironically, they could have achieved their goal. The manager of the metrics program didn't think that enhancements were part of maintenance. Enhancements make up about half the activity of maintenance. So, by redefining maintenance to exclude enhancements, they could have reached their goal. However, this meant that the enhancements would have to be done by projects. Projects are much more expensive than the close, trusting cooperation that existed between the maintenance programmers and their users. Thus, the result of the apparently lower maintenance costs would be that total costs would go way up.

- We know of yet another organization that sent its managers to Japan to consult with software development managers there. However, they never talked with their own programmers about the day-to-day problems that programmers face here. This is an example of international stratification. (It turned out, however, that the Japanese managers politely asked the Americans not to come back. Could they have been sending us a message?)

- We even know of a vendor who had so much influence in his customer's organization that he caused an employee, who objected to the vendor's position on software development, to be fired. Since we have correspondents in both these companies, we were able to verify the story. The fired employee was closely working with a staff of software developers and knew they were using prototyping and evolutionary software development. The vendor was influencing the employee's company to use a Waterfall, which his tools supported. The employee knew that, if introduced, this method would completely disrupt the current work. When he brought this up with his management and challenged their association with the vendor, he was asked to resign. It became an issue of not being able to do an honest job for his boss because his boss was paying more attention to the vendor's claims than to the reports coming to him from those who were actually doing the work.

A very, *verrrry* distant management, indeed.

High Overhead Costs

Overly Roman organizations have very high overhead costs. The many levels of management themselves contribute to this. In addition, each level has its own staff being supported on overhead. *Super staffs* also spring into existence in an attempt to coordinate all the various activities. These also contribute to overhead. Here are some examples:

- The two organizations we discussed earlier both had very high overhead costs, even though they were constantly trying to lower them. The employee information project is an example of such a try.

Each level of the management strata we discussed earlier had its staff of bureaucrats. In addition, as we stated above, there were *super staffs* that attempted to span the breadth of the organization, and never the depth. In fact, the effort of lowering overhead costs not only spawned the failed project, but yet another costly bureaucracy that collected metrics on costs.

- CASE is supposed to help software development organizations lower costs. However, in one of the organizations we looked at, there were at least half a dozen different groups all looking at CASE tools. Any vendor with a good product had to face many separate evaluations and selling jobs. A vendor with a not-so-good product could simply try again with another group if he met with sales resistance. All these groups cost money and contributed to overhead costs.

- Another organization established a "high technology" organization that set about looking at technology and trying to transfer it into the enterprise. They spent most of their time looking for technology and very little time asking programmers what they needed. As a result, they were constantly running around with solutions looking for problems to solve.

Project Orientation in an Overly Roman Organization

The stratified structure of an overly Roman organization is reflected in their projects. There are many layers of software development: systems engineering, system architecture (sometimes), analysis, design, coding, test, configuration management, and librarian functions. Each level of the development has its own specialists ... its own tasks ... and produces the materials to be sent to the next and lower level. The various specialists are often physically separated from each other.

Just as *planning* is valued as much or more than *doing*, so too is *analysis* valued over software *design and construction*. The message is clear: being an analyst and breaking things down is where the rewards are. Building something, designing something, perhaps even flirting with beauty, well, these are just barely tolerated steps toward becoming an analyst.

Analysis is important. The trick, of course, is to analyze the correct things and analyze them correctly. Sometimes a user/customer approaches the developers with the "solution" already in hand. For example, he might say he needs a mainframe database system, but analysis would reveal that he actually needs an inexpensive PC system.

But, sometimes problems are analyzed too far. In classic Structured Analysis the problem is analyzed down to "primitive" processes, which are then passed on to the designers and coders to be implemented into software. This might work with a well-defined problem or a problem with well-defined processes. However, if the problem is not well-defined, or if it is misdefined, or if it has unknown processes, or if it might have to take into account unknown interactions, then *analysis* of the classic structured type will go too far. It would have been better to have started with a more general goal, such as "we need *an* inventory control system," rather than "we need *this* inventory control system."

After analysis, the requirements are thrown over to the designers, coders, and others who are to "simply" code up the solution. In these organizations, design is an extension of analysis and actual coding is considered a "no-brainer." (We hope that Chapter 3 demonstrated how wrong-headed these folks are.) The result is that coders, who come in cold, do not have a chance to see the total system and, thus, aren't able to give the resulting software the integrity it requires.

Some projects have system architects who are supposed to provide that integrity. However, in overly Roman projects, system architects become mere paper shufflers, administering the "methodology" in use.

The overall structure of the software system produced in an overly Roman organization is thin and shallow, rather than the normal, effective structure, which is approximately as deep as it is wide.

We need to digress here a moment to explain a little more about design and construction. This explanation is shown in Figure 4-10.

The Infinite Step

Managers often miss the point that design and later work are different in *kind* from analysis. True, analysis decomposes problems into atomic parts and eventually describes what must be done. But, actually building the software is another matter altogether. When a system is built up from nothing (or from very little) into something that is useful to others, we call this "making the *infinite step*." It is called this because the distance between nothing and something is infinitely long.

The infinite step is very Greek-like; it is the most creative of all the software engineering activities. It relies heavily on intuitive, creative processes that are not well understood, even now. It certainly has to do with being fully engaged in the process. But, it's more than a mere adjunct to analysis. Consider these examples from Susan Lammers's book, *Programmers at Work* [1986].

"*You have to simulate in your mind how the program's going to work ...*" [ibid, Bill Gates, p.73] "*I believe very strongly that one person ... should do the design and high-level structure. You get a consistency and elegance when it springs from one mind.*" [ibid, John Page, p.98] "*... I can do anything that I can make an image of in my head.*" [ibid, Jonathan Sachs, p.169] "*To do the kind of programming I do takes incredible concentration and focus. ... keeping all the different connections in your brain at once ... .*" [ibid, Andy Hertzfeld, p.260]

The infinite step is going to the immensely tractable medium of a computer programming language with a problem in hand, discerning the structures and order you want, yanking them into our world, and then creating a computer program from them. The resulting program may still be somewhat ill-formed and "dripping" with disorder. And that's perfectly okay because then comes the finishing process, which will debur and dry off the code. (See Chapter 3 for some ideas on how to do that.)

Figure 4-10. The Infinite Step

Getting back to our main discussion, there is a lot of documentation in overly Roman projects. In one project, there were 80 different types of documents and many of these could be repeated dozens of times in the course of the project. Sometimes, documentation was measured in terms of linear feet by developers who were having trouble seeing any value in most of it.

There are many formal procedures in this type of organization. Each procedure is written in third person, passive voice, as if any one of them would be suitable to be chipped in marble. These come regularly from the TEMPLE MOUNTS OF THE CORPORATION, written by the bureaucrats, who usually don't have to follow them, and then are foisted on the workers. The procedures and standards become a straight jacket composed of things one *must* do, not guidelines that *might or might not* be observed as the situation dictates.

We estimate that for our earlier employee information system example, the project overhead was 40% of the costs incurred. Because management was distant, this overhead substituted for much of what we feel they were supposed to be doing.

After a system is up and running, it is given over to the users. If they don't like it, well, the excuse is that they should've been more precise about their requirements in the first place. Actually, the users have little real standing. Hasn't the system actually been done by technical specialists? And, if the system doesn't please the users, well then they obviously simply don't understand software systems (poor people!). Besides, given the stratified environment in an overly Roman organization, the users' *management* talks to the development staff's *management* more than it does to the *users*, so the user's complaints are less likely to find a friendly ear.

Types of Software Development

An overly Roman organization uses FORMAL METHODS—for example, the Waterfall—and actually expects work to be done according to these methods! The Romans expect analysis, design, and construction to be done in a top-down way. But, programmers do not always work that way, and problems are not always amenable to top-down work. The *results* of a programmer's work should be expressed in a top-down fashion; but, not always (perhaps not even often) actually done that way.

Formal methods were attempted in both of our example projects. However, neither of the example problems was amenable to top-down work. The reliability problem was a essentially a bottom-up one, and the employee information problem was a "wicked" problem that had no real formulation until *after* solutions were offered to the users to try.

Both projects attempted to use the Waterfall. They made their schedules according to the phases of the Waterfall and expected reports to be based on these phases. But, as we indicated above, the programmers had to use other means to get their work done. Yet, they had to waste time making reports according to a wall chart.

The programmers felt they were working out of their region of greatest skill. They were not able to easily get a "picture" of the system. We'll discuss these areas more fully in the next chapter. However, for now it's important to understand that FORMAL METHODS disrupted the normal approaches to problem-solving and program-building used by many of the programmers we talked to. As we indicated earlier, Formal Methods are sometimes appropriate. However, they need to be leavened by experience and wisdom, not formed into straight jackets for the developers who use them.

Types of Tools

From our point of view, one of the main effects of an overly Roman organization is when software engineering tools are acquired and used. To set the stage for our discussion, we will first describe how tools are sometimes selected elsewhere. We will then relate these experiences to our discussion.

First, we begin with the story of the short hoes.

Once upon a time in California, farm workers had to use tools that were specified and provided by the growers. The hoes were short, and the workers had to bend over to use them. As the workers used the tools, they began to experience back pain. Over a period of time, the workers experienced many crippling back conditions. Over the objections of the growers, a law was finally passed to change this.

The result was not poorer crop production (although we can't say there was *improved* crop production either). The improvement was in a reduction in the amount of back pain that the workers had to suffer.

The growers who originally selected the tools weren't interested in making people suffer; they were only interested in the most efficient crop production. They contended that the tools were designed to bring the workers closer to the ground so that weeds would be easier to spot. They were trying to make things *easier*, not *harder*.

So, how could such good intentions produce such opposite results? The growers simply hadn't taken into consideration the tool users themselves. This is an example of the goal displacement we discussed in Chapter 2. Rather than simply *imagining* how workers should work, the growers could have *watched* them, noticing what it took to spot and pull the weeds. They could have noticed what happened when people used the short hoes. They could have asked the workers how it felt to use them. They themselves could have tried both methods and observed the results.

The growers were the overly Romans in this story; Romans who knew what *should* work but didn't really know what *actually* worked.

Okay, so what does this have to do with CASE and the methods we use to produce programs? Well, there are some overly Romans in the CASE field who select tools based not on what the programmers actually need, but on what they *think* the programmers need. We have seen this repeatedly.

One of the projects we studied introduced a CASE tool that had exactly the opposite effect from what was originally intended. It had a high learning curve, it continuously got in the way, and it added a lot more time and other resources to an already devastated schedule.

One might say, "Come on ... these tools might not have been productive, but they couldn't have caused the programmers actual *pain*!"

Well, because we've seen it, we say, "They sure do! Especially those tools that are used to enforce a methodology or someone's view of what *should* work." They have resulted in mental anguish and stress-related disorders like high blood pressure, tension headaches, sore shoulders and stiff necks from muscle tension, depression, etc.

Many of these tools were created to force formal STRUCTURED STUFF to be done. However, as we observed earlier, many programmers use an opportunistic approach to development and observe the principles of simple structured stuff. So, the tool's introduction and the tool Centurions forced these programmers into difficult situations. They were required to produce the soft-ware, but felt they were being inhibited by the METHOD. So, they simply did double duty. They did what had to be done to get the software built, and they also fulfilled the requirements of the method that was being enforced by the tool.

This type of situation leads to high stress and a great deal of anxiety. There is not enough time for the programmers to do the best they can because they must do two developments. Also, the two developments are timed differently. It is easy to see that while the programmers are still wrestling with the requirements or other upstream documentation, they could also have a prototype running. So, the signals they are passing back to the "method

Centurions" are inconsistent with those they are passing back and forth with the user.

But, even if the tool doesn't cause actual pain, it can still get in the programmer's way if the tool selector's expectations and valuations don't match those of the programmer. Here is an example of what we mean:

We know of a project where a tool was evaluated and its score was sent to management so they could decide whether or not to purchase it. The tool was a source code fixer-upper designed to turn spaghetti code into "structured" code.

For management, there were two criteria of equal weight: first, that the tool did not damage the functionality of the code and, second, that it improve the readability of the code. It could get a rating, say, of 100 on the functionality issue and 50 on readability. Combining the scores on a scale of 100, the functional safety would come in at 50 and the readability at 25 for a final rating of 75, which is a C-grade tool. That's not too bad; the tool probably should be purchased.

But, to the programmer, the story is entirely different. Her context doesn't allow the entry of tools that could damage the functionality of her code. She has other headaches. For her, the question of rating comes only *after* the tool is evaluated for functional safety. Only *after* it is judged safe should it be allowed into the environment for evaluation.

Therefore, the rating would consist of only the readability improvement portion. She would rate it 50, which is an F-grade tool that probably shouldn't be purchased.

Notice the difference in context and the results. In this case, management, trying to get tools for programmers, ends up buying a tool that a programmer sees as a poor one. This results in managers wondering why programmers don't use the tool, and programmers wondering why the manager bought the tool in the first place. This is a condition that is rich in possibilities for misunderstandings.

In general, we did find that the Olduvai Imperative is strong indeed. In organizations with several mainframes, data centers, or networks, we found that programmers "illegally" acquired tools; they "worked" the system to buy the ones they needed, "borrowed" them from one place or another, or built their own. With home-built tools, we found a substantial amount of duplication. Essentially the same tools were created in several places. We found tools not being used yet being paid for, and useful tools "pirated" to platforms other than those to which the tools were licensed. If you add to this the many tool activities described above, you have a rather chaotic situation which, if it is ordered the way the overly Romans want it, will be even worse.

A Final Word

We are not the first to have noticed these ineffective structures in our business enterprises. Here is a conclusion from an EDN magazine article entitled "Production Oriented Management Stifles Innovation": "Thus, the company that is logical, analytical, orderly, decisive, aggressively single-minded, and always *right the first time,* [their italics] paradoxically is taking the biggest risk of all: being blind sided by innovators." [EDN Magazine 1992, p.62]

We also found this, from Harvard Business Review, explaining why certain kinds of change programs don't work: "In a 1991 survey of more than 300 electronics companies sponsored by the American Electronics Association, 73% of the companies reported having a total quality program under way; but of these 63% had failed to improve quality defects by even as much as 10%." [Schaffer and Thomsom 1992, pp.80-89]

The authors go on to explain that the quality programs of these organizations weren't tied to the results of the enterprise itself. The programs were "too large and diffuse." They used "delusional measurements which measure the quality program activities and equate these with actual improvements in performance." They are "staff- and consultant-driven," and are "bias[ed toward] orthodoxy, not empiricism." This sounds *very* Roman.

We have tried to point out how these affect the IS field. And, we've done it from the bottom up to show how these organizations get themselves into trouble.

While we have no fixes for these organizations, Andrall Pearson has. Besides being a professor of Business Administration at Harvard, he used to be the president of PepsiCo, so he has pretty good credentials. He has been watching from the top level and has made much the same observation that we have. He has something to offer that may help. He starts by listing the seven deadly sins [Pearson 1992, p.65]:

1. Inconsistent product quality

2. Slow response to the marketplace

3. Lack of innovative competitive products

4. Uncompetitive cost structure

5. Inadequate employee involvement

6. Unresponsive customer service

7. Inefficient resource allocation

Sound familiar? He suggests six things to do to fix the problem of what we call the overly Roman organization:

1. "[Decide] what the company stands for that is special and competitively significant." You do this by really focusing on the company's values, skills, and mission.

   - Fill in the value gaps. A company cannot get away with saying, for example, that "our employees are our greatest asset" and then lay off thousands of employees. You've got to figure out what your values are in this changing environment, make sure everybody knows what they are, and then stick to them.

   - Get yourself a world-class set of those "special skills" on which your company can pride itself. This "builds pride and commitment within the organization and helps to focus and energize the people."

   - Finally, get yourself an exciting mission or cause that can bring the work force together because they feel their jobs are at stake. For example, Toyota targets General Motors [as the organization to beat].

2. "[Set] higher competitive performance standards, then [enforce] them and [raise] them." Do not simply "notch your expectations up a bit but ... set the kind of standards that drive your business to world-class levels, focus your managers on the specific means to achieve them, and be very tough minded about each year's progress toward your goals."

3. "[Adopt] organizational concepts that stimulate constant innovation—not just adding a few new ideas each year." He gives Honda's approach as an example. Honda management sends a consistent message to workers to let them know that:

   - What matters are big differences in product performance.

- The key to these big differences is technology. Technology, in turn, is driven by small ideas added together to produce big breakthroughs.

- Small ideas crop up everywhere in the organization, not just at the top.

- Management's function is to move ideas quickly upward so they can be debated, decided on, and implemented.

- Coordination and improvement result from egalitarianism and legislated interaction. Honda executives work at desks in open rooms and spend their time in plants, labs, and with customers. *Honda Circles* and the *Honda Way*—formal interaction techniques—ensure that information and ideas move across functional boundaries.

- Disagreements produce better ideas. Honda promotes and manages debate and conflict, rather than avoiding disagreements.

4. "[Involve] top managers in the substance of the business, not just the administrative processes ... they are competitive leaders who have passionate feelings about their businesses and who focus their time mainly on what is critical to their company's success. ... Despite style differences, these leaders have one big thing in common: everyone in the organization acknowledges their involvement and welcomes their contributions. They not only add value, but they add it in critical places."

5. "[Recruit and develop] more than your share of the right kind of talent for your company."

6. "[Create] a reward system that emphasizes performance and ties the other elements together."

We think Mr. Pearson has something important to say about overly Roman organizations and how to fix them. His fixes restore the balance to the Greco-Roman organization.

Much of this chapter has been a polemic against the overly Roman view of software engineering which, in our view, contributes substantially to the malaise we've been encountering having to do with software development tools and the "software crisis" in general. Good management calls for orderliness and for logical, analytical administration; in other words, for the Roman point of view.

But, when management runs out of Greeks (or runs the Greeks out), it finds itself presiding more and more over mere shells of what once was, spending all of its energy conserving what is left. This process is exacerbated in times when great stress is placed on commercial structures. The 1990s are a time of such stress, as the Japanese and others are kicking our butts commercially. This process is also exacerbated whenever there is a major technological shift, such as the computer revolution.

We believe an imbalance between the Greeks and Romans accounts for much of the difficulty that exists in accepting CASE tools in our field. However, we know of many organizations in many different areas that have achieved the appropriate balance and maintained the necessary tension between the Roman and the Greek points of view.

In the next chapter, we will look at the Greek side of things and we will have something to say about overly Greek organizations. ✇

Chapter 5.
Software Engineering:
The Greek View

In this chapter, we look at the Greek view of software engineering. The last chapter dealt with the Roman view by concentrating on an external feature: the organizational characteristics of software engineering. In this chapter, we will deal with the Greek view by concentrating on an internal feature: problem-solving.

Problem Solving

Do you ever wonder how people come up with the solutions to problems? Now, we're not shrinks and we don't pretend to be, but there is a lot of information around that explains something about what really goes on when we are doing our jobs. We're going to present some of it here, especially as it applies to solving problems and producing programs.

We will start with a particularly narrow view of our world. It comes from one of the best of us, Edsger Dijkstra, in a paper that appeared in the *Communications of the ACM* [Dijkstra 1989, pp.1398-1414]. In this famous paper, Mr. Dijkstra describes what he calls *radical novelties*. These are historical discontinuities where the usual methods of understanding—metaphors and analogies—break down. He argues that "Computing Science" is this type of discontinuity, and that our field of Software Engineering is composed, to a large extent, of "frantic—but as we now know, doomed—efforts at hiding or denying the frighteningly unfamiliar."

He says:

- That Software Engineering should be known as the "Doomed Discipline"

- That its charter is: "How to program if you cannot"

- That we use our name—*software engineering*—as a primitive means of gaining control over unknown, malicious demons, whistling in the dark

- That we believe programs are just like other devices but that their manufacture might require a new type of craftsman

He decries programmer productivity, quality control, software maintenance, and programming tools as yet another dimension of the snake oil business.

He then goes on to say that computers are nothing more than symbol manipulators, and that programs are abstract symbol manipulators connected to computers to make them concrete. He defines *computing science* as "concerned with the interplay between mechanized and human symbol manipulation usually referred to as computing and programming respectively."

He sees computing science as a *form* of mathematics and logic, but expects it to transcend them by "effectively realizing a significant part of Liebniz's dream of providing a symbolic calculation as an *alternative* to human reasoning, which is not a suitable model to mimic by computers: 'I would rather see [computers] mimic something better.'" He then proceeds to decry the use of anthropomorphisms: "if this guy [say, some subroutine] wants to talk to that guy [another routine]." [ibid] He calls this *operational reasoning* and insists that it's wasteful.

To prove his point about mathematics, programming, and the waste of "operational [anthropomorphic] reasoning," Dijkstra gives us a puzzle (the first of four we will look at in this chapter):

"Consider the plane figure Q, defined as the 8 by 8 square from which at two opposite corners, two 1 by 1 squares have been removed. The area of Q is 62, which equals the combined area of 31 dominos of 1 by 2. The theorem is that no placement of 31 dominos will yield the figure Q.

"Another way of stating the theorem is that if you start with squared paper and begin covering this by placing each domino on two new adjacent squares, no placement of 31 dominos will yield the figure Q.

"So, a possible way of proving the theorem is by generating all possible placements of dominos and verifying for each placement that it does not yield the figure Q: a tremendously laborious job.

"The simple argument, however, is as follows. Color each square of the squared paper as on a chess board. Each domino, covering two adjacent squares, covers one white and one black square and, hence, each placement covers as many white squares as it covers black squares. In the figure Q, however, the number of white squares and the number of black squares differ by two—opposite corners lying on the same diagonal—and, hence, no placement of dominos yields figure Q.

"Not only is the above simple argument many orders of magnitude shorter than the exhaustive investigation of the possible placements of 31 dominos, it is also essentially more powerful, for it covers the generalization of Q by replacing the original 8 by 8 square with any rectangle with sides of even length. The number of such rectangles being infinite, the former exhaustive exploration is essentially inadequate for proving our generalized theorem.

"The moral of this story is: deal with all the elements of a set by ignoring them and working with the set's definition. Returning to programming, our recent moral says: deal with all the computations possible under the control of a given program by ignoring them and working with the program.

"In other words, the main task of the programmers is 'to give a formal proof that the program he proposes meets the equally formally derived functional specification.' " [ibid]

Mr. Dijkstra sure is tough on us, and we think he has something valid to say on these points, especially about radical novelties. And, his example is a good one. Certainly his proof, or algorithm, is an extremely efficient and powerful statement of the solution to the problem.

However, we believe his central view is essentially erroneous and that he has made a category mistake. He believes that computing science lies in the direction of, yet goes far beyond, formal mathematics and applied logic. We think that computing science certainly draws from mathematics and logic, but that its center lies in another direction. It is not just another, yet much larger form of, mathematics and logic. It is a tortuous view of programs to see them that way. The main task of the programmer is not "to give a formal proof that the program he proposes meets the equally formally derived functional specification."

And, while we agree that his solution to the domino problem is valid, we still question how the solution *first* presented itself. Was not the algorithm created after some *insight* was arrived at first? Is not the description of the algorithm, especially the part about coloring the squares like a chess board, an artistic approach offered to help the observer *see* the solution? Is there any mathematical or logical analysis that can conclude that the square *ought* to be colored as a chess board? Can any set of formal syntax with proof rules that define its semantics—the things about computing science that Dijkstra wants us to reason about—*ever* devise the solution to the problem?

No! All they can do is reiterate and verify the solutions arrived at by other means.

This is because they are formal: math, logic, and rules. Their very nature disqualifies them from devising solutions to problems: they can only deal with the *form*, not the *essence*, of problems and their solutions.

We believe (and will offer some proof that) computing science lies exactly in the direction of human thought, of which mathematics and logic are but a part; that programs are not simply formulas, but expressions of language that might *contain* formulas; that the main task of programmers is to extract an acceptable problem description from an almost always incomplete problem description and then to devise an acceptable solution expressed in a form suitable for both computers and human beings to sense (or read, if you will).

Even some of Dijkstra's colleagues view things this way. "... it turns out that English majors are as likely to be as successful at programming as mathematics graduates are." [ibid][9] "Dijkstra excoriates 'software engineering' by deliberately comparing it to his conception of mathematics rather than to, say, *'effective writing'* [our emphasis] which I feel is a far better analogy." [ibid][10]

As evidence for our view, we offer the next puzzle, the elevator cabin controller problem described in a report of a study done by Raymonde Guindon at the Microelectronic and Computer Technology Corporation [Guindon 1989]. In the study, three very experienced and highly educated software designers were asked to design the control system of an elevator system with *N* lifts in a building with *M* floors. They were videotaped, and their "thinking aloud" reports, written reports, and diagrams were analyzed to determine how they discovered knowledge. Figure 5-1 shows the experience of designer *D1*. There are several things to notice about how this designer did his job.

First, the process involved "mental and external simulations of scenarios in the problem domain (i.e., the Lift domain)." The designers built prototypes in their minds to simulate the action of the elevator.

Second, they used these simulations and other notes and diagrams to gain an "understanding and elaboration of the requirements ... The designers' activities related to the understanding of the requirements include: a) testing the consistency of the requirements with their own general knowledge; and b) abstracting the critical points."

Third, "the developers produced ... mental or external simulations of the design solution at various levels of abstraction. By levels of abstraction, we mean the vertical partitioning of the functions accomplished and information processed by the software system such as found in the design at the end of the session. The high level of abstraction concerns the adopted control scheme (e.g., central vs. distributed) and ways of handling individual lift functions.

---

[9] M.H. van Emden, University of Victoria, Victoria, B.C., reply to Dijkstra in the same article.

[10] R.W. Hamming, Naval Postgraduate School, reply to Dijkstra in the same article.

The medium level of abstraction concerns how these functions are divided into subfunctions. The low level of abstraction concerns how these subfunctions are further subdivided, how system functions are realized in the hardware, and details about data structure."

Fourth, "Figure 1 [our Figure 5-1] shows that the designers elaborate their solutions by *interleaving design activities associated with different domains (problem spaces) or at different levels of abstraction* [their emphasis]. In other words, *our designers did not exhibit the well-known strategy of stepwise refinement, with a top-down breadth-first decomposition of the system into functions and subfunctions during the session. Neither was problem understanding a fully completed process preceding design* [our emphasis]. The gray bar in figure 1 represents what the shifts would be like if the designer followed a prescriptive top-down approach, such as stepwise refinement, preceded by understanding the problem as a separate and independent block of activities. [It corresponds to Dijkstra's view of separate steps, each completed before the next can be done, i.e., a formal specification, a proposed program, of formal proof of correctness.] Instead, the observed design process can be described, behaviorally, as *opportunistic ...*" [ibid]

Fifth, and "more relevant to this paper, the episodes which are annotated with a light bulb in figure 1 are interesting instances of knowledge discovery or insights during design. These insights led to unplanned addition of new requirements, new knowledge about the problem domain, new design goals, or new partial design solutions. These insights, in turn, frequently *triggered* a reformulation of the problem by the designers. These insights also *triggered* changes in the agenda of activity of the designers, as new information modifies the priority or relevance of already set goals ..." [ibid] Notice the use of the word *triggered*; we'll use that again shortly.

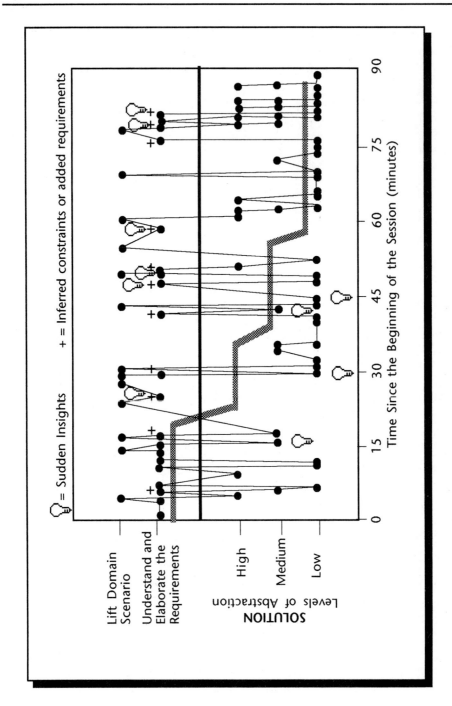

Figure 5-1. Shifts in Domains and Levels of Abstraction of D1

Neurons and Problem Rendering

In programming, we abstract essential features of problems into our minds' space, somehow synthesize a solution, and then express it in a language. How much data is required to abstract the problem? Well, if you're an experienced person, less than you might think; certainly less than the enormous requirements documents we sometimes find ourselves trying to cope with. That's because we can recognize in the present problem familiar features of other problems we solved long ago. This is called *associative memory* [Smith and Dietrich 1990].[11] Designers use associative memory when they compare requirements with their general knowledge.

As Guindon shows, we don't acquire knowledge about problems smoothly, as the steps of the Waterfall suggest (although it is a good idea to always express our knowledge as if it were arrived at by the Waterfall). Rather, we seem to take in information in chunks and then process them to one level or another (take in a chunk and process it, take in another chunk and process it, and so on). This might take longer because we reconcile the new stuff with old stuff. In any case, we apparently fit new stuff into old patterns. The designer in the elevator system example was doing this when he "interleaved" problem space with solution space in order to test his partial solution or his understanding of the problem when he mentally simulated the elevator system.

Our brains are made up of cells called *neurons.* Neurons are connected to each other in networks; one neuron might connect to 10,000 others, and we have trillions of them.

"Nerve cells [neurons] have two major tasks: computing, and then speeding the results of the computation to the far end of the nerve cell so that they can be passed on to another nerve cell. Both tasks run on electricity. ... The electrical signal is called an impulse. It is only 1/10 of a volt ... it lasts only 1/1000 of a second (quicker than most camera shutters), and it races along ... at speeds of as high as 500 kph (300 mph) ... The impulse is passed from one nerve cell to another by an electrically *triggered* [our emphasis] squirt of a chemical ... As in a checkbook, balance is what counts. If the voltage balance is big enough in the positive direction, another impulse will be *triggered*. Each nerve cell is thus a simple computer, adding and subtracting influences from many inputs, sending its new message on to many other cells." [Calvin and Ojemann 1980, pp.13-17]

---

[11]This is an excellent introduction to the ideas about neural networks and computers. For information concerning how our brain works, see Calvin, *Inside the Brain*, and other works by him in his search for consciousness and how we are who we are.

The designer experienced this when insights he gained triggered new requirements, priorities, etc. However, we're not suggesting that any *single* neuron triggered the designer's response; one or more sets of *interconnected* neurons did.

These neuron networks are arranged roughly in layers: an input layer, a "hidden" intermediate layer that "filters" the signals from the input layer providing a feed forward, and an output layer. Does this sound familiar, like the input, process, and output of a computer?

Well, these layers are not like the simple I/P/O features we're used to in serial computers. These layers act *in parallel* to solve problems quickly. And, they can be trained. It is the *training* that produces associative memory. Given some part of the problem, the network pulls out all the related information. The requirements document might only say something like "Here we have a system problem #3" and we can know what that is based on our experiences and associative memories. The designer in the Guindon experiment used this process to test requirements and build mental simulations. And, it was probably the combined effects of one or more neuron networks that triggered the designer's response.

We got some other real world support for this minimalistic approach to information transfer from a computer game maker we know. He told us about what makes up a good computer game. He indicated that one game he developed, which had exceptionally good rendering of the game's participants (they looked almost like characters from a Disney cartoon) didn't do very well. The high-resolution rendering didn't provide the players with the information they needed or, rather, it provided *too much* information. Players apparently needed just enough rendering to make the figures recognizable from the background. More than that somehow interfered with their play. So, a good game maker doesn't have good renderings of the figures in his scheme; he provides less, but optimum, information than he could in order to facilitate the play.

Right Brain ... Left Brain

Our brains are composed of two halves—hemispheres—each with its own specialties and way of thinking. The left side is where language skills are lodged; the right side has spatial skills. The left brain "not only thinks in words; it excels at the kind of one step at a time logical sequences that are the basis of language. Because the right brain thinks in images, it has a tremendous advantage for recognizing and manipulating complex visual patterns."

[Blakeslee 1980, p.9] Another analysis technique the designer in our example used was *visualization*, when he mentally simulated the operation of the elevator system.

There is a special test done on special patients. Normally, we have communication between the hemispheres mainly by means of a connecting band of nerves: the *corpus callosum*. Certain medical conditions, such as epilepsy, sometimes require that the hemispheres be disconnected in order to limit the effect of seizures. Patients with these conditions provide a means of glimpsing into the workings of the brain.

Each hemisphere is connected to the opposite eye and hand. Images can be presented to one visual field and not to the other. When different visual fields are presented with figures and the patient is asked to draw what they see, they produce very different results. See Figure 5-2 [ibid, p.11]. Notice how the left brain, which drives the right hand, seems to think in just two dimensions, while the right brain, which drives the left hand, can easily recreate three dimensions (even though there are muscle control problems associated with using one's unfamiliar hand).

However, the development of language (left-brain specialization) in human beings is probably one of the most important functions that distinguishes us from other species. Language is powerful in that it enables us to more precisely communicate ideas over space; for example, the source and direction of a threat. By orally passing the contents of memory from generation to generation, illiterate societies can also communicate over time and, thus, can speed up the rate of development through social memories. But, with written language, this development is accelerated many times over. Add to this the facility for abstract thought and the development of abstract, symbolic languages such as mathematics, and we have powerful tools indeed for investigating the world. This is as Dijkstra would have it; using mathematics to investigate the world.

This language specialty has some interesting consequences coupled with the human need—an absolute *compulsion*—to make up stories about anything and everything in order to make sense of the world:

"When we ask a split-brain patient to explain actions that we know were done by their right brain, they sometimes explain their actions with rationalizations that we know are untrue—but they obviously don't. Evidently, their left-brain consciousness has constructed a false world in which it is responsible for all actions. When it observes a left-handed response that we know came from the right brain, it will often make up a story to explain the response.

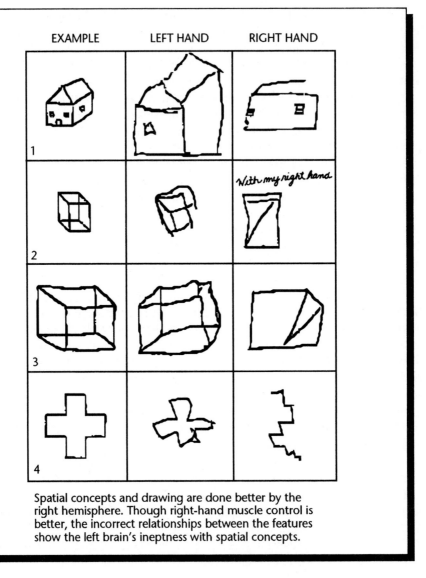

	EXAMPLE	LEFT HAND	RIGHT HAND

With my right hand

Spatial concepts and drawing are done better by the right hemisphere. Though right-hand muscle control is better, the incorrect relationships between the features show the left brain's ineptness with spatial concepts.

Figure 5-2. Right Hand vs. Left Hand

"For example, in one experiment different pictures were flashed simultaneously on the left and right of a screen, and the subject had to choose simultaneously a matching picture with each hand. In one case a snow scene was flashed on the left while a chicken claw was flashed on the right. As expected, the subject's left hand chose a snow shovel while his right hand chose a chicken. When asked why his left hand picked a shovel, he answered, 'I see a claw and I picked a chicken, and you have to clean out the chicken shed with a shovel.' Since the split-brain patient's left brain doesn't hesitate to rationalize and take credit for actions that are obviously the work of his right brain, one can't help wondering how often normal people do the same thing." [ibid, p.15]

But, there are tasks that simply can't be done logically. See Figure 5-3 [ibid, p.40]. "An average person can look at each drawing of a hand and decide whether it is a left or right hand in only a couple of seconds, yet the largest supercomputer known would be incapable of doing this task at all. Though we can easily solve the hand problem with visual thinking and even answer verbally 'left' or 'right,' our left brain is simply receiving the answer from the right brain. This becomes apparent if we try to explain verbally how we got the answer. The fact is that we don't know verbally how we got the answer because the task is impossible to do verbally ... The best explanation for how we got out answer would be by " 'intuition'." [ibid, p.39]

Perhaps, by now, the most powerful computer *can* solve this problem, but think of the problem and the step-by-step processing involved. It would take a very powerful machine indeed to duplicate what we are able to do so easily!

"One of the benefits of having two kinds of thinking is that they can often work together in a task. ... For example, a visual task took more than twice as long if the answers were given visually rather than verbally. Yet a verbal task was 40 per cent faster when answers were given visually." [ibid, p.43]

It is this working together that interests us. Some heavy hitters in mathematics were asked what kind of thinking they did. Here is a summary of their responses. The questioner, Jacques Hadamard, said: "Practically all of them ... avoid not only the use of mental words but also the use of algebraic or other precise signs ... The mental picture of the mathematicians whose answers I have received are most frequently visual, but they may be of another kind—for instance, kinetic." [ibid, p.45]

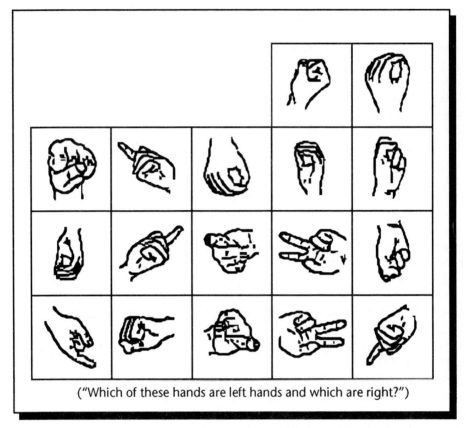

("Which of these hands are left hands and which are right?")

Figure 5-3. Thurstone's Hand Test

Here's what Albert Einstein replied to the question:

"(A) The words or the language, as they are written or spoken, do not seem to play any role in my mechanism of thought. The psychical entities which seem to serve as elements in thought are certain signs and more or less clear images which can be voluntarily reproduced and combined.

"There is, of course, a certain connection between those elements and relevant logical concepts. It is also clear that the desire to arrive finally at logically connected concepts is the emotional basis of this rather vague play with the above mentioned elements. But taken from a psychological view-point, this combinatory play seems to be the essential feature in productive thought—before there is any connection with logical construction in words or other kinds of signs which can be communicated to others.

170

"(B) The above mentioned elements are, in my case, of visual and some muscular type. Conventional words or other signs have to be sought for laboriously only in a secondary stage when the mentioned associative play is sufficiently established and can be reproduced at will." [ibid, pp.45-46]

"The two halves of the brain thus have a kind of partnership in which the left brain handles language and logical thinking, while the right does things difficult to put into words. By thinking in images instead of words, the right brain can recognize a face in the crowd or put together the pieces of a jigsaw puzzle, which would totally baffle the left brain." [ibid, p.6]

In many people, the right brain isn't used much. Our culture seems to favor logical, left-brain thinking. "There is a decadence in the field of higher education that is the natural result of an ignorance of the 'unconscious' [right] side of the brain. A sort of academic dream world has been created in which purely left-brain thinkers admire each other's 'scholarliness.' Many students [who] earn their Ph.D.s become so habitually 'left-brained' that they are unable to do anything but become 'scholars' themselves. The system thus feeds itself and becomes more and more scholarly and less and less intuitive." [ibid, p.56]

Even when it is recognized that creativity is necessary, many teachers are unable to enhance their students' abilities with it. As a physics professor said at the conclusion of one of his lectures: "I can teach you the methods and processes of science, but I cannot give you the *imagination*, the *creativity* [emphasis ours], the judgment, nor the commitment to work that it takes to be a physicist. Please bring those with you to the next lecture." This statement brought knowing laughter from the students.

We offer now another problem for you to try. Please pay attention to how you *think* about the problem and its solution. See how much you visualize, and try to notice when you get ideas, or inspirations, or flashes of insight. See for yourself how *thinking* about thinking shows that there is a lot more going on than simply cranking out formulas and proofs.

Consider now the famous Twelve-Ball Problem. Let's suppose you have twelve balls. They are identical except for one, and it is either heavier or lighter than the others. You also have a balanced beam scale; but you may only make *three* weighings on it. How do you determine which is the odd ball and whether it is heavier or lighter?

We will give a solution later. But, for now (assuming you don't know how to solve the problem), how would you go about solving it? Most people start by weighing six balls against six and work the possibilities until they run out of trials. Then, they start searching for another path. Most are aware that weighing six against six is probably a dumb thing to do (us included), but we do it anyway. This is the wrong path to a solution, since how do you know which six to set aside?

But, remember what you were thinking about when you realized it was the wrong path. Isn't the Twelve-Ball Problem like a programming problem? There is a combination of searching for and sorting data, constraints, and a goal. There is input data, processing to be determined, and a piece of required output data.

From our interviews, we found other methods for approaching the problem. One person we interviewed is an extremely strong visualizer. She was going to start out by weighing six against six but "saw" that it didn't provide any new information. Most of the other respondents also used some sort of visualization.

The following is a list of known ways people go about finding things out and solving problems. Many of them involve using visualization:

Induction	Reasoning from particular facts of individual cases to general conclusions [Webster's New World Dictionary 1979, p.718].
Deduction	Reasoning from a known principle to an unknown, from the general to the specific [ibid, p.368].
Socratic method	A dialectical method of teaching or discussion used by Socrates that involves asking a series of easily answered questions that inevitably lead the answerer to a logical conclusion foreseen by the questioner [ibid, p.1352]. It is also a part of the Continuous Quality Improvement movement that is becoming popular in our field.
Analogy and metaphor	Similarity in some respects between things otherwise unlike [ibid, p.49], and a figure of speech containing an implied comparison in which a word or phrase ordinarily and primarily used of one thing is applied to another [ibid, p.893]. Always be careful to assess the extent of the comparison's validity.

Appeal to authority	Ask a knowledgeable or expert person to give you the answer.
Prayer	Appeal to a final authority practiced by project managers and others who haven't a clue about how things work.
Oracle	Appeal to an authority through an intermediary. In our day, they are consultants. You know who we mean; they are the guys you hire to tell you the time and the first thing they do is borrow your watch.

Here is a list of concepts and methods useful in computerized problem-solving. It's from another one of the best of us, Donald Knuth, from his three-volume work, *The Art of Computer Programming* [Knuth 1973]:

Fundamental Algorithms
- Information Structures
  - Linear Lists
    Stacks, Queues, and Deques
    Sequential Allocation
    Linked Allocation
    Circular Lists
    Doubly Linked Lists
    Arrays and Orthogonal Lists
  - Trees
    Traversing Binary Trees
    Binary Tree Representation of Trees
    Other Representations of Trees
    Basic Mathematical Properties of Trees
    Free Trees
    Oriented Trees
    Path Length
  - Lists and Garbage Collection
Multilinked Structures
Dynamic Storage Allocation

Semi-numerical Algorithms
- Random Numbers
    - Generating Uniform Random Numbers
        The Linear Congruential Method
        - Choice of Modulus
        - Choice of Multiplier
        - Potency
        Other Methods
    - Statistical Tests
        General Test Procedures for Studying Random Data
        Empirical Tests
        Theoretical Tests
        The Spectral Test
    - Other Types of Random Quantities
        Numerical Distributions
        Random Sampling and Shuffling
    - What is a Random Sequence?
- Arithmetic
    - Positional Number Systems
    - Floating Point Arithmetic
        Single-Precision Calculations
        Accuracy of Single Point Arithmetic
        Double-Precision Calculations
        Distribution of Floating Point Numbers
    - Multiple-Precision Arithmetic
        The Classical Algorithm
        Modular Arithmetic
        How Fast Can We Multiply?
    - Radix Conversion
    - Rational Arithmetic
        Fractions
        The Greatest Common Divisor
        Analysis of Euclid's Algorithm
        Factoring Into Primes
    - Polynomial Arithmetic
        Division of Polynomials
        Factorization of Polynomials
        Evaluation of Powers
        Evaluation of Polynomials
    - Manipulation of Power Series

Sorting and Searching
- Sorting
  - Combinatorial Properties of Permutations
    - Inversions
    - Permutation of a Multiset
    - Runs
    - Tableaux and Involutions
  - Internal Sorting
    - Sorting by Insertion
    - Sorting by Exchanging
    - Sorting by Selection
    - Sorting by Merging
    - Sorting by Distribution
  - Optimum Sorting
    - Minimum-Comparison Sorting
    - Minimum-Comparison Merging
    - Minimum-Comparison Selection
    - Networks for Sorting
  - External Sorting
    - Multiway Merging and Replacement Selection
    - The Polyphase Merge
    - The Cascade Merge
    - Reading Tape Backwards
    - The Oscillating Sort
    - Practical Considerations for Tape Merging
    - External Tape Merging
    - Two-Tape Sorting
    - Disks and Drums
- Searching
  - Sequential Searching
  - Searching by Comparison of Keys
    - Searching an Ordered Table
    - Binary Tree Searching
    - Balanced Trees
    - Multiway Trees
  - Digital Searching
    - Hashing
    - Retrieval on Secondary Keys

Returning to the Twelve-Ball Problem, when our correspondents described their solutions, they made up logical stories about what happened after they discovered the solution. Their solution stories are decoded records, as it were, of another process.

We know two things about solving the Twelve-Ball Problem. One of the authors of this book, Peter, *did* solve the problem. (We'll show his solution a little later.) In solving the problem, we know that he used some trial and error, which helped him gain insight into the problem. Second, he is only dimly aware of how he really solved it; but, a part of him (his left brain) has made up a story explaining how to arrive at a solution and tries to pass it off as what actually happened at the time. The story his left brain made up is perfectly logical and, if you follow the instructions in his solution, you will solve the problem. However, it is not what actually happened when he solved it.

It's a lot like studying literary criticism. We can create all kinds of explanations of what an author "had in mind" when she wrote her book. But, that type of supposition is mere speculation. It is an artificial structure we impose on the writer's product to help us better understand the writing. When we do a literary critique, we say (and even believe) that we are explaining the writer. However, in every case we studied, when an author was actually *asked* about what was going on in their mind when they were writing, they either didn't know or wouldn't say.

Here is where "structured stuff" reveals one side of its power. The training we receive provides one anchor of the "bridge" between the hemispheres of our brains over which passes information generated in non-verbal form. When the information reaches the verbal, conscious side of our brains, it tumbles into the templates provided by our SASD training. We can then analyze this information for appropriateness and errors and can send it to others who need it.

Peter's Solution to the Twelve-Ball Problem

Incidentally, here's Peter's story about how to solve the Twelve-Ball Problem. The key is to determine which are the good balls and then use that information in isolating the bad one. Also crucial is remembering *how* the balance beam scale pointer moves for each trial and interpreting each outcome: it doesn't move at all, it moves one way, or it moves the other way.

The way to solve the problem is this: Do the first trial by weighing any eight balls, four on each dish. The results are that either the eight being weighed are good (the pointer didn't move off center) or the remaining four are good (the pointer moved one way or the other). In either case, note the direction of the pointer (straight up, left, or right).

In the case where the eight measured balls were good, remove five leaving three in one dish. Now, compare them with three of the four unmeasured balls; one of the four must be the bad one. If the pointer still remains on center, then the bad ball is the remaining unweighed one, and the last trial will tell you whether it is lighter or heavier. (If it is lighter, the pointer will move toward the good ball; if it is heavier, it will move away from it.)

If the pointer moved off center in trial two, then you know the bad ball is in that group compared with three good ones and, even though you don't know which of the three it is, you can still figure out whether it is lighter or heavier by the same interpretation of pointer movement as above.

For the third trial, compare any two balls from the suspect group against each other. If the pointer returns to the center, then the third ball was the odd one and you know from the second trial whether it is heavy or light. If the pointer *moves* in the third trial, it will point toward the odd ball if , from trial two, it was heavy, or away from it, if it was light.

Now, let's take the case where the odd ball is in the group of eight compared during the first trial. You know the unweighed four are good. Now note the direction the pointer moved, remove three balls from one tray, move three from the second to the first tray, and place three good balls on the second tray. If the pointer changed direction, then you moved the odd ball; if it went to zero, you removed the odd ball; if not, then the odd ball is one of the two you didn't move.

To determine which of the two balls is bad, compare either of them with a known good one. If the pointer remains off center, then the odd one is on the scale and you can figure whether it is heavy or light by familiar criteria. If the pointer centers, then the bad one is the other of the two and from the pointer's position from the second trial you can figure whether it is heavy or light.

If the pointer pointed in the opposite direction after the second trial, then the odd ball was one of the three moved from one tray to the other. If it moved back to center, then the odd ball was one of the three removed for the second trial. In either case, you can determine which one was bad and whether it was heavy or light by the procedure for the third trial.

Creativity

Finally, we offer a friendly jibe to mathematicians about their vaunted problem-solving powers explained by Dijkstra:

Marilyn vos Savant (who has the world's highest IQ) printed the following brain teaser in her column, "Ask Marilyn," in 1991 in *Parade Magazine* [Posner 1991, pp.342-345].

"Suppose you're on a game show, and you're given a choice of three doors. Behind one door is a car; behind the others, goats. You pick a door—say No. 1—and the host, who knows what's behind the doors, opens another door—say No. 3—which has a goat. He then says to you, 'Do you want to pick door No. 2?' Is it to your advantage to switch your choice?"

Marilyn answered, "Yes, you should switch," explaining that "obviously, there is a 1:3 chance that the original choice, door No. 1, is the correct one. Therefore, there must be a 2:3 chance that, since door No. 3 has now been eliminated as a possibility, the car is behind door No. 2."

Lots of folks didn't agree with her, and many of them were mathematicians. She printed some of their scathing letters (the asterisks below are in place of where the writer's names originally appeared to help protect the identities of the guilty):

"I'm very concerned with the general public's lack of mathematical skills. Please help by confessing your error. ... " *******, Ph.D., George Mason University.

"You blew it, and you blew it big! ... You seem to have difficulty grasping the basic principle at work here. ... There is enough mathematical illiteracy in this country, and we don't need the world's highest IQ propagating more. Shame!" *******, Ph.D., University of Florida.

"Your answer to the question is in error. But if it is any consolation, many of my colleagues have also been stumped by this problem." *******, Ph.D., California Faculty Association.

Marilyn then tried what she evidently thought was a clearer explanation, describing the "shell game," which simulates the same condition. This did not end the thing. " ... in her February 17, 1991, column, we were treated to the following:" [ibid, p.343]

"I am in shock that after being corrected by at least three mathematicians, you still do not see your mistake." *******, Dickinson State University.

"... Albert Einstein earned a dearer place in the hearts of the people after he admitted his errors." *******, Ph.D., University of Michigan.

"... Your answer is clearly at odds with the truth." *******, Ph.D., Millikin University.

"May I suggest that you obtain and refer to a standard textbook on probability. ..." *******, Ph.D., University of Florida.

"... I am sure you will receive many letters from high school and college students. Perhaps you should keep a few addresses for help with future columns." *******, Ph.D., Georgia State University.

"You are utterly incorrect. ... How many irate mathematicians are needed to get you to change your mind?" *******, Ph.D., Georgetown University.

"... If all those Ph.D.s were wrong, the country would be in serious trouble." *******, Ph.D., U.S. Army Research Institute.

"Maybe women look at math problems differently than men." *******, Sunriver, Oregon.

Apparently, these were only a sample of the letters she received; all were willing to correct her, many were irate with her, and many of *those* were mathematicians; you know, those people Dijkstra wants us to be like.

And, here from the mighty *Mensa Bulletin*, the journal of the IQ heavy-hitters, is another statement responding to a question about her answer:

"... The door with the goat is now irrelevant, leaving a binary problem: Two doors remain, each with an equal probability of concealing the coveted prize. The contestant neither gains nor loses advantage by changing her mind. Marilyn's error may be the most common one made in probability problems: assuming that eliminated options still affect the probabilities for the remaining options." [Mensa Bulletin, July/August 1991, p.13]

Well, this might surprise you, but Marilyn was right, and all those other folks were wrong; and many of them are people we're supposed to be emulating!

However, other mathematicians eventually came to her defense, as if she needed any: "Mathematicians at the Massachusetts Institute of Technology came to vos Savant's defense. 'You are indeed correct,' wrote Seth Kalson, Ph.D. 'My colleagues at work had a ball with this problem, and I dare say that most of them—including me at first—thought you were wrong.' The same thing happened at the University of Oregon. After 92 percent of the letters vos Savant received expressed the belief that she was wrong, Frank Anderson, head of the University of Oregon's Mathematics Department, said: 'Consensus is not the issue. She is 100 percent right.' " [Posner 1991, p.344] In other words, one does not vote on the *truth*.

The most frequent error we got from the non-mathematicians to whom we showed this problem was that they thought the probability of a winning original selection could be changed from one in three to one in two by showing the door with the goat behind it; in other words, what happens in the future affects the past. The second selection would indeed be one chance in two to a contestant they dragged in off the street, after the game show host opened the second door. But, to the original contestant, the probability remained one chance in three if she didn't switch, and was two chances in three, much better than one in two, if she *did*.

The other most frequent error was that folks either misunderstood the effect of new information when the game show host revealed a door with the goat behind it, or didn't even see that it *was* new information. And, they expressed this feeling very loudly, vociferously, and, sometimes, intimidatingly and rudely.

We have been struck by the patronizing way most mathematically inclined "systems analysts" teach basic probability theory. However, most programmers, even though they weren't able to logically or visually solve the problem when they were first shown it, immediately set about constructing programming simulations; and, many *then* saw the "logical" solution as they began to construct their program.

This problem received a lot of publicity: the *New York Times*, the *Skeptical Inquirer*, and many other newspapers, magazines, and newsletters have run articles on it. The largest online bulletin board service, CompuServe, had an entire forum dealing with this problem. It has been discussed and verified at any number of cocktail and dinner parties and in classrooms all over the country. Here is the simplest explanation, given anonymously, we might say [Mensa Bulletin, p.42]:

"If you don't switch, the only way you can win is by choosing the car. If you do switch, the only way you can win is by first choosing a goat. Because there are twice as many goats as there are cars, [and you can never switch from goat to goat], switching gives you twice as many chances of winning."

Our point in telling this problem is to illuminate the other part of visualization, the solution side. We've talked about simulating the world, or the problem description, and even testing a solution by simulating it mentally, but now we're talking about arriving at the solution by using both halves of the brain: the right side to come up with possibilities and the left side to analyze and verify them.

One writer breaks the creative process into four stages: preparation, incubation, *illumination*, and verification. "The preparation stage consists of gathering relevant information and narrowing the problem until the obstacles are *visible*. Incubation is a period in which the unconscious processes of the mind seem to work on the problem. During this time, it is permissible to think occasionally about the problem, but generally there should be no pressure for a solution. The *illumination* stage may come spontaneously or as a result of conscious effort. This is where intuition and *insight* produce possible solutions to the problem. Finally, in the verification stage the *intuitive* solutions are logically tested for validity, then organized and elaborated into a finished solution." [ibid, pp.49-50] Notice how frequently terms related to *sight* were used in this description.

Have you ever encountered any incubation phases in any methodology you've ever heard of? Are there any instructions to just think, imagine solutions, simulate things? We find there is mainly a request to create more and more documents. Yet, is not the above description of the creative process similar to the observations of Guindon in the elevator problem experiment reported earlier in this chapter?

All At Once

There is one more thing yet to say about how problems are solved. Several times in the article on neural nets there appeared the phrase *all at once*.

"The brain—any brain, from a slug's on up—is more like a medieval kitchen in a great lord's palace on the eve of a feast. A multitude of helpers bustles at a variety of tasks shouting advice and instructions to one another. Everything happens *all at once*, and the banquet emerges almost spontaneously from the coordinated actions of many individuals.

"Neural nets, both man-made and biological, work fast. By exploring their options *all at once*, rather than scrutinizing each one in turn, they give you a pretty good answer immediately instead of the best possible answer in a week." [ibid, pp.49-50, in a discussion of G. Wallas's book, *The Art of Thought*. [Emphasis added.]

This *all at once* business has a mystery to it and we do not pretend to understand it fully, but we can say that *all at once* means that things happen in parallel, as was indicated in the Guindon article. Also, in our first book on software engineering paradigms [DeGrace and Stahl 1990], we noticed one group of methods that we called *all at once* because, as we observed it working, things happened all at once. This one set of paradigms fits comfortably into the nexus of our brain's operation.

The preceding has been a description of what we call the Greek approach to software development. It involves a lot of mental work, visualizing the problem and its solution, and then expressing the solution in language. But, there is an extreme approach which we will discuss next.

The Overly Greek Approach

The overly Greek approach to software development appears to be chaotic; and to some extent it is. As we explained in the previous chapter, the resulting program may still be somewhat ill-formed and "dripping" with disorder since it has been *yanked* out of chaos. That's okay, but thinking that still "wet" code is "finished" code is not okay. In Chapter 3, we discussed what finishing code involves. Unfortunately, the overly-Greek approach leaves code in an unfinished state: brittle, not well tested, and subject to failure when it is placed into a mode for which it has not been tested.

We have found several reasons for this. First, it is darned hard to do programming; going through the finishing process adds a great deal of effort to what already has been a lot of work. Second, many programmers are ignorant of what to do to finish code; we hope Chapter 3 will help correct that. Finally, many programmers aren't able to empathize with those who will come after them: the user, the documenter, or the maintenance programmers. They aren't able to project their personality into that of the next person in order to better understand him and his feelings. And, finally, there is seldom the time or resources to finish the code anyway.

As a result, the program is poorly documented, is not configuration managed well, and it is hard to maintain. The error rate is not likely to go down over a period of time; it will be hard for the maintainer to learn the program; and the program will be hard to convert and to enhance.

In one overly Greek project we know about, most of the front-end development work was carried on inside the programmers' heads (which is a very Greek thing to do). They did their coding from this internal information.

The problem was, the project was simply too big to let the Greeks have complete control. It needed some Roman order.

The project was made up of six loosely organized teams. Each team was responsible for its own product. The six products were all supposed to work individually as standalone products, but they also needed to work together as modules of an integrated product, sharing data among all six modules.

You would think that a product like this would have very clearly defined naming conventions, interfaces, and other standards so that all the modules would have the same look and feel when they were integrated. Instead, each programming team had its own set of conventions, and they were only loosely followed. The conventions followed by the members of one team often were different from the conventions followed by the other teams. There were no guidelines for the *whole group* to follow.

Standards had been talked about, but none were ever established. The older team members knew how the parts of the program were *supposed* to fit together, but it was difficult for newer team members to absorb all of this unwritten information. Also, it was hard to transfer this information to support personnel (such as QA and documentation) since so little had been written down.

To document the system, the technical writers had to wait until they could run the finished code. There were no design documents they could work from to get a head start on the user's guides. As a result, the code was finished long before the user's guides were ready to accompany the software. The developers used this time to begin making changes and enhancements, but did not document the changes as they made them. (These changes had to be "discovered" later by the technical writers and users.)

The technical writers also became the people responsible for testing the user interface. Many inconsistencies and problems were discovered only *after* the writers and editors had a chance to look at the menus. When bugs and interface problems were discovered, they were noted for future releases of the software. However, since a process for fixing these problems was never put in place, nothing was ever done about them. A configuration management system was only put in place after major bugs were found and there was no way to back out the code that caused the bugs.

Like the ancient Greek city-states, these developers were unable to unite into a single unit. They only formed alliances where portions of the code overlapped. Users complained about the non-uniform interface, so fixes were hacked out. A fix in one area would cause a crash in another, since the links needed by one module were renamed, moved, or removed and could no longer be found.

Software crashed, schedules slid, documenters tried to document moving targets, QA people threw up their hands, and upper management believed the programmers were "running wild." When the users complained, it somehow became *their* fault; the users (poor people) were simply too stupid to figure out how to use such a sophisticated system.

Much too late in the process, an overly Roman methodology was applied in attempt to forge order out of chaos. The overly Greek developers rebelled; some were fired and others quit. In the end, upper management assigned a new program manager. He was told to start the program over, using the old, "wet" code as the basis for a new and improved version of the system. Obviously, this simply passed the problem down the line. The code was finally bought by another company, where it became somebody else's problem.

Implications for CASE

Suppose you were in an environment where there was no look-ahead and no visualization because management didn't allow for any of that; where management pushed down methods that squeezed out any kind of creativity; where the tools and processes management asks (or even forces) you to use leave you exhausted at producing documents but not any software; where there is no time to think; and where you are expected to produce results, but as if you were on an assembly line.

Isn't this the kind of environment we mostly have now? One of the most frequent problems with CASE tools is that people simply don't use them, even though they are available; or, if they do use them, they use them in their simplest, most rudimentary forms. They will use a $10,000 CASE tool to draw pictures. We are convinced that to a large extent this is because using the tool interferes with actually producing results.

To the extent we are correct, and we believe this chapter points out that we are, then tools that are simple to use, that are "intuitive," and that can aid in visualizing are the tools that people will use. People will not use those that interfere with or attempt to take the place of thinking.

It's as if the formality of methods, and the tools that support them, are an attempt to provide the structure that's missing when you do software rather than hardware. But, these formalisms are cases where the user's hand is forced to fit the tool (which is the antithesis of the Olduvai Imperative). Instead, we should be producing methods and tools that fit the hand. Modeling tools (such as Stella), CASE tools for the Macintosh platform (such as those from Iconix Software Engineering), and action diagrammers (or outliners like More II) are useful, but they are useful because they help us engage our brains (or at least they don't interfere with our brains' work).

Here are some requirements for tools that we believe will assist Greek programmers in producing finished code and good documentation for others and themselves to use:

- Creating programs

    - The tool should provide a means for creating standard diagrams such as data flow diagrams (DFDs), structure charts (SCs), and entity relationship diagrams (ERDs). Rather than having the programmer create all the figures, the tool should allow her to select from a palette of "standard" looking diagrams from which she can select the number of boxes, the number of inputs, the number of outputs, and the number of levels of decomposition. It should try various mappings of DFDs into a structure chart that can then be edited for the problem at hand. The programmer should be able to associate each box on the structure chart with associated control structures from language-sensitive editors or mini-specs from the DFDs.

    - The tool should have a library of standard programming functions such as those in Knuth's *The Art of Computer Programming*. It should also contain libraries of standard mathematics and business functions. It should also have libraries to facilitate creating graphics, creating GUIs, and communicating using modems, networks, manufacturer's protocols, and various printers.

    - The tool should allow automatic compiling, testing, debugging, and editing in a smooth, seamless environment with an intuitive user interface.

♦ The tool should also have a library of standard, classic problems, already solved and documented. And, it should allow programmers to add to it from those problems they have already solved. The tool should keep track of the versions of these. This enhances reusing previous results whether they be analyses, designs, or programs themselves.

♦ The tool should have language-sensitive editors of the main languages with various editing modes such as:

- syntax checking as you type

- look-ahead, which makes sure ending statements and parentheses are balanced

- automatically inserting functions and other known code fragments as it becomes evident they are to be used in the code

• Instruments

♦ The tool should provide control graphs of source code, and orthogonal graphs of the data flow diagram decomposition, seen in Figure 5-4. It should also provide graphs of the data model, file, and record structures obtained from the data dictionary.

♦ The tool should provide complexity measures, and other measures such as commentary, and module count. It should advise of dangerous coding practice and inefficient design if it detects them. It should report on the position and number of unbalanced data flows.

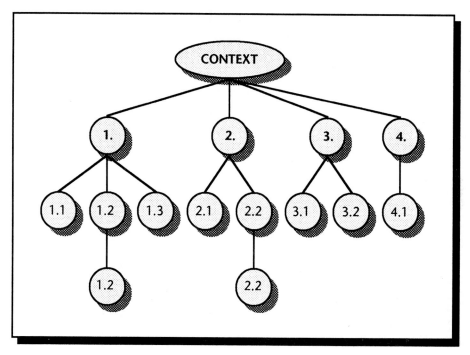

Figure 5-4. Data Flow Diagram Decomposition

- **Housekeeping**

    - The data dictionary/directory is an important part of software development no matter how you do it. The tool should be able to pick out such things as data elements and the relationships among them, file descriptions, and record and data structures, and at least make an entry in the dictionary for them. It should also contain statistics of the emerging program, lines of code, number of modules or paragraphs, number and types of branching statements, and an indication of the complexity of the code modules or paragraphs.

    - The tool should clean up graphs, making them neat, with evenly distributed boxes/bubbles and minimized line/arrow crossings.

◆ The tool should bubble up new data flows as far as possible and mark them as being entered at a lower level with options to unmark them when any conflicts are resolved.

◆ The tool should provide navigation aids in the data models, data flow diagrams, and structure charts showing where you are in the model and allowing you to select another place in the model and "go" there; for example, a small window with diagram and nodes that show where you are and that you can select to move to.

◆ The tool should produce no show stoppers. It should allow you to do opportunistic design without requiring the current status to be corrected if there is something wrong or missing. And, it should produce simple, readable reports on irregularities in the context of the programmer with no cryptic messages.

Final Thoughts

We believe that overly Roman methods—indeed, even some reasonable Roman ones—produce software that costs too much, takes too long to develop, and doesn't work very well. The Romans, of course, dispute this because they see nothing with which to compare their methods. They argue that after seeing how the Greeks screw things up, their methods simply try to bring order out of Greek chaos. They ask the Greeks: "What do you bring to the table? Where's your paradigm?"

We hope this chapter helps clear up what Greeks bring to the software development process: creativity, insight, right-brain stuff, and a willingness to deal with the chaos endemic to creating anything. Yet, the question of paradigms remains. Of course prototyping, hacking, and other opportunistic approaches can be offered as Greek paradigms. But, prototyping has already been taken over by the Romans and, anyway, opportunistic approaches are all reactions to the Waterfall; they do not arise from the way programmers behave.

But, there is something that might qualify: object-oriented (O-O) stuff. O-O stuff came from attempts to improve computer simulations. It continues this tradition by offering programmers the opportunity to model the world more closely than do traditional methods of software development. Traditional methods abstract the world to a level they can deal with.

O-O stuff also lets a partial solution show the way to the complete solution. So often, the problems we have to deal with are wicked problems that need partial solutions in order to finally be solved. In addition, O-O stuff closes the gap between analysis and synthesis by encouraging programmers to begin synthesizing soon after being aware of the problem to be solved. These have the Greek-like character of experimenting and otherwise experiencing the real world.

Of course this might bring on the Roman response: "Yes, but doesn't this simply bring on the chaotic situation we are trying to avoid? How does O-O stuff help?"

But, we reply, "O-O stuff is very orderly, nonetheless." It allows you to create *user-defined* data types that follow *rules* you set up. It does this by encapsulating what might be called "private data" and the processes that can act on them in a single container of code called an *object*. The ability to create and use objects is embedded in languages like Smalltalk and C⁺⁺. This results in loosely coupled, highly cohesive code, which is a hallmark of good software. In addition, O-O stuff helps you cast the solution in the same terms as the problem.

But, more than that, O-O stuff allows you to quickly extend the objects you have created by allowing the new object to inherit the data and methods of objects already extant. This means that if you have been dealing with, say, squares, you can add the ability of dealing with rectangles by inheriting all the data and processes from the square base type, and simply add the new rectangle data and processes. You can now build or acquire libraries of base types, or object classes, and use these to reduce the distance between the user requirements and the eventual solution. You bring these object classes to the table and extend them to meet the customer's requirements. And, the eventual solution itself can be easily and more safely changed by merely extending what already exists.

Obviously, there is much more to O-O stuff and we are simply introducing it here since there is an already large body of literature on the subject and much new development is being done in O-O methods. In fact, one of our correspondents, a salesman/consultant, gave us his calendar of business calls for a three-month period. Ninety-five percent of his calls were to be at enterprises with O-O projects just starting up.

O-O Cautions

However, we do have some cautions to offer on O-O stuff. First, it is very important to get the base types, or object classes, right. Our correspondents report that they have had to make three tries before they got it right. There is a common notion first put forward by Fred Brooks that in software development by traditional methods you ought to plan to throw the first attempt away. This means that traditional methods might require only two attempts to "get it right" while O-O stuff could require three. We're not sure why this is so. It might be because O-O stuff is one step closer to the real world, and this closeness somehow causes it. It could be that our correspondents were stumbling over traditional methods in their early attempts at O-O stuff. Nevertheless, be aware that you might have more initial work to do when you first embark on O-O stuff.

Second, O-O stuff is a clear contradiction to the Roman way of doing things. However, there are already overly Roman approaches to O-O stuff. These have to do with scant descriptions of the part of the real world being modeled and lots and lots of analyses and designs resulting in delays before even partial solutions are available, and then a higher chance of requiring much rework. Long discussions about arcane or obscure aspects of O-O stuff substitute for driving the forklifts, having coffee with the pickers, and watching trucks unloading in some warehouse whose system is to be automated using O-O stuff. O-O guys ought to get their hands dirty; it's the Greek way.

Close to this is the "guru" effect noticed by one of our correspondents. O-O gurus are divided into analysis, design, and programming camps. Each guru has his own approach and attempts to differentiate himself from others. But, this differentiation might lead you astray. We believe object-oriented orientation should concentrate on actually *doing* O-O stuff and actually programming as soon as possible. These experiences ought to be supported, but not determined, by Object-Oriented Analysis and Design.

A lot of this differentiation among gurus is done by using new words or old words in new ways. These cause the long discussions mentioned above that distract programmers from the task at hand.

Then, there are the Object Oriented Data Base Management Systems (OODBMS). One of the goals of databases was to decouple data from the functions that work on them. O-O stuff has the goal of tightly coupling data and the processes that work on them. Both of these approaches appear to be in reaction to the loosely coupled data and processes in traditional programming.

One of our correspondents told us that a major part of her career was in reformatting files produced by one program for use in another. Thus, the structure of the data was a result of the program using it rather than the relationships among the data elements themselves. This is the loose coupling both O-O stuff and databases are trying to avoid.

But, notice, aren't these two approaches fundamentally opposed to each other? How can you have no coupling and tight coupling at the same time? (See Figure 5-5.) It isn't clear exactly what an object is in an OODBMS. And yet we hear about OODBMSs frequently, especially in relation to CAD/CAM systems.

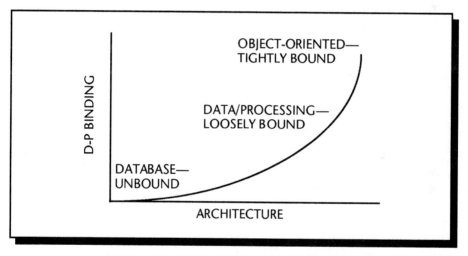

Figure 5-5. D-P Binding vs. Architectures

Be careful here. If you confront an OODBMS, make sure of your ground, of what the OODBMS thinks objects are, and how it manages them as opposed to object managers of O-O systems. There is a good discussion of these issues in "Fitting Round Objects Into Square Databases," by D.C. Tsichritzis and O.M. Nierstrasz [1988].

These cautions notwithstanding, O-O stuff holds a lot of promise for the Greek approach to software development and represents a paradigm that should warm the hearts of the Romans.

Our O-O Recommendations

If you are considering getting into O-O stuff, we recommend doing some "doing" and doing some reading.

First, we recommend learning and using some language like C⁺⁺ that has been extended to incorporate O-O methods. This gets you to the "doing" part of the thing. You might practice making objects by using Jean-Claude Corbeil's *Visual Dictionary* [1986]. For example, pages 217 to 221 show groups of kitchen utensils organized so that you can see both the relationships among them and their parts.

Here's what we would recommend reading:

- For the Greek approach, we recommend Gary Entsminger's *The Tao of Objects, A Beginner's Guide to Object-Oriented Programming* [1990], and Brad Cox's *Object Oriented Programming, An Evolutionary Approach* [1987].

- For a more Roman analytic view, we recommend *Object-Oriented Analysis*, by Peter Coad and Edward Yourdon [1991], and *Designing Object-Oriented Software*, by Rebecca Wirfs-Brock, Brian Wilkerson, and Lauren Wiener [1990].

- Finally, you might consider reading *Object-Oriented Technology: A Manager's Guide*, by David A. Taylor, Ph.D [1990].

This chapter has looked at the other side of programming: the Greek side. In the next chapter, we will look at an environment where the two sides naturally come together. It is the most common environment in our field: the software maintenance environment. ❧

Chapter 6.
Software Maintenance:
The Greco-Roman Balance

Maintenance is probably the predominant activity in our field. Some observers attribute eighty percent of the total costs of software to maintenance [Vick and Ramamoorthy 1986]. (See Figure 6-1.) And, as we shall see, maintenance programmers must achieve a balance between the Greek and Roman approaches.

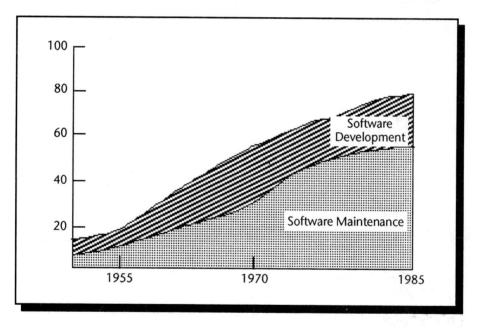

Figure 6-1. Maintenance Costs

Some folks deal with the large maintenance problem by trying to do away with maintenance altogether. One of their arguments is that you don't need to maintain code if you are using a fourth-generation language (4GL); you only need to maintain the *specifications*. But, there are three large difficulties with this argument.

First, most 4GLs simply cannot do the whole job and the developers must add *custom* code to make a satisfactory program. This means that the code the 4GL produced must be changed to include the *custom* stuff. The custom stuff must be maintained in the normal manner along with the specifications. So, maintenance programmers have yet another interface to deal with: that between the specifications and the custom code. This is normally called *perfective maintenance.*

Second, there are all the optimizations that have been done (we hope) to make the analytical solution a slick, nifty, real-world program. We do not know of any 4GL that can do that kind of stuff; indeed most of their code is, to put it mildly, less than optimal when it comes to maintenance.

Third, simply maintaining the specifications themselves isn't so simple. They are usually harder to read and understand than English (or natural language); they are affected by incomplete and incorrect requirements, just as third-generation languages; and, finally, one is simply pushing back to a more abstract level the problem of maintaining some sort of program description, which might be harder to deal with in connection with the real world.

Given that maintenance will continue to be the main activity performed by programmers, it has nowhere nearly the attention paid to it as its impact would warrant. Maintenance programmers are considered *meatball* programmers, not in the same class with *real* programmers. For one thing, maintenance programmers deal with all that old stuff—you know, the spaghetti code. For another thing, maintenance is not original; nobody thinks there are any infinite steps here. And, after all, it *is* only maintenance.

If you've ever had the experience of finally discovering what some pasta programmer had in mind when s/he first produced the program, then you know the work that went into figuring it out; there is some kind of infinite step here, only it's more like a detective story.

Maintenance programmers think they are not paid enough and they might be right. They often are not respected as much as the gurus and the Holy Grail guys we have all around us [Parikh and Zvegintzov 1983, p.339]. But, as you will see in this chapter, there is a lot going on to keep things going. There is even more that might go on once maintenance is thoroughly discussed.

There is a lot of lurching about in our field from one buzz word to another, from one Holy Grail method to another, and from one "productivity" solution to another. Most CASE (and other lurching about for that matter) has to do with software *development,* not *maintenance.*

When methodology consultants come into an enterprise with their new "holy book," they are sometimes challenged to apply their wisdom to maintenance. Most of them simply proceed to adapt their "method" to what maintenance *should* be, not to what it actually *is*. In this chapter, we look at what maintenance is in some depth and talk about the processes.

Maintenance is usually considered an on-going support activity, and so it is budgeted on an annual basis rather than on a project basis. We have sometimes heard the term *level of effort* applied to maintenance assignments. This means there is no specific task assigned to maintenance programmers, only the general task of keeping the program "up and running."

The literature [ibid][12] describes three types of maintenance:

corrective   debugging code (also known as *rat-killing*)

perfective   adding enhancements to code (also known euphemistically as *extended development*)

adaptive   porting code to new environments such as hardware or operating system versions (also known as the dreaded *conversions* we must bear from time to time to account for new technology, especially new hardware)

But, as a matter of fact, there is one activity that is more important than the three listed above: learning the software. One of the authors of this book re-discovered this during a series of team meetings in which he participated in 1990. The purpose of these meetings was to bring some understanding to the maintenance process.

Learning is an issue because the maintenance programmer must understand the software in order to make the changes required by the other types of maintenance. The programmer who does the maintenance usually hasn't developed the software and initially doesn't understand it. Even if s/he has developed the software, there is often such a significant time lag between the development period and the maintenance activities that keeping "current" in the software is an on-going activity. This learning is done in parallel with the other three maintenance tasks previously described.

---

[12] This reference is somewhat dated, but it looks to us like nobody is paying attention to it. See especially p.339, "I'm OK, You're OK, Maintenance is OK," by G.M. Bronstein and R.I. Okamoto for some insight into attitudes about maintenance. See also *Part I: The World of Software Maintenance; Part II, Understanding Software;* and *Part III: The Modification of Software.* Our chapter here can only be an introduction, such as it is, to this important material.

If the task is truly trivial, such as correcting a format error in a report or doing a simple recompile and test after trivial changes to an operating system, the opportunity and need to learn the software are small.

But, if the programmer's job is to be the maintenance programmer for the program, then, over time, s/he will have to learn it. If it is *active* software (in the sense that many folks are using it and want changes made), then the programmer has a large need to learn as much of it as s/he can. However, learning software competes with the on-going requirements of maintenance.

Figure 6-2 shows how learning software relates to the on-going maintenance process. Incidentally, much of the material in this chapter is from a team effort in which one of the authors of this book participated. The team members graciously allowed us to use it.

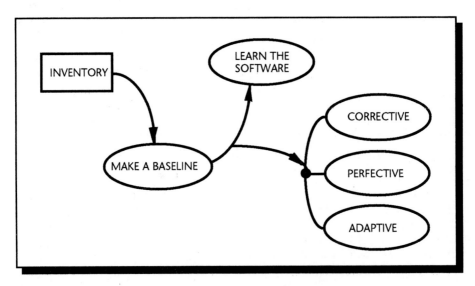

Figure 6-2. The Maintenance Effort

Figure 6-3 shows the jump in total effort and the decline in maintenance actually done when a new maintenance programmer is assigned to a program. Relative values are shown; the actual values depend on the programmer and the condition of the code. Even if little gets done, a lot of learning is going on.

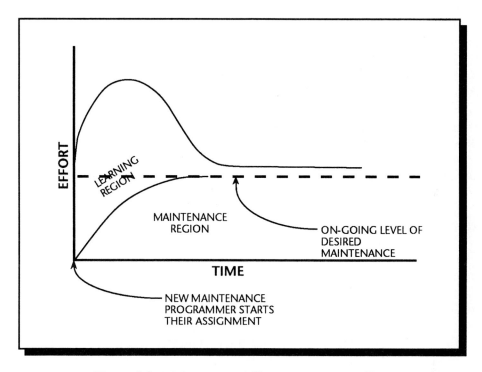

Figure 6-3. Maintenance Effort vs. Learning Effort

Figure 6-4 is a flowchart of the learning process. Immediately following the chart are: an explanation of each step on it, a list of some tools that might be useful during those steps, and some self-test questions that we think would help a maintenance programmer determine how well s/he is doing. We selected a flowchart presentation because it isolates each activity from all the others in the diagram and enables the viewer to concentrate on the essential processes involved.

This is a Roman device that helps clarify things. But, we know that each of the steps in the flowchart can be performed in parallel just as learning occurs in parallel with the three maintenance tasks. So, the flowchart shows the learning processes in their rough sequence.

The flowchart cannot be a procedure for proceeding with maintenance. If it were used that way, there would be no parallel activity. No maintenance would be performed while the programmer was learning the software. And, within the process itself, no succeeding step would be performed until the preceding one was completed.

None of these situations reflect the real world. But, the flowchart shows the kinds of activities that a maintenance programmer must eventually perform to become knowledgeable about software and productive in maintaining it.

Even though her or his first days as a maintenance programmer on an "active" program will probably be hectic, s/he will eventually establish a baseline, routinely assess and update portions of the code, and will frequently test it to verify the baseline. Once that is established, the programmer has a foundation for doing maintenance confidently, quickly, and efficiently.

Notes for Figure 6-4

(In the following discussion, we are assuming that *you* will be the maintenance programmer. That way, we don't have to worry about which personal pronoun to use.)

Step I (Acquisition)

To start, you will have to obtain the elements you will need to establish a baseline. You should try to obtain the following items:

1. Source code image

2. JCL (compile, link, and execute job instructions)

3. Required inputs

4. Test cases (I/O)

5. Documentation

    - User's guide

    - Programmer's document

    - Requirements document (old requirements for corrective and adaptive maintenance)

    - New requirements (for perfective maintenance)

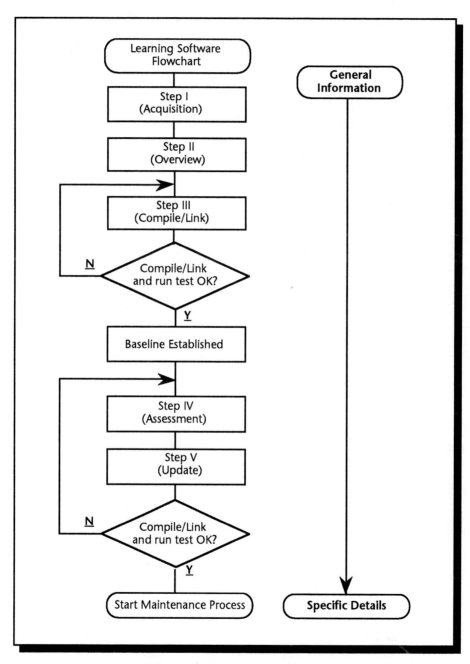

Figure 6-4. The Learning Process

- Updates, notes, diaries, notebooks, etc., from all the previous lives of the code

6. Names of the previous programmers

Over a period of time, you will acquire this basic information about the program and its history. Some of it must be re-created, some you can do without after a while. But, initially, the above list represents the main elements of the information you need to know.

Step II (Overview)

As the maintenance programmer, you will review the information gathered in Step I. Here are some of the questions you are likely to ask yourself:

What do I have?

How docs it work?

What's missing?

What do I need to know to understand the program?

What domain knowledge must I acquire?

How can I get a "picture" of the program?

Can I spot the optimizations, the patches, the vestigial, the active code?

Finally, as you answer these questions (many of which are felt more than asked) you slowly becomes the "owner" of the program, and your confidence builds. You find that much of the information you initially needed is no longer important.

Step III (Compile/Link)

The next step is to compile, link, and test the program to gauge its completeness and correctness. Are the tests okay? Turn on all the compiler messages. What happens? Are volumes of warning and information messages produced? Are there any "dangerous" use messages? Can you understand what they are and what to do about them?

This provides an initial baseline for learning the software and concurrently performing the three types of maintenance: perfective, corrective, and adaptive.

Step IV (Assessment)

Over a period of time, you will determine the standards you want to apply to the program to make it maintainable to you. Assess the code for the following features:

- Readability (which is made up of completeness, consistency, simplicity, modularity, and self-descriptiveness)

- Correctness

- Interconnection

- Learnability (another neologism we coined to be consistent with the other "ilities")

Here is a list of tools that might help:

- A code analyzer

- A call tree generator for producing maps of the interconnections of the modules or paragraphs of a program

- A tool for checking the consistency in arguments between the calling routines and the called routines

- For languages with global data, a tool that analyzes global data for consistency and locates where they are used and set

- Perhaps a flowchart maker (we know of a very experienced programmer who makes flowcharts of the most unmaintainable code in order to learn it)

Step V (Upgrade)

Over the period of rat-killing and other work, consider the following activities to upgrade the code to these standards:

- Restructuring the code

- Improving its readability and control flow (see the guidelines later in this chapter under the discussion of re-engineering)

- Interpreting the output of the tools and incorporating it into the code, if necessary

- Adding meaningful commentary as you uncover the secrets of the program

Here is a list of tools that might help:

- Restructurers that remove GOTOs and replaces them with block structures

- Commentary form: injectors, header makers, and statement renumberers (simply inserting places in the code where comments should go adds to the consistent look of the program even if the programmer can't add meaningful commentary at the time)

Last Step

As a final step, you would compile and link the program and run test cases. Compare the execution and results with the baseline:

- Does the program run OK?

- Do you understand why it runs OK?

- Do you understand the code?

The Baseline

The *baseline* is a version of the program and the data input that produces a correct solution. This does not mean that all the data sets will run correctly, nor that all the paths in the code are tested by the data sets. It simply means that the baseline version of the software and an ever-growing number of test cases will provide correct results.

Establishing the baseline is most important; it provides the reference to which you can compare the results of test executions. It provides a basis for knowing how the software functions. With a baseline, you can remain sane; without one, you are adrift on an uncharted sea full of "craziness monsters." Lose your reference and you might as well start over.

Corrective Maintenance

Corrective maintenance, or *rat-killing* as we sometimes call it, is most prevalent right after the software is released and declines over a period of time to become the least prevalent form of maintenance. The length of the rat-killing period is determined by how correct and how maintainable the software is. The average or mean time between failure (MTBF) is sometimes used as an indirect measure of quality and an indicator of the amount of corrective maintenance performed on the software.

Rat-killing involves more than just tracing code back from an anomaly detected during test or reported in discrepancy reports. It is a process akin to detective work as G. M. Bronstein and R. I. Okamoto put it in their article [ibid, "I'm OK, You're OK, Maintenance is OK", etc.]. "The triumph of a maintenance programmer over a program bug and the successful modification of an undocumented program illustrate the reward that comes from solving a tough maintenance problem."

Maintenance programmers are supreme head scratchers:
"Now why did he do it that way?"
"Why doesn't this work?"
"The compiler says this code line is wrong; I can't find it, can you?"
"This should work, dammit."

Faced with software that is seldom written in their own style, the maintenance programmers are always challenged by the styles of those who have built the thing in the first place.

Maintenance folks have to understand what the original programmer had in mind, the theory of the problem, what subsequent programmers were trying to do, and how the users are currently trying to use the software. They must understand what the user is telling them and the user's needs.

They must understand code, and they must be good at it; better even than the programmers who wrote the program. The original programmers usually are approaching the program from a narrower point of view. They've got a problem to solve, not a system to build. But maintenance people must work within the current system, extending the solution to all users.

Also, although the original programmer built the software with a large range of data states in mind, s/he usually tested it for a rather small subset. However, the maintenance programmers must correct the errors that keep the software from being used over the entire range of data that are actually used.

Here's an example. One of the authors of this book, Peter DeGrace, worked with a programmer-engineer who had just built a complicated plumbing program. About ten percent of the time it would give bad results. The engineer said: "You know, it does that sometimes." He had tested his program, Peter estimated, for only about three to five percent of the cases likely to be seen in real use and errors showed up when he tried to use a new network. Peter had to redesign the program to take into account a far greater range of plumbing networks.

In a similar example of poorly tested software, another engineer said: "I wrote that [huge, 1500 line] loop; but I don't understand it. Sometimes it doesn't work; I can't figure it out."

So, the maintenance programmer must:

- Be able to see beyond the view of the original programmer

- Make the program work for the intended range of data

- Know how to trace code and, these days, how to use a debugger

- Bring all these things together to keep the software up and running

The maintenance programmer must be both a Roman and a Greek. S/he must establish a structure—his or her own baseline—within which to work. S/he depends on the organizational structures as much or more than the developers. Configuration management is extremely important. The program must be managed and protected, and made available to the users. All this requires the stuff of the Romans. But, when it comes to fixing it, or enhancing it, or moving it, or making it beautiful, well, then you are in the realm of the Greeks.

Maintenance is not for the purely Greek or the purely Roman. Here we find that the "golden mean" is necessary: the best balance of the two forms. Its application is in the recognition of patterns in structures (the Greek view) and the recognition of structures in patterns (the Roman view).

Perfective Maintenance

Perfective maintenance is software development using an extensive prototype. Where error correction extends the solution to the originally conceived range of input states, perfective maintenance extends the range itself, sometimes allowing new kinds of data. A monthly forecast also becomes an annual one; analyzing metal fatigue now includes composite materials; an insurance advisor also becomes an investment advisor, etc.

These new requirements occur for several reasons. One reason is the "report effect." This is the condition where the user has not been able to specify all the requirements in advance. S/he needs to see something before the other requirements come to mind.

Another reason is the existence of "wicked problems." These are problems that can be explained only *after* they are at least partially solved. Many engineering and business programs have this characteristic. In engineering programs, wicked problems come about because it might not be known if the computation can be done at all. In this situation, intermediate results are needed to get a better understanding of the problem at hand. Also, the engineer or scientist might not know what the solution even looks like and, therefore, can't know beforehand when the problem is solved.

In business programs, wicked problems occur for similar reasons and also because customers and users don't completely know their processes and data. They have been operating somewhat intuitively until the computer system comes along. Now they must make their unconscious processes and data explicit. Folks are uncomfortable doing this; they can easily feel threatened. And, it is hard to do anyway since they can't know the unconscious stuff. So, the program must produce the data in such a way that the customers and users can get acquainted and feel comfortable with the results. This solution also becomes an aid to discovering the unconscious processes and data that are in use.

Here again the maintenance person must know what the original program was intended to do and get a feel for how extendible it is.

Adaptive Maintenance

In *adaptive maintenance*, you take the existing solution (such as it is) and adapt it to new environments; for example, new or changed operating systems, platforms, communications schemes, user interfaces, or database schemes, etc.

In Chapter 3, we listed some of the "ilities" of software that make adaptive maintenance easier. But, there is a caution here. Remember the three parts of programs discussed in Chapter 3: active, inactive, and vestigial? All this code can be a source of problems when you port because you must compile, link/load, and test *all* the code, not only the familiar portions. Problems such as machine dependencies, language extensions, or incompatibilities can occur anywhere in the program. A programmer must therefore pay attention to all the code. This is why there are so many nasty surprises when conversions occur.

Conversions are one of those times when folks think that they can do a *might as well.* Here, you might find budgets that were allocated for conversions being devastated by the notion that, as long as the code is being opened up, we *might as well* do all those things we've wanted to do for some time. We *might as well* make the code maintainable, or portable, or more efficient, or whatever.

This sounds laudable, but has the unfortunate effect of adding complexity to the conversion, damaging or even destroying the baseline and, as a result, causing budgets to burn out of control. That's because you affect the code whenever you *upgrade* it: you might introduce errors, the code certainly requires a new understanding by the programmer, and the *might as well* distracts the programmer from the problem at hand, which is to convert the code.

If you want maintainable code, pay for it; don't think that it comes free, riding piggyback on a conversion. That's one reason why conversions are so dreaded.

Implications for CASE

More maintenance tools are coming on the market, but most CASE tools are intended for software development. Maintenance programmers tend to build many of their tools, such as reformatters and various analyzers. Below are some ideas for doing the three types of maintenance and some tools that might help.

For rat-killing, many folks use the code itself, a compiler that was used to establish the baseline, and a test data set. They put print statements in the code at strategic points, compile the code, attempt to execute it, save the results, and then examine intermediate values and states for anomalies. Then, programmers use their understanding of the code and the theory behind it to resolve anomalies and errors. They repeat this process until the anomaly or error condition is resolved.

Tools that might help here are debuggers, some of which are so good that developers purposely convert their code to run on the platform where the debugger runs. We were told that this is the case with the debugger on the Apollo platform. Debuggers, like compilers, are mostly offered by the platform vendor, are optimized for the vendor's hardware, and can be used only there.

Configuration managers are other tools that might help. These tools usually aren't welcomed in an environment until they are needed, and then they sometimes are an answer to a prayer: "If only *you* would save my code, I'll always backup in the future. Oh please. Oh please. Oh *pleeeeeese!?!?!?!*"

For perfective maintenance, most of the same tools apply. Configuration management tools are important here because adding new features to existing code is more destabilizing to the baseline than fixing errors that prevent the software from operating as expected.

For adaptive maintenance, the best advice we can give is to simply attempt to compile your code on the new host and see what happens. Languages are getting good enough that if you use a standard one and avoid machine dependencies, you have an excellent chance of doing a conversion with little trouble. Machine and operating system independence will also help a lot here, and compilers that mark their source code output files with non-standard code and dependencies are helpful.

This has been a description of maintenance as we've seen it in our field, and of the growing influence of reusable software. There are some related issues we also need to discuss. These are the "R" words.

The "R" Words

There are four "R" words: *restructuring, reverse engineering, re-engineering,* and *reusing software*. There is some disagreement about the definitions of these words, but it is generally accepted that restructuring code is the activity that precedes any of the others.

Restructuring includes all the improving activities that maintenance programmers perform on the code they maintain. *Reverse engineering* is an activity that attempts to extract design and analysis information from the existing code. *Re-engineering,* which is a more controversial term, sometimes means a more comprehensive form of restructuring. It would be an activity to be undertaken before reverse engineering is attempted. Sometimes it means changing an existing software system into a better one: one with better technology or performance.[13] As such, re-engineering would be performed after reverse engineering, when the design and analysis recovered from the code is available. *Reusing software* attempts to eliminate duplicate effort by reusing code in various forms instead of re-developing it. Together, these four notions include or are based on maintenance activities.

Figure 6-5 illustrates the relationships among the four "R" words and highlights an area of substantial risk in attempting to implement some of these notions. We describe these risks in the sections that follow.

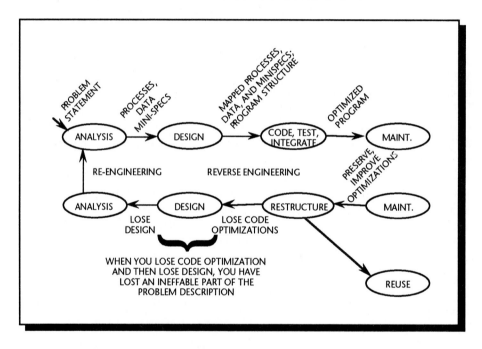

Figure 6-5. Relationships Among the "R" Words

[13] The definitions of the four "R" words are largely from *American Programmer*, Vol. 2, No. 4 (April 1989): Children's Computer Company, Ltd., 161 West 86th Street, New York, New York, 10024. This journal is one of the best in the business. It's produced by Ed Yourdon, ably assisted by Toni Nash. It's expensive, but we think it is worth it because it deals with what *we* deal with: what we really have to put up with and not the moral questions of what we *should* put up with. The articles do lean toward the guru side of things; nevertheless, you easily get the feeling of familiarity as you read it. If you work in a large enterprise or, perhaps, if you are a member of a professional organization, Ed will offer a site license to it for a price that will reduce the overall cost.

Restructuring

Restructuring is a term that has been around for 20 years. It means: "Reorganizing the procedural logic of a computer program so that it conforms to the rules of structured programming." [ibid, p.3] Practically, this means getting rid of GOTO statements and replacing them with block structures such as IF-THEN-ELSE statements. It also means optimizing cohesion and coupling, adding effective commentary, and all the things maintenance programmers do to code to establish their baselines. It is a well understood technology. Software that does restructuring is typically grouped with maintenance tools.

Reverse Engineering

Reverse engineering is the process of producing the intermediate products of forward engineering. It hopes to recover from the code the functional specifications or even the user requirements. It is very dubious that this can happen easily or effectively. Besides, after the software exists, the value of the intermediate products is questionable.

Most other engineering fields do not pay much attention to the reverse aspects of their areas. Some notable exceptions are home remodeling, auto repair, airplane restoration, and decoding encoded messages. But, usually, the work is *forward.*

Software reverse engineering has an application in data resource management by attempting to extract the data models embedded in programs. To the extent that reverse engineering is successful, it is a valuable tool especially in trying to manage the information resources of an enterprise. The success of data resource management is very important, in our opinion. The information represented in the data is a *resource* that must be better managed.

Sometimes, reverse engineering is performed in order to do some *post mortem* requirements tracing, or to extract functional specifications in order to use code generators. And, there are efforts reported by some of our correspondents to use reverse engineering to prepare existing systems for substantial changes in computing architecture, such as moving to a new database management system or to multiple parallel processors.

But, these functions are still on the "bleeding edge" of technology, and their promise, especially code generation from functional specifications, hasn't yet been realized.

We are also told that it is another white knight rushing forward to rescue us from the dragons of complexity and huge maintenance costs. The claim is that one can solve the software maintenance problem by first reverse engineering existing programs and then re-engineering them "correctly" to produce maintainable software. We take exception to this claim.

The reverse engineering strategy usually described in the literature is based on the assumptions that *reverse* engineering is the *inverse* of *forward* engineering; that forward engineering steps are well understood (and are understood to be of the Roman variety); that we really go through or should go through the Roman steps of forward engineering to produce code; and that the intermediate products of software development—the *artifacts*—are important after the software is produced, especially if the proper steps weren't done in the first place.

These assumptions are just not true in most of the real cases of software development that we know and hear about. Therefore, the claims of reverse engineering are in doubt. Here are our arguments about this issue.

First, forward engineering produces something starting from nothing. It starts with the most abstract and least concrete representation of the software. It proceeds through some not very well understood processes to something that is as concrete as software will ever be: the program itself and its associated files.

Reverse engineering, on the other hand, starts with something that exists. All the decisions that were made during analysis, design, construction, test, and maintenance are present in the code. As you reverse the process, you retreat from the current state of the solution. So, you could end up with a poor representation of the design, showing the patches that were made as an expedient maintenance technique rather than as part of the design.

When a reverse software engineer withdraws across the design-analysis border, all the optimizations are lost and the results are the sterile problem descriptions stripped of their expressions in the real world. The pity is that programmers frequently had to steal the resources to put these optimizations into their software in the first place because it isn't usually understood by customers and managers that it is necessary to optimize code. Therefore, many of the advantages of well-optimized code are lost. And, these very often were the reasons why the code was valuable in the first place.

Next, forward engineering is not done in the same consistent manner. As stated earlier, there is a wide continuum of approaches.

The orthodox method is called the Waterfall. In addition, there are many variations of the Waterfall itself. And, very frequently, when the Waterfall is claimed as the method used on a project, investigation reveals that the software was actually done some other way and recorded in the traditional way [DeGrace and Stahl 1990].

There are various types of prototyping. There are the *all-at-once* methods: hacking, handcuff, and scrum [ibid]. Most of these involve an opportunistic approach that is unbalanced, not step-wise, etc.

Given the problems inherent in the Waterfall, and the industry's dismal record using it, there is no reason to believe that rational people will select it most of the time if they are given an opportunity to do so. So, reverse engineering is claiming to assist in a process that is not universally, or even, we suspect, frequently used.

Next, all the artifacts that were created when the system was originally built are not necessarily needed even if they *were* created. For example, functional specifications, which represent the final user view of the system before preliminary design, are not as useful as the system itself when it comes to user verification. This is one reason why prototyping has been so successful and has received so much attention recently, because it goes beyond stuffy documents to actual system operation.

In addition, low-end tools, rather than high-end tools, tend to be used to accomplish the goals that reverse engineering claims to assist us with. Compilers are one example. They optimize code for vector computers. You would think that reverse engineering would have a market here rushing in to save FORTRANers from themselves as they attempt to use the new vector computers. And, initially, it *was* thought that this optimization would have to be done manually, and that special tools would have to be used or the software would have to be redesigned. However, recent improvements in compilers, which are lower-level tools, accomplish much that is necessary to do the job.

Therefore, it isn't clear that intermediate artifacts of software development are useful or that the tools that produce them are appropriate technology. In our opinion, the most useful *artifacts* are: the code itself, a *call tree* diagram, the structure of the data, and a context diagram. We already have tools to get these artifacts. We know this both from our review of the literature Schneiderman 1982][14] and from our correspondents.

Finally, there is the notion of *notational hysteresis*. This is the effect we have noticed in many of our correspondents who perform maintenance when they are working in code and want to stay with lexical representation as long as possible. This is the reverse of forward engineering where, if they began their work in graphics, they would stay with graphics as long as possible. So, the graphics, which have been touted as the savior of us all, aren't really all that necessary for maintenance folks.

---

[14] Ben Schneiderman found that data structure documentation was more helpful to programmers than control flow information, such as pseudocode, in program comprehension.

In our opinion, the main, practical goals of reverse engineering are to extract enough design information from the code to enable the maintainer to *understand* and, perhaps, *reuse* it. We conclude that reverse engineering is not very useful except in the special situations we described previously. Even then, we believe it has limited usefulness and that claims for it are exaggerated (so what else is new?).

Reverse engineering is another blind alley that the gurus of our field are causing us to lurch down. They would like us to extract the form, and not the substance, from software and to reconstitute the software simply from the form alone. It looks like those who run our industry hope to eliminate the unpredictable and unmanageable human programmers by automating the entire process. They believe in the fallacy "… we can devise a system that is so perfect that nobody has to be good." [Bork 1992]

Re-Engineering

There is some disagreement about the definition of *re-engineering*. Some see it as having evolved from *restructuring*. In that context, the term has a high hype content because the word "engineering" lends a certain authority. It includes restructuring, but means more. It means decomposing large routines and removing patches and dead code. It includes: identifying the essential data structures, reporting where global data occurs, checking that this data has the same structure in every routine in which it appears, and checking where elements of global data are used and set. It also includes identifying redundant code, adding improved layout features, reducing the complexity of the code, and creating a call tree and context diagrams.

Re-engineering also includes reformatting the code to make it more readable. This means adding commentary, white space, and indentation. The commentary is usually put at the beginning of each routine, before each call to another routine and, perhaps, before each conditional statement. White space is composed of blank lines that are inserted into the code to set off the structures. In FORTRAN, you might insert blank lines before and after loop constructs, calls to other routines, and block structures. You usually do indentation to show structure within some larger structure. In FORTRAN, you might want to indent the code *inside* DO loops, or block structures. You need to be careful about adding too much re-engineering to code, though, because this can again make it unreadable.

In the other context, re-engineering is the next step *after* reverse engineering. It is re-engineering that uses the information derived from reverse engineering to produce better programs. With functional specifications and a data model it might attempt to use code generators to produce the next transaction processing system. It is re-engineering that tries to produce better and more technologically improved programs using the information from reverse engineering, or to redesign existing systems for substantial changes in computing architecture, such as moving to a new database management system or to multiple parallel processors.

We think the latter meaning is more appropriate because it appears to be the more current one.

Reusing Software

Reusable software is very important. It can provide a substantial savings in software development and maintenance by making already canned partial solutions available to developers. It is, by our estimation the most important thing we can do to reduce costs and shorten the time to develop software.

We already reuse a lot of stuff. As we write software, we are reusing the machine, the operating system, and system services (lower level, primitive functions).

When a developer uses libraries of functions, especially in object code form, he begins to apply powerful levers to his work. Some of these larger solutions in libraries include various kinds of sorting, whole groups of standard calculations, windowing operations, and graphical functions. When source code is reused, the size of the levers grows. Object code is not considered to be portable because it is usually dependent on unique (or uniquely implemented) features of a certain computer model. However, source code can be portable if it is in a standard language and the standard is rigorously followed. This makes the program more valuable, since it can then be executed on many platforms.

Finally, when you reuse whole programs you get the most benefit from reusable software. One of the trends we've noticed is the availability of software to provide general, customizable solutions to business problems. You buy the application, say a general ledger system, modify it to suit your needs by providing parameters to it, and then proceed to use it.

The following are some things that can be reused:

- The machine and/or the operating system.

- System services: time, largest number, smallest number, etc.

- Default library and/or intrinsic language functions.

- User owned (or controlled) and selected libraries for such things as the user interface, graphics, mathematics, and special functions such as those for business or structural engineering, usually in object code form.

- Routines and/or modules (source code) of application-specific or language-specific functions, such as real estate or construction contracting and basic mathematical functions in Ada.

- Programs (remodeled), such as entire applications moved to new platforms or redesigned to use new types of data, such as a structural application originally designed to model steel now redesigned for composites.

- Documentation, especially excellent examples of such difficult-to-write items as trade studies, usability reports, technical feasibility reports, environmental impact statements, and grant proposals, where you might be able to reuse both the form of the documentation and the content. In addition, you can reuse tables, figures, and other charts.

- Portions of designs, such as DFDs, structure charts, etc. There are two types of design reuse that are of interest here: (1) empty diagrams already nicely laid out and sized by several menus that select different diagrams and the elements for each (the Roman form); (2) example systems designs stored as, for example, a standard cruise control in DFDs and structure charts already fully populated with data and processes decomposed and named to use (reuse) as starters for new designs (the Greek form).

- General-purpose applications.

Figure 6-6 shows the relationship between forward engineering and the processes needed to produce reusable code. These processes are similar to making a baseline. Notice how deeply involved reusability is in the maintenance process. And, if you have already optimized code for maintenance, you have practically optimized it for reusability.

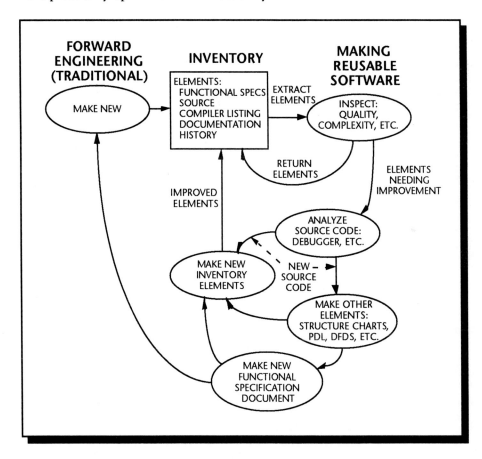

Figure 6-6. Maintenance and Reusability

Reusable stuff can be a resource to take the place of programmers who are in short supply. Of course, you have to do more work to make programs reusable and to capture, inventory, advertise, and distribute the stuff. (See Figure 6-6.)

A rule of thumb we use (and which makes sense) is: if something is a candidate for reuse, then do whatever is necessary to make it reusable if you can reasonably expect to reuse it three times in one year. Make sure that it has all the characteristics of reusable code (discussed in detail in Chapter 3), which are: generality, modularity, software system independence, machine independence, and self-descriptiveness.

In our opinion, the closest we can come to silver bullets for solving our software problems is to adjust our software development environments to make reusable software easier to make, find, and use.

In the next chapter we will look at one of the most underrated yet important activities in which a software engineer can engage: documentation.

Chapter 7.
Documentation:
It Is Written

To introduce this subject, we'd like to share with you an article we found in *PARCBench*, a compilation of articles from Xerox Corporation's quarterly magazine, *Benchmark* [Feinstein 1988].

My Life as a Document (as told to Debra Feinstein)

The traditional view of documents is one of static objects that exist on sheets of paper. Xerox has a different vision—of living, evolving organisms that carry people's knowledge, decisions and intentions and that affect their fates and fortunes. Here, a document expresses that vision in its own words.

I feel lucky to have been born during this modern, high tech era. My ancestors had to spend their entire lifetimes on the walls of caves, but these days, a document can really cut loose.

I'm well past my prime now. I live inside a manila file folder, but I can't complain. My life has been illustrious and exciting. And early retirement is giving me a chance to reflect on all that I've seen and done...

I was conceived in a moment of passion. The marketing team was meeting to talk about a major contract our company was hoping to win from TNX Industries, the aerospace firm. The boss told the group they would have to submit a proposal to TNX's vice president of engineering by the end of the month, and it would have to knock his socks off.

Suddenly, everyone started getting very worked up, and the next thing you know—there I was. Not the final document, of course—I had some growing up to do before I would be ready to act as our company's ambassador to TNX. At that point, I was just the *idea* for the proposal. But written or not, I felt a life-force surge through me.

Everyone at the meeting felt it. They started bouncing me back and forth, spinning me around, twisting and turning me. I lived my entire childhood during that meeting. By the time someone scribbled me down on the conference room easel, I had shape and form, identity and a sense of direction—even if all there was to me were three sentences and two bullets.

Week One

Next, it was time to build my character. As my coordinator, Frank was responsible for my education. Under his able guidance I set out to accumulate knowledge and life experiences.

The first thing Frank did was type me into his personal computer. A strange feeling—moving from the material, fixed medium of paper to the ephemeral, mutable electronic world inside the computer. I think it's what Shirley MacLaine calls an *out-of-body experience.*

Frank brought meaning into my life. He organized my scribbles into an outline and gave me a beginning, middle and end. He also gave me a family: memos that carried news of me to all the department managers who would contribute to my education.

During that week, I was the center of attention throughout the entire company. I got crash courses in engineering, finance, scheduling, quality, manufacturing, purchasing, accounting and shipping as one by one, each of those departments fed me their knowledge and expertise.

It was a lot to absorb in a short time, but Frank helped me put it all together. As pages came in across the network from each department, he revised them to make them consistent and understandable and to give me a logical structure.

All went well until we received the section from purchasing. I guess the purchasing manager likes to be different—that department is on an incompatible system, so they sent their pages in on paper. The whole section had to be rekeyed from scratch, which made Frank mad. He asked Nancy to type it, which made her mad, too.

My first real crisis came on the day before graduation. I was to be presented to the president and his executive committee on Friday, and on Thursday we still hadn't received the finance section. When Charlie finally turned his information in late Thursday morning, wouldn't you know it—it was *raw data.* Rows and rows of figures.

Frank began to sweat. He couldn't send *data* to the executive committee! And Nancy, who knew how to make charts out of data, was very busy and still mad at Frank. I have to hand it to that guy—he knows how to make things happen. He took Nancy to lunch; they were gone for more than two hours. That afternoon, she turned Charlie's data into two pie charts and a bar chart while he worked on the copy.

By closing time they had finished the Finance section, but Nancy still didn't feel I was ready to go upstairs. She said, *"They never even take their coats off up there. You need to fix this proposal up."*

If you've ever gotten dressed up in a tuxedo or ballgown, you can imagine how I felt. They decked me out in a Classic (10 pt.) body, did my titles in Helvetica bold, justified my right margins and gave me headers and footers. Seeing how much they cared for me made me feel even more special. After all, how many documents would you stay at work until 10 P.M. for?

Before taking me up to the meeting, Frank made 10 copies of me. It was my first experience with reproduction—talk about an identity crisis! I got even more upset when I heard Frank tell the executives that I was only a "first draft" and that he wanted to get their input before the next set of revisions. The news that I had more growing up to do came as a shock. Like a typical teenager, I thought I already knew everything there was to know.

Week Two

The executives promised Frank they would return me with their comments by Monday. He was a nervous wreck when he arrived at work, but as soon as he saw, *"Great job! Thorough and well organized,"* scrawled across the top of the president's copy, he relaxed. Everyone's comments were positive, but there were a lot of suggestions for revisions and additions. Our work for the week was cut out for us, and most of it was done in meetings.

My favorite was the meeting we held with all the department managers. They each brought letters, reports and memos they had written about me. It was the first time I'd had a chance to meet most of my relatives.

Another memorable event took place when I got "faxed" to the president's executive assistant who was visiting the Los Angeles office. I had some trepidation about traveling so far so fast, but it was a breeze. Okay, I was a little blurry when I arrived, but when I think that only a few years ago I would have had to sit in an envelope for an entire week to get from the East Coast to L.A.—well, it renews my faith in office technology.

By the end of the week, my content was in great shape. The engineering designs and a few miscellaneous diagrams had been scanned in, and all the plans, budgets, schedules and facts from each of the departments were clear, concise and complete.

Now that I had the substance of a mature document, it was time to concentrate on my form. After all, I was going to be my company's representative to its largest customer. And this wasn't just any contract I was going after. Winning it would take the company out of the slump we'd been in since a competitor had stolen two of our biggest accounts. Everyone was depending on me. I *had* to look great.

That's why Frank scheduled me for a makeover with Dorothy, the best graphic artist in the publishing department. I wondered what was in store for me.

Week Three

To the casual observer, it may have looked like all Dorothy did was make a few cosmetic changes on her desktop publishing program. She gave me a new set of fonts, moved my margin settings and played around with my layout and other features—but the changes weren't just skin deep.

Where before I had been opaque, now I was transparent. It was if my soul had been laid bare.

The big day finally came—I was delivered to TNX. I made my way through several layers of staff, causing a stir everywhere I went. Several people attached complimentary notes to me. Finally, they put me in a stack with proposals from three competing suppliers and handed us all to Arnold, the engineering vice president who would make the final decision on the contract.

Arnold spread us all out on his desk. Thanks to Dorothy's magic touch, he was attracted to me right away, singling me out from the rest of the group for immediate attention. Thanks to the work of Frank and the others, I stood up well under close scrutiny, too. He read me from cover to cover.

My company received the news of Arnold's decision a few days later. It was like a party back here. Everyone was so excited about getting the contract that no one could do any work.

I was excited too, but my excitement was laced with a touch of sadness. I had served my purpose—now it would be up to the next generation to carry on. By the time Frank put me away in the filing cabinet, I was prepared. Still, it was a poignant moment for both of us—we had been through so much together.

* * *

It's not so bad in here. I'm surrounded by friends and family. News from the outside world filters in. Last week, I found out that Frank and Nancy are dating.

This morning, I heard that our company is up for a big contract from Granx Corporation to manufacture a part for their new jet. Someone said that Frank suggested using me as the model for the proposal—imagine, a shot at immortality. I'm trying not to get too excited, because it will probably never happen.

Wait a minute, what's that sound....? Who turned on the light....? Someone's opening my drawer. Frank, is that you....?

Debra Feinstein is a freelance writer based in Los Angeles. She is a frequent contributor to Benchmark.

We felt the need to tell this story here because it gives so much valuable insight into what goes on in a typical documentation project. Although the process will be slightly different from product to product and organization to organization, the fundamentals are basically the same. We'll re-address many of the issues raised in that article later in this chapter.

Documentation is one of the key indicators of software quality. (The others are Software Quality Assurance (SQA) and reviews [Card et al 1987].) In spite of that fact, it has frequently received low priority and its power to help programmers has been poorly understood. The most up-to-date version of the code is the last one, the one you throw away when you are done with it. The most up-to-date version of the documentation is often the first version of it because it is never updated.

There are many different types of documentation produced during the life of a project. And, the focus of the documentation varies depending on whether it is being developed in a Greek or Roman environment. Here is a partial listing of the types of documentation that may be produced [DeGrace and Stahl 1990, pp.54-55]:

- Original problem statement
- Options analysis document
- Cost-benefit analysis document
- Requirements document
- Preliminary program plan
  - Statement of work
  - Work breakdown structure
  - Management plan
  - Documentation plan
  - Visibility and tracking plan
  - Schedules
- Alternatives analysis document
- Functional specification document
- Preliminary design document
- User's guide
- Programmer's guide
- User test plan
- User training plan
- Test plan outlines
- Test reports
- Installation plan

Then, there is the software itself and all the associated software, such as support libraries, job control language, configuration control programs, etc.

Here is what the Department of Defense wants in the way of documentation [ibid, from DOD-STD-2167A]:

- Preliminary system specification
- System specification
- System/segment design document
- Preliminary software requirements specification
- Preliminary interface requirements specification
- Software development plan
- Software requirements specification
- Interface requirements specification
- Software design document (preliminary design)
- Software test plan
- Preliminary interface design document
- Software design document (detailed design)
- Software test descriptions
- Interface design document (detailed design)
- Source code listings
- Software test descriptions (procedures)
- Software test reports
- Operation and support documents (there could be lots of these)
- Version description document
- Software product specification

That's a lot of documents! And, depending on whether they are Greek or Roman, programmers find different documents important. The Romans want the planning and status-reporting documents, and the Greeks are more interested in programmer and end-user documentation. The overly Romans we described earlier in the book want *everything* documented. The above lists are just a starting point for them. Conversely, the overly Greeks are anti-documentation. It is difficult to get them to keep historical records of anything, much less produce the design documents that help the technical writers create user documentation.

We asked a large, diverse group of software engineers what they considered to be the most effective and common forms of documentation to produce. Their response was almost unanimous: commented code and user's guides. All the other types of documents fell far behind, such as project schedules, specifications, design documents, etc. Therefore, in this chapter, we will focus on comments in code and user's guides.

Documentation in Code

Comments in the code usually describe what is actually going on inside the program. Generally, documentation inside code involves noting what decisions were made about the code in the context within which they were made. This type of commenting is very important not only to tell *that you chose* to do one thing over another, but *why you chose* to do it the way you did. Often, comments involve explaining exceptions to what would normally be expected for common computations.

Commentary throughout a module does not seem to be as effective as commentary at the top of a module because it interferes with scanning the code and breaks the programmer's concentration. Besides, programmers have little trouble understanding each line of code; what they are interested in is how all the lines work together toward the goal of the module. There are exceptions to this: for example, when you are calling another module, sometimes it is useful to explain why it is time to call another module. Sometimes when you call the error-handling routines, it is useful to explain what the error was and why you are calling the routine. This is particularly useful for large programs with many modules, or for programs that have evolved over a long period of time. In this way, the history and logic behind the software can be maintained even after program personnel have changed. And, documentation people can use the comments in the code to help them in creating user's guides. Some of the best programmers' code is so well commented that it is self-documenting.

The documentation inside a program is composed of preambles to modules, comments associated with the code where necessary, and layout features. Preambles to modules are blocks of comments explaining the data the module expects to get, the data the module expects to deliver, error conditions and what the software will do with them, a description of the processing to be accomplished in the module, and small blocks of commentary for each enhancement. Other material that programmers frequently put into a preamble are a list of modules that *call* the current module and another list of modules that are *called by* the current module.

In the body of the code, the comments associated with lines of code involve explaining variations in accepted procedures, calls to other routines, etc., and white space (space between lines at appropriate spaces and appropriate indentation levels to aid in legibility).

These comments must be legible (readable) and should follow some typographic conventions for the programmer to use them effectively. One of our correspondents offered us some tips for improving code readability:[15]

- In C and Lisp programs, use boldface type for comments using the filters CBOLD (in C programs) and LBOLD (in Lisp programs).

- Use comments as titles for the major sections of a C source file. These are:

  - Include Files
  - Constants
  - Types
  - External Variables
  - Variables
  - Macros
  - External Functions
  - Functions (this implies that you group all `#include` directives together, all external-variable declarations together, and so on)

- Use comments as titles for subsections, such as groups of related constants, types, or variables.

- Use comments as titles for important individual items, such as structure types, and for all function definitions.

- Use comments as headlines for significant or difficult-to-follow sections of code within a function, indenting the headline comment according to the nesting level of the following statement. Leave a blank

---

[15] These tips and the code sample given in Figure 7-1 were provided courtesy of Daniel N. Ozick. He also has written a very useful article entitled "How to Make Program Printouts Easier to Read." For information on how to obtain a copy of this article, you can contact him at: 1 Jackie Court, Chester, NY, 10918.

line after a headlined code section and after significant un-headlined sections as well.

- Use the two-column, line-by-line style of commenting only to document simple constants, variables, and the members of structures.

- Use three blank lines to delimit coherent sections of the source file.

"The visual appearance of a printed program affects its readability, which in turn affects how easy it is to develop, debug, maintain, and improve. You can use layout and typography to provide visual cues that help reveal the underlying structure of a program and make it easier to read. In particular, by using comments as titles and headlines, and by printing them in boldface, you can provide effective visual markers that help you navigate through the printout of a complex program." [Ozick 1990] Figure 7-1 is an example of Mr. Ozick's style of commenting.

In addition to the comments inside the code, there is often material outside the code, which is closely associated with the program: a context diagram, a call tree diagram, and descriptions of data structures. A *context diagram* describes the way a program interacts with the external inputs and outputs of the program. A context diagram might have one or two levels of subordinate decomposition in diagrams. They begin the process of illustrating the eventual decomposition of the program. The externals to the context diagram are: files of various types (disk, tape, card, and files entered by human beings) and interactions with the machine itself (such as instructions to an NC drilling machine).

```
/* apply — apply a ("pure" Object) FUNCTION to a list of args
(max of 8) */
Object apply (Object f, Object args)

 {
  return ((*function (f)) (nth (args, 0), nth (args, 1),
                          nth (args, 2), nth (args, 3),
                          nth (args, 4), nth (args, 5),
                          nth (args, 6), nth (args, 7) ));
 }



/* eval — evaluate a Lisp-syntax expression (see notes above) */
Object eval (Object expr)

 {
  Object first_element, f;

  /* () is self-evaluating */
  if (is_null (expr))
   return (expr);

  /* symbol ==> symbol's value, other atoms are self-evaluating */
  else if (is_atom (expr))
   {
    if (is_symbol (expr))
     return (symbol_value (expr));
    else
     return (expr);
   }

  /* lists are function applications or quoted expressions */
  else if (is_pair (expr))
   {
    first_element = first (expr);

    if (first_element == quote)
     return (first (but_first (expr)));

    if (is_symbol (first_element))
     f = symbol_value (first_element);
    else
     error ("eval: first element of list is not a symbol");
```

Figure 7-1. Example Code Listing

```
      if (is_function (f))
        return (apply (f, map (eval, but_first (expr)))));
      else
        error ("eval: symbol value is not a function");
    }
  }



/* main (REPL) — interactive read-eval-print loop (Tiny Lisp Inter-
preter) */
int main (int argc, char *argv[])

  {
  printf ("A Tiny Lisp Interpreter using the Lisp-Style Library for C
\n");
  printf ("Copyright (C) 1991 by Daniel N. Ozick \n\n");


  /* initialize internal symbol tables and read-tables */

  mark_persistent ();

  install_internal_symbols ();
  init_internal_read_table ();
  set_internal_reader ();
  install_function_symbols ();

  quote = intern ("quote");

  unmark_persistent ();

  /* do read-eval-print loop until user interrupt */
  while (TRUE)
    {
    mark ();
    printf ("\n> ");
    write_object (eval (read_object ()));
    free_to_mark ();
    }

  /* return "no errors" */
  return (0);
  }
```

Figure 7-1. Example Code Listing (cont.)

Figure 7-2 shows a somewhat idealized context diagram. Usually, there is more information such as more explanation of the sources of data in and sinks of data out. Also, there are frequently more realistic figures, such as a warehouse in place of, say, Data2, to show where the information is coming from. There are a number of ways of pictorially presenting this context, and this is only one.

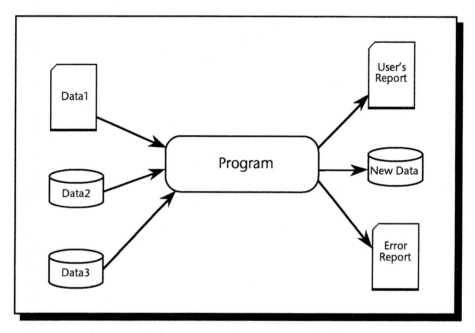

Figure 7-2. A Context Diagram

There is another type of document called a *call tree diagram* or *structure chart*. It shows the complete decomposition of the program, but it does not show the externals. It shows which module calls which module. (Context diagrams and call tree diagrams usually go in the maintainer's manual.)

Figure 7-3 shows an idealized call tree diagram. (The routines labeled *Ln* represent the routines "called" from a library.) The order of execution is roughly from the left to right and top-down (library routine *L4* will normally execute before, say, routine *BB*). There is very little other information concerning the actual operation of the program itself; there are no conditional executions; for example, library routine *L32* might execute only under unusual circumstances, while routine *BB* might unconditionally execute whenever routine *B* is called. The call tree tells you which routines are called by which other routines. If routine *L4* changes, it affects both *AA* and *BB*. In addition, if you are working in routine *CA*, you know it is "called" by routine C and "calls" library routines *L15, L12, L1,* and *L9.*

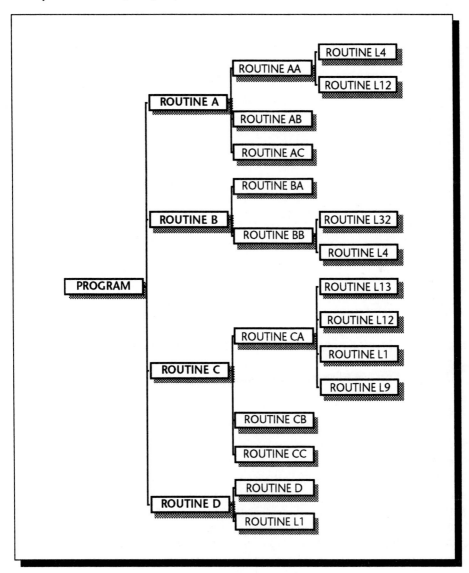

Figure 7-3. An Idealized Call Tree Diagram

Another type of documentation is a description of the data structures that exist in the external files and in the internal routines of the program. This description would be in the maintainer's manual, in the data dictionary (if there is one), and in the routines where the data is used along with descriptions of global data, local data, and parameters.

User's Guides

User's guides tell the users of the software how to operate it. They usually start with a seed document, often written by programmers and from a programmer's perspective. That perspective is not necessarily useful for the end user. The programmer knows how the program works from the inside out. What the user needs is a view of how the program works from the outside in. It's important to start the user's guide early to keep the development on track because it acts as a surrogate for user requirements.

Creating good user documentation is a very Greek activity that engages the creative side of the brain. However, to do it well requires a number of Roman tools. In this section, we will make some specific recommendations on how to create good user's guides. Some of these recommendations address *form* and others deal with *content*.

The reason we are including this discussion here is because many of us do not have a team of documentation specialists available to help us with our manuals. Some of us work in small code shops or are self-employed. Often, we must create the user's guide and other necessary project documentation ourselves.

If you end up producing user documentation, we hope you will find this information useful.

Templates and Standards

Just as there are CASE tools available to help with the code portion of the product, there are many documentation aids available to help with the project documentation including templates, standards, and style guides. An example of a document template is the DOD 2167 Data Item Description (DID) template set. We've included an example of the CRISD (Computer Resources Integrated Support Document) DID in Appendix D. The CRISD describes all the resources required to support the software being delivered by the project.

It describes the required support software, hardware, facilities, personnel, and many other resources. System planners use this document to deploy, integrate, and operate the software to be delivered.

Templates will help to ensure that you have included at least the minimum amount of information the user needs. There are many different standards available from a number of sources and organizations: in particular, you might find the IEEE documentation standards useful. We've listed some standards in more detail later in this chapter.

You can also get a great deal of help from *style guides*, which offer style guidelines and conventions for producing different types of documents. All style guides offer similar help on diverse topics, but the "flavor" of the help varies from guide to guide. All of the flavors have been tested and found widely acceptable through common usage. However, individual preferences dictate which flavor *you* choose. We prefer the *United States Government Printing Office (GPO) Style Manual* for government projects, and the *Chicago Manual of Style* for commercial projects.

In general, style guides offer specific help on approved terms and terms to avoid; rules of capitalization, punctuation, spelling, and compounding; rules for abbreviations; lists of the required elements for different types of documents; how to set up bibliographies and cite references; guidelines for indexing; and much more. There is an electronic style guide that is available on both the DOS and Mac platforms called the *American English Writing Guide*. It offers some very comprehensive help and would make a reasonable substitute for a traditional printed style guide.[16]

A Document Quality Model

The basic requirement of a document is to tell you what you want to know when you want to know it. How do you know, though, if the document you created is of good quality? There are some scientific indicators that you can apply to a document to determine its quality.

There was a case study that determined how to assess the adequacy of project documentation through document quality indicators. The study was the result of a research effort funded by the Naval Surface Warfare Systems at Dahlgren, Virginia. The results of the study were reported in the proceedings

---

[16] One of the authors of this book uses the Mac version, which is HyperCard based. We haven't tried the DOS version. The *American English Writing Guide*, is from Nova Development Corporation, 23801 Calabasas Road, Suite 2005, Calabasas, CA, 91302.

from the IEEE Conference on Software Maintenance. We've reproduced the results in their entirety in Appendix E. (For convenience, from this point we refer to that study as the *IEEE report.*)

The authors of the IEEE report state that the qualities of good documentation are *accuracy, completeness, usability,* and *expandability.* The report addresses each of these qualities in detail. The results of the report are summarized in Figure 7-4. Although the entire report offers some useful insight and is worthwhile reading, it does *not* address aesthetics issues nor does it offer specific recommendations on how to achieve those four qualities. Therefore, we will do so in the section entitled *The Elements of Adequate Documentation.*

It is noteworthy, however, that when we ran a random sample from the IEEE report through a grammar-checking program, it didn't score very well on readability and vocabulary.[17] It was written at a graduate school level (grade 17), which means that its vocabulary would probably be too advanced for most of us to read comfortably. It's not that we are incapable of reading at this level, it's just not very fun to do so. *This* book is written at only a tenth-grade level, and it's not exactly light reading.

We believe that *readability* is one of the most important aspects of a document's *usability,* and this is one area they did not adequately cover in the report. (In fact, in light of our analysis, we feel that the authors of the IEEE report failed dismally in the area of readability.) Therefore, we will be offering some specific recommendations here on improving readability.

---

[17] Correct Grammar by Lifetree Software, Inc.

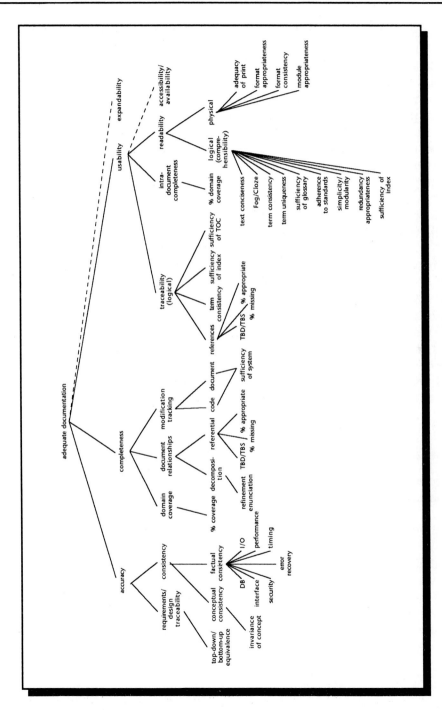

Figure 7-4. The General Evaluation Taxonomy Tree

The Elements of Adequate Documentation

The first question to ask yourself when you are beginning a user's guide project is: "Who is the audience and what is their level of expertise with the software." You should always write to the lowest common denominator. By that we mean if the average user has moderate experience with the software but some of the users are beginners, then you should write the guide for the beginners. The best thing you can do for your readers—regardless of their level of experience with the software—is to use plain English and make the document "good."

Use Plain English

It's important to use plain English regardless of the type of documents you are producing, and regardless of whether it is written for other programmers or end-users. Even though programmers are perfectly capable of understanding extremely technical material, why should we have to struggle through 45-word sentences in our test reports? Is the typical end user (who is resistant to reading manuals anyway) likely to bother to read something that's loaded with techno-babble? Our goal should be to write material that cannot be misinterpreted by anyone. This is especially critical when dealing with technical data that describes procedures that could cause software or systems to crash.

Here is an example of what we're talking about:

> *"It is equally important that there be no seasonal changes in the procedures, as, although aircraft fuel system icing due to water contamination is more often met with in winter, it can be equally dangerous during the summer months."* [Stahl 1992]

What exactly did this say? How many times did you struggle through it before you were able to get the writer's point? Or, did you just give up on it? When this information is translated and presented in plain English, it becomes the following:

> *"Use the same procedure all the time. Water in the fuel system can freeze during both Summer and Winter."*

234

When you use plain English, you use clear, simple, and familiar words in a conversational tone using active voice verbs (whenever possible). If you use a passive voice, it sometimes becomes fuzzy who is the subject and who is the object of the action that is going on. Consider the following example:

"The use of this equipment is not encouraged."

Whoa! First of all, who's using the equipment? Does this mean it is not recommended for anyone, or for anyone without proper gear, or for inexperienced people, or what? And, this use is not encouraged by whom? (Who's in charge here and who's responsible?) What will happen if it *is* used? Does this mean it's dangerous? What's going on here?

You can see why you should avoid this type of ambiguity.

Then, there are the issues of *jargon* and *acronyms*. There is an entire vocabulary inside the computer industry that is rarely understood by people outside the computer industry (interface, database, gigabytes, paradigm, etc.). If the documentation might be used by people with limited computer experience, then try to reduce your use of jargon.

Also, try to reduce the number of acronyms, wherever possible. When you can't avoid acronyms, be sure to completely spell out each one before you use it the first time. The computer industry's vocabulary is filled with acronyms formed from computer-related terms, such as *CD-ROM* (compact disk, read-only memory).

The purpose of words, whether written or spoken, is to communicate ideas. Although *you* might understand the term or be familiar with the acronym, you cannot assume that the user will. So, every time you introduce a new acronym, you should clearly spell out what it means. Any time you introduce a term that could possibly be new to the user, display it in italics to show that it is unique and then define it. It is also helpful to include all unique terms and acronyms in a glossary.

Then, there is the problem of wordiness. There are many expressions that are long and needlessly complex. They "puff up" the material, making it more formal and complex than is really necessary. These expressions are commonly used in business writing. Besides being wordy, some are redundant and trite. Terms like these do not make the writer seem more intelligent. Instead, they make the writer seem stuffy, formal, or pretentious.

Table 7-1 is a list of commonly used verbose terms and their plainer forms. However, exercise personal taste and judgement in using the alternate forms; use the suggested word or phrase only if it truly expresses your intended meaning.

Table 7-1. Verbose and Stuffy Expressions	
Instead of this	**Say this**
accordingly	therefore, so
advance planning	planning (besides, this is redundant)
aforementioned	these, those, previous
am going to	shall, will
am of the opinion	believe
as a result of	because
assistance	aid, help
at the present time	now
by means of	by
consequently	so
correspondence	letter, memo, note
due to the fact that	since, because, due to
during the time that	while
facilitate	help, ease
foregoing	this, these
inasmuch as	because, since
in connection with	with
indicate	show
in lieu of	instead
in order to	to
in regard to (in reference to)	about, regarding
insofar as	because, since, as
in the event that	if
in the near future	soon
in view of the fact that	since, because
I would appreciate it if	please
prior to	before
provided that	if
terminate	end
transmit	send
utilize	use
whether or not	whether
with regard to	about
with the exception of	except

You get the general idea. Keep it plain and keep it simple.

Finally, there is the matter of clichés. Avoid them "like the plague." They add nothing to your writing and they're boring. Table 7-2 lists some particular irksome clichés and trite expressions that sometimes appear in technical writing. (We couldn't resist commenting on some of the worst of them.)

Table 7-2. Trite Expressions

all in all
all things being equal (*What is the purpose of this saying, anyway?*)
at one fell swoop
avoid like the plague
best foot forward
better late than never (*Not in polite company, it isn't!*)
bottom line
clear as mud
conspicuous by its absence
draw the line at
each and every
easier said than done
few and far between
first and foremost
foreseeable future
hale and hearty
have a nice day (*No thank you. I have other plans.*)
if the truth be told
it goes without saying (*Then why say it?*)
it stands to reason
last but not least
moot point
more easily said than done
necessary evil
needs no introduction (*Then don't bother.*)
plain vanilla (*Not very nice considering that vanilla is a distinct flavor —
    therefore not plain—and is even* **preferred** *by some people.*)
rack your brains
suite of tools (*Suites refer to bedroom furniture and musical compositions,
    not tools or applications.*)
try it, you'll like it (*Maybe ... maybe not.*)
you know

There are many good books available on how to use plain English and good grammar. A few of our favorites are:

- Joseph, A. *Put It In Writing.* Fourth Edition, International Writing Institute, Inc., 1989.

- Shaw, H. *Dictionary of Problem Words and Expressions.* Revised Edition, McGraw-Hill Book Company, 1987.

- Johnson, E.D. *The Handbook of Good English.* Facts on File Publications, 1982.

- *The Written Word II.* Based on The American Heritage Dictionary, Houghton Mifflin Company, 1983.

Make the Document "Good"

There are some specific characteristics of good user's documents. If you are responsible for producing end-user documentation, following this list will help make them good. This is a somewhat Roman list that you can adapt for your documents and consider for other types of documents.

- Include a thorough, detailed table of contents.

- Provide a map through the document.

- Enhance readability. This can be aided by the design of the document, including a generous use of white space, proper font selection, running headers (which serve as navigational aids), and folio numbering (page numbering by section).

- Use plain English (which we've already discussed).

- Avoid clichés "like the plague" (which we've already discussed).

- Include a good glossary.

- Use footnotes where needed for clarity.

- Use graphics generously.

- Use a good grammar checker, which includes an analysis of "fog factors."

- Include a detailed bibliography.

- Offer a well written, thorough index.

- Use a project style guide and follow standards.

You can map these characteristics to the qualities of good documentation given in the IEEE report (*accuracy, completeness, usability,* and *expandability*), as follows:[18]

- *Accuracy*

  - *Provide a map through the document*—This ensures that all of the topics that need to be covered *are* covered.

  - *Use a good grammar checker*—A grammar-checking program not only helps identify grammatical problems, it also catches spelling errors and problems with punctuation capitalization, and doubled words.

  - *Use a project style guide and follow standards*—Many standards have already been established.

- *Completeness*

  - *Include a thorough, detailed table of contents*—This helps to ensure that all of the topics that need to be covered *are* covered. A thorough table of contents also provides a simple map through the document and, therefore, helps to eliminate redundancy.

  - *Include a detailed bibliography*—This will also help the reader keep track of references.

---

[18] Each of these qualities and their matching characteristics are described in detail in the paragraphs immediately following this list.

- *Offer a well written, thorough index*—Absolutely necessary for a complete document.

- *Usability*

  - *Enhance readability* (with all this implies).

  - *Use plain English with active voice verbs.*

  - *Avoid clichés.*

  - *Include a good glossary.*

  - *Use footnotes.*

  - *Use graphics.*

  - *Offer a well written, thorough index.*

- *Expandability*

  - *Enhance readability*—By using folio numbering, you can easily add chapters without having to reproduce the entire document.

Each of these qualities and their matching characteristics are completely described in the following paragraphs (with the exception of "use plain English" and "avoid clichés," which we discussed in the previous section).

Accuracy

Besides the issues discussed in the IEEE report, there are some other things you can do to help improve the *accuracy* of a document:

- Provide a map through the document.

- Use a good grammar checker.

- Use a project style guide and follow standards.

Provide a Map Through the Document

A good way to keep the more experienced users from becoming bored is to write a "getting started" or tutorial for the beginners, and a "quick start" for the experienced users. The more experienced users would skip the getting started/ tutorial and jump to the more advanced sections. At some point, the separate paths through the document would meet and merge. In such cases, a "map" through the document is particularly helpful.

A document map could be a graphic, like a tree chart, showing the key branches (chapters) of the document highlighted. It could be a graphical table of contents, with the branches for beginning users highlighted.

A document map could also be a text description. It should include recommendations about which chapters each type of user should read: for example, you might say, "Everyone should read the Preface, Introduction, and Chapter One. If you already know how to use MS-DOS, you can skip Chapters Two and Three and continue with Chapter 4. If you are a beginning user, please be sure to read Chapters Two and Three."

If both beginning and experienced users would use the document the same way, the document map can be basically a table of contents with amplified descriptions of what is in each chapter.

In any case, user's guides should always include a brief outline in the preface or introduction describing the layout of the manual. For example, Figure 7-5 is the document map from the *FastTask™ User's Guide*. FastTask is a CASE tool from Iconix Software Engineering, Inc. that performs real-time structured analysis.

Use a Good Grammar Checker

A good grammar-checking program is a valuable documentation tool. Grammar-checking software can help you identify passive voice, spelling errors, punctuation errors, missed capitals after periods, doubled words, and other common errors. The better grammar checkers employ artificial intelligence to help identify problem areas.

For example, you should always spell check your documents, but you should never, *ever* rely on your spelling checker to proofread your documents. That's because a spelling checker can only catch blatant typographical errors (like *automtic* instead of *automatic*), but cannot catch errors where a word is *spelled* correctly but *used* incorrectly. Some good candidates for this type of error are: *form* and *from*, *statue* and *statute*, *an* and *and*.

- Chapter 1, *Introducing FastTask,* briefly describes FastTask and its relationship to the other tools in the Iconix PowerTools tool set.

- Chapter 2, *Real-Time System Development,* provides an overview of state transition analysis.

The following chapters provide detailed information about using FastTask:

- Chapter 3, *Using FastTask's Menus,* gives an overview of the program's main parts: the main menu functions, their associated pull-down menus, and how to start and stop the program.

- Chapter 4, *Using the Diagram Editor,* describes how to use the diagram editor to create state transition diagrams.

- Chapter 5, *Using the Dictionary,* describes how to add, edit, delete, and report on dictionary entries associated with the symbols on the diagrams and how to generate dictionary reports.

- Chapter 6, *Using the Language-Sensitive Editor,* describes how to edit the text files associated with the symbols on the diagrams and how to create data definitions for database management systems or conventional programming languages.

- Chapter 7, *Opening, Closing, and Saving Files,* describes how to open, close, and save FastTask files.

- Chapter 8, *Printing Files,* describes the printing functions available in FastTask.

- Chapter 9, *Networking and Multi-User Versions,* describes how to use FastTask in a networked, multi-user environment with a file server.

A *Glossary* and *Index* are located at the back of this guide.

Figure 7-5. Example Document Map

These are all real words and are correctly spelled, but if you meant one and used another it would look pretty stupid. That's where a good grammar checker comes in. Good ones employ artificial intelligence to help root out this type of error. Some checkers are better at this task than others, but every checker has its own strengths and weaknesses. It is important to evaluate the strengths of each product and then determine which is the most appropriate for the types of errors you make most often.

Our two favorite grammar checkers for the Mac are *Gram•mat•ik™ Mac* by Reference Software International and *Correct Grammar* by Lifetree Software, Inc. For the PC, we like the DOS version of *Gram•mat•ik™* and *RightWriter* by Que Software.

One of the authors of this book makes two common writing errors: using passive voice constructions (all of these products accurately identify this problem) and making typos that cause real words to be used incorrectly (like *form* instead of *from*). One thing to keep in mind, though, is that although most grammar checkers will point out passive voice constructions, they won't offer alternative wording suggestions *in context*. Instead, they will just point out that it is passive, and will give an *example* of passive vs. active voice. However, after you've corrected a few of these errors, you'll easily become proficient at spotting and correcting them.

After using a spelling checker and a good grammar checker, you should still carefully proofread your documents. There will still be instances of missed or erroneous punctuation, layout problems, missing articles (a, an, the), weird or inappropriate words (sometimes left when you delete a blob of text), and other errors that you'll only spot by actually carefully rereading the material.

There is another factor you need to consider, called the *Fog Index* or *Readability Index*. The Fog Index was developed by Robert Gunning. In many studies, it has proven to be very reliable in evaluating readability [Ready 1991]. Most grammar checkers will automatically calculate the Fog Index for you and will display a Fog Index numerical value.[19] However, some of the grammar checkers don't tell you what that numerical value actually means so we'll tell you here.

The numerical values of the Fog Index correspond closely to levels of reading difficulty by school grade. Table 7-3 shows the Fog Index equated to grade levels. The table also shows the Fog Index for some popular magazines

---

[19] If you are interested in seeing the formulae for determining the Fog Index and the other readability scores described in this section, just drop us a line and we'll be happy to send them to you.

to give you an idea of the level of effort required to read at that grade level. The data for the table was taken by Gunning and his staff from hundreds of samples. Table 7-4 shows the results of an analysis of a one-paragraph example from each of five other periodicals.

Gunning also carried out a nationwide survey of scientists, engineers, and technical management people in twenty prominent research, development, and manufacturing organizations throughout the country. The panel members ranked the examples on a scale of *very poor, poor, fair, good,* and *very good.* Those in the *good* range had Fog Index levels close to 15. This is the average level of Scientific American. Examples that had a Fog Index with levels much above 15 were rated by the panel as *fair* to *very poor.* Those below 15 were rated *good* to *very good.*

Some grammar checkers use other readability indexes than the Gunning Fog Index. Figure 7-6 shows an example analysis from Gram•mat•ik™ Mac. (By the way, this analysis is also of a sample from the IEEE document quality study.)

Table 7-3. The Fog Index and Reading Levels of Popular Periodicals

Fog Index	By Grade	By Periodical	Range
17	College graduate		Area of technical and
16	College senior		professional journals.
15	College junior		No popular magazine is this difficult.
14	College sophomore		Good
13	College freshman		
12	H.S. senior	Atlantic Monthly	"Class"
11	H.S. junior	Harper's Magazines	
10	H.S. sophomore		Time
9	H.S. freshman	Reader's Digest	Easy (very good)
8	Eighth grade	Ladies' Home Journal	
7	Seventh grade	True Confessions	
6	Sixth grade	Comic books	

Fog Index	By Grade	By Periodical	Range
		Table 7-4. The Fog Index and Reading Levels of Five Other Periodicals	
28	Genius	Physiological Zoology	Difficult to the point of pain (very poor)
25	Ph.D.	Biological Bulletin	
24	M.S.	Science	Extremely difficult (very poor)
14	College sophomore	Scientific American	Good
13	College freshman	Saturday Evening Post	

The Flesch-Kincaid rating determines the grade level required to comfortably read the material. The most effective reading range is between sixth and tenth grade. Higher grade scores mean that most readers will find the writing difficult to understand.

The Flesch Reading Ease score is on a scale of 0-100. The lower the score, the more difficult the writing is to read. The ideal range here is between 60 (fairly difficult) and 70 (fairly easy).

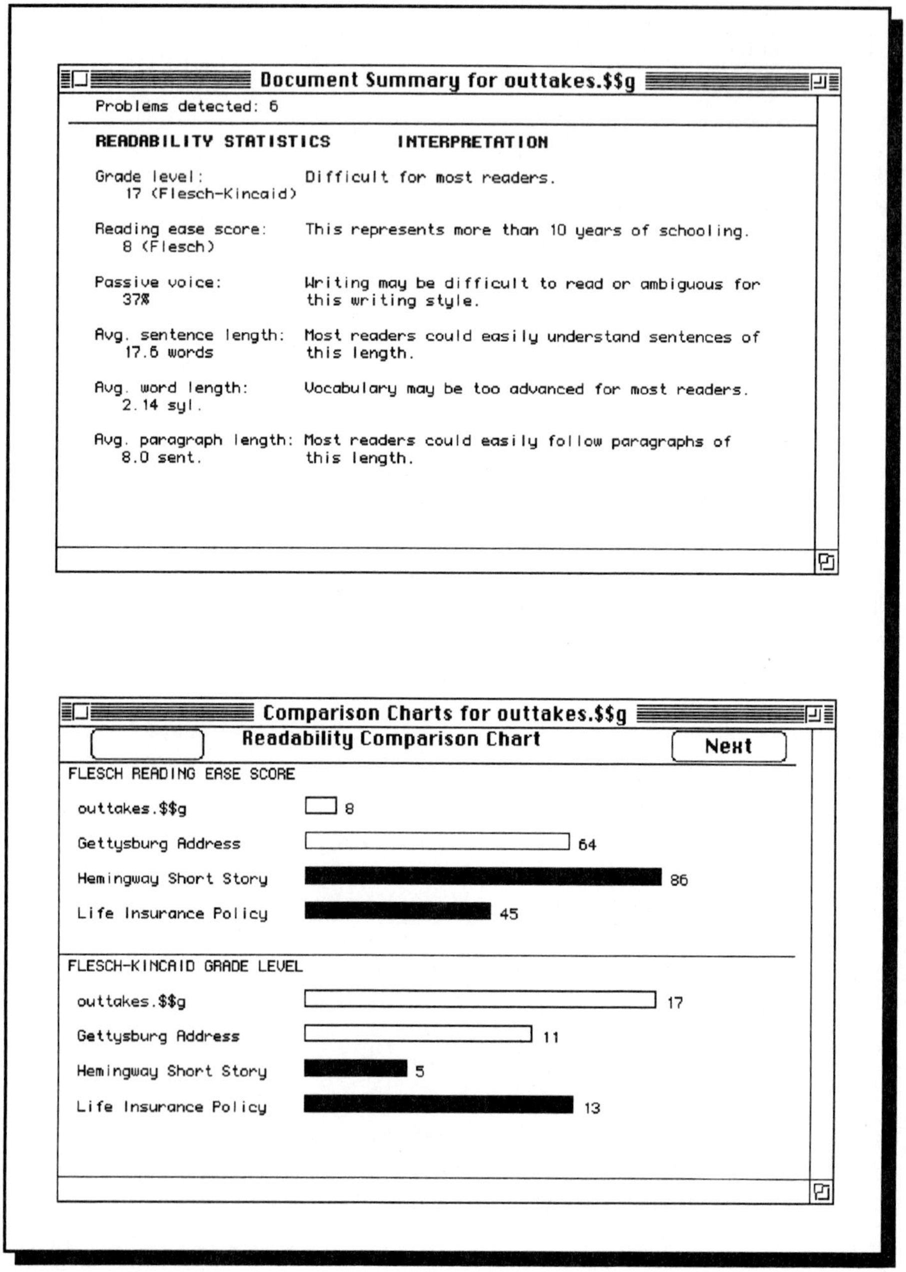

```
▤▯▤▤▤▤▤▤▤▤▤ Document Summary for outtakes.$$g ▤▤▤▤▤▤ ▣▯
  Problems detected: 6

  READABILITY STATISTICS        INTERPRETATION

  Grade level:          Difficult for most readers.
    17 (Flesch-Kincaid)

  Reading ease score:   This represents more than 10 years of schooling.
    8 (Flesch)

  Passive voice:        Writing may be difficult to read or ambiguous for
    37%                 this writing style.

  Avg. sentence length: Most readers could easily understand sentences of
    17.6 words          this length.

  Avg. word length:     Vocabulary may be too advanced for most readers.
    2.14 syl.

  Avg. paragraph length: Most readers could easily follow paragraphs of
    8.0 sent.            this length.
```

```
▤▯▤▤▤▤▤▤▤▤ Comparison Charts for outtakes.$$g ▤▤▤▤▤ ▣▯
  ┌──────────┐      Readability Comparison Chart      ┌──────────┐
  └──────────┘                                        │   Next   │
  FLESCH READING EASE SCORE                           └──────────┘

  outtakes.$$g          ▭ 8

  Gettysburg Address    ▭▭▭▭▭▭▭ 64

  Hemingway Short Story ▬▬▬▬▬▬▬▬ 86

  Life Insurance Policy ▬▬▬▬▬ 45

  FLESCH-KINCAID GRADE LEVEL

  outtakes.$$g          ▭▭▭▭▭▭▭▭ 17

  Gettysburg Address    ▭▭▭▭▭▭ 11

  Hemingway Short Story ▬▬▬ 5

  Life Insurance Policy ▬▬▬▬▬▬ 13
```

Figure 7-6. Grammar Analysis from Gram•mat•ik Mac

Use a Project Style Guide and Follow Standards

Using a project style guide and following standards are important components of the *accuracy* quality described in the IEEE report.

Besides the commercial style guides, like the *GPO (Government Printing Office) Style Manual* and the *Chicago Manual of Style* mentioned earlier, you should also have a *project* style guide. Many different people throughout an organization can contribute to a user's guide or documentation project. By using a project style guide, you can ensure the overall consistency and cohesiveness of the document.

A project style guide should contain key information about all of the components of the user's guide. This could include details of the document's design, words or phrases that are unique to the project that might be hard to remember, and all of the acronyms used in the manual completely spelled out. The style guide can (and should) also include any problem words or expressions that are common in your environment.

We've included an example of a project style guide in Appendix F. The page layout details are from a hypothetical project. The list of problem words is extracted from the actual style guide that one of the authors of this book created to use for our own projects.

You might also find it useful to use checklists when producing documentation. With a checklist, you can make different passes through the document checking that certain things have been done. For example, you might want to change any occurrences of the word *execute* to *invoke*. You might want to check that all of your chapters start two carriage returns below their headings. You might want to make sure all of your periods are followed by only one space instead of two. You would enter all these items onto the checklist and then review the checklist for each chapter. An example of a project checklist is also shown in Appendix F.

In addition to using a project style guide, you probably will want to follow some type of documentation *standards*. Your company might have its own documentation standards. If not, many standards for documentation have been established that you might find useful:

- *American National Standard for Guidelines for the Documentation of Digital Computer Programs,* American National Standards Institute. ANSI-N413-1974, American Nuclear Society, 1974.

- *Guidelines for the Documentation of Software in Industrial Computer Systems,* The Institute of Electrical Engineers, 1985.

- Poschmann, A.W., *Standards and Procedures for Systems Documentation,* American Management Association, 1984.

Completeness

Besides the issues discussed in the IEEE report, there are some other things you can do to help improve the *completeness* quality of a document:

- Include a thorough, detailed table of contents.

- Provide a map through the document.

- Include a detailed bibliography.

- Offer a well written, thorough index.

Include a Thorough, Detailed Table of Contents

A thorough table of contents is the foundation for the entire document. The table of contents should be detailed enough to serve as a supplement to the index, aiding users in quickly and efficiently finding the material they need. A thorough table of contents also provides a general map through the document.

The example table of contents shown in Figure 7-7 is an excerpt from the user's guide for FastTask™, a real-time structured analysis tool from Iconix Software Engineering, Inc.

CONTENTS

Figure 7-7. An Example Table of Contents

Figure 7-7. An Example Table of Contents (cont.)

Always be sure to include a list of figures and tables in your table of contents.

Provide a Map Through the Document

See the earlier discussion under the *Accuracy* heading.

Include a Detailed Bibliography

A bibliography can include more than simply material that was cited in the body of your text. It can also include other source material that you found useful. It offers the reader a handy place to go to review references.

Offer a Well Written, Thorough Index

An index is required for the document to be considered complete. Besides, it can determine the *usability* of the entire document. The reader *must* have a good index available to help locate key concepts. The index also serves as a supplemental map through the document.

A good index is absolutely crucial to the success of a user's guide. If you can, hire the best *technical* writer you can to create your index. This is a highly specialized skill and even many experienced general writers do a bad job of it. The writer you assign to this task must have the technical expertise to understand the meanings of the terms in the document, particularly in knowing when to group similar concepts.

If you *must* create your own index, keep these two points in mind:

- Use adequate cross referencing. For example, individually list each command name, but also have an entry entitled *Commands* with each command separately listed under it.

- Include enough entries to help the user find the key points (yet without indexing *every* occurrence of a word).

Usability

Besides the issues discussed in the IEEE report, there are some other things you can do to help improve the *usability* of a document:

- Enhance readability.

- Use plain English with active voice verbs.

- Avoid clichés.

- Include a good glossary.

- Use footnotes.

- Use graphics.

- Offer a well written, thorough index (described in the previous section).

Enhance Readability

Readability is one of the keys to a document's *usability*. The readability is greatly enhanced by the document's design. There are a lot of issues here including the generous use of white space, proper font selection, running headers (which serve as navigational aids), and folio numbering.

White space—In a user's guide, white space is generally the amount of space allowed for the margins of the page and between sections. The greater the amount of white space, the more "rich" the document will look and the more legible the document will be (just as white space aids the legibility of comments in code). In general, you should have no less than one-inch margins all the way around an 8.5x11" page. If the document will be printed two-sided, include a more generous margin along the inside edge for binding. If you think the user will want room for notes, you can use an extra wide outer margin or leave a blank half page at the end of each chapter for notes.

Proper font selection—Selecting the appropriate typeface for a document is an arcane matter that is extremely important to documentation people, but might not appear to be important to the programmer who is responsible for writing end-user documentation. If you can't ship this responsibility off to a technical writer, graphic artist, or typesetter and you get stuck doing it yourself, we have a few hints. This is a very Roman discussion so, if you don't need to get involved with user documentation, you can skip this discussion entirely (unless you're interested in this kind of stuff.)

You might be thinking, "So what's the big deal? How can picking a typeface be hard? You've got lots to choose from!"

Well, that's the point, actually. Which, of all the fonts on your machine, should you choose for your user's guides?

For example, here are the three most common typefaces:

> Times
> Helvetica
> `Courier`

You could use any of the three to create a user's guide, but there are reasons why you might not want to use two of them—the Helvetica and the Courier—for the text.

Times is a nice, legible typeface that has "serifs" at the ends of the strokes of the letters. These serifs help lead the eye from one letter to the next. They help improve the readability of the text. This is a good "body" typeface.

Although Helvetica is a nice, clean looking typeface and is highly legible, you probably shouldn't use it for long passages of text because there are no serifs to help lead the eye. The text will be legible, but your eyes will tire more easily.

Courier has serifs, but it is what's called a "monospaced" typeface. That is, each character occupies the same width of space on a line. If you look through the text of this book, you'll notice that a letter like *l* is much narrower than say an *m*. Well, with a monospaced typeface, all the characters are the same width.

Why is this important? Monospaced typefaces resemble typewriter type or computer printout. It's a good typeface to use for showing code examples, but not really appropriate for user's guides that should look *typeset* not *typewritten*.

Then there are typefaces you shouldn't use for technical documentation at all. They are simply inappropriate, because they are hard to read, or too ornate, or special-purpose, such as 𝔐edusa, or *ZAPF Chancery*.[20]

The type of computer equipment you are using to create your documentation, and the typeface (font) selection you have available, will probably have a lot to do with your choices. It is generally considered good design practice to use a conservative, serif typeface for the body of the text (like Times or Palatino), and a bolder, sans serif typeface for the headings (like **Helvetica Bold** or **Franklin Gothic Bold**). The sans serif headings will contrast with the serif body text, making them stand out from the rest of the text.[21]

---

[20] ZAPF Chancery by Adobe Systems, Inc.; Medusa™ by Lorvad; Helvetica™, Times™, and Palatino™ by Linotype AG and/or its subsidiaries; ITC Franklin Gothic® by International Typeface Corporation.

[21] We have available a list of ten typeface and layout tips that you might find useful. If you are interested, please send us a stamped, self-addressed envelope and a note requesting them. Our address is given at the back of the book.

Running headers and folio numbering—*Running headers* and *folio numbering* help to enhance readability by serving as navigational aids. On a document that is printed two-sided, running headers will show the chapter name on the left-hand page and the current section's name on the right-hand page. Or, you can have the chapter's name at the bottom of the page and have the section and subsection names in the headers. However you decide to set up your headers, use them consistently throughout the document.

Folio numbering is page numbering by section. That is, each chapter's numbering begins over again at page one. The chapter's number is added as a prefix to the page number; for example, 6-1, 6-2, 6-3 or 11-1, 11-2, 11-3, etc. Folio numbering is also an important aspect of the quality of *expandability*. By having each section's pages individually numbered, you can more easily add material to the end of a section or add new sections to the end of a document. In this way, you only have to reprint the new pages and then insert them at the appropriate place.

Include a Good Glossary

The glossary is where you will define new or complex terms, and where you will spell out *every acronym that appears in your document,* no matter how common you think it might be. A good glossary can greatly enhance the user's understanding of your material.

Use Footnotes

Use footnotes throughout the document for references. Use footnotes to amplify material that appears in the text and to reference quoted material. Any material that is quoted and has a citation in a footnote should also appear in the bibliography.

Use Graphics

The better user's guides have one thing in common: the generous use of graphics.

- Use as many as you can.

- Try to use at least one figure, table, illustration, or example per page.

- Set them off from the basic text with a box or a change in typeface. Whatever method you use to set them off, use that method consistently throughout the document.

If you cannot come up with illustrations or examples, try breaking the words of the text into bulleted lists. This will add visual interest to the page. Long lists of "things" or "actions" are good candidates for bulleted lists. Graphics and text work well together because they engage both sides of the brain and make for very effective use of the reader's time.

Summary

Documentation is a sophisticated practice similar to programming in many ways, and yet is often misunderstood by programmers. Programmers provide a means for the machine to sense the solutions to problems. Documentation experts do the same thing for humans.

Often, the documentation that is complained about most is programmer-written documentation. This is partly because the documentation is then written from a programmer's perspective, rather than from the perspective of what is useful to an end user. And, unfortunately, programmer-written documentation is often unusable even by other programmers, much less end users. Many programmers are so accustomed to communicating with machines that they are unable to communicate directly with humans without the machine as an intermediary.

Writing for a human is vastly different from writing for a machine. Software engineering is a communication from the mind of a human being, through a machine, and back again to a human being. The activities associated with software engineering and the use of computers is a much more human tool than is a screwdriver, for example. What is really important is the connection of the minds.

It is when professional technical writers get involved early on in the project that award-winning documentation is produced [Deaton 1990; Dieli 1989; Slivinski 1988]. Just as a programmer needs to have an in-depth understanding of both programming and the application domain for which the software is being written (such as business or accounting), the documentation people need to have expertise in documentation *and* programming *and* the application domain for which the software was written.

While programmers might be capable of producing excellent documentation, most are human and can't do everything; their expertise *is* programming, after all, and their time is better spent in "doing" software. Just as writers are not usually expected to be expert programmers, neither should programmers be expected to be expert writers. That is not their particular area of expertise and there is no shame in not having that expertise. Both technical writing and programming are highly skilled areas of expertise in themselves.

If, however, the programmers *must* write their own documentation, there are some resources available to help them. The standards, templates, and style guides available provide the equivalent of a methodology for technical writers or those who must do technical writing as part of their jobs.

Implications for CASE

One of the key values of CASE, especially Upper CASE, is that it aids in documentation. The various diagrams produced, the information in the data dictionary, and the documents generated during a project can help customers, users, downstream developers, maintainers, and managers understand what is going on in the project and in the software being produced by the project.

Unfortunately, the people who actually are most concerned about useful documentation, such as comments in code and user's manuals, are quite often folks who have little say in setting priorities. Those who *have* the say are often those who care more about documentation of little or transient value. These are the overly-Romans. They like to measure documentation by the pound and not by its ability to communicate, and they use CASE to obtain the documentation they require.

Documentation and the Olduvai Imperative

Language is a tool and documentation is the written expression of language. Documentation itself is a tool. We have had language tools for thousand of years. Our tools have evolved from stone tablets to clay tablets, from papyrus scrolls to paper, from the typewriter to computers, and from the printing press to paperless electronic publishing. This is this historical context in which we work. Hopefully, the material presented in this chapter will also serve as a tool that you can adapt to your environment. ❧

PART III.
Pomp and Circumstance

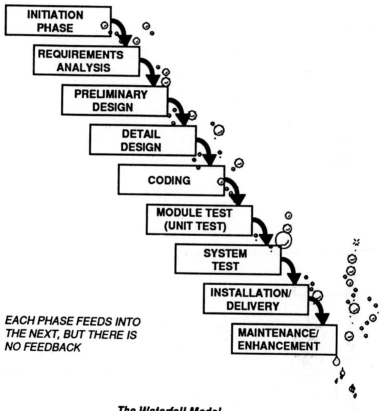

INITIATION PHASE

REQUIREMENTS ANALYSIS

PRELIMINARY DESIGN

DETAIL DESIGN

CODING

MODULE TEST (UNIT TEST)

SYSTEM TEST

INSTALLATION/ DELIVERY

MAINTENANCE/ ENHANCEMENT

EACH PHASE FEEDS INTO THE NEXT, BUT THERE IS NO FEEDBACK

The Waterfall Model

Chapter 8.
Deltas: The Differences and
the Differences they Make

In this chapter we will distinguish between software and hardware and, within software, between business systems and scientific programs. The former separates software from other commercial activities (what a Roman needs to know). The latter shows the extremes of the world of software (what a Greek needs to know).

Software vs. Hardware

Many observers of our field, especially Romans, often make analogies between software and hardware and between the processes that produce them. They relate software development to building a house, or making cameras, or any number of other kinds of hardware. But, these analogies break down quickly. Software is really quite different from hardware.

Troubles occur when the limits of these analogies aren't understood. One type of trouble is a burdensome software development "methodology" practiced in projects where software development is seen as a form of hardware development. Another type of trouble is when a tool is introduced into such an environment to support such an idea. Here are some of the differences between hardware and software that we've found.

Simplicity

Some hardware is complicated; a watch, for example, is extremely so. Some software is very simple; a routine to extract and display the time from the computer's clock is very simple. However, hardware is generally much simpler than software. Typically, a program has more unique parts and it functions in many more ways than hardware. That is one reason why hardware is computerized: so it can do many more things with much more data. The old accounting machines were replaced by computers for precisely that reason.

Anyone who has ever had to program the control panels of accounting machines knows this.

If you were to break down hardware, say a house or a VCR, into its constituent parts, you would find many parts repeated. This is necessary because these parts are needed all the time in the hardware. All the 2x4 studs in the house are needed all the time and are therefore repeated. In software, when something needs to be repeated (for example, a date function), it is simply referred to again. The computer program points to the function and it is fetched and re-executed. So, if you were to count all the parts of a house and all the parts of a program and come up with equal totals, there would be vastly more *unique* parts of the program than the house. The interrelations of all these parts is what makes up the complexity of software.

Entropy

Hardware wears out. It runs down, usually because of heat. It falls apart. This is known as *entropy*, and it doesn't happen to software. Although software "rides" on hardware, it is not subject to the wear problems of hardware and will never wear out. This distinction has some other interesting implications, which are discussed below.

Scope of Defects

The scope of a particular defect is frequently limited to that particular piece of hardware. Of course, if there is a design problem with a certain piece of hardware (for example, a car), then it affects all the cars produced using that design. But, ordinarily, when you have a flat tire you are the only one around who does. A software defect often has much larger and wider implications because it usually affects *all* the copies of that software. The defects seldom occur because of the media on which the software is "riding." Usually, they are because writing and testing software is so difficult and bugs remain.

Maintenance

Many folks assert that since software doesn't wear out, there is no maintenance on it. Strictly speaking, they are right if they are thinking of software in hardware terms. However, the limited scope of influence described above, combined with the problem that hardware wears out, defines the kind of maintenance required on hardware. It is usually to replace or adjust individual parts of the thing.

But, because software is so complex, because it can theoretically be used with many operating systems and on many platforms, and because it is very tractable (see the later discussion on tractability), we can define maintenance on software as rat-killing, conversions, and enhancements. However, it is maintenance nonetheless. No one we know in the field would call it anything else, except for some folks who suggest that enhancements to software really ought to be done on a project basis and not on the usual "level of effort" found in maintenance shops. As we said earlier, this drives up the costs of enhancing software while lowering the costs of maintenance.

Continuous vs. Discrete Functions

Hardware or, rather, mechanical things, usually operate over a continuous function. You steer your car from one direction to another through one sweep of motion; one position is very much like the position just before it and just after it. Software is based on discrete states and merely *simulates* smooth motion. However, any one of these states may be completely different from the preceding or succeeding one. When you test software, you test as many states as possible. And, because software can be so complex, it is practically impossible to thoroughly test it. Yet, it is usually easy to test hardware; some tests can be performed quickly by simple observation.

Manufacturing Processes

Software is produced very differently from hardware. It is produced automatically from instructions supplied to a compiler, assembler, or code generator. Hardware has an assembly process, which is preceded by a drawing process that provides information to the shop about what to build. (See Figure 8-1.)

This difference in how stuff is actually produced causes much confusion in organizations that are primarily hardware shops but also produce software. It causes them to over burden the documentation stage of producing software with manufacturing processes. In addition, the instructions for software are for people *and* machines while those for hardware are for people only (drawings).

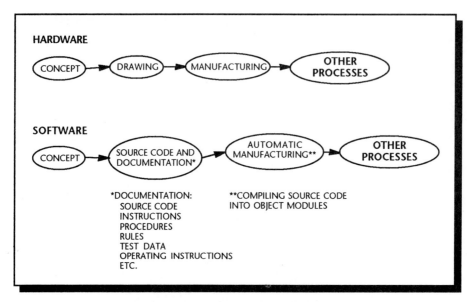

*Figure 8-1. The Hardware Manufacturing Process
vs. the Software Manufacturing Process*

Finished Product vs. Finished Design

Hardware processes produce a finished product; software processes produce a finished *design*, which is then manufactured into a hardware form by being impressed onto some media, say a floppy disk, for production. This is what makes software more like literature than like mechanical production.

Very Old vs. Very New

Hardware is very, very old; software is very, very new. We know a great deal about hardware and hardware processes. We know how these processes affect us. In fact, much of our culture is affected by hardware processes. Our schools are still set up like factories; so are our offices, although this might be changing somewhat. Software and how it is produced is so new that, in spite of the fact that it is pervasive, it hasn't affected the form of our culture very much yet.

Personal computers are still aids in factory-like offices. Perhaps someday this will change, but into what we don't know. However, there might be a hint about the future discussed later in this chapter.

Hardware-Software Models

Hardware, or mechanical things, are essentially mimics and are extensions of our limbs. The more sophisticated mechanical things mimic and extend our senses. Software, on the other hand, starts at the high hardware functions and goes on to become extensions of our minds. This puts a premium on mind-centered things and will eventually have an affect on the environment in which software is produced and used. It will also affect our culture generally. In the software making and consulting business, there is a move back to the cottage industry from which the Industrial Revolution and its factories started because it appears to be a suitable place to do the work. The term *software factory* seems so out of place when you consider what is going on.

Dependence

Software is completely dependent on hardware to execute; but, hardware doesn't need to have anything to do with software to be perfectly useful. This one-way dependence makes it all the more likely that naive mechanical folks will mistakenly make hardware dominant over software so that software is merely an adjunct of hardware. They simply don't understand that much of the hardware produced today is possible only because of software, or it was produced to support software.

Nevertheless, it is still possible to picture a world without software and it is not possible to picture it without hardware.

Tractability

Software is clay to hardware's marble; it is very tractable. By *tractable,* we mean that software is something that is easily worked like clay; not the connotation applied to problems describing them as solvable.

Our world of problems and solutions does not have the natural, physical constraints of the mechanical world. When we are confronted by having to make something new, we draw from Chaos, what the Greeks called "a rude and undigested heap." [Dictionary of the History of Ideas, p.297] It is this consultation with the great unknown, this Great Gob of unorganized *stuff*, that really distinguishes us from engineers of the mechanical world. This is where the radical novelty of our field shows itself. (See Figure 8-2.)

Even the greatest violin maker has just few things to keep track of when making violins: maybe 25 or 30. He must know a lot about each of these things and how to fit them together well. For example, he must know how to properly place the sounding column and use the appropriate varnish. Still, his stuff is really limited compared to the creative processes of the music composers.

The composers have no such constraints. They have produced an enormous literature of music, much of which is played on the same instrument: the violin. From Beethoven to Bluegrass, they all deal with the Great Gob. They suffer for it, they are driven by it and, after they wrestle with it, they create music. Mahler is often quoted as saying after someone asked him a pointed question about why he composed a certain way: "I didn't choose the music; it chose me."

When we are confronted by a novel problem or solution, we don't simply crank out solutions, although we are sometimes cranked around by them. We draw from immense possibilities: solutions that sometimes have all the beauty and harmony of the great music compositions. This communication with Chaos is what sets us apart; we must remember this and not let those from the mechanical world dictate to us how we are to create.

Here is what Frederick P. Brooks has to say about the tractability of our medium and the problems it implies [Brooks 1982, p.14]: "More software projects have gone awry for lack of calendar time than for all other causes combined. Why is this cause of disaster so common? ... our techniques of estimation are poorly developed. More seriously, they reflect an unvoiced assumption which is quite untrue, i.e., that all will go well.

"In many creative activities the medium of execution is intractable. Lumber splits; paint smears; electrical circuits ring. These physical limitations constrain the ideas that may be expressed, and they also create unexpected difficulties in the implementation.

"Computer programming ... creates with an exceedingly tractable medium. The programmer builds from pure thought stuff: concepts and very flexible representations thereof. Because the medium is tractable, we expect few difficulties in implementation; hence our pervasive optimism. Because our ideas are faulty, we have bugs; hence our optimism is unjustified.

"In a single task, the assumption that all will go well has a probabilistic effect on the schedule. It might indeed go as planned, for there is a probability distribution for the delay that will be encountered, and 'no delay' has a finite probability. A large programming effort, however, consists of many tasks, some chained end-to-end. The probability that each will go well becomes vanishingly small."

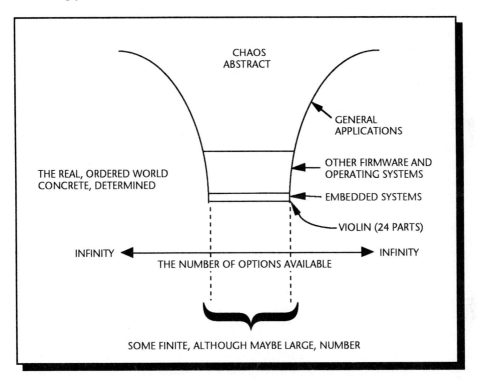

Figure 8-2. The Great Gob

The differences we noticed are summarized in Table 8-1.

Table 8-1. Deltas	
Hardware	**Software**
Simple	Complex
Wears out	Doesn't wear out
Limited scope of defects	Unlimited scope
Maintenance: Replace worn out things and parts	Continuously fix found bugs, move to new platforms, enhance
Continuous functions	Discrete functions
Manufacturing process	Automatic production
Finished product	Finished design
Very old	Very new
Mimics arms and legs	Mimics brains
Does not need software description for people: drawing	Needs hardware for people and machines
Relatively intractable	Very tractable

Differences Between Business Systems and Scientific Programs

One of the authors of this book, Peter, had a dream that he couldn't figure out until he came to this chapter. He dreamt that he was flying through mountains and could see a swarm of people climbing some of them. The mountains were very steep and the climbers were proceeding slowly up the nearly vertical faces of the steepest parts. They appeared to be shouting to each other. Some of them were tied together and were trying, with different gestures, to coordinate their ascent. There appeared to be no coordination in spite of all the shouting and gesturing.

Peter could also see beyond the mountains to the plains beyond. There, farmers were working the land, busy bringing in a harvest (it was a dream, remember). Each farmer had his own plot, each was minding his own business. But, Peter had the feeling that each farmer knew the other farmers were there and had nodding acquaintances with them. There was a just barely noticeable humming of activity coming from the farmers, and things seemed calm and peaceful. (See Figure 8-3.)

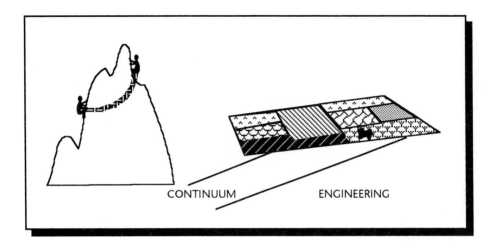

Figure 8-3. Peter's Dream

One day, Peter ran into one of our correspondents who wrote engineering applications, usually by himself or in a small team. When it came to programming, our friend was always composed, worked closely with his customer, had few communication problems, was extremely productive, and otherwise managed well. He had recently attended a motivation-raising meeting involving teams. There were all kinds of folks there; many of them wrote business applications. After listening to their views of programming, our correspondent commented that he had nothing in common with business programmers. They worked on very large projects, mostly on large teams, had communication and coordination problems, took forever to get things done, and seemed to always deal with tricky things. There are notable exceptions, of course, such as command and control systems and real-time systems. But, generally speaking, there did seem to be these distinctions.

Peter was reminded of that hum from the farmers in the dream. And then it came to him. The dream was about programming: the farmers in his dream were the engineering guys, and the mountain climbers were the business programmers to whom our friend was referring.

We sympathize with our correspondent's feeling about having nothing in common with business programmers, but we also believe that if he looked at programming from a distance he would see that he is on a continuum with them. The business programmers are at one end of the continuum and the scientific programmers on the other end; he would see what Peter saw in his dream. We all share this continuum. In this chapter, we will describe the ends of the continuum; we assume that all programming lies somewhere along it.

Not much has been written on this subject. We've conducted two intensive literature searches, but have found no significant work. However, bits and pieces are spread throughout the literature. What we found seems to reveal major differences between the two areas.

Our conclusions are based on data that we collected or computed from what literature *is* available. The most important source we used is from *Data Processing Technology and Economics,* by N. M. Phister, Jr. [Phister 1979]. This work was originally published in 1979, and was updated in the mid-eighties. This must have been a labor of love for Phister since he did so much scut work. There is precious little hard data about our field; here is a good source. We hope it is updated regularly.

Some of our data is *quantitative* and some is *qualitative. Quantitative* data is clearly preferable because you can easily compare the things described by the data. However, it is the most expensive and time-consuming type of data to produce. And, it lacks a sense of descriptive completeness. For example, a Mercedes Benz is considered to be a good, high-quality car. All of its parts can be quantified and some of them might even be somehow less (shorter, heavier, rougher, etc.) than those on other cars. Nevertheless, the characteristics of *good* and *high quality* are applied to the whole car.

Qualitative data has a sense of completeness, but it often depends on anecdotal accounts of people's experiences ("This is good code!") or subjective data. Subjective data is not bad if it comes from someone who is knowledgeable about the subject. This qualitative sense accounts for much of a customer's buying decision. Japanese car sales are so high because of the perception of overall high quality that is built into them.

It is important, here, to note several things. First, we are dealing with *applications,* which is what people mean when they talk about computer software. An application does a specific job for a customer. For example, both a payroll system and a fuel tank analysis program are *applications*. However, the modules that comprise the applications can be quite different. The *payroll application* is probably composed of several programs, while the *fuel tank analyzer* application is composed of a main routine and many subroutines. Nevertheless, they are applications in the sense that they each do a job for a customer. Exceptions exist, but this is the way things typically are.

Second, the data was validated in interviews with people experienced in one or the other area. In some cases, they are experienced in both. While there are exceptions and overlaps, nevertheless, we believe the data depicts the situation broadly viewed.

Third, special conditions might apply to embedded or CAD/CAM systems, robotics, computer-integrated manufacturing, or other *dedicated* applications. Nevertheless, we still think they lie somewhere on the continuum.

Application Size
(Business systems are 47 times larger than scientific programs. See Figure 8-4.)

Figure 8-4. Business Programs vs. Scientific Programs

Business systems are extremely large compared to scientific programs. This size difference is one of our most surprising and important findings. We made the measurement in an heterogeneous environment (mixed business and engineering programming) by examining the size of many examples of each type and then averaging them. The measure we used was the total lines of code (TLOC). We have more to say about this measure in the chapter on metrics. We also confirmed this ratio with several of our correspondents.

267

This size difference has many consequences. Take communications for example. The great size of business applications (typically about 650K LOC) requires a large team of developers and often a team of customers. This situation makes communication among all the players very important, yet all the more difficult because there are so many combinations possible among the communicators. In the judgement of one of our correspondents—a project manager—producing successful business systems requires a lot of very high quality communications. Our view of *high quality* communications is the kind that enables or aids one person to do their work without affecting or duplicating others' work. We found that the quality of the communication could very easily degrade from the slightest problem.

Time and again, we found folks bound together affecting each others' work in trying to put together a typical business system; like the mountain climbers, tied together, gesturing and shouting but only slowly edging up the cliff face. Now, this is only anecdotal information, but it was pervasive. Yet, when the application is one-person size, then communication goes down and the time devoted to it can be used in other places.

This great difference in size between the two application areas is one of the causes of misunderstandings between the business and scientific areas. It affects the approach to solving problems, the skills required by programmers, the way work gets done, the cost of doing work, and the risks involved.

It is one of the few examples where economies of scale operate backward; that is, the larger the project the higher the cost per line of code because of the complex communication patterns involved. It probably has other effects. For example, business areas tend to be dominated by one vendor, IBM, while the scientific areas have a more heterogeneous mix [Phister 1979, p.407]. The barriers to entering the business systems market are very high because only an enterprise with deep pockets can invest the money it takes to produce a line of equipment that can manage the complexity and size of business problems.

Trends:

Scientific programs are getting larger while the typical business system seems to be getting smaller. We mean systems that have recently been developed, not the so-called *legacy systems* that were built in an earlier era. What we are talking about here is not the size the *computer* sees, but what the programmer has to write and otherwise deal with. It isn't because the problems have changed. Except for computer-integrated manufacturing (CIM) and decision support applications, we haven't found that business problems have changed much over the last ten years.

In our opinion, there are two reasons for this down-sizing of business programs. The first reason is the use of fourth-generation languages (4GLs). Using a 4GL, one produces between 1/10 and 1/100 the lines of code as COBOL. 4GLs don't always do the whole job; however, they are improving all the time. Some of them produce pretty good code and they are becoming more and more popular.

The second reason is that data resource management (DRM) is finally having an affect in the business programming environment. More and more data needed by the enterprise are being collected into information systems that provide "user views" of it for programs to use. In other words, data are being unbound from applications. This enables the smaller, one-person jobs to become more frequent because the application is no longer involved with data management. Business programmers no longer must build and maintain intermediate files of data. And, they need not build those reformatting programs that "connect" two of the programs in the application system.

The techniques used in scientific applications haven't changed much in the past ten years. They are still based on mathematical descriptions of nature. But, the problems they try to solve have certainly changed. And, this is why scientific applications are becoming larger. A typical scientific application might remain person-sized, but the latest ones are becoming very large, dwarfing the large business applications. Some examples of huge application systems are:

- the Strategic Defense Initiative (SDI)
- the space station
- computer-aided design/computer-aided manufacturing (CAD/CAM)
- weather forecasting
- computational fluid dynamics (CFD)

Many of these applications require super-computer vector machines to run them. In addition, these applications are demanding more and more memory in the computer and depend on larger and larger amounts of data for input.

Dr. John Manley, Professor of Industrial Engineering at the University of Pittsburgh, compared the sizes in LOC of some of the larger systems. For example, where the B-1B program was 1.2 million LOC, the space station will be 10 million. And, he thinks this trend is just getting started [Manley 1988, pp.115-124].

These trends have important implications. 4GLs and DRM will become ever larger influences. Business and scientific techniques will overlap more. And, while complexity for business systems will start to decrease, complexity for scientific systems will increase.

Type of Operation

(Business programming is I/O bound; scientific programming is compute bound. See Figure 8-5.)

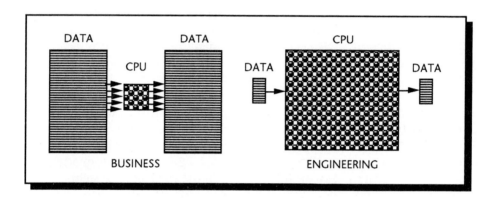

Figure 8-5. Scientific vs. Business Programming

It should come as no surprise that scientific programming deals mostly with mathematical functions and algorithms and business programming deals with a lot of data about business processes.

In science and engineering, many states can be described by one function: a pocket-sized algorithm specifying how to generate every possible state for that function. One function can easily generate many millions of states.

Here is an example of producing lots of states from a small thing: snow machines. You turn one on, point the nozzle in the direction you choose and, voila, in a little while you have a hillside covered with individual ice crystals.

In business, you are usually keeping track of individual things, individual products, employees, buildings, accounts, customers, categories of these things, etc. In our snow machine example, you would be cataloging and filing each crystal, and keeping track of such things as when the crystal was created, how cold it is, where it is, what type of crystal it is, and so on. That's because, in business, the discrete states are what are hauled around, usually in some sort of database. And, since there might be many millions of discrete states, the database is hardly pocket-sized.

Our example is not realistic. However, here is one example that *is* realistic: ordering some equipment.

Some of the states you might encounter are:

- the requested state

- the ordered state

- the purchased but not delivered state (which itself might have many states, such as the shipped state, the enroute state, and the received state)

- the states involving the equipment being delivered

- the states for setting it up to operate and, finally,

- the operating state

You have to keep track of all that stuff; and, that's just for one piece of equipment. Very often, each state described above is recorded somewhere on a form or represented on a computer screen and is then transferred to a file.

What we described above are very few states compared to those held in, say, an employee information system for a medium-sized business. People, of course, are frequently what all the *data* in business applications are about.

With a mathematical function, any state is not much different than the one before it or the one after it. But, with people, there could be a *lot* of differences; we are individuals. And, when we are categorized based on one characteristic or another, such as race or gender, we object (or ought to) because over-simplified categorizations do not do us justice. It is hard to see how any algorithm can account for the information about each of us that is necessary to run a business.

Nevertheless, the business and engineering sides of an enterprise are very often cheek by jowl, feeding each other. For example, a fairly simple go-ahead to the engineering side for a new product could very well result in an extremely large amount of data about the new product. The data could include its size, shape, performance, specifications for parts to be purchased from other businesses, and so on. (See Figure 8-6.)

The business side takes this information and uses it to plan production. For example, purchasing would use some of the data to order the parts. They keep a great deal of information around on file in order to process the purchases; they do not regenerate most of it.

When we say that business programming is input/output (I/O) bound, we mean that when you look at the program, most of the activity is involved with getting data to flow across the program's boundary, both from the outside inward and vice versa. (See again Figure 8-6.) Usually, these flows are associated with rather simple processing steps inside the program itself. This means that the input data maps to one or only a few processing steps inside the program and then to the output data. You can see how the output was produced from the input.

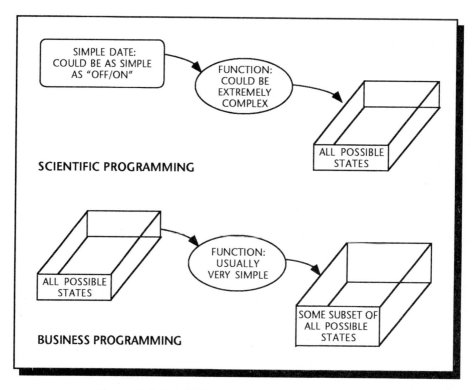

Figure 8-6. Scientific vs. Business Programming

In the scientific areas, this is not so effective because these applications tend to be *compute bound*; flows across the interfaces are not very representative of the state of the system. This means that you can expect many processes to result from one or only a very few number of inputs. The mapping, therefore, is not simple; it is not likely to show how an output was produced from any one input [Ledgard and Marcotty 1981, p.7].

Another way of putting it is: "Where is the most complexity that must be managed?" If it is in the data, then you likely have a business system on your hands. If it is inside the program, then it is probably a scientific program.

Trends:

The advent of decision-support systems, executive information services, operations analysis, and applications involving statistical methods will have some impact on internal complexity and will make some business systems more processing bound. Likewise, large amounts of data for engineering purposes will also affect the data-processing attributes of scientific systems. Knowledge-based systems (KBS) will affect both.

Nevertheless, the characteristic of business programs managing data and external complexity, and scientific programs managing processes and internal complexity, remains rather stable. This stability comes from the basic difference described earlier; that is, scientific programs involve functions and algorithms that can produce a large number of states but don't store these states, while business programs are involved with storing and otherwise processing large numbers of states. If that were to change, then maybe this characteristic would also change.

Number of Files Used

(Business systems use five times as many more files than scientific systems. See Figure 8-7.)

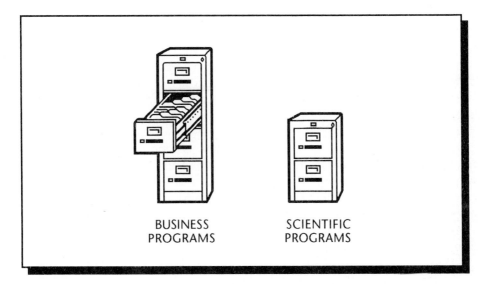

BUSINESS PROGRAMS   SCIENTIFIC PROGRAMS

Figure 8-7. Business Systems Use Many More Files Than Scientific Systems

This characteristic is important because it affects the hardware environment, storage planning, system accounting, and management, and it contributed to the rise of Data/Information Resource Management.

The literature clearly shows that, from the start, scientific programming emphasized calculating over file management [Wexelblat 1978, pp.25-71]. The opposite is true with business programming [Ledgard and Marcotty, p.7]. (See Figure 8-7.) There wasn't much quantified data found in the literature to support this characteristic. Our normal source, Phister, wasn't much help here, although we could find tabular data concerning business file *sizes* [Phister 1979, pp.126-127]. The data we present is from our own knothole. We looked at a library of scientific applications, and we talked with as many business programmers as we could find with whom we could discuss this matter.

Our survey of the scientific applications library we examined showed that the average number of files per program was five. But, see the Manley reference [Manley 1988]. He indicates that the International Ultraviolet Explorer produced 23 gigabytes of information, while NASA's Materials Sciences data volume has 23,125 terabytes of information; presumably, all this stuff is stored in many files [Phister 1979, p.116]. Our business correspondents indicated that business systems require forty or fifty files per system.

Trends:

Here is some more switching around. As data resource management (DRM) gets more and more data resources under control, the number of files required to run an enterprise will decline to an essential set. The number of files required to execute a business program will also decline because the DRM folks will be able to present the view of the data required by each program; the reformatting programs, which are sometimes a major portion of one's career, will become extinct.

In the scientific side, more and more data is required to investigate structures of all types under many varied conditions. Some scientific problems, such as weather forecasting, are becoming possible only because there is enough data to "run" through the analysis programs.

We expect a crossover, probably by the end of the century or sooner depending on when DRM gets its act together and when CAD/CAM and other scientific systems get their data.

File Manipulation

(Business programming is good at it, and needs to be; scientific programming is not so good and doesn't need to be.)

In the business area, a programmer's knowledge of the file shape, record size, and file access methods are much more important than in scientific areas. Many more software tools are available for doing file-related tasks. Much more training is also required. And, over time, the required knowledge, tools, and training have grown because the environment that programmers face has grown. In Figure 8-8 we see a picture of the environment faced by a business programmer in a mature environment. Over time, new terminal programs, data access methods, and operating systems have been added without removing the old ones. Their interrelationships have also grown.

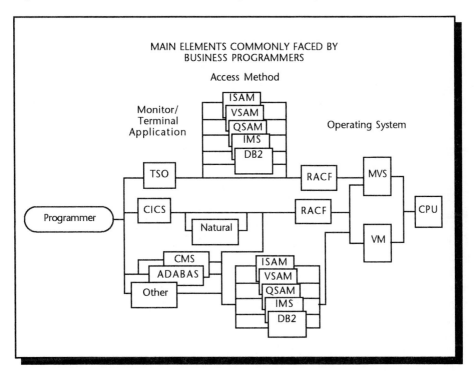

Figure 8-8. File Manipulation/Business

In the scientific area, many file attributes and manipulation tasks are transparent to programmers. This is one of those quality attributes that, while it was verified in the interviews, was not supported quantitatively in the literature [Phister 1979; Ledgard and Marcotty 1981, p.7]. (See Figure 8-9.) Compare the two figures. Which one would you rather face?

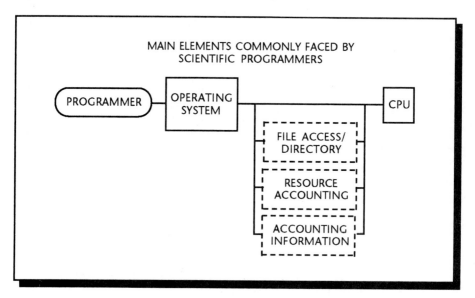

Figure 8-9. File Manipulation/Scientific

Trends:

This will probably remain a stable attribute of the differences between business and scientific programming. This could be unfortunate because, as scientific programs grow ever larger and require more files, they will find good file-management facilities and languages that support them to be of great utility. But, their environments will become more and more complex.

Quality of Solutions

(Business is exact; scientific is approximate with varying degrees of precision. See Figure 8-10.)

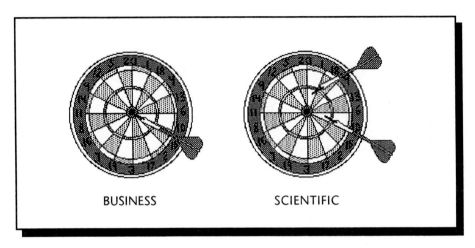

BUSINESS   SCIENTIFIC

Figure 8-10. Business is Exact, Scientific is Approximate

By discussing the *quality* of the solutions, we are not making any judgements about the goodness or badness of the answers you get from the two types of programming. Indeed, none are warranted. We mean the basic nature of the solutions; what's different about them. This is a complex subject, but we believe it lies close to the heart of the differences we've been discussing.

Portions of both types of programming produce solutions in natural languages; for example, English or Japanese. We are not concerned with these. What we *are* concerned with, though, are the *numbers* that form the rest of the solutions.

There are many types of numbers ranging from simple to complex. The simplest are the counting numbers: 1, 2, 3, 4, 5 ..., infinity. These are the *positive integers*. Add zero and all the negative integers and you get the set of integers. There are "spaces" between the integers, just like there are tones between the keys of a piano. Some of these spaces are filled by fractions and numbers formed by integers and fractions together: the *mixed numbers*. These fractions and mixed numbers can be expressed as quotients of two integers and are called *rational numbers*. The rest of the spaces between the integers are filled by *irrational numbers*. Pi (π), which describes the ratio of the circumference to the diameter of a circle, is an irrational number.

All of these together make up the *real numbers*. There are other numbers, such as *complex numbers*, which have a real and an imaginary part, and *transfinite numbers*, which are larger than any positive integer. Figure 8-11 is a picture of the number types we've been discussing.

Business programs deal mostly with the integers and simple rational numbers. Integers are so important because they are used for counting and ranking things, cardinality and ordinality, respectively. You use them to answer questions such as, "How many things do I have?" and "What is the first one, what is the second one?"

The simple rational numbers express money in dollars and cents, interest in percentages, and transactions in much-used fractions such as 1/2, 1/4, 1/8, 1/16, and 1/32, which are used in stocks and bonds transactions.

To be sure, one can do some pretty sophisticated business calculations. Try calculating the present value of some money that is promised to you at some future time, or the amortization of a mortgage over a period of time. They're not simple calculations; but, their answers are expressed in dollars and cents, or percentages, or common fractions of dollars.

Scientific programming uses all the numbers we discussed above, plus all the other numbers, especially *all* the real numbers. Answers are usually expressed in decimal form with many places to the right of the decimal point; not simply two as in business.

Then comes the accuracy and precision of the answers. *Accuracy* has the quality of either being exact or not exact. When my pay check gets to me, the solution to the problem of getting it to me is exact; either it got to me or it did not. *Precision* has the quality of being minutely exact. Here, we are talking about real numbers, which are frequently expressed with some amount of error. The trick is to figure out when this error is not important for your purposes.

When men first landed on the moon, the distance between us and the moon was expressed in a form such as 400,000 kilometers plus or minus so much. The size of the error relative to the quantity being expressed is the *precision*. The distance to the moon could have been expressed as 400,000 kilometers plus or minus one thousand kilometers, or plus or minus one kilometer, or something else.

Most business applications seek exact solutions; they want to find one particular pigeon hole. In this case, *precision* and *accuracy* are identical: any loss of precision results in a loss of accuracy and vice versa. On the other hand, scientific applications often seek good approximations with varying degrees of precision. Here, the accuracy of the solution diverges from the precision with which it is expressed.

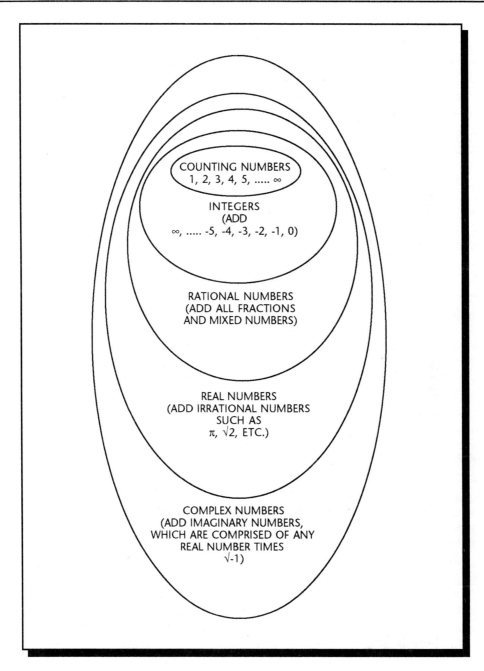

Figure 8-11. Number Types

Business folks don't always understand the precision used by engineering folks, or that errors are not necessarily bad. Scientific folks, on the other hand, think that the problems of business folks are simple *yes* or *no* propositions, and fail to understand the incredible complexity of the data on which these programs act.

Trends:

We don't think much will change about the quality of the solutions. The nature of business requires the simpler numbers to aid in managing the tremendous complexity of the data that business people deal with all the time. Science people stuff *all* the numbers into functions and algorithms and use real numbers mainly to describe Nature.

Types of Development
(Business tends to be phased; scientific tends to be incremental.)

Obviously, the sheer size of business applications makes project control more important. Therefore, a phased development model, usually called the Waterfall model, has become very popular. (See Figure 8-12.) Another reason for the use of the Waterfall is because the user has so much say about the system being produced. Development proceeds logically and sequentially according to phases and produces a final product. But, there are problems with this development method. We discussed the Waterfall model and its advantages and disadvantages in our last book, *Wicked Problems, Righteous Solutions* [DeGrace and Stahl 1990].

In scientific applications, the incremental or prototyping approaches (also discussed in the *Wicked* book) are more popular. (See Figure 8-13.) In both of these models, a program representing an incomplete set of functions is produced and put into service. Then, over a long period, it is perfected.

Another reason why the incremental or prototyping approaches are popular is because they are able to produce intermediate results, and users often need this type of information to help them understand all the requirements of the program. With these models, the distinction between development and maintenance becomes blurred.

Trends:

We believe that the differences between business and scientific methods of development will eventually go away; that developers will choose an approach to development because it fits the problem and the person trying to solve the problem. For this to happen, we will need to understand more about the nature of solving problems and writing programs. But, for now, you can expect to see the Waterfall used, or attempted, in business and DoD development efforts and other approaches in scientific and engineering efforts.

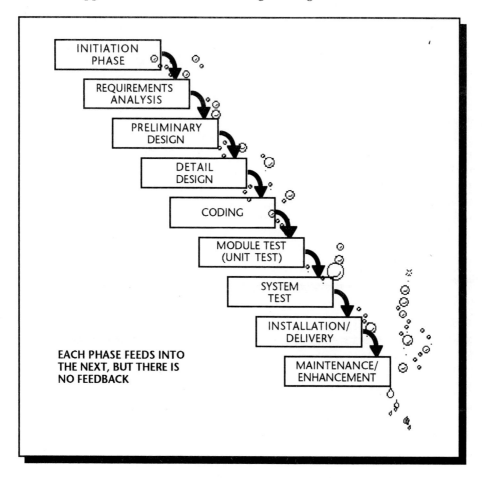

Figure 8-12. Business Uses a Phased Approach

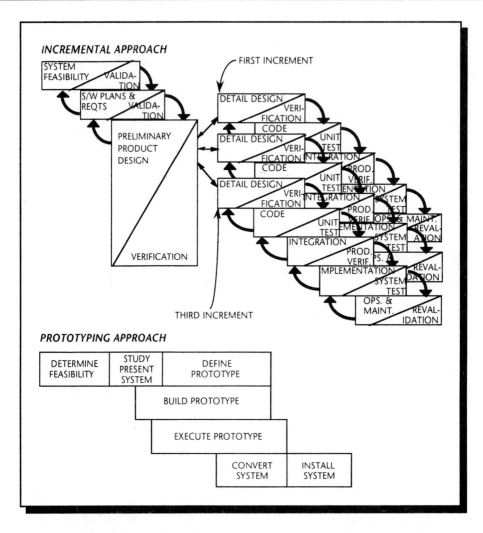

Figure 8-13. Scientific Uses Incremental or Prototyping Approaches

Modularization

(Business tends toward project-sized modules; scientific tends toward function-oriented modules. See Figure 8-14.)

In business applications, work is usually assigned in one- or two-week packages. The resulting modules are large and have many functions stuffed into them. And, all the functions share the same data.

In scientific areas, the work tends to be decomposed by function. This is reflected in the module sizes, which are much smaller, and in data sharing, which can be minimized.

In software engineering, modularity is expressed in terms of coupling and cohesion. One goal of good design is to produce modules that are functionally cohesive and loosely coupled. Business system modules tend to have less cohesion than engineering modules. We are not sure about coupling characteristics; there simply was no data available and our own investigations turned up no information on this side of the coupling-cohesion couplet. We did find, however, that wherever cohesion was optimized, coupling seemed to be also.

Figure 8-14. Modularization

Trends:

We see this modularization difference remaining rather stable. Even though training (which shows the need for modular code) will improve, and the inventory of programs in maintenance (which would profit from modular code) will continue to grow, the culture of business programmers and the language they use will mitigate against improving the modularity of the code they deal with.

Language
(Business uses COBOL; scientific uses FORTRAN. See Figure 8-15.)

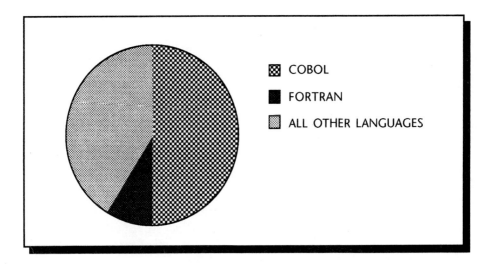

Figure 8-15. Business Uses COBOL, Scientific Uses FORTRAN

The main language used in business applications is COBOL (an acronym formed from COmmon Business Oriented Language). In engineering applications, the main language used is FORTRAN (another acronym, formed from FORmula TRANslation, or some such thing). COBOL accounts for at least 50% of all applications programs, while FORTRAN accounts for about 9% [Phister 1979, p.83]. Other languages make up the rest.

But these aren't the only languages around. Between 1952 and 1972, over 200 "high level" languages were introduced [Phister 1979, p.82]. Most of these have fallen by the wayside. There were some noble experiments: ALGOL (yet another acronym that we will let you decipher for yourself) is one of these.

FORTRAN appeared before COBOL. It was simple and compact, but lacked many features and contained the infamous GOTO as the main feature for transferring control. It was, however, difficult for business specialists to use, and COBOL was specifically invented for them. COBOL had many modern features. But, its Data Division was the most important because it allowed the data complexity found in business problems to be better managed.

Soon, however, FORTRAN appeared with subroutines that aided in modularizing code. A subroutine is accessed by using the verb *CALL* along with the subroutine's name and some data known as arguments. When executed, the CALL statement caused the program to transfer to the address of the "called" routine. Subroutines could be compiled separately, and they had some data (or rather process) hiding characteristics.

In addition, variables inside a routine affected only the code in that routine. This is known as *limiting the scope of effect of the variables*. Data is delivered to the subroutines in two ways. First, it is delivered through a global facility of common data blocks. Whenever the common block appeared in a routine, that routine had access to all the data in the common block. Of course, if twenty routines had the common block in them, then all twenty had access to all the data. This is known as *common data coupling*, an undesirable form of coupling because it causes code changes to produce surprising consequences.

Second, data is passed in the form of arguments to the "called" routine by the "calling" routine when the CALL statement was executed. This second method allowed programmers to control and optimize the most desirable form of coupling; namely, simple data coupling. The effect of this is to make modules more independent of others. This makes maintenance easier because you don't need to trace out so many implications of a change when you know exactly what data could be affected. Many fine libraries for mathematical analysis, graphics, user interfaces, etc., have been created to take advantage of this subroutine feature.

COBOL also has a subroutine facility. But, at first there were problems because the Data Division had to go along with the module and, therefore, the advantages of using subroutines in the same way as FORTRAN were not as great. One of our correspondents reported that using the subroutine feature in COBOL was almost the same as writing another program, so why use it.

Nevertheless, notice how the main features of the languages were set to manage the important sources of complexity in the environments where they were to be used, data for COBOL and functions/modules for FORTRAN.

Both languages were "standardized" in the sixties. FORTRAN finally received block structures, such as IF THEN ELSE, in the version known as F77. It was now possible to remove the GOTOs if you wanted to. Yet, with all the new features put into these languages, we found that programmers tend to use simple features rather than complicated ones [Phister 1979, p.93].

When the two languages are compared, the differences are impressive. COBOL is verbose: it takes about five times more code to do the same work as it takes in FORTRAN [Martin 1982, pp.182-183].[22] In addition, COBOL manuals are much bigger than FORTRAN and there are about five times more words to remember, such as the COBOL Reserved Words, than in FORTRAN.

Trends:

We have noticed a trend toward abandoning these venerable old languages. For FORTRAN, the trend is to convert some programs to the C or C++, Pascal, and Ada languages. This is due to the difficulties of "modernizing" FORTRAN (see Chapter 10, *Standards,* for a more complete discussion), its relative ungainliness compared to C, and its difficulty in operating in the UNIX environments that are becoming so common today.

COBOL is being replaced more and more by fourth-generation languages, application generators, and query languages in sophisticated database-management systems. The user interface and programming facilities of Microrim's R:base is one example.

---

[22] This reference shows the same sample problem coded up in five different languages. This is skimpy evidence by itself; but, our correspondents had no trouble verifying it. Here is another case where our research institutes could be of some help to us.

Size of Modules

(Business is large; science is smaller. See Figure 8-16.)

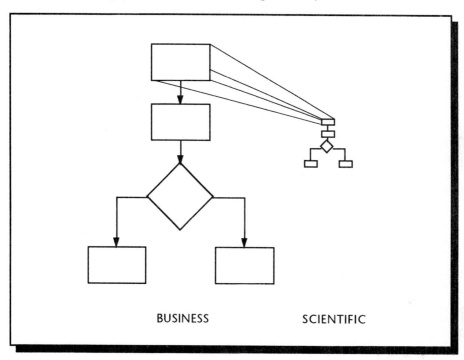

Figure 8-16. The Size of Modules

The modules that make up business applications are about eight to ten times larger than those that compose scientific ones. We weren't able to find much support in the literature for this conclusion; we based it on our observations and by confirmation from our correspondents. But, it *does* make sense; remember that business systems tend to be parceled out according to some level of effort—say a person month—and COBOL doesn't support modularization the way FORTRAN does.

This characteristic is important because it affects the qualities of cohesion and coupling, which contribute to overall software quality. We are not saying that business systems are lower quality products than engineering programs; however, practice and the language involved make it tougher to produce code with optimized cohesion and coupling characteristics. Because of COBOL's data-handling facilities, it seems a worthwhile trade off.

Trends:

The trend here closely follows the course of language replacement discussed in the preceding paragraphs. The newer languages are more compact—except for Ada—and lend themselves to better modularization. There is another effect, however. As DRM succeeds, we will see smaller one-person projects in the business side along the lines of engineering programs.

Sources of Tools
(Business tools are purchased; scientific tools are built by the programmer. See Figure 8-17.)

BUSINESS   SCIENTIFIC

Figure 8-17. Business Programmers Buy, Scientific Programmers Build

Business areas tend to buy more software tools than do scientific areas. And, scientific programmers tend to build tools more than do business programmers. A scan of a tools catalog (the ACR Productivity Aids catalog) shows that most of the tools are targeted at IBM programming environments, which are the predominant ones. This confirms our own experience: scientific programmers build many of their own tools while business programmers buy theirs. Not *everyone* we interviewed agreed on this but, as we explored this issue, it was confirmed over and over again.

There is another reason for this difference in the source of tools, especially if your enterprise is heterogeneous. If your managers are drawn from predominantly one side or the other (we have found that at the levels just below V.P., business folks predominate), their perceptions of the tools required will not match the practice of the side they are not familiar with.

For example, one of the authors of this book requested some resources to take the tools made in the engineering side of the house and make them into "products" that could easily be used all over the enterprise. Management thought that the resources he requested were rather low and that he had seriously underestimated what would be required. But, while they had water-cooled, 400 horsepower, eighteen wheelers in mind, he was thinking of air-cooled, seventy-five horsepower, four-wheeled tools that zip in and out of the environment and do just one or two jobs; more like the tools you find in the UNIX environment.

This type of perceptual problem creates serious miscommunication. It could also lead to funds being misallocated, particularly if a vendor gets wind of what is going on and convinces the big shots that they should buy big tools.

There is also a problem with the perceptions people have of the tools themselves. Some people think that the tools are somehow different from other software; that software purchased on the outside is much better than anything that can be built inside their firm.

This is just not true. Software engineering tools are *software*. The people who make them are programmers no matter where they work. The tools are composed of ones and zeros whether they are home grown or purchased from an outside vendor. And, while a vendor might have a better grasp of the *theory* in which the tool is supposed to assist (or, in hard-luck cases, impose), the toolmakers in the firm, who are producing for themselves and their colleagues, are closer to the problem at hand.

Trends:

We have found that the activity of buying tools from the outside is spreading to the engineering folks. This is because of the Roman trait we call *push-down* technology; a lower grade form of technology transfer. What happens is that folks who are no longer current with the field, but are high in the corporation and are constantly courted by vendors, attempt to solve problems by making assumptions about the state of the art and matching the vendors' tools to these assumptions. They then try to impose their solution on the entire enterprise; and, it usually fails, for obvious reasons. Rather than trying to understand and perfect the processes currently being used, they bank on what they think programmers *should* do and turn programming into a moral issue. Once this happens, all the dimensions of religious strife enter the issue and it becomes almost impossible to back away from the situation.

Two things could help to limit the effects of push-down technology. The first is the UNIX environment and its culture. UNIX was designed to be simple, portable, and useful. The culture that has grown up around UNIX is very powerful and acts to counter the trend toward extremely large and extremely powerful tools.

The second is the new emphasis on *quality*, especially the notions of continuous quality improvement. One of these important notions is to understand the processes of one's enterprise that are really being practiced. The people who are buying tools for us ought to understand how software is really developed and maintained. Gaining this understanding counteracts push-down technology because it gives some hope for bubbling-up requirements for tools. The effect would be to improve the technology transfer because people would have a better idea what the hell they are trying to do.

Estimation of Effort

(Business programming is most difficult; scientific programming is least difficult. See Figure 8-18.)

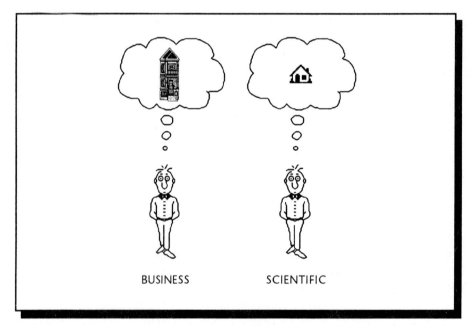

Figure 8-18. Business Programming is More Difficult,
Scientific Programming is Least Difficult

The difficulty of estimating the effort required to build business systems is due to the nature of the development approach, the size of business projects, and the unpredictably changing requirements for the systems. The Waterfall model does not handle iteration very well and, since development must iterate through several phases, original estimates fall apart. Folks cannot predict very well how the changing requirements affect things in a development environment. Changes that appeared simple on the surface have consequences far beyond what was originally anticipated. And, because these changes must be accounted for, estimates frequently fall out of bed.

One of the people we interviewed wrote down his experience with four major business systems. Two of them were seriously underestimated while the other two had conditions that usually lead to underestimating.

The incremental approach, which is popular in the engineering side, is much easier to estimate. In fact, in many cases, it is downright trivial. The idea here is to get something up and running and in use as quickly as possible, observing as much good software engineering practice as possible. Once the program has gone through test and is in use, experience with it yields new requirements that are used to perfect the requirements for the program.

In addition, experience with the program builds confidence in the solutions it produces. This confidence becomes the basis for establishing the baseline we discussed in Chapter 6, *Maintenance.* Now you have a platform to use to perfect the application. What remains is the task of adding the optimizations that make maintenance easier.

Combine this with a budgeting process aimed at getting as much bang for the buck as possible—"do as much as can be done in one year"—and you have a simple, effective, and inexpensive process of estimating the effort. In that year, enhancements, rat-killing and, perhaps, conversion are performed. As time goes by, the programmer puts in the enhancements that are possible given the circumstances. Perhaps a lower priority enhancement is placed ahead of a higher priority one because the programmer happens to be examining the part of the code where the lower priority change would go.

Anyway, at the end of a year, you've got a program that was useful at the start, was maintained over that period, had some improvements installed, and was more useful at the end. All of this was accomplished without burdening project management, interminable meetings, change boards, reports, and the cursed Gantt charts. Not a bad deal!

The problem here is that management would have to trust the programmer and would have to empower the programmer to make the best decisions s/he can for the program. This is not very common, especially in the business side of the house. From our own experiences, we still remember (and our correspondents verify) the terrible lack of trust and extremely wasteful project practices in business systems development.

Trends:

As engineering projects become larger, those large projects (especially for NASA and the DoD) will probably institute Roman-like project control over software development. Perhaps there is no other way for large projects. But, then our question becomes, "Why are there large projects?" Can't system engineering produce better work packages to reduce the project size to more manageable levels? We have no problem with sophisticated and comprehensive reporting on systems engineering projects; these seem to be in the very nature of the beast. But, there is something very disheartening about the stress we notice when Greek-like people spend most of their time talking about the job and not doing it, which is a Roman characteristic.

Development Costs
(Business systems spend more per LOC [approximately $30]; scientific systems cost less per LOC [approximately $20]. See Figure 8-19.)

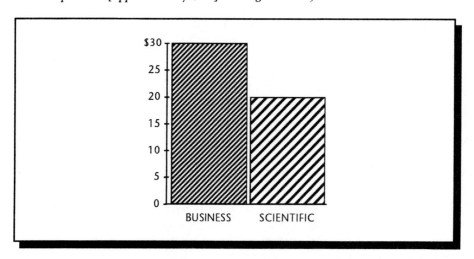

Figure 8-19. Business Spends More per LOC Than Science

For business systems, we calculated the figures the following way:

- A high-level language generates an average of four object instructions per instruction [Phister 1979, p.214].

- The cost per object instruction using a high-level language was $2.39, $2.62, $2.99, $3.13, and $3.22 in the years 1960, 1965, 1970, 1972, and 1974 [Phister 1979, p.504, table II.4.22.3].

- Therefore, the cost per line of a high-order language using the four times calculation described above was: $9.56, $10.48, $11.96, $12.52, and $12.88. Since COBOL has the largest representation in the nation's inventory, we assume these costs are the most relevant to it.

- We then calculated the figures in 1983 dollars. The values are: $22.65, $24.83, $28.35, $29.67, and $30.52.

We know it is very dangerous to assume that the costs translate proportionately upward as the languages used go from the object level to a higher level such as the third-generation level of COBOL. This was a preliminary figure, to be checked out by someone else's experience. We verified these numbers by means of our correspondents who agreed that they were reasonable. We also used a report from *Computer World* [1985]. GTE replaced COBOL with application generators, ADFII from IBM, and MARK IV from Informatics General Corporation. They claim that a stock replacement program produced with these generators cost $780,000 for 90,000 lines of code, or $8.67 per line. Their costs for COBOL code was between $25 and $35 per line. Notice that GTE's figure falls around the latest cost we calculated above.

For FORTRAN, we know the figure is smaller, but we don't know how much; generally speaking, there isn't much to go on. One of the authors of this book calculated for his environment, which was $20 per line in 1985. Others claim lower figures still. This is one figure we are leery of, and we hope that someone has more to substantiate our claim.

If we are correct, then the lower figure has to do with the way the software is produced, the problem-solving skills of the programmers (they are already knowledgeable in mathematics), and other characteristics described in this chapter. But, we suspect the main reason is not that engineering code is so economical to produce, but that business code is so difficult to produce because of data complexity.

Trends:

We see engineering systems' costs going up and business systems' costs declining somewhat or remaining much the same. The GTE report [Computer World 1985] showed that using an application generator cut their costs by two thirds. This is hopeful news indeed.

Maintenance Costs

(Business and engineering both cost about $1.25 per line per year. See Figure 8-20.)

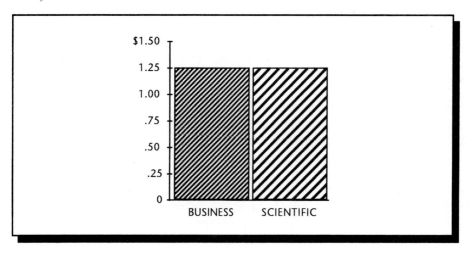

*Figure 8-20. Business and Engineering Maintenance Costs
Are About the Same*

By examining both sides of the house, we found that maintenance costs were roughly the same per line of code per year for both business and scientific systems. But, again our data is based on a small sample; there is not much in the literature about any differences.

Trends:

We don't expect this to change much except that as our practices improve, our costs will go down. Our practices give us a feel for the code, the sense that we know it. It is this feel that allows us to do maintenance quickly and efficiently, mainly in our heads with a few tools assisting.

Job Size

(Business systems use more programmers per application; scientific systems use more applications per programmer. See Figure 8-21.)

Figure 8-21. Business Uses More Programmers per Application,
Science Uses More Applications per Programmer

Producing business systems requires teams of developers, and maintaining them requires somewhat smaller teams. Producing scientific programs requires small teams, and maintaining them requires part of a programmer's time so that s/he is usually assigned to several programs. Certainly, many COBOL shops assign one programmer to several of their systems, especially the smaller ones; and, many FORTRAN shops do large initial developments similar to business development. But, we have discovered that most business development is attempted by a large development project, and a very substantial portion of scientific development is done by a single programmer or small team.

In addition, business programmers tend to specialize in certain software engineering aspects of the systems—telecommunications, database design, etc.—because, as team members, their assignments tend to be specific *chunks* of the system. Scientific programmers specialize in domain knowledge but tend to be less specialized in the software engineering aspects of their jobs because their responsibility extends to the whole context of the job: all analysis, all design, all database design, all configuration management, etc. Besides, their programming environments are simpler than the business environments. (See also Figure 8-8.)

Trends:

As business programs grow smaller and scientific programs grow larger, the ratios of programmers to programs will tend to equalize between the two types of programs. This trend indicates that software development will become more and more bureaucratized, which is unfortunate. However, we hope that all software jobs are sized for one person to produce, because this size job minimizes communications and burdensome overhead and maximizes the advantage of the best tool of all: our mind.

The Nature of Problems
(Business is arbitrary; science is determined. See Figure 8-22.)

Figure 8-22. Business is Arbitrary; Science is Determined

Business systems operate in a world of human beings interacting with each other. People are subject to fashions and other changes. They create laws, rules, and conventions that change in unpredictable ways; where each person and their activity is counted, recorded, and kept track of to one degree or another; and where the communication medium is imprecise and ambiguous. Scientific systems operate in Nature's world of orderly systems; where laws are immutable; where unpredictable activity is more the exception rather than the rule; where measurements are of averages, totals, and typical; and where the communication medium is precise and unambiguous.

Trends:

We don't see this changing much at all. We think it makes for the rich environment in which we work.

Workers' Skill Emphasis
(Besides programming skills, the two types of programmers tend to develop different skills. See Figure 8-23.)

Figure 8-23. Business Programmers Lean Toward File Management, and Scientific Programmers Lean Toward Calculations

All programmers draw from the same central set of programming skills, but the business programmer is shaded toward file management and the scientific person toward calculations. Moreover, because of the size of projects, the reporting required, and the types of problems to be solved, business programmers find they need interpersonal skills, which have long been associated with the service industry. They develop communications, planning, and management skills.

Scientific programmers use the language of Nature: mathematics. They find themselves closely allied with engineers. It is easier for them to understand the computer and how it operates. They develop "math sense," but find themselves without the natural opportunity to develop business sense and communication skills. The result is a situation like where our friend, the scientific programmer, felt he had nothing in common with business programmers. They talked a different language. It is also the reason why we perceive that business programmers rise higher and more often in the enterprise than scientific programmers.

Trends:

We don't see this changing much either.

Summary of Programming Characteristics

Table 8-2 has three columns. The first column lists the characteristics of programming that are being measured or compared. The second and third columns list the values for business and scientific applications, respectively. Each characteristic and the values associated with it were explained in the preceding paragraphs.

Table 8-2. Business vs. Scientific Applications

Characteristic	Business	Scientific
Application size:	650K LOC	14K LOC
Type of operations:	sorting, searching, summarizing	arithmetic, logic
	compute bound	I/O bound
Number of files used:	large	small
File manipulation:	extensive, well done	restricted, not so good
Quality of solution:	exact	approximate
Type of development:	phased	incremental
Modularization:	task-oriented	function-oriented
Language:	COBOL	FORTRAN
Size of modules:	very large, more like overlays	small, <100 LOC
Source of tools:	external	local
Nature of problem:	arbitrary, conventional	determined
Workers' skill:	interpersonal emphasis	object-oriented emphasis

Size and costs

Est. development:	most difficult	least difficult
Development costs:	more per LOC ($30)	less per LOC ($20)
Maintenance costs:	$1.25 per LOC	$1.25 per LOC
Job size:	More programmers per application	More applications per programmer

Implications for CASE

What this chapter clearly shows is one of the reasons why CASE is having trouble. The types of programming that we do are so different that any one tool can't possibly cover them all.

In the business side, you can expect the huge, water-cooled types; in the engineering side, you can expect the smaller ones. In business, there will be data-oriented, entity-relationship diagramming aids and the like to help with the external complexity. On the engineering side, tools will concentrate on the complexity of the process. However, different problems within these super domains also vary and overlap. When you are selecting tools, you must be careful that they indeed apply to your problem.

Another thing that is clear from this chapter is that tools must be managed, reasonably and realistically. Whether you build them or buy them, you need to do configuration management on them to give them good technology characteristics; namely, that they will be spread where needed, and not duplicated. They should be ported to appropriate environments and maintained like any other software. This almost never happens because there is seldom enough time to make the tools good.

And, finally, wherever possible, try to get tool usage reports regularly. This will give you a feeling for the state of the practice. We have often noticed tools being hauled into the environment and not used. You've got to be able to spot these things and find out why they are happening. Programmers have pretty good reasons for what they do. If they're not using your best-picked tool, there's probably a good reason why not.

Final Thoughts

Scientific people bring problem-solving skills to programming in addition to a knowledge of the domain. They simply need to adapt these skills to programming. Business people, on the other hand, bring mostly problem *statements*, and must frequently learn how to solve problems in addition to programming.

Of course, this is a gross generalization, but we have frequently observed that business people tend to think that what can be stated can be done. This is not very realistic, but it is *very* Roman.

This chapter describes the things that separate the business and scientific sides of programming. We hope that we have shown that these are really differences in *degree*, not in *kind*. When we look at what programming is—how invisible it is, how all programs are made of the same stuff, and how we are all turning computers into virtual machines and changing our world—we can see that there are more things about us that are *alike* than are different. ❧

Chapter 9.
Metrics:
Spans, Cubits, and Stadia

When we use the term *metrics*, we mean "the extent, dimensions, capacity, etc., of anything, especially as determined by a standard." [Webster's New World Dictionary 1979, p.895] In software engineering, we are referring to items such as lines of code, errors, problem reports, and the amount of time it takes to do things. We also mean such project management items as milestones, deliverables (usually documents), and resource consumption (such as man-months).

There are many metrics in our field. In fact, they are frequently seen as a panacea. People all over the place have been put to work making measurements, and then talk about it as if just making the measurements will improve things. And, there are controversies about what metrics mean and how they are used.

But, some good work has been done. There are two excellent books that describe the creation of a software metrics program for the Hewlett Packard Company [Grady and Caswell 1987; Grady 1992]. These books do a better job than we could ever do in describing a company-wide program. See specifically Chapter 8 of the Grady and Caswell book on metrics tools and how simple they can really be. Another look at metrics appears in the article we've reproduced in Appendix B [Côté et al. 1988, pp.121-131]. It is essentially a bodacious bibliography with a concise introduction and description. It is so good that we have included the entire article as a pointer to the available literature.

We cite these references to provide you with pointers to a traditional view of metrics. However, we are going to continue our Roman-Greek approach to describing the state of the art. In this case, we'll describe metrics, the problems with them, and how these problems affect tools and tool users.

We will start with a discussion of some metrics we use. Then, we will discuss problems with metrics and offer a way to determine which metrics you should use.

Two of the most important metrics we need to understand well are *customer satisfaction*, which is important in every market, and *software size*.

Customer Satisfaction: Money is a Direct Measure

Customer satisfaction is our customer's degree of acceptance of our product or service. Although nebulous, our customer's satisfaction is the most important measure of all. It is their satisfaction that we seek because they ultimately pay the freight. It is the true measure of our work. And, it is often measured in dollars, or pesos, or whatever.

A computer game maker once gave us his criteria for customer satisfaction: "Does my game cause a boy between five and fifteen to put another quarter in the machine."

That's a very simple metric. You get the game out there and you count the quarters. If you get a lot of quarters, your customers are satisfied; if not, they're not.

Some other criteria are: "Will the customer put the first quarter in?" and "Will the customer buy the software?"

Money is still the most effective measure of customer satisfaction. If you were Bill Gates of Microsoft, you would have to conclude that customers are satisfied with your products because they keep buying them. After you become a billionaire, it is hard to conclude otherwise as the money keeps rolling in.

But, there is an indirect measure, too. It is what we call the *smile metric.*

When you are in an IS shop, nobody is going to pay a quarter to run your program. So, you've got to find another measure of satisfaction. One method that is pushed by the Romans is the *smile metric.* It purports to measure customer satisfaction by interviewing customers and getting testimonials from them that are favorable to the product or service being measured. Sometimes it works, but it is always tricky to ask customers to talk about whether or not they're satisfied.

Suppose, for example, that a customer says he doesn't like the position of the *Name* field on one of the screens you provide. Placing it in a different location might improve his liking of your software and you might get a smile to report out of it. But, if he never liked the time it took you to get the software to him in the first place, or if this improvement is swamped by other unfriendly (or even hostile) characteristics of the software, then fixing the field's location is not going to help much and asking the question did not elicit a good measure.

Another effect occurs when customers are pleased simply because they are asked questions about the products they use and try to be as cooperative as possible. However, in trying not to offend the questioner, they frequently give misleading information about their level of satisfaction.

The *smile metric* is a wicked cousin of customer satisfaction. It is indirect because it does not measure the customers' behavior, only their future intention to act.

The Software Size Metric

Software size is important because, unlike hardware production, most of the cost of software production goes into designing and constructing the first copy. Subsequent copies are inexpensive and easily made. And, of this first copy, size is the most important feature for estimating costs. So, when someone is deciding to develop some software, an estimate of its size is important for allocating resources.

There is a controversy in our business about the *software size* metric: how big is the software or how big will it be? Some predictions of size are really stunning. Right now, many business systems are extremely large. In fact, one of the distinguishing characteristics we found between business and scientific software was the very large size of typical business applications compared to typical scientific applications.

But, now there is definitely a shift the other way. Engineering systems are getting larger. And, their growth appears to be exponential. In June of 1988, at the CASE Symposium for Aerospace, Defense, and Engineering software in Los Angeles, Dr. John Manley predicted that the Space Station will require at least ten million lines of code, and stated that NASA has 23,000 terabytes of data in its Materials and Sciences data [Manley 1988, p.116].

Lines Of Code

One way of measuring size is simply to measure what the programmer produces: the programs themselves. This includes the number of program modules, such as subroutines; various lines-of-code measures; and tokens, the distinguishable units of a language expression such as operators, variable names, and control structure indicators.

The most frequently used measures are the lines of code. The least often used, we find, are tokens. Tokens measure the intrinsic characteristics of the software.

The various measures of lines of code are some of the simplest and cheapest size measures. They come in several flavors:

LOC	lines of code
KLOC	thousands of lines of code
SLOC	source lines of code
DeSLOC	delivered SLOC
ELOC	executable lines of code
KELOC	thousands of executable lines of code

And, our choice:

ALOC	all lines of code (total lines of code) including JCL, TLOC, commentary, test data, and even user's guides

The term *LOC* is ambiguous. Does it mean *all* lines of code? All *executable* lines of code? All executable and *specification* lines of code?

KLOC has the same problem except that it is multiplied a thousand times. SLOC and DeSLOC are still ambiguous, but are usually composed of executable and specification statements.

ELOC does not include specification statements, JCL, commentary, or formal headers. Executable statements were an important measure when computers were slow. Then, storage wasn't any problem; magnetic and paper tapes were already well-developed media, and while their transfer rates were low, their capacities, especially that of magnetic tape, were high relative to the needs of the computers. Faster storage didn't matter as long as the computer was slow.

ELOC was the most important measure for optimizing software because it was a measure of time on the CPU, and the machine was relatively expensive compared to a programmer's wages. But, as CPUs speeded up, the need for fast retrieval grew quickly. Soon, real core memory was replaced by much faster and smaller integrated circuit memory chips. The cost of the machine dropped dramatically, and both time (the speed of the CPU) and space (memory) were getting cheaper (but were still more expensive than programmers). So, uncommented lines of code (SLOC), including specification statements, became the measure.

Then, about 1985, things changed again. Programmers became dear, and optimizing machine time and space wasn't as important as programmer time. But, ELOC and SLOC are still used. We believe the measure ought to be what we produce; it ought to be all lines of code (ALOC), which includes everything in the source file, all the code the programmers produce, all the commentary in the code, JCL, test data, etc.

There is some evidence for this. The modules in a simulation project averaged 69 lines of third-generation language code and 114 lines of commentary, JCL, and formal headers. The development team discovered that the cost of this other stuff was equal to the cost of source code. In other words, commentary, JCL, and formal headers in a module cost about 60% of a code line, where a line of code could be either an executable or a specification statement [Shrock 1983, pp.831-834].

In addition, the cost of the programmer's commentary in the code itself has a considerable effect on maintenance costs. For every extra dollar spent in the design and implementation phases of development (where commentary is written), a dollar and a half is saved in maintenance. (See Figure 9-1.) All this adds up to a case for using what a programmer produces: ALOCs.

Function Points

Function points are an extremely complicated Roman metric intended to be a size metric. They were invented by Allen Albrecht at IBM in the early seventies. He was looking for a way (other than lines of code) to measure the size of a software inventory.

He perceived that, properly weighted, the inputs to an application, the outputs from the application, inquiries by users, the data files to be updated, and interfaces to other applications should represent the common concerns of the users: the functionality of the application. These characteristics could be combined and summarized to give an indication of the functional size of the software: its function points.

Function points are a measure of the extrinsic characteristics of the software. They are based on the assumption that there is a simple mapping of each input to one or very few internal processes and to an output. This is not the case for most engineering software.

Computing the function points for a system is extremely complicated. And, there are variations. The variation that we will summarize here is taken from "Function Point Analysis" by Productivity Management Group.

Function points are the product of an unadjusted function point count (UFP) and a value adjustment factor (VAF): UFP × VAF. The unadjusted function point count is the sum of five products. The VAF is the sum of the weights applied to 14 general system characteristics. This VAF is then adjusted to zero plus or minus 35%.

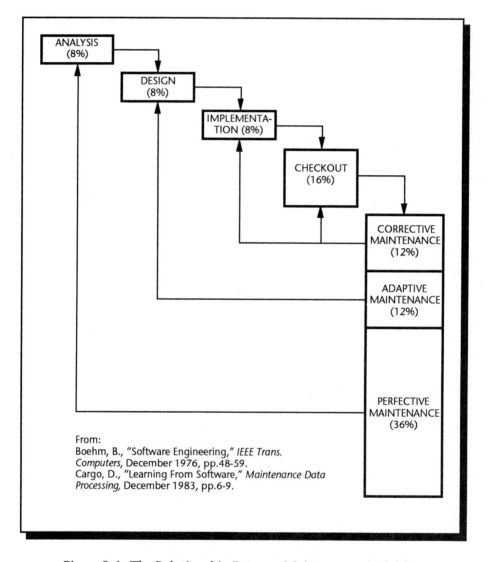

*Figure 9-1. The Relationship Between Maintenance Activities
and the Development Activities that Preceded Them*[23]

---

[23] Analysis takes up 8% of total cost, but affects 36% of downstream costs, i.e, perfective maintenance.

To compute the unadjusted function points, sum the weighted values of the number of system components: internal logical files, external interface files, external inputs, external outputs, and external inquiries. The weights applied to each of these components are determined by the numbers of data elements in each file: low, average, and high.

Weights	Low	Average	High
internal logical files	7	10	15
external interface files	5	7	10
external inputs	3	4	6
external outputs	4	5	7
external inquiries	3	4	6

The file definitions themselves are complicated. For example: an internal logical file is a group of logically related data or control information than can be identified by the user and is used inside the software. This appears to be inconsistent. If the file is used inside the application, how can the user be aware of it and why should s/he be? The user uses information *outside* the application, not inside it. At any rate, this is the UFP.

To compute the VAF, rate on a scale of 1 to 5 the 14 general system characteristics. They are: data communications, distributed functions, performance, heavily-used configuration, transaction rate, on-line data entry, end user efficiency, on-line update, complex processing, reusability, installation ease, operational ease, multiple sites, and facilitate change [ibid; sic]. We will not define these here, but you can obtain more information on them from Productivity Management Group. The general system characteristics appear to be a good list of risk factors; at least they would be a good starting place for building a table to evaluate the risk of doing a project.

The calculation is:

Function Points = (sum of the weighted values of system components) * ((.01 * (sum of the weights [from 1 to 5] of the 14 general system characteristics) + .65)

The unadjusted function points are, therefore, adjusted up or down by as much as 35% by the weights of the general system characteristics.

As you can see, function point counting is extremely complex, and the tools available to help simply record the results of work done by other means. One of our correspondents said that once you've done a function point count, you don't want to do any more. In UNIX systems, there is a utility that counts the carriages returns and all lines of code in any file. Compare this to the calculation above. Which would you rather do?

Ordinarily, organizations have a function point lead group to train the developers and build the database needed to support function point counts. In Chapter Four, we talked about overly Roman organizations and their super staffs. Well, function point counting is a good example of this.

The Problems with Metrics

There are some problems with metrics.

- We have frequently heard the claim from participants at metrics conferences and seminars that some programmers are more verbose than others. They feel that if lines of code are used to measure their performance, then programmers will "pad" their programs with commentary, blank lines, and other text *irrelevant* to the machine's operation.

- One guru we know of claims that lines of code aren't "economic goods."

- Others claim mystical, magical powers for the function point and defect metrics.

- Still others are so enthralled with the measurement activity that the actual software production appears to take a back seat.

So, we are going to take the time here to correct these ideas.

How to Measure Programmers' Performance

In our opinion, programmers should be measured by the *quality* and *timeliness* of their solutions, not on the *size* of their programs. But, size is a popular measure.

This whole issue is very difficult to sort out. And, it reveals, oddly, a schizoid temperament on the part of many managers in our business. On the one hand, these managers think programmers will work to maximize the lines-of-code measure with *unnecessary* code. They will, in effect, defraud the company of honest product. This is called the "padding effect."

Yet, in public, they often eschew using the line of code metric to measure programmer performance because they claim (correctly in our view) that programmers will take this and not the quality and timeliness of their solutions as the measure on which their performance will be rated.

As a result, there is a desire to do with function points what would be too obvious with LOC. With function points, programmers can be *controlled* from the design phase. Function points supposedly enable managers to concentrate on the functionality of the product and not the size of the program. Yet, function points are indeed a size measure and, whenever we press managers on the issue, they reveal that some of their programmers are lazy so using function points will identify their recalcitrant workers.

Here is a message to managers: *Programmers are not dumb!* If you measure them based on lines of code and they are *indeed* padding their work, then wait until you see what they can do with function points! Any cursory look at the function point calculation we described earlier shows how chock full of padding opportunities they are.

But, let's take that padding argument head on. We'll stipulate that different programmers produce various sizes of software for the same problem. In fact, we'll stipulate that a good programmer indeed does produce differently sized solutions for the same problem depending on circumstances. Why?

Our answer comes from the famous Weinberg-Schulman experiment reported by Barry Boehm, who produced one of the most important works on economics in our field [Boehm 1981, p.318]. In that experiment, six programming teams were given the identical task to perform, but they were also given different objectives to optimize. The results are summarized in Table 9-1.

Table 9-1. The Weinberg-Schulman Experiment			
Team Objective	**Program Size**	**Man Hours**	**Productivity**
Program Size	33	30	1.1
Memory Required	52	74	0.7
Program Clarity	90	40	2.2
Execution Time	100	50	2.0
Effort to Complete	126	28	4.5
Output Clarity	166	30	5.5

If a team were to optimize for *program size*, it produced the smallest program (no padding). If, however, they optimized for *program clarity*, they produced a program almost three times bigger than the smallest. Program clarity is for fellow programmers. If they optimized for *output clarity*, they produced a program 5.5 times larger than the smallest. This is for the customer.

Is there padding in these last two examples? It would seem so. But, notice the two teams that padded their programs are following what we would call good programming practices.

Software size is important to programmer performance only later on when testing and maintenance occurs and "levels of effort" are set up. For example, one maintenance programmer could easily keep ten programs comprised of about 10,000 lines each of well laid out FORTRAN running and constantly improved. But, when a programmer is at work *developing* a program, you cannot take her lines of code (or function points) per day as any indication of her productivity, unless it is a trivial job. This is because the lines of code or function points are produced at the end of a long, difficult, invisible process used by the programmer. So, these measures per day have no meaning until the job is done; they just aren't produced uniformly as a result of each day's effort.

If you can't measure quality and timeliness, you are missing some key points of the field; but, see Chapter 3 for some ideas about quality and how to measure it.

Lines of Code (LOC) vs. Function Points

Now, let's take on the business about LOCs not being "economic goods." This argument is made by T. Capers Jones. A version of it appeared in *System Development* [1989]. In his article, Mr. Jones builds an example to demonstrate his contention that LOCs are neither goods nor services in the "economic" sense, but that function points are. In his example, there are two software development projects. The only difference between them is the language used. One uses assembly language and produces the result in 10,000 lines of code. The other uses COBOL and produces its results in 3,000 line of code. He makes some calculations on both examples; the results are shown in Table 9-2.

Table 9-2. Lines-of-Code Analysis		
Activity	**Assembler Version (10,000 lines)**	**COBOL Version (3,000 lines)**
Requirements	2 months	2 months
Design	3 months	3 months
Coding	10 months	3 months
Integration/Test	5 months	3 months
User Documentation	2 months	2 months
Management Support	3 months	2 months
Total Months	25	15
Total Costs	$125,000	$75,000
Cost per Source Line	$12.50	$25.00
Lines per Man Month	400	200

Mr. Jones complains that even though the lines of code per man month have gone down from 400 to 200 in the move from Assembler to COBOL, the cost per source line has gone up from $12.50 to $25 per line. This shouldn't be, he argues, because when you change to new technology, your costs should go down, not up. He says this is because there is a large percentage of fixed costs (requirements, design, etc.) and a declining output (from 10,000 lines to 3,000 lines), and that the cost per line must go up because the costs must be distributed over fewer units of output. Therefore, he concludes, one cannot measure real productivity with LOCs; they are neither goods nor services in the "economic" sense.

He then produces another table (shown in Table 9-3). This time, he uses function points. The number of function points per month goes up (from 1.2 to 2.0) and the cost per function point goes down (from about $4,200 to $2,500). This result corresponds with his expectations that, as the number of units produced goes up, the price per unit goes down.

We believe that Mr. Jones has made a mistake in his analysis. The statement about unit costs going up when there are large fixed costs and a declining output is generally true. But, the declining output must truly be a decline and must be caused by something *outside* the enterprise. This is known as the "buggy whip" argument and explains why, when people switched to automobiles, the costs of buggy whips went up. The demand for horse-drawn buggies went down and, therefore, the quantity of buggy whips demanded went down. So, the fixed overhead costs were spread among fewer units of output and costs went up.

But, Mr. Jones changed the inputs of one of the projects by changing its technology and didn't account for the change in his calculations. He didn't hold all the inputs constant or account for any change; "all things being equal," as it's often said.

Suppose, for example, new technology was developed so that the enterprise could produce buggy whips packaged by the dozen with half the manpower as before. One would get similar results: the cost per output unit (dozen) would go up and the effort per unit would go down. Yet, one would still say that buggy whips are economic goods.

Table 9-3. Function Points Analysis		
Activity	Assembler Version (30 function points)	COBOL Version (30 function points)
Requirements	2 months	2 months
Design	3 months	3 months
Coding	10 months	3 months
Integration/Test	5 months	3 months
User Documentation	2 months	2 months
Management Support	3 months	2 months
Total Months	25	15
Total Costs	$125,000	$75,000
Cost per Function Point	$4,166.67	$2,500.00
Function Points per Man Month	1.2	2.0

What he should have done is something like the following:

- Do the calculations of the lines-of-code example.

- Calculate an efficiency figure to account for the difference in technology inputs: the languages.

- Apply this efficiency figure to the first analysis.

One of the authors of this book did this and produced results comparable to those Mr. Jones' function points example.

In our opinion, a brewery would have been a better example. If you switch from producing beer by the can to beer by the six-pack, the cost of your product goes up by the cost of six cans *plus* packaging, even though the units you produce goes down to about one-sixth of the previous production. This is equivalent to Mr. Jones's first example because, when you write in a third-generation language, each line decomposes into several lines of assembly language, which is a second-generation language, just as a six-pack decomposes into individual cans. Yet, one would hardly say that a can of beer is not an economic good, no matter how it's packaged!

Another part of the problem is that arguments such as Mr. Jones's have a quality to them of needing to *beat* or *exclude* the other guy; not just establish one's own position. "One should use function points and *not* lines of code he concludes."

We see Mr. Jones's argument as a further example of the overly Roman approach to our field. It detaches the producer from his product and forces him into some La La Land of abstract "ought" thought. It's hard to imagine that what someone produces, whether it is beer or code, is *not* an economic good.

The Misuse of the Defect Metric

At code inspections, programmers who are acting as inspectors are asked to locate errors in the work being submitted to them for inspection. These errors are reported to the original programmer, who then has a chance to correct them. Code inspections are an effective way of locating errors and correcting them before they can be sent downstream. As long as this information stays in the reviewing group, then the review can be a positive experience.

But, sometimes overly Roman organizations require that the errors detected by the inspectors be reported outside of the reviewing group as defects attributed to a specific programmer. In that type of atmosphere, reporting defects undermines the purpose of the inspection and can be damaging to the individual and their environment. How can someone ask her peers to review her code *knowing* they are required to report any defects to the metrics Romans? Worse, does anyone really expect that the reviewee will *voluntarily* submit her stuff if she is also expected to report her defects?

Programmers, like all of us, make errors as they work. These errors don't become defects until they are passed off to the next process: testing, the customer, or whatever. After they are passed on to the next process as defects, they become fair game for reporting; but, until then, programmers ought to be allowed to find and correct their errors before they become defects, and to use effective methods of doing so.

In the type of environment where any error is reported, there is no longer any time to do program sketching, or to imagine solutions to problems, or to consult with peers. We get the feeling that we are in a tribunal of the Cultural Revolution and are required to denounce ourselves for our own sake. It is not a very healthy environment, it seems to us, but one that comes to us from frenetically chasing after external recognitions such as the Baldridge award.

Chasing the Indicators

There is a kind of goal displacement (described in Chapter 2) known as *chasing the indicators*. It is a term used in aviation to describe the error a pilot makes attempting to change the position of the airplane by fixating on a single indicator rather than on the main one. As a result, the pilot may not be able to make the change effectively or, sometimes, safely.

The cockpit of an airplane is *full* of controls and indicators. (See Figure 9-2.) Usually, there is a cluster of about seven major indicators that deal with the airplane's movement through the air. The central instrument is the attitude indicator, which shows level flight and deviation from it in pitch (nose up or down) and roll (banking). Six other indicators are: airspeed, power, turn coordinator, horizontal situation, vertical speed, and altimeter. To make a change in the aircraft's movement, the pilot decides what changes are needed, puts in the pitch, roll, and power required to give the desired results, monitors the attitude indicator, and scans the other instruments as the airplane changes its position. As the aircraft reaches the desired position, the pilot modifies the pitch, roll, and power to maintain the new desired position.

If you don't do it this way, you will overshoot or undershoot the desired results and you won't end up in the desired position. So, you have to correct again and from an undesirable attitude.

Here are some examples from our field:

- Over-analyzing or over-normalizing data
- Producing stacks of short-lived documents
- Using a CASE tool to produce an endless stream of graphs
- Writing a huge, unreadable requirements document

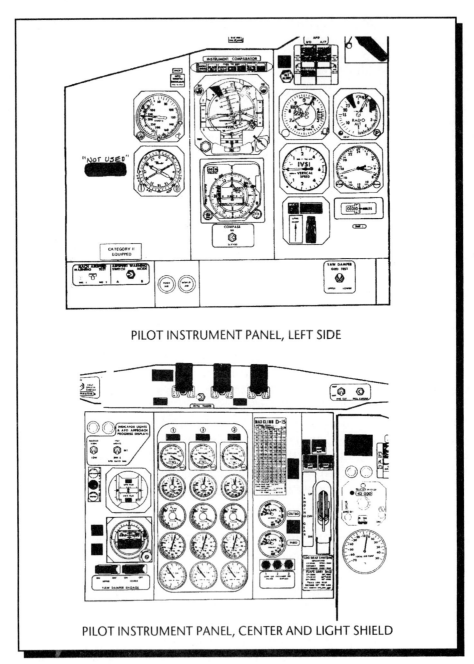

PILOT INSTRUMENT PANEL, LEFT SIDE

PILOT INSTRUMENT PANEL, CENTER AND LIGHT SHIELD

Figure 9-2. Airplane Controls and Instruments

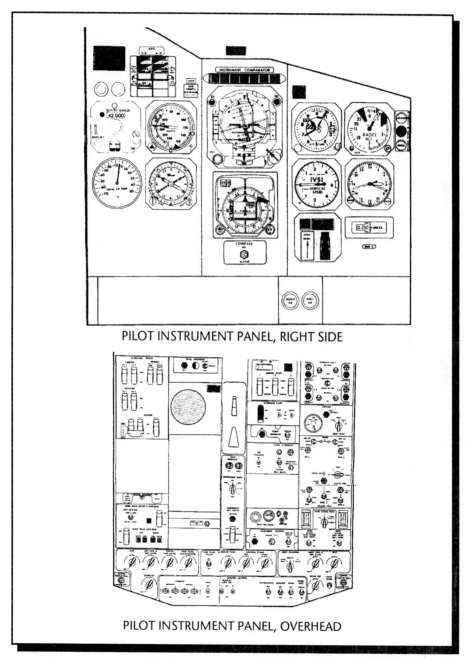

PILOT INSTRUMENT PANEL, RIGHT SIDE

PILOT INSTRUMENT PANEL, OVERHEAD

Figure 9-2. Airplane Controls and Instruments (cont.)

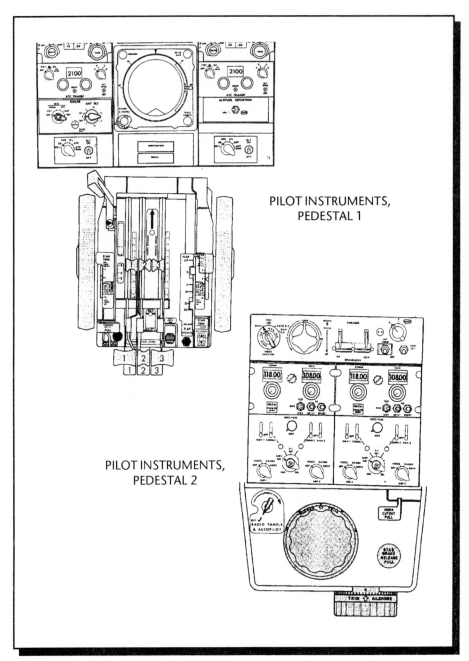

PILOT INSTRUMENTS,
PEDESTAL 1

PILOT INSTRUMENTS,
PEDESTAL 2

Figure 9-2. Airplane Controls and Instruments (cont.)

Other examples could be: using function points with its super-staff of counting specialists, and requiring defect reports without understanding the process as we described earlier. Even chasing after the Baldridge award is an example if focussing on it distracts you from understanding what's happening in the enterprise, which is the goal displacement we discussed in Chapter 2.

The results of this displacement can be very dangerous for the organization. John Akers, IBM's Chairman, is said to have once remarked to a group of IBM managers: "All the indicators are up but our market share is still going down." Apparently those managers were spending their time optimizing the wrong measures. Now this anecdote might be apocryphal, but it illustrates the results of chasing the indicators. And, IBM has reorganized, cutting its work force substantially.

In business, whether it is directly or indirectly measured, customer satisfaction is the main indicator. But, if you spend too much time and too many resources financing some super staff (such as a metrics operation) and neglect customer satisfaction, you are "chasing the indicators." You might get glowing reports about heroic efforts to count the function points in your company, but your customer is likely to vanish.

In an airplane, the attitude indicator gives the pilot a picture-like indication. In business, management's main indicator should be a picture of satisfying his customer's needs.

Which Metrics to Use

Some important questions about metrics are which measures to use and when to use them.

Project or Level of Effort

When you write programs, is your business context a *project* or a *level of effort*? When we say "write programs," we mean in the broader context of all the stuff that goes on in programming such as understanding the problem, imagining a solution, expressing it in some computer language, and then testing and documenting it.

Projects are used for new systems. They have relatively fixed goals and allow time to vary in achieving them. Folks in projects assume that these goals are known. Projects tend to be formal, are often involved with some standard development method (usually a Waterfall), and require extensive documentation. They also add management and accounting overhead costs to the effort.

Projects are interested in milestones, deliverables, and schedules. Success is often measured in meeting these schedules, not necessarily in reaching the project's goals.

The fact that the project exists or ever existed is often perceived as the most valuable aspect of the project. If it happens to fail, the manager is insulated and is often promoted. We have seen too much of this nonsense. Here are some facts:

- Many (perhaps all) of the planners of the failed desert rescue mission in Iran were promoted.

- We know of a large project cancelled by the DoD for poor performance. The project manager was promoted to V.P. afterward.

- We know of a V.P. who left a string of "systems from hell" in his wake as he travelled through his career. We were told that he was "kicked" upstairs to get him out of the way. This is an old custom, but it sets a bad example. Yet, in smaller organizations, or in organizations that must satisfy the general public, if you screw up you are *history*. What a dichotomy of effects to try to make sense out of!

Levels of effort, on the other hand, are used for maintenance activities such as rat-killing and "enhancements." (Conversions to new platforms, the third type of maintenance, are frequently *projects*.)

Here, time is fixed and results vary. Progress is frequently made opportunistically. The goals usually aren't known completely, and those that are known are fuzzy. Intermediate results are used to generate new goals. Levels of effort tend to be self-managed, with low overhead. Documentation is sparse. Methods include prototyping, incremental development, and hacking [DeGrace and Stahl 1990].

Levels of effort have the goal of maintaining an initial useful product and improving it over time. Success is measured by keeping the system on the air and accomplishments in improving it in the background. It's a neat, nifty way to do things, but it gets no press because it isn't "orthodox." Yet, if it is true that most software engineering is maintenance, then most effort in our field is done by means of *level of effort* organizations.

Now, as we promised you earlier, we can help you determine which metric to use by translating all this stuff into software terms. Figure 9-3 shows the metrics we will look at and how they relate.

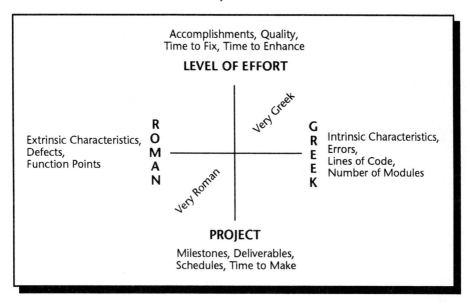

Figure 9-3. Metrics and How They Relate

If you are a Roman and are doing *projects*, then you'll probably want to use defects, defects per cycle time, function points, milestones, deliverables, and schedules. If you are a Roman doing *levels of effort*, then leave off the project stuff and add accomplishments, time metrics, and quality.

If you are a Greek doing product development at *levels of effort*, then use levels of effort and Greek measures. If you are doing product development under a project structure, then leave off the level of effort stuff and add the project metrics that were initially used.

Of course, no matter how you view your work or how you account for the resources you use, the ultimate goal is *customer satisfaction*.

Implications for CASE

Measuring what you are doing can help you determine how well you are doing. If you are Greek, the measures might not always be simple but they are straightforward. If you are Roman, they become sophisticated. In either case, there is software available to help you make software metrics.

You can use LOCs, but use *everything* the programmer produces. Between the programmer and the machine, the programmer's time is the most valuable.

Metrics *themselves* are tools, and there are software tools that help you collect them. *Project metrics* are the most expensive. A metrics program starting at the programmer level can be based on practical things. Rolling them up into larger and larger units is also very expensive and obscuring. Function points are more expensive than LOCs because you get LOCs with most compiler listings, but you have to count function points and much of the effort must be done manually.

Defects could be either inexpensive or expensive. If they are collected along with trouble reports, they are inexpensive. If they are collected as a result of indirect means, such as customer satisfaction interviews after the fact or intrusion into the programmer-analyst's process of visualizing the problem and its solution, then they are expensive and can be very damaging psychologically.

When you look at the state of practice, you see many metrics, many arguments about them, and many challenges about selecting and using them. Romans tend to use metrics such as function points, and Greeks will use those such as lines of code. Where the Romans can look at software generically, Greeks take another view.

In the next chapter, we'll look at standards as they apply to the state of practice. ❧

Chapter 10.
Standards:
The Greek-Roman Rosetta Stone

You might be asking, "What are *standards* and why is a book on CASE talking about them? Isn't that a little out of the scope of this book?"

We believe that these are good questions, and they have been raised by some of our correspondents. But, our purpose is to describe the state of practice in our field. Standards are a part of all that. In this chapter, we will give a definition of standards and a description of their benefits. We then end with a description of the four types of standards themselves.

Definitions of *Standards*

Our dictionary has ten definitions of the word *standard*. But, the ones that interest us are the following:

1. "Something established for use as a rule or basis for comparison in measuring or judging capacity, quantity, content, extent, value, quality, etc.;"

2. "The type, model, or example commonly or generally accepted or adhered to;"

3. "A level of excellence, attainment, etc. regarded as a measure of adequacy." [Webster's New World Dictionary 1979]

We use all three meanings in our field, but the most common meaning is the second: "The type, model, or example commonly or generally accepted or adhered to."

The Benefits of Standards

Standards are important to selecting and using tools, and here are some reasons why. First, if you're Greek, standards enable *uniformity*; if you're Roman, they enable *conformity*. In either case, you get a certain sameness and predictability that ease communications as well as make it easier to hook disparate things together. The total effect is to reduce the real (or sometimes the apparent) complexity in the environment in which you are working.

Second, there is the uncovered opportunity to pay attention to the important, unique aspects of the task at hand. Thus, mundane tasks aren't elevated to important levels of activity and programmers have a better chance of working in the higher quality regions of their skills and talents.

Third, standards can free us from the tyranny of vendors. By enabling us to connect together disparate hardware and software, they also enable us to select software and hardware that better match our requirements even though they might be produced by different vendors.

Fourth, many standards exist in our field, and many more are coming our way. The software and hardware we get and make will be affected by these standards and those who make them. Appendix C contains some excellent data on CASE standards organizations. It is a reprint of the minutes from the July 6, 1992, CASE Standards Coordination Workshop by David Sharon and Myer Morron [1992]. It provides useful pointers to those who are setting standards in our field and what their goals are.

In addition, there are about 130 communications standards, no telling how many hardware standards, and a growing number of software engineering standards, including data transfer standards and the most important standards of all, language standards. (We know this to be true because we asked a lot of programmers which standards, if any, they regularly try to adhere to. More than *two-thirds* said language standards, while any of the others were less than one-tenth).

Types of Standards

There are four basic types of standards in our field:

- Common-usage standards
- Fiat standards
- Monopoly standards
- Consensus standards

Common-Usage Standards

The world of standards is a typical Greco-Roman one. Standards start out Greek; they are used voluntarily by many folks because they see the benefits of common usage. We call these *common-usage* standards. The common ways of doing things in the UNIX culture is a good example of common-usage standards.

Common usage is a popularity contest. Does the typical person usually have this thing or do this thing? Some examples of common usage are IBM PCs, DFDs, graphical user interfaces (GUIs), mice and, of course, UNIX.

When you buy a computer these days, you're likely to get some or all of these standard, commonly used items. Common usage is a cultural thing ... a Greek thing. It grows from successful use, which attracts other users either by example or by word of mouth. After it attracts enough users, it becomes a *common-usage* standard.

Of course, common usage is a relative thing. You could easily have a group of folks isolated from most others adopting certain conventions and using or adhering to them faithfully. At that local level, they are common usage.

In the larger world, one of the best examples is the UNIX culture. These folks are the "Greekest" of us all; they regularly build and exchange tools and other software they make. And, they have many far-flung networks over which to make their requests.

If the thing being represented by a common-usage standard is seen to be very useful and popular (for example, primitive FORTRAN), then it becomes a candidate for standardization by the American National Standards Institute (ANSI). (See Figure 10-1.)

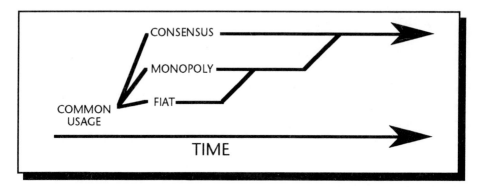

Figure 10-1. Common-Usage Standards Evolve Over Time

Fiat Standards

Frequently, Romans take over and impose standards on Greeks and Romans alike. They codify and promulgate and define and get the usual response: folks avoid things that are imposed from the outside and are not internalized. These are the *fiat* standards.

Project standards are often set by fiat. Here, the Romans enter the picture imposing order. This order is a good thing; it manages complexity and provides a clarity to activities and communications, which makes it easier to cooperate with others efficiently and quickly.

The project manager, or chief guru, establishes a standard to suit her own sense of goodness in the environment she is creating for the project. At the local level, there may be perfectly good reasons for this and it gets things settled quickly. After all, that's what the manager or guru is being paid for.

But, our correspondents report that when the project's members have a say in setting these standards, they find it easier to adhere to them. When they don't, the project's players live with the standards, but find ways of defeating their purpose which, in projects, is to get folks to communicate or do things in a uniform way according to rules with which everybody agrees.

However, there are problems with this approach. It has a "push down" characteristic: "Who the hell are those ?!@# guys, telling *us* how to do *our* work?"

Here's an example: It is the Pentagon's fiat that Ada be used in mission-critical applications. Yet, in an announcement of an Ada Colloquium, the text started off with, "In contrast to other languages, Ada did not come with a set of intrinsic or built-in math functions. It is hard to imagine a scientific or engineering computation that does not require square roots, logarithms, exponentials, or trigonometric functions, and that is why compiler vendors have included their own math libraries (often as Ada shells around pre-existing C or FORTRAN code). While this approach meets the immediate needs of application programmers, the larger problem of portability of application remains unsolved, primarily the vendor supplied libraries vary widely in composition, names of individual components, parameter/result profiles, and even the use or avoidance of genericity."

Why are we not astounded by such a revelation? Why is the "mission-critical" standard language of the Pentagon not prepared to do mission-critical work without a lot of reinventing the wheel?

Worse, our correspondents report that developers (at least in 1990 and earlier) purposely *don't* use the features that the Pentagon wants for mission-critical work because there is simply too much overhead still involved.

Monopoly Standards

Another type of standard is the *monopoly* standard, so called because those who set the standard have monopoly power. Industry leaders who produce the first product often have the only say in how is should be. IBM's System Network Architecture (SNA), SAA, and AD/Cycle are examples. Here, an industry leader is able to set the standard and enforce it through its products. A big advantage with the monopoly standards is that they can insulate you from problems with consensus standards (described later in this chapter).

In the early eighties, there was a huge donnybrook over a new COBOL standard: COBOL-80. The battle was mainly waged in the pages of *ComputerWorld* in 1981 and 1982 by Joseph Brophy, a senior vice-president at Traveler's Insurance Companies. In one report, in the March 15, 1982, edition of *ComputerWorld*, he stated that the new standard would not be compatible with earlier standards and would cost fifty cents per line to convert. However, *ComputerWorld* reported in January 1983 that the IBM VS COBOL II Compiler, which was to be available in 1985, was based on the existing COBOL-74 standard and included many extensions that were part of the original draft standard for COBOL-80.

In other words, let the bureaucrats do what they want; IBM promised to stand behind its customers, providing them with incremental enhancements and improvements to its current line of COBOL compilers rather than making huge step changes that cause so much heartburn.

To do this, IBM was faced with supporting three different compilers for the same language. That type of customer support is one reason why Big Blue remains *Big*.

Monopoly standards have a lot more going for them. They bring regularity and reduce complexity to a much wider scope than local fiat standards and can have the same range as large scale consensus standards.

Monopoly standards frequently arise from one or a small number of minds that have been concentrating on certain technical problems. For some unknown reason, this has kept complexity low. FORTRAN was a good example.

Monopoly standards have the breakthrough quality of a large step in technology because they very often come about as a result of technical breakthroughs. An example is the Polaroid camera and its film. Our patent laws protect and encourage this sort of innovation by promising the rewards of monopoly control to those who are willing to take the risks involved in making breakthroughs.

How do monopoly standards become common-usage standards? Here's an example: We asked one of our correspondents which laser printer he would recommend. He replied that any one would do as long as it had a Canon engine in it. For him, all the other engines gave you problems you don't need. He said we should get one of the Canon types: "because it's standard!"

We joshed him a little: "Whose standard is it? ANSI, ISO, or what?"

He said, of course, "Because everybody uses it."

Consensus Standards

Finally, there is a fourth type, called *consensus* standards. These are made by a group of people getting together for the sole purpose of making standards. These people should be Greek, but very often are taken over by well-meaning Romans who want to "improve" things.

By the way, we have frequently illustrated the Rome vs. Greek idea to show the split in our ranks. But, consider the following quote from Marshall Rose concerning the Open Systems Interconnection (OSI) standards makers [Rose 1990, pp.585-586]:

"Consider who actually gets sent to standards meetings. When a technology enters the standards process, vendors send their best and brightest to safeguard their proprietary interests. Once the course is set, the Doers are called back to the office where they can perform more productive tasks for their employers. To finish off the process, the vendors then send persons they can afford to have out of the office, the professional standards Goers. The Goers have likely never implemented anything in their professional careers (if they have, it was so long ago as to be unworthy of mention, e.g., when vacuum tubes were the rule). There is a propensity among the Goers not even to use computers, the very technology they are working to enhance. A Goer attends meetings to deal with weighty political issues, travel, and have many fine lunches and dinners.

"The caricature of the Goer is someone who pops into the office Monday morning to pick up mail, and then jets off to a standards meeting, liaison session, workshop, or symposium. On the airplane, the Goer reviews the numerous written contributions and gets ready for the next meeting, all around the in-flight movie.

"In 1988, the Goers were commonly referred to as nitwits (genus *nitwitus vulgaris*). A nitwit in the standards sense is someone who thinks that just because you write something down, it is implementable and workable.

"There are notable exceptions. The landmark standards on message handling are the result of a few key persons, combination Doer/Goers, who were able to come to the table with savvy technology and then keep the discussion focused, regardless of the political influences. This is but a stellar exception, not the rule.

"A large number of Doers boycott standards meetings because they are afraid of being tainted by nitwits. Instead, Doers are sending their colleagues, who in turn report back, thereby letting them ruin their careers. Nevertheless, without the few combination Doer/Goers in attendance, OSI would simply be unimplementable, as opposed to being mostly unimplementable.

"What happens when a Doer meets a Goer makes for an interesting vignette. When one of the OSI subcommittees invited experts from the Internet suite of protocols to attend a meeting, the result was: You guys really need a sanity check.

"The 'OSI sanity check' could probably be a very popular gift. It would probably be a lapel pin containing a very loud, obnoxious buzzer. Whenever a Goer utters nonsense, the buzzer emits an ear-shattering sound until a Doer resets it. This is a superb example of a self-correcting system: if the ratio of Doers to Goers is high enough, then lots of productive work occurs. If the reverse is true, especially if there are no Doers on the committee, then eventually the Goers will be rendered completely incoherent and no documents will ever be produced. Considering some of the OSI standards that do exist, it is clearly better to have no standards than to have bad ones."

Consensus standards are created by a divers group of volunteers who are, at least initially, experts and are intimately associated with the topic of the standard. The method of producing the standard is through a consensus process in which everyone has his or her say and votes are taken.

Then, politics set in to smooth ruffled feathers and to try and reach a unanimous vote. If that isn't possible, then the largest possible majority will do. The standard's scope is national or even international. The authority and excellence of the standard is determined by those of its creators.

ANSI is the main standards-coordinating body in our country. To actually create the standard, it makes use of other organizations specializing in the topic of the standards. For example, the Association of Computing Machines (ACM) and the Institute for Electrical and Electronic Engineering (IEEE) both have ties to ANSI and do standards work for it. The International Standards Organization (ISO) is the organization for international standards that are adhered to by local national bodies, especially in Western countries.

ANSI is an old institution. It was formed in 1918 by five professional technical societies and three federal agencies. These organizations wanted to avoid conflicts and duplication in the standards-making processes.

ANSI guides the efforts of over 250 standards-developing organizations at the national and international level. It has guided the creation of standards in areas as diverse as telecommunications, safety, health, information processing, petroleum, banking, household electrical appliances, electronics, and more.

Figures 10-2, 10-3, and 10-4 are some illustrations of the ANSI organization as it concerns us.

- Figure 10-2 shows the general organization of ANSI.

- Figure 10-3 shows the composition of the X3 Information Processing Systems committee.

- Figure 10-4 shows the languages committees, *X3Jn*.

If any of these interest you, you can reach ANSI at (212) 354-3300 or write to the Director of Development, ANSI, 1430 Broadway, New York, NY, 10018.

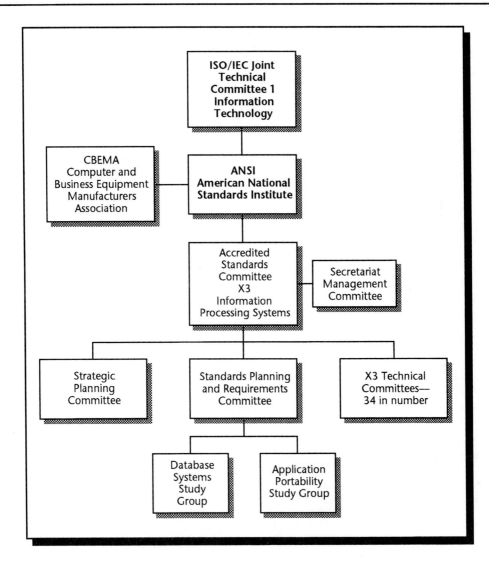

Figure 10-2. ANSI—General Organization

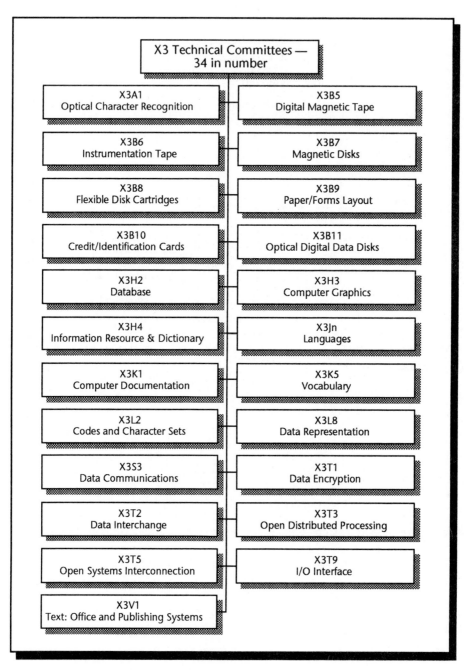

Figure 10-3. The ANSI X3 Information Processing Systems Committee

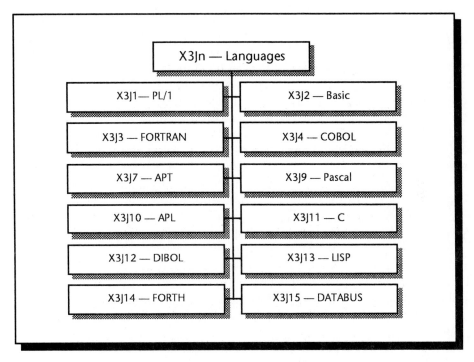

Figure 10-4. The ANSI Languages Committees, X3Jn

The Trouble with Standards

Standard is a very misused word in our field. It conveys a feeling of authority, a certain augustness that evokes a grand conservation of mass or energy or something, an approach to the fundamental values of Nature. And, it seems whenever one of us needs to evoke this awe in our fellow workers, we use the word *STANDARD* in all its uprightness and thereby blow away all objections.

Sometimes, we take our "standardness" even further and use the word *Bible* to raise our standard to even greater heights. It's as if by using the word *Bible* we are raising ourselves to be closer to God, fully justified and saintly.

One time, one of our correspondents wanted to show us that the COBOL standard to which he was referring was the last word in standards; he called it the *Bible* for COBOL. It was the IBM version of COBOL.

Now, IBM seems to have cornered most of the business market for computers and associated software, and it does a great job of supporting customers using its language products. So, in some respects, its version of COBOL could be called the *Bible*. But, it was *IBM's* Bible; there was yet another level of standardness—the American National Standards Institute (ANSI) version—from which, depending on your view of history, IBM built its own version of COBOL (or defended us from the ANSI version).

Another correspondent, wanting to impress us with his notion of standards (why do we need to impress others with the "standardness" of our stuff?), commented that in computing organizations we don't really know what standards are because they change so often. *"Real standards* don't change," he said, as he pointed out the engineering standards he had been using for some time. When we objected that these were but one kind of standard, he overruled us by citing his standards credentials: "I go to all the meetings," he said.

In another case, an organization we know of decided to make APS, from Intersolv, its *standard* for code generators. When a peer organization heard about this, it decided to have a *standard* of its own; so, it named Excelerator its CASE tool standard. Now, APS is a fine product and so is Excelerator; but, this was a case of political "me too-ism," taking standards to a new depth of absurdity.

In our field, we frequently misuse the word *standard* and then find ourselves confused about the issue. We take it to those absurd extremes, use it for purposes for which it was not intended and which damage our standing as a serious emerging field of engineering. We then stand back, scratching our heads, wondering why things aren't going well.

We mention these things not to poke fun at our correspondents, whom we deeply respect, but to show that there is a woeful misunderstanding among ourselves concerning what we mean by certain important words. This misunderstanding causes much mischief. In our opinion, we won't grow up until we learn to respect the words we use. We simply *must* have words that stand for something we can count on, that everybody has access to, and that are broadcast to the widest possible audience.

Standards move around a lot. For one thing, our software engineering standards *do* change frequently. They are just emerging, taking tentative steps toward the approval that only time and usage can grant. Some standards are like *constants*, never changing; others are like *parameters*, changing as conditions change.

Here are some examples of standards that have gone bad. We know of one vendor whose CASE tool product was made a fiat standard in a large, heterogeneously constructed business where one of the authors of this book (Peter

DeGrace) worked. A user's group was established and a meeting was arranged with the top management of the CASE tool vendor to cement the relationship.

One of the problems with this product was that it had a proprietary user interface (and, in Peter's opinion, it was clumsy and hard to use). At the meeting, the vendor announced no plans to improve the interface; instead, he announced partially implemented new features. When Peter challenged him about his decision to increase the complexity of his tool (rather than helping regular folks), the vendor hemmed and hawed and finally blurted out that it was a *Strategic Decision*, as if calling it that lent credibility to the decision. This must have worked on Peter's boss because he uninvited Peter to the later management follow-up meeting.

Selecting that tool as a standard, and the vendor's response, caused the tool's complexity to increase and closed the communication paths that were necessary to correct the situation. It is hard to see how such a *standard* could be effective.

Languages are strange birds to standards organizations. You usually can't unscrew a FORTRAN program from an IBM machine and then screw it into a VAX without changing the program. Yet, the resulting programs could both be called "standards-conforming." This is because there was a policy for languages to be "minimum standards":

- You had to be able to dimension an array to at least three dimensions, but you could have your compiler accept any number larger than that.

- You had to have certain input/output statements, but you could have others.

This meant that if you satisfied the minimum, you could claim to be "standards-conforming" with all the marketing value that brings. Nowadays, ANSI is changing things a little. Now, both programs would be called non-standard if they contained any extensions; however, the compilers on both machines can still be called "standards-conforming," satisfying the minimum of the published standard.

In addition, the FORTRAN Standards Committee is attempting to "modernize" FORTRAN. It is an old language and a lot could be said for the desire to modernize it. But, the steps needed to do so would have severe consequences for the inventory of code already in existence. Either you'll have to keep old features along with their replacement new features, or you'll have to remove old features. The effect will be that you'll have a large, complex language and compilers with many bugs in them, or you'll get a new language with all that means for the dreaded *conversions* that would have to be done to bring the old programs up to the new standard (causing much the same problem that occurred with COBOL-80).

Standards Domains of Interest to Us

The standards that most interest us are those dealing with:

- communications
- windowing
- languages
- data transfer
- graphics interfaces
- data dictionary and information resource systems
- tool environments

Here are our recommendations of what to do with them.

Communications standards (OSI, SNA, consensus, and monopoly): There are many communication standards, and you might quickly become absorbed by them. If your organization is small, pay attention to your network and data communication folks and, perhaps, your vendor (if you trust him). Try to keep things simple. We counted 131 standards here.

Windowing standards (X-Windows, Windows, common usage, and consensus): These are important because they affect programmers so much. Be prepared to participate here and to ask programmers what works and what doesn't work for them.

Language standards (consensus, fiat, monopoly—IBM shops use IBM CO-BOL): This could be a real mess. Take a conservative approach here, especially if you have lots of software to maintain. It's okay to accept monopoly standards, but be aware of what it means. For example, see our comments about COBOL-80 in the section on Monopoly Standards.

Data transfer standards (EDIF, CDIF, attempt at consensus): These are very important for tool flexibility. If you have bought into one vendor's line, then this isn't so important. If you want to keep your options open, then pay attention here.

Graphics interface standards (PARC style, common usage): We have the same recommendations here as for communication standards.

Data dictionary and information resource systems (IRDS) (IBM's Repository Manager, DEC's CDD Repository, monopoly and consensus): These are important in regulating the way central dictionaries store information. They are especially important in business. However, there have been long delays in bringing fully-functional standards to the market.

Tool environments (Portable Common Tool Environment [PCTE], consensus). These are important for near-term improvements in CASE usage in complex networked environments. Keep a watch on these; they could be very important. But, there are more important standards to be concerned with.

Implications for CASE

If your organization is large, you will have a large stake in the standards business. Be prepared to have a staff of specialists doing standards work such as interfacing with standards bodies and participating in making them. If your organization is small, you cannot afford this and have to take what the standards community gives you.

However, there are several thing you can do. First, you can consider tying yourself to a vendor you trust, like IBM, and expect that they will provide you with all the standards support you require. Second, you can pay attention to the *important* standards. The most important standards for programmers are *language standards*. Finally, you can insist that your vendors demonstrate support for standards. The vendor should tell you what current standards their products support, what their standards support plans are, and which standards activities they are participating in.

The significance for CASE buyers is that the vendor must support standards, have a plan to meet them as they evolve and, most important, support trying to find a way to minimize the number of standards required and streamline the process of creating them. The vendor should be ready to show you their plan and strategy in writing.

A final word: we have not seen one standard—not one—for the *usability* of CASE tools. Here is what we mean by the term: *usability* is the measure of the effort required to learn, operate, prepare the input, and interpret the output of a program; the less effort, the better. Most of the CASE tools we've seen and used could profit from such a standard. ✒

Chapter 11.
How to Deploy CASE:
Hoeing the Rows

In this chapter, we are going to discuss how to deploy CASE in an organization. We will discuss the perils of selecting tools, describe the environment of a not-so-mythical software development organization, and then offer two approaches to deploying CASE.

The Perils of Selecting Tools

There was a time in California when farm workers used the tools specified and provided by the growers. Hoes were short and required the workers to bend over to use them. As a worker used the tool, he began to experience some back pain. Over a period of time, the workers experienced many crippling back conditions. A law was finally passed to change this over the objections of the growers.

The result was not poorer crop production, although we can't say there was improved crop production either. The improvement that was made had to do with reducing the pain of the workers—constant back pain.

The growers who selected the tools weren't interested in making people suffer; they were interested in the most efficient crop production. They contended that the tools were designed to bring the workers closer to the ground so that weeds would be easier to spot. They were trying to make things easier not harder.

So, how could such an intention produce such opposite results? The growers simply hadn't taken the tool users into consideration. This is an example of the functional distortion we discussed in Chapter 2. Rather than simply *imagining* how the workers should work, the growers could have *watched* them, noticing what it took to spot and pull the weeds. They could have noticed what happened when people used the short tools. They could have asked the workers how it felt to use them. The could have tried both methods and observed the results.

The growers were the Romans in this story; Romans who knew what *should* work but didn't really know what *actually* worked.

Okay, so what does this have to do with CASE and the methods we use to produce programs? Well, there are some Romans in the CASE field who select tools based not on what the *programmers actually need*, but on what *vendors say they need*. We have seen this happen repeatedly. Our correspondents have corroborated it, and so have the vendors themselves a time or two.

You might say, "Come on … these tools might not have been productive, but they couldn't have caused the programmers actual pain!" Well, because we've seen it, we say, "They sure do! Especially those tools that enforce a methodology or someone's view of what should work."

Many of these tools were created to allow STRUCTURED STUFF to be done. Many programmers use an opportunistic approach to development and observe the principles of structured stuff. So, the introduction of the tool and the tool centurions forced them into difficult situations. They must produce the software, but they think they are being inhibited by the Method. So, they simply do double duty: they do what must be done to get the software built and then they also try to fulfill the requirements of the method being enforced by the tool.

This situation leads to high stress and a great deal of anxiety. There is not enough time to do the best they can do because they must do two developments. Also, the two developments are timed differently; it is easy to see that while the programmer is still wrestling with the requirements or other upstream documentation, he could also have a prototype running. So, the signals he is passing back to the "method centurions" are inconsistent with those he is passing back and forth with the user.

But, even if the tool doesn't cause stress-related illness, it can still get in programmer's way if the expectations and valuations of the tool selector don't match those of the programmer. Here is an example of what we mean.

One enterprise we know about evaluated a tool and sent its score to management so they could decide whether or not to purchase it. The tool was a source code fixer-upper designed to turn spaghetti code into "structured" code.

For management, there were two criteria of equal weight: first, that the tool did not damage the functionality of the code and, second, that it improve the readability of the code. It could get a rating, say, of 100 on the functionality issue and 50 on readability. To get a total score on a scale of ten, the functionality would come in at 5 and the readability at 2.5 for a final rating of 7.5, which is a C-grade tool. That's not too bad; the tool probably should be purchased.

But, to the programmer, the story is entirely different. His context doesn't allow the entry of tools that could damage the functionality of his code. He has other headaches. For him, the question of rating comes only *after* the tool is evaluated for functional safety. Only *after* it is judged safe should it be allowed into the environment for further evaluation. Therefore, the rating would consist of only the readability improvement portion. He would rate it 5.0, which is an F-grade tool that probably shouldn't be purchased.

Notice the difference in context and the results. In this case, in trying to get tools for programmers, management ends up buying a tool that the programmers see as a poor one. This results in the managers wondering why the programmers don't use the tool, and the programmers wondering why the managers bought the tool in the first place. This is a condition that is rich in possibilities for misunderstandings.

A Mythical Software Development Organization

We are going to describe a mythical software development organization that we will use in our description of how to deploy CASE. This organization is part of a much larger enterprise and produces software for internal customers only. The environment in this organization would be split along the lines of Rome and Greece we've been referring to all throughout this book. For example, there would be processes put into place to pay lip service to the desires of management, and then there would be the *real* processes performed to get the work done.

The tools would be selected by those who don't actually use them and, typically, they would select short hoes when the programmers require violins.

You'll find the management to be rather distant and highly bureaucratic. They practically never talk directly to programmers, particularly almost never one to one. They get their information from gurus, vendors, competitors, and goers, not from the programmers who are doing the work. This mythical organization is a composite of real ones we know about. Here are some examples:

We know of an organization that couldn't come up with a good set of requirements for their universal workstation and, therefore, left it up to vendors to specify it. We know of another organization that, without consulting programmers, suddenly decided to reduce maintenance costs by 50% as part of a Continuous Quality Improvement program. And, they could do it, too, because the manager of the metrics program didn't think that enhancements were part of maintenance. So, by *redefining* maintenance to exclude enhancements, they could have reached their goal.

We know of yet another organization that would rather send its managers to Japan to consult with software developers there than have them talk with their own programmers about the day-to-day problems programmers face. We have even heard of a vendor having so much influence in his customer's organization that he caused an employee, who objected to such intrusion, to be fired. Since we had a correspondent inside the vendor's company, we were able to check it out. A very, *verrrry* distant management.

There would be many formal procedures in this organization, written in third person, passive voice, as if any one of them would be suitable to be chipped in marble. These would come regularly from the TEMPLE MOUNTS OF THE CORPORATION, written by the goers, signed off by the do-nothings, and foisted on the doers.

Oh, yes, there would be the *quality* programs: Quality Circles, Total Quality Commitment, Continuous Quality Improvement. But, management would find wonderful ways of defeating the basic purpose of these programs. They would pay lip service to them and would cause processes to be put into place that are worthless to the Greeks. These programs would become occasions for setting goals without consulting the programmers who must attain these goals. Such programs would first raise and then dash the expectations of programmers. Yet, these are the very programs that enable the Japanese to beat the pants (or skirts) off us.

You would find recognition programs skewed toward the *goers*; those who live on overhead costs and who don't actually *do* work but only *talk about* doing work. "Technical excellence" would be used to describe the efforts of these non-workers. These recognition programs would give the *doers* exactly the wrong signal: that a programmer's career is in the direction of doing less work, not more, and of burning profits rather than making them.

In this environment, claims are accepted as verified if they are based on anecdotal evidence or vendor claims.

Finally, in this environment, truth is not sought out, but dogma is tenaciously defended.

Deploying CASE The Roman Way

We now present our notion of how a Roman would approach implementing CASE in such an organization (and we *don't* recommend it). Our notion was adapted from Watts Humphrey's Software Maturity Model [Humphrey 1987] developed at the Software Engineering Institute (SEI) and his report on CASE planning [Humphrey 1989].

"The SEI of the Carnegie-Mellon University was established in December 1984 to address the well-recognized need for improved software in U.S. Department of Defense operations." [Humphrey 1987, p.1] Although it is heavily supported by the DoD, the SEI has influence throughout our field.

Accordingly, the SEI was asked by the DoD for a means by which it could assess the capabilities of software organizations. At the SEI, Watts Humphrey produced the Software Process Maturity Framework to be used by the DoD and other software organizations "to assess their own capabilities and identify the most important areas for improvement." [Humphrey 1989, p.1]

Mr. Humphreys identifies five levels of software process maturity: Initial, Repeatable, Defined, Managed, and Optimized. These are referred to as Levels 1, 2, 3, 4, and 5, respectively. He claims that these levels were "selected to reasonably represent the actual historical phases of evolutionary improvement of real software organizations." [Humphrey 1987, p.2] He indicates that each subsequent level represents improvements over the previous ones.

He says that such improvement is the result of statistical process control, and that the software development process is as amenable, with some important differences, to such statistical control as the production of automobiles, cameras, wrist watches, and steel making [ibid].

Here is a description of the levels as best we understand them. We quote and paraphrase from the report [ibid, pp.3-5] to get the most accurate and concise description, but the going is a little heavy.

"The *Initial Process* could be properly called *ad hoc* or chaotic. Here, the organization typically operates without formalized procedures, cost estimates, and project plans. Tools are not well integrated with the process or uniformly applied. Change control is lax and there is little senior management exposure or understanding of the problems and issues. Since problems are often deferred or even forgotten rather than solved, software installation and maintenance often present serious problems."

The *Repeatable Process* is a stable process with a repeatable level of statistical control achieved by initiating rigorous project management of commitments, costs, schedule, change, and product assurance in the Level 1 environment. Mr. Humphrey asserts that the Repeatable Process "is such an enormous advance over the Initial Process that people in the organization tend to believe they have mastered the software problem." However, some risks, such as the impact of new tools and methods, lack of experience developing a new product, and lack of information about what is going on, still face Repeatable Process Organizations.

The *Defined Process* assures consistent implementation and provides a basis for better understanding of the process. Here, it is probable that advanced technology can usefully be introduced. When faced with a crisis, the defined process group would probably remain with the defined process rather then reverting to Level 1.

You get to this level by establishing a process group whose exclusive focus is to improve the software development process, establishing a software development process architecture that describes the technical and management activities required for proper execution of the development process, and introducing a family of software engineering methods and technologies including design and code inspections, formal design methods, library control systems, and comprehensive testing methods. Mr. Humphrey indicates that prototyping should be considered for inclusion. Very generous of him, but prototyping has been going on all the time; didn't he notice?

However, even at this level, you will have problems figuring out what is going on and how effective the process really is. So, you then advance to Level 4, the *Managed Process*.

The *Managed Process* makes it possible to initiate process measurements. To get here from the Defined Process, you must establish a minimum basic set of process measurements to identify the quality and cost parameters of each process step, establish a process database with resources to manage and maintain it, provide sufficient process resources to analyze this data and advise project members on the data's meaning and use, assess the relative quality of each product, and inform management where quality targets are not being met. The trouble here is in selecting the right data to measure, and management is still presumably focusing on the product rather than on the process. So, you move on to the final level, the *Optimized Process*.

The *Optimized Process* makes it possible to collect the right data and refocuses management to the process, not the product. Mr. Humphrey calls the move to this level a "paradigm shift."

Mr. Humphrey goes on to say that CASE should not be introduced when the organization is at Level 1 [ibid]. The earliest should be at Level 2; but, Mr. Humphrey is a little inconsistent here. He says you should "develop your [software] process before or during CASE installation, but not after." [Humphrey 1989, p.9] This indicates to us a Level 3 organization; but, Mr. Humphrey suggests you can do this at Level 2 when he says you can introduce CASE while you are formalizing configuration control and setting up procedures for requirements control.

He says that not training the people is the most common single weakness of Level 2 organizations. He also suggests that CASE installation is never completed but will change and evolve along with business requirements and the software development process itself.

He then goes on to describe how to plan and install CASE systems. Start with an orderly study of the requirements, which should "clearly state management objectives for the CASE system [nothing here about programmers' objectives] and define the critical functions." [ibid, p.13] But, since there are likely to be so many requirements that they will provide little guidance, he suggests prioritizing them according to those essential for the first installation, those required as an early enhancement, and those desirable for the future [nothing here about consulting with programmers].

He thinks that, over time, CASE systems are likely to be the most expensive capital investment a software organization makes. He believes that ultimately CASE system costs "will exceed those of the organization's other software, computing systems, and terminals combined." [ibid, p.13] Therefore, a justification is needed and he recommends an economic justification; he offers a ten-step example.

1. Make a task map consisting of a structured picture of the software process. Identify each key task and the tools and methods used in performing it. [Since you haven't deployed any CASE tools yet, this list is likely to be skimpy.]

2. Identify the current resource expenditure profiles for each task.

3. Assemble a team of experts [presumably Marshall Rose's Roman goers] to determine the resource impact of the new CASE system and its associated support tools and methods.

4. Review each project's migration plan to determine the accrual rate of savings.

5. Get each project's commitment to this savings schedule. [How can you honestly commit to something as probabilistic as the ultimate savings realized from using CASE the first time?]

6. Establish a new schedule of estimating factors for project planning.

7. Estimate planning, training, installation, and support costs.

8. Construct a composite savings schedule for the organization as a whole.

9. Get competent financial advice on the methods used and the results anticipated.

10. Go to management for approval.

He says that "there is no way to absolutely prove the economic value of a CASE system ... when the executives are convinced of the soundness of your *logic*, they will not require absolute proof." [ibid, p.15] He says to be careful about promising dramatic early savings because "there is evidence that enforcing a comprehensive design discipline will actually increase early costs." In addition, "the early costs are likely to be inflated by the added time required for the professionals to become familiar with the new system and the procedures and methods involved in its use." The actual benefits come later with reduced testing and improved product quality.

Now, let's review all this stuff. Watts Humphrey assumes that software development is like producing cameras, wristwatches, or cars because they are all amenable to the same statistical control processes. He says there are five levels of the software maturity framework: Initial, Repeatable, Defined, Managed, and Optimized. He suggests that CASE is important in automating the process and should be introduced no earlier than Level 2. There ought to be a list of CASE requirements made up and prioritized.

He goes on the say that there ought to be a ten-step justification for acquiring and installing a CASE system, which he means as fully integrated, operational software environments. He says to use logic to convince executives to buy CASE. Finally, do not expect dramatic early savings because benefits accrue downstream in other processes. This, of course, requires a little more clever logic than if CASE tools aided the process into which they were introduced.

This is all extremely logical. We know many organizations are trying it out. But, we would not follow it and advise you not to. We question Mr. Humphrey's assumption about the statistical control processes of camera production being useful in software development. We question that the software maturity framework represents actual real-world descriptions of a software maturity process. We question his description of the process maturity levels themselves; they neither make sense to us nor reflect the real world we see. For example, he completely leaves out processes involved in the "level-of-effort" environments we typically see in maintenance shops. And, software maintenance is the most common software process going.

We think his requirements gathering and economic justifications are typical of those done by bureaucrats who have no notion of how software is really done or, if they ever did have, they've forgotten. He talks about getting requirements that clearly state management's objectives. But, he never says a word about talking to the programmers and finding out about *their* objectives.

Here are our arguments. First, about the applicability of hardware statistical control procedures to software development, the closest hardware analog to software development we've ever been able to find is lithography. In lithography, you have a process where wood blocks, or stone, or metal plates are somehow inscribed with a design. Then, they are inked and have paper sheets pressed on them transferring the design to the paper. The paper is then dried, coated (sometimes), and then packaged and shipped to market or the warehouse. This pressing process is well known, and perhaps statistical control processes can be applied here, although the use of inks is still a skilled job. But, control processes have no place in deciding what and how to inscribe the media. These are still done by the artist or engraver and involve a myriad of imaginings and decisions not amenable to hardware processes.

So it is, too, with software development. After the software is made, it can be transferred to many forms of media, usually tape or disks. These transfer processes are amenable to the statistical control procedures used to make cameras. But, before it is made, the software is still in large part in the minds of the user as a need, or in the minds of the producers as potential solutions. These mental processes have no history of being controlled by statistical control procedures.

Second, he says the levels of the maturity framework reasonably represent actual historical phases of evolutionary improvement in real software organizations. Yet, he does not give any data from which he observed this framework in use. How many organizations did he canvass? It must have been one hell of a job to get enough data to represent a reasonable sample and we haven't heard of it. No, Mr. Humphrey has a wonderfully logical model that "should work" but that, as far as we can tell, he has not observed.

For example, why does he *not* include an organization to locate, catalog, and distribute reusable software as one of those project controls that are needed to advance from Level 1 to Level 2? In our opinion, this is vital to improving things because we simply *must* reduce the levels of development that typically exist between the user's requirements and the final solution.

Even he cannot say there are any more than a few organizations at Level 5. So, how does he know such a level even exists in more than his own imagination?

Third, trying to implement this model can become a case of chasing the indicators. (See Chapter 9.) We have seen, and have heard from our correspondents, that the SEI maturity model becomes the central activity of some software engineering organizations. Management of these has lost sight of the main indicator of customer satisfaction apparently believing that by achieving some high maturity level, customer satisfaction will automatically follow. The Department of Defense colludes in this by requiring that its vendors achieve at least Level 3 in the model.

Do you get the idea here? The software maturity framework is a Roman's idea of how we should proceed; it does not represent the real world. Therefore, it might be accurate and, then again, it might not. But, to represent it as being historically accurate is very disappointing. One explanation could be that if we all followed the framework, then at some future time, he would claim, it would be historically accurate. However, this is a moral argument, not a technical or scientific one.

In the Initial level, he thinks that chaos should be removed from the process. But, whenever there is novelty involved, chaos comes along with it; that is where novelty resides. If you are developing software where there is no novelty, then you have a problem that isn't new to you and, therefore, has already been solved. If this is so, why are you solving it again? Why aren't you reusing the old solution? You can't do that with bridges or cameras (except maybe to reuse a design), but in *our* business you *can* do that and you should.

On the other hand, if you are reusing software, chaos might be minimized but not entirely eliminated because there is still some uncertainty about which software to select. And, if you are doing maintenance, there is always some chaos present. One never knows when the software will fail, or how, or where. One never knows what delightful tortures are in store when you bring software up on new platforms or under new operating systems. One never knows what the user will do, or want, next.

Mr. Humphrey also says that the Level 1 organization operates without formalized procedures. He is correct here, but it is not because there aren't any. We have never seen a software development organization without formal procedures; what we see is the wholesale disregard of them in order to get the work done.

You are supposed to use formal procedures to stamp out chaos. But, the more formal the procedures get, the less the user gets, the angrier he gets, and the more dissatisfaction you get. Many times we've observed a non-chaotic procedure taking a week of labor to get a ten-minute fix. On the other hand, when the crunch comes (and it inevitably does in these cases), all formality ceases and people are set to get the job done, in slightly chaotic, non-procedural ways. This is what attaining Level 3 should prevent; but we suggest that attaining Level 3 will cause it to happen.

At the Repeatable level, he says you have put processes in place that cause software development to be repeatable. But, this is not reasonable. You don't know what you'll drag out of chaos, and handling it might be different at different times. For example, in prototyping, new requirements occur at different times, at different places, and at different rates. A repeatable process would have them occur at the same time, place, and rate.

One thing that should be repeatable is a system for locating, cataloging, and distributing reusable software because you don't want to solve the same problem over and over again. But, he doesn't talk about that.

At the Defined level, you have a process group, a development architecture, and methods and technologies. But, as we have alluded to before, those who are doing the defining are often *not* those doing the software. The definers are usually Marshall Rose's goers [Rose 1990] or David Parnas's Technocrat managers [DeGrace and Stahl 1990, p.207] trapped in a LaLa land of inconsistent and conflicting claims of vendors and the desires of executives who don't understand what is going on.

At the Managed level, you should be able to measure progress. However, as Chapter 9, *Metrics*, discusses, the measures depend on your point of view, and the proponents of the maturity framework have a point of view that is usually not well connected to reality. For example, see our earlier description of the metrics organization that could realize its goals by simply redefining what maintenance is.

Then, at the Optimized process, we have Nirvana; this is the goal we must all seek if, of course, we are moral people. Never mind the real world intruding and making over the environment every few years; and, by the way, adding chaos to it. Never mind the major actors in this play: the programmers. If you get to Level 5, you will be optimizing the production of general ledger programs, one after the other, until the world is hip deep in the stuff. We ask you, does this seem reasonable or even sane?

Finally, it is clear that he is describing a top-down approach where all requirements can be known before other development processes occur; that all processes are projects; and where one method fits all programmers and problems. And, he obviously believes that what can be written down can be done. This is simply not true.

The Greek Approach

If someone were to make Peter DeGrace (one of the authors of this book) the King of Computing, Sultan of System Engineering, Maven of Management Information Systems, Duke of Documentation, Prince of Programming, Admiral of Analysis, Dictator of Design, Count of Coding, Marquis of Maintenance, and Tyrant of Testing, he would do some system things and some programming things. Let's talk about the programming things first.

Programming Things—Internal

If Peter were all of these things, he would ask the programmers in his organization how they actually produce software, what works for them, what doesn't work for them, what would help them, and what information he would need to understand their answers. These questions were actually asked of a group of programmers. The questions themselves came from a correspondent, who used them to define the goals of a survey that was conducted by a process improvement team. The team used the information to characterize a programming environment.

Here are some other questions Peter would ask to get expansive answers to the main questions above:

- He would ask what kind of software each programmer produces and how formal is the process?

- He would ask each programmer to diagram their basic software process. He would offer some standard diagrams that they could change or allow each an opportunity to draw their own.

- He would ask them what standards they use; why do they follow them; and what they get out of conforming to them?

- He would ask them what tools they use, why, and what are the benefits?

- He would ask them how they get their software requirements; where do the requirements come from; how are the requirements communicated; and how involved are they in producing the requirements?

- He would ask how complete are the requirements before starting design? How formal are they; what design procedures do they follow; who reviews the design; how formal are the reviews; why are they held; and what are the benefits?

- He would ask how complete is the design before starting the coding?

- He would ask how complete is the software before testing begins? How much of it is tested before it is released? Who tests it? How formal are the procedures and how do they measure the quality?

- He would ask what type of maintenance is done? How do they learn the software? What tools, documents, and assistance is helpful in code maintenance? What are the major issues they face doing maintenance? What tools, documents, and assistance would help solve these problems?

- He would ask what documentation is produced; why is it produced; and what are the benefits of each type? Is there a documentation template used and what is the quality of the documents produced?

- He would ask how successful is the software they produce? What would help with the development? What improvements should become standard?

- He would ask if there were a development standard and how they would support it? If not, why not? If so, how would they want it implemented? And, what training, publications, and other help would be important to them?

- He would then ask for some general demographic information and, finally, for some personal information; especially if they would want any feedback about his survey.

We have some hunches about the answers we would get. We would find that software is produced in much less formal circumstances than many people think. Programmers probably try to avoid standards or use them only under duress. They probably use low end CASE tools unless they are doing real systems engineering. They work from incomplete requirements, probably averaging no more than 70% complete. They're probably split on whether they use reviews, mainly because of time and other constraints, but probably indicate many benefits from using them. They will be tentative about how well the testing goes and will have strong opinions about how to learn code in maintenance.

We tentatively grant some validity to our hunches because this survey has already been given to 60 programmers. It was as part of a Continuous Quality Improvement team's effort to define the processes software used in an organization. The team graciously allowed us to review it and the information collected from it.

As an aside, many people probably think they are bad or dumb people because the way they do their work isn't like the way it's shown in the books and magazines of our field. It's a lot like looking at the pictures of the beautiful people we all see in magazines at supermarket checkout lines. They are the way we all hope to look; but, how many of us actually do look that way or want to take the time to look that way. It's interesting that these ideals are placed in the locations we will be at when we are most likely not to be at our best; at least, Peter usually notices them when he is in his gorilla disguise at 3 A.M. on writing days. Leslie (the other author of this book) notices the irony at the check-out register when she has a pile of snack food stacked on top of the latest issue of Vogue. We hope that the information in this book will reassure you that many of us work in non-standard ways.

Peter then would take the time to understand the answers to his survey; for example, does the answer that most of the time programmers begin design and coding with less than 70% of the requirements mean that there is a defect in the system or in the way the world really is? Peter would figure it out by adapting and using a Total Quality Control process known as *managing the previous process*:

"Managing the Previous Process—Because of its preoccupation with data rather than results, TQC encourages people to go back to the previous process on the production line to seek out a problem's causes. Improvement requires that we always be aware of what comes from the previous process. In the factory, problem solvers are told to ask why not once but five times. Often the first answer to the problem is not the root cause. Asking why several times will dig out several causes, one of which is the root cause.

"Taiichi Ohno, former Toyota vice president, once gave the following example of finding the real cause of a machine stoppage.

"Question 1: Why did the machine stop?

"Answer 1: Because the fuse blew due to an overload.

"Question 2: Why was there an overload?

"Answer 2: Because the bearing lubrication was inadequate.

"Question 3: Why was the lubrication inadequate?

"Answer 3: Because the lubrication pump was not functioning right.

"Question 4: Why wasn't the lubricating pump not working right?

"Answer 4: Because the pump axle was worn out.

"Question 5: Why was it worn out?

"Answer 5: Because sludge got in.

"By repeating "why" five times, it was possible to identify the real cause and hence the real solution: attaching a strainer to the lubricating pump. If the workers had not gone through such repetitive questions, they might have settled with an intermediate countermeasure, such as replacing the fuse." [Imai 1986, p.50]

Peter would interview the requirements givers to determine why requirements are incomplete. He would work back from there to the need for the requirements. He would continue back until he found the reason. However, there are many legitimate reasons why requirements are incomplete. For example, the problem to be solved might be a wicked one. For more reasons, see our book, *Wicked Problems, Righteous Solutions*, Chapter Four, *Problems with the Waterfall Model* [DeGrace and Stahl 1990].

If following the defect back to its root causes shows that there was indeed a defect in the process, then perhaps traditional CASE or some other approach would improve it. But, if the root cause is simply the human condition, then software must be designed and coded to be extendible right from the start to accommodate human frailties. Should that not be one of the key general requirements of software?

Peter would then do two things: For the Greek side, he would find out what would help the programmers, get the stuff, and then give it to them. For the Roman side, he would follow the six steps recommended by Beer, Eisenstat, and Spector in their article, *Why Change Programs Don't Produce Change*. [1990]

"1. Mobilize commitment to change through *joint* diagnosis of business problems."

Get as many people as possible *from as many levels as possible* involved in defining a business problem to solve.

"2. Develop a *shared vision* of how to organize and manage for competitiveness."

Get everybody to sign up for the problem. See *The Soul of a New Machine* [Kidder 1982] for how this happens in the computer field.

"3. Foster the *consensus* for the new vision, *competence* to enact it, and *cohesion* to move it along."

This is where leadership from management—especially senior management—comes in. Essentially, they must support what is known as "task alignment," which means that the employees' roles, responsibilities, and relationships are organized to solve specific business relationships. They must make it clear that task alignment is the way they are going to do business; any manager who wants to help gets support; those who don't get outplacement counseling.

"4. Spread revitalization to all departments *without pushing it from the top.*"

Let the new way of doing business spread from the organization doing it to those who interact with it.

"5. Institutionalize revitalization through formal policies, systems, and structures."

Don't be too quick to do this; let the Greek types make the improvements, then "Romanize" them.

"6. Monitor and adjust strategies in response to problems in the revitalization process."

This is the touchiest of all. Management, Romans at heart, must make, foster, and care for organizations that are Greek at heart. This is some task! However, if it can be done, then you have a chance of making CASE or any other change work. Remember, it must be oriented toward solving some business problem or it doesn't work. It relies on reorganizing roles and responsibilities to solve that business problem. It can't be done by pushing it down from the top; it must be accomplished by those who have signed up to solve that business problem.

System Things—External

Peter would plan for a small staff to provide information about the external world to those in software engineering. The plan would include a Software Engineering Information Center, a technical library with a professional staff to help the organization obtain useful information from the many books and journals in our field. The plan would also include keeping an eye on vendors, standards organizations, consumer organizations (user groups), the national economy (Defense Department build down, etc.), and market information in general. Peter wouldn't actually put this plan into effect until the signals from the programmers indicated so.

System Things—Internal

Peter would allow programmers to choose the hardware and software they use. But, he would support their choices with internal organizations dedicated to keeping programmers on the air, communicating with the people and machines they need to communicate with.

Here's how this support would proceed. First, he would find out who the smartest and wisest programmers are and he would gear the organization toward them, rather than toward the lowest common denominator.

It's hard to assess wisdom. But, here is one measure: wise folks avoid the situations smart folks can get out of. Both are important. Smart folks push you along; they represent new juice, they don't know what can't be done so they have a habit of doing it. Wise programmers can provide a quality of tradition; they provide an ongoing record of things that work and those that don't: "If you do this, you will stay out of trouble." Or: "There's a better approach." Or: "I did it that way once. You can get my code from the library."

Peter would like to form a programmers' Senate from these smart and wise folks to help make decisions about programming. They would be given real power to make changes.

Peter would plan to improve technology transfer. He would use the market watch described above to discover new technology. But, those doing the looking would be prompted by programmers, through one-on-one conversations or from requests from the Senate. He would use the Senate to assess how appropriate any new technology would be for his organization. He would let playing with the new technology be a reward to programmers for good service. The Senate would have the main say in selecting tools and other technology.

The distribution and integration of the tools would be left up to a Central Software Engineering organization, which would be Roman in the best sense of the term. This organization would create a place—a software engineering repository—for programmers to put their applications, tools, and reusable software.

For tools, this organization would locate those built by the programmers, "productize" them, maintain them, catalog them, and make the catalog available to all the programmers. For tools purchased from the outside, the only change would be that instead of "productizing" them, this organization would perform an incoming inspection, including a usability test. There would be an internal programming staff to do maintenance and integration.

How does someone determine whether a tool works? In the Roman way, they depend on theory and usually pick short hoes. In the Greek way, they depend on observation; they listen to the music. For tools purchased from the outside, here are some of the more or less standard criteria that would be used by an "incoming inspection" team in the Central Software Engineering Organization:

- *Usability* would be most important. This usually means the programmer interface. Peter would make Macintosh-like interfaces standard because they provide a conceptual model of how the tool works, good mapping between controls and the conceptual model, good constraints and safeguards to minimize error and disaster, and good feedback that matches the operator's expectations with the operation of any control. Especially prized tools would be those that help programmers think. At the very least, these would pick up after the programmers. But, they would also detect coupling and cohesion problems, assist in decomposing problems and solutions, aid in locating software to be reused, and provide palettes of blank diagrams and libraries of basic designs.

- There would be connection to other developers where necessary. This communicating aspect of the CASE tool would include the facility to connect to the technical library, repository, and appropriate electronic bulletin boards around the world. The team would check for networking capability and for multi-user access with "check-in" and "check-out."

- Tools should be able to handle many notations. Here are some examples:

    ◆ Action diagrams

    ◆ SASD—Data-flow diagrams and structured charts

    ◆ Structured Analysis and Design—Data-flow diagrams and structured charts

    ◆ OOD—Such as Buhr and Booch diagrams

    ◆ STD—State Transition diagrams

    ◆ Miscellaneous techniques by means of a customizable graphics editor

    ◆ Language-sensitive language editors able to handle many languages

- Where necessary, the tools would support multiple phases of the life cycle including requirements gathering, requirements traceability—especially a requirements traceability matrix—analysis, design, coding, and maintenance. But, see what we hate about CASE in the following paragraphs for more criteria.

- There would be high priority requirements for any tool to support reuse of any artifact, especially code. The vendor would have to show how his tool helps programmers really reuse software.

- Maintenance tools would be examined to determine how they help programmers really do maintenance. The actual requirements would come from the programmers or the Senate, but Peter would plan for tools that restructure code, examine it for the quality features we discussed in Chapter 3, and help produce and keep track of the maintenance baseline discussed in Chapter 5.

- The incoming inspection team would look at how well any tool can be integrated, how well it talks to other tools and the software engineering repository. The team would look for popular output formats such as: ASCII, EDIF (Electronic Data Interchange Format), especially CDIF (Computer Data Interchange Format).

- The team would also determine how the vendor plans to keep up with changing technology. For example, does his tool run on several platforms? Of course, all vendors will probably answer *yes*. But, if the vendor has only plans for each platform or a separate version of his tool for each platform, then it really isn't part of the vendor's strategic plan, it's probably part of the marketing plan. On the other hand, if the vendor uses a toolkit composed of sets of low level routines for all the platforms and keeps these and only one version of his software, then he has a commitment to all platforms. These routines usually consist of the user interface and other machine-dependent system character-istics of each platform. Sets of these routines are sometimes known as a "virtual toolkit."

The software engineering repository would also include a place where reusable code could be deposited. It would be collected by appealing to programmers to contribute candidate reusable software. They would be re-warded for contributions that were accepted. The repository staff would do all the collection work, they would "productize" the software, and then they would catalog and distribute it. Peter would give rewards to the folks who reuse code.

If you already have most of your code written and in maintenance, then Lower CASE is probably where you should concentrate. If you are making software from scratch, have a homogeneous environment, and are using a top-down approach, then Upper CASE is where you should concentrate. If you are going to be making and maintaining software, then investigate ICASE.

From a systems point of view, any of these approaches is appropriate; but Peter would make sure the programmers have the main say in selecting methods and tools.

That's how Peter would implement CASE if he were King, Sultan, Maven, Duke, Prince, Admiral, Dictator, Count, Marquis, and Tyrant.

Final Thoughts

Here are some things here that don't work:

Pushdown Technology Transfer for Deploying Tools

Pushdown technology transfer is the process described earlier where those who don't presently understand the process have the say about which tools to use in it. Those who receive the technology will resist this because they have no stake in it. They had no stake in selecting or developing the tool, and they most likely have not internalized the method behind the tool as part of their training. The tools are often short hoes.

Requiring Extreme User Involvement

Most of the time, an organization uses software to help it get another product out the door or do business. The most difficult part of doing this is actually *getting the product out the door*: not talking about it, not meeting about it, not guessing at it, not predicting it, but actually *doing* it.

The Romans among us sometimes ask those responsible for getting the product out the door to concentrate on being the "owner" of the software that is but an aid to them. When that happens, those who are getting the product out the door must spend an inordinate amount of their time understanding our processes. We ask them to divert their attention from their main task to a subordinate one, which is the functional distraction described in Chapter 2.

One Method Covers All

There are many methods of producing good software. The reason these are not usually explored is because of the "Holy Grail" impression of **The Methodology**, which is supposed to be suitable for all software development situations. No one who knows the business can believe this. The pushers evidently *do* believe this.

Things We Hate about CASE Tools

CASE tools enforce a method rather than offer support to programmers to help them understand the problem they are solving and approach a solution.

Most CASE tools require a strict top-down approach. If, for example, you're at the fourth level in some data-flow diagram (DFD) and discover you need another input—say, some kind of enabling signal—most DFD editors require that you enter it at highest level first and then show it all the way down (balance it, they say). If you discover this missing piece of data, you must either disregard it until you complete the diagrams and then remember to go back up to the top level and enter it, or you must go back to the top immediately and stop the current analysis.

But, why is *this* the rule? Why can't a programmer enter a new kind of data anywhere and let the editor figure it out? If it can't, it should do the best it can and notify you at a time that suits *your* processes, not the machines'. Here's a message to the CASE developers: you are writing tools for people ... please give us a break.

Most CASE tools make *you* do everything. For example, they have no galleries of blank DFDs of various sizes. If someone is decomposing their DFD down a level, none of the tools we have looked at offer you pre-drawn, generically labeled DFDs composed of various bubbles and different data arrangements. These could be neatly drawn and nicely distributed across the drawing space. Such a scheme could be combined with a feature of some DFD editors that automatically show the data entering and leaving the level.

Why don't the CASE people offer design libraries? They almost always show some example in their promotional literature.

Why can't the software clean up after us? Heck, we're trying to make something; we're not trying to show how morally responsible we are by following the order of the DFD. We would ask the tool to let us proceed and, if it can't figure us out, then tell us later. It shouldn't make us pay attention to it until we're ready. We must be able to sketch ... to muse about the problem. Our tools should *help* us.

Our Picks

We've been talking about tools throughout this book without mentioning any specific ones, and now we are going to fix that. Here's our experience with and preferences for tools. We're offering Peter's picks first, since he has the most experience with the tools themselves. Then, Leslie will offer a few additional picks of tools she has used, particularly those she found useful in preparing this book. We offer these picks so you can get an angle on our point of view in this book.

Peter's Picks

Peter started out in a Greek environment doing maintenance on mainframe applications. His main tool was the editor supplied by the vendor. It was his only friend in a stormy sea of listings and documentation. The compiler stood out like a dangerous rock and the linker loader like some mystical land emerging from the mists. Soon, he came to understand the language and these tools; they became transparent to him.

About that time, out came source code managers and symbolic debuggers which, he saw, had real potential for helping him. In fact, he used the operating system to integrate them together with the editor, compiler, and linker into what he calls a primitive "language processor." One merely had to execute the processor with the name of the program and module to be changed and the processor started the editor with the source code. When the code was ready, the processor would compile, link, and execute the program, all while it sensed the state of system variables to detect any compiler, linker, or execution errors. When any of these errors occurred, the processor signaled the terminal, displayed the error indication, and executed either the editor or the debugger with the offending module. If there were no problems, the processor would ask if the source, binary, and test files should be updated, and it would do all the updates necessary if commanded to do so.

This reduced the amount of keystrokes required to do the work by 80%. But, alas, this was a time when computers were 90% more valuable than people and his "computer budget" couldn't take the hit.

Soon, he found himself in a Roman environment "managing" some of the first front-end CASE tools that were independent of a platform vendor. Then, he discovered the Macintosh and the tools offered on that machine. Greek-like memories came back to haunt him. He then evaluated some maintenance tools for assessing and improving whole inventories of software.

Finally, he found himself on the very front end of application development trying to understand customer's goals. Outliners and presentation software became important here.

As a result of all this, here are the tools he likes to use. For software development in the Greek world, he uses MORE II™ from Symantec™ for sketching, for yanking stuff out of chaos, and for structuring and presenting initial ideas. MORE II combines many of the useful qualities of an action diagrammer with superb presentation features. It even turns outlines into structured charts with a simple command.

Next comes a language processor for quickly expressing these ideas in code that executes. Peter prefers Microsoft products but, if he were purchasing a new language processor, he would wait until the last minute to pick either Microsoft or another product. This is because there are many very good ones out there, they are improving all the time, and they are to some extent platform dependent. (He would also acquire more software libraries.)

For maintenance, he would use Logiscope for assessing whole inventories and ACT for improving individual elements of it. Logiscope is more on the Roman side and provides all the metrics needed to adequately assess the state of an inventory. Management can then use this information to plan inventory improvements. ACT, on the other hand, is more on the Greek side and is useful for actually improving existing code.

In the Roman World, he uses Iconix PowerTools™ on the Macintosh. These allow straightforward, Roman kinds of analysis, design, and programming without damaging the Greeks. There are ten modules that cost about one kilo-buck apiece. They cover traditional structured stuff, data management, and O-O stuff. They are easy to use, and they make us feel like we are using a tool rather tnan the other way around, which is what you get with the big, water-cooled, hugely expensive tools.

Peter would not look at I-CASE yet for the reasons we gave earlier, but he is keeping an eye out for improvements in CASE integration. The emerging CASE data exchange standard (CDIF) is one.

By the way, many of the graphics used in this book were created with MORE II and PowerTools.

Leslie's Picks

For software configuration management (including document configurations), Leslie likes the Aide-de-Camp™ (ADC) software management system. It has versions that run under UNIX (including A/UX on the Mac), VAX/VMS, and PRIMOS operating systems.

To keep track of all of our partnership information, she uses HyperCard® on an Apple® Macintosh® IIsi to create custom databases. For this book, she created a number of custom HyperCard stacks for vendor information, personality profiles, glossary entries, contact lists, style guides, and the initial bibliography. For hypertext development on the PC, she likes both Asymetrix® ToolBook® and Guide™ from OWL International. And, there is a really great tool for getting your HyperCard stacks converted into ToolBook format. It's called ConvertIt!™ from Heizer Software.

To create this book, she used Macintosh-based applications:

- Microsoft® Word for word processing
- Aldus PageMaker® for page layout and typesetting
- SuperPaint 2.0 from Silicon Beach Software for graphics

Summary

In this chapter, we have looked at how to deploy CASE tools. We've used information developed in previous chapters to focus our attention on programmers and tools that would assist them. We've shown that a programmer's world is very complex and that there is no Roman Silver Bullet, but that there are tools that can help Greeks make software.

If Romans and Greeks can work together, they can improve things. But, until Romans respect Greeks, it is not likely that this will happen. In our opinion, organizations that already have this cooperation or can cause it to happen will be successful; those who don't, or can't, will fail. Since software is playing an ever-increasing role in the operation of businesses, those who fail in their software processes are risking causing the entire enterprise to fail. ✤

Chapter 12.
Epilogue

We've taken this unusual approach to CASE because we have discovered that tools aren't used as frequently as we'd originally thought, nor in the numbers advertised, nor as intended by theorists. Yet, tools are important to people and always have been. We call this the *Olduvai Imperative*. We've found that some of the most important tools are very simple and are built by programmers themselves.

We see the Olduvai Imperative channeled into two worlds that we call *Roman* and *Greek*. The Roman world has been captured by the vendors who sell to the Corporate Romans who are infatuated by "front-end" tools. These folks buy the tools and try to push down the technology on producers. The Greek world has few spokespeople; the Greeks tend to use "back-end" tools and are interested in producing software.

There are a lot of folks around, especially the Romans, who love to make up arguments about how the world works; it is their specialty and their special advantage. However, these folks are more than a bit reluctant to check the truth of the premises in their arguments. If they had lived in *Pax Romana*, during the Age of Faith, or in the United States in the mid-twentieth century before competition had its say, then argument was all they needed. In those days, the truth of their premises would have already been checked out, sometimes over a period of generations. But, in times of rapid change, you can't be sure of your ground. It keeps shifting, so you must check and recheck your assumptions. Here are a few assumptions from our field that need checking:

- Software engineering is like other engineering.

- Programming is or should be like building cameras.

- There is or should be one method of software development.

In the previous chapters, we encountered these arguments over and over again, as when systems engineering and software engineering were argued to be the same thing; that reverse engineering was the inverse of forward engineering; that you don't have to maintain code if you use a code generator, only the specifications; that one method of doing software applies to all cases; that simply by calling something *standard* makes it appropriate to use in all cases; that software quality is the same as the number of smiles you can get from your customers; that the lines-of-code metric is not an "economic good"; that when software is "up and running" it is finished; that one style of thinking is done by all people; and that documentation is nothing more than a necessary evil.

In the period of time between the fifth and fifteenth centuries, after Rome fell and before the Renaissance, there arose a school of philosophy called *Scholasticism*. This view of the world used argument and logic to defend dogma. The Scholastics were some of the most brilliant minds we know of, among them Thomas Acquinas. They turned their powerful minds to the service of defending faith, and the revealed truth. From this period, we hear of arguments about how many angels can dance on the head of a pin. To us, this argument seems trivial; however, at that time, the issues were real, the fires hot, and people died over arguments such as these. Heresy was an intellectual activity of important consequence.

As clever and ingenious as these philosophers were, they never had to search for the truth, only defend what was revealed to them. Their Truth did not describe the world as it was, only as it should be. They argued from the perspective of fallen angels trying to regain sanctity.

The inconsistencies between the world as it was and as it should be began to wear on intellectuals until the classical world was rediscovered. People could once again search for truth and use argument to uncover truth as it was. The humanists of the Renaissance argued from the perspective of the risen ape, a happier position not requiring the *mea culpas* of a sinner trying to become a saint.

We have a sort of scholasticism in our field. We find that how software is produced has been neither completely nor correctly characterized. We have found that our schizophrenic world has those who don't ask for evidence but who know how software *should* be produced. Not actually producing software themselves, they try to force others to work using "short hoes."

Where is the proof that structured stuff works? Where is the evidence that formal methods are actually used? Where is the evidence that actually using formal methods improves things?

There are any number of claims, sometimes even backed up by anecdotal reports of how good this approach is or how well that tool worked, but there is no *reliable* supporting evidence. We grant that some tool supporting some method will be used successfully by someone sometime. But, we have not seen evidence that some tool supporting some method works *all* the time or even a substantial number of times. The success we have seen usually depends on the programmer, not on the tool or method.

The formal methods and tools of software engineering are essentially arguments in support of revealed truth: a truth with little support in the world that we found and have described in this book. Until we actually come to terms with reality, until we figure out what producing software is all about, we cannot hope to affect major changes in a field of endeavor that holds so much promise and can affect so positively so many lives. Until we can ask, "Where is your evidence," and expect to actually receive some, we will never get our Romans and Greeks together.

And the Olduvai Imperative? Well, it keeps chugging along, expressing itself as it can, always with us. ✦

Appendix A.
CASE Tools or Techniques vs. Applications

Legend:
  x = Okay to use
  ? = Maybe
  * = Definitely not
  ▓ = Incomplete data

Tools or Techniques	Business applications	Engineering applications	Scientific applications	Computer operating systems	Embedded systems	Real-time systems	Asynchronous systems	Telecommunications	Network systems	Games	User interface	Database analysis	Database design	Database construction	Information resource management	Enterprise modeling	Systems engineering	Object-oriented stuff	Maintenance	Reusable code	Program enhancement	Program transitioning
Decomposition diagrams	?																					
Dependency diagrams	?																					
IDEF0	?																X					
IDEF1	?																X					
IDEF1X	X											X	X	X			X					
IDEF2	?																					
Data-flow diagrams	X	X	X	X	X	X	X	X									X					
Booch diagrams	*	X	X	X	X	X	X	X										X				
Buhr diagrams	*	X	X	X	X	X	X	X														
Entity-relationship diagrams	X	X	?	*								X	X	X			X					
Data structure diagrams	X	X	X									X	X									
Data navigation diagrams	X	X	X									X	X									
HIPO charts	X	X	X																			
Structure charts	X	X	X	X	X	X	X	X											X			
Warnier Orr charts	X																					
Control flow diagrams	*	X	X	X	X	X	X	X			X											
Michael-Jackson charts	X																					
Flow charts	X	X	X	X	X	X	X	X	X													
Structured English	X	X	X	X	X	X	X	X											X			
PDL	X	X	X	X	X	X	X	X											X			
Nassi-Schneiderman charts																			?			

(continued on next page)

(continued from previous page)

Legend:
x = Okay to use
? = Maybe
* = Definitely not
▓ = Incomplete data

Tools or Techniques	Business applications	Engineering applications	Scientific applications	Computer operating systems	Embedded systems	Real-time systems	Asynchronous systems	Telecommunications	Network systems	Games	User interface	Database analysis	Database design	Database construction	Information resource management	Enterprise modeling	Systems engineering	Object-oriented stuff	Maintenance	Reusable code	Program enhancement	Program transitioning
Action diagrams																						
Database action diagrams													?	?								
Decision trees and tables		X	X	X	X	X	X	X														
State-transition diagrams		X	X	X	X	X	X	X			X											
Gane and Sarson	X																					
Mellor Schlaer diagram set		X	X	X	X	X	X	X										?	X			
Behavior diagrams																						
Simulation																						
Cost/estimation																						
Project support																						
Code generators																						
4GLs																						
Compilers																						
Parsers																						

Appendix B.
Software Metrics Overview

Software Metrics: An Overview of Recent Results

V. Côté, P. Bourque, S. Oligny, and N. Rivard
Université de Sherbrooke, Québec, Canada[*]

The groundwork for software metrics was established in the seventies, and from these earlier works, interesting results have emerged in the eighties. Over 120 of the many publications on software metrics that have appeared since 1980 are classified and presented in five tables that comprise, respectively, (1) the use of classic metrics, (2) a description of new metrics, (3) software metrics through the life cycle, (4) code metrics and popular programming languages, and (5) various metric-based estimation models.

1. INTRODUCTION

The groundwork for software metrics was laid in the seventies. The earliest paper on the subject was published in 1968 [100]. From these earlier works, interesting results have emerged in the eighties. This paper aims at classifying the wealth of publications in the active field of software metrics since 1980. The term software metric designates here "a unit of measurement of a software product or software related process" as defined by Hamer and Frewin [64].

General introductions to the field of software metrics can be found in [31, 108, 4, 64, 98, 71]. Brown et al. [31] offer a brief overview of this field that is of particular interest to the software practitioner. Shooman [108] presents software metrics as it relates to software engineering. Arthur [4] introduces specific guidelines for Assembler,

---

[*]Address correspondence to: Vianney Côté, Département de Mathématiques et d'Informatique, Université de Sherbrooke, Québec, Canada J1K 2R1.

The Journal of Systems and Software 8, 121-131 (1988)
© 1988 Elsevier Science Publishing Co., Inc.

COBOL and PL/1. Hamer and Frewin [64] offer an excellent overview and criticism of the field. Robillard [98] proposes a brief introduction to the field in French and presents an interesting discussion on a statement interconnectivity metric. In [71] Jones discusses software metrics in detail from a productivity standpoint.

Previous classifications of software metrics publications can be found in [106, 22, 40, 17, 47]. Shaw [106], Cook [40], and the DACS report [47] also introduce extensive annotated bibliographies. Basili et al. [17] propose in their paper a framework for analyzing software experimental studies.

Pioneering work such as Halstead's software science [63] and McCabe's cyclomatic complexity [86] have been examined from a theoretical and empirical standpoint in a large number of papers. The publications that have studied these "classic" metrics and others are summarized in Section 2.

Although much effort has been invested in code metrics, researchers are developing metrics available at other phases of the software life cycle. An excellent example of a metric available early in the life cycle is Albrecht's function points [1, 2]. Function points can be used for software sizing, a most important input parameter in all software project estimation models, and for productivity studies [80]. Another area that is benefiting from research in software metrics is software quality assurance (SQA). DeMarco states it very clearly in the first sentence of his book [49]: "You can't control what you can't measure." The Quality Assurance Institute [91] emphasizes software metrics considerably in their program. Section 3 thus studies software metrics throughout the life cycle.

Software metrics researchers have studied software code in detail from a number of varied approaches. They have developed code metrics because code can be measured by automated code measurers. The use of code metrics can greatly help in depicting the features and layouts embedded in thousands of lines of code, in much the same way that gauges and dials give a nuclear plant operator an idea of what is going on inside a reactor. Therefore Section 4 elaborates on code metrics.

A good indication of the sustained interest in the software metrics field is the proliferation of new metrics. In fact, Ramamoorthy et al. explain in [94] how software metrics will play an important role in future software development methodologies. Section 5 summarizes these newly developed metrics.

Software project managers are interested in software metrics because of their ability to predict or describe overall characteristics of software systems. They are generally interested not in a particular metric but rather in combinations of these metrics in a model. Today macromodels like COCOMO [24] are used by large corporations such as TRW and Fujitsu [87]. Therefore, Section 6 puts forth publications dealing with software process estimation models.

Even though our bibliography is extensive, we do not claim that it is complete. We are also aware that our classification may be concise, but we believe that this paper can serve as a quick reference guide to software metrics researchers and practitioners.

2.   CLASSIC METRICS

Section 2 classifies the publications by examining the particular metric studied. This classification is displayed in Table 1. This section is titled "Classic Metrics" because we considered Halstead's software science (HSS), McCabe's cyclomatic complexity (MCC), lines of code (LOC), and Albrecht's function points (AFP) as "classic" metrics. This is due to the large number of publications on these four metrics. The DISC column is checked as empirical (E) if the publication contains some empirical validation; otherwise it is checked as theoretical (T). The last column (labeled "Other") functions as a cross-reference to Table 4, which contains a brief description of the metrics in question; for certain publications, however, there were simply too many new metrics to list them in Table 4.

It is clear from the information introduced in Table 1 that there are a large number of newly developed metrics. Enough, in fact, that we submit them in Section 4.

Another point is that software metrics is generating a growing flow of publications over the years. This is a good indication of the sustained interest in the field.

Table 1. Classic Metrics						
	DISC	HSS	MCC	LOC	AFP	Other
MCCA76	E/T		•			
HALS77	E/T	•				
JONE78	T			•		
YINB78	E		•			AI, FFIN, FFOT, L, Ni
ALBR79	E			•	•	
CURT80	T	•	•			Entropy, Zipf
BASI81B	E				•	DL, M, NL, NM
BASI81D	T	•				
BELA81A	E					Clustering Complexity
CURT81B	T	•	•			
GAFF81	E	•	•			

ID	Type	1	2	3	4	Description
MOHA81	T					McClure's Complexity, Chapin's Q, Entropy
TROY81	E					X1 .. X21
BESE82	T	•				
KAFU82	E	•	•			Direct Local, Global & Indir. Flow, Inter. Complexity
LASS82	E/T	•				
TYLE82	T	•				
WOOD82	E	•	•	•		TL
ALBR83	E	•		•	•	
BASI83A	E	•	•	•		
BASI83B	E		•			CALL, DECS, SYNC
BEHR83	E				•	
BOWE83	E/T	•				51 metrics for distributed systems
CURT83	T	•	•	•	•	
EVAN83	T	•	•	•		
HALL83	T	•	•	•		
POEL83	E					S
ZWAN83	T				•	
ALBR84	T				•	
BASI84A	E		•	•		ECE, ERMO
BEAN84	T					Path, Stress Point
BOYD84	E			•		BALnew, BALmod, BALunch, HOLnew, HOLmod, HOLunch, MODmod, NM
DUNS84	T	•	•	•		
HALL84	T	•	•	•		
HENR84	E	•	•			See KAFU82
PRAT84	T	•	•			mu
REYN84	T	•				
SZUL84	E/T	•	•			
YAUS84	E/T					DSM, LSM, MS, MC, PSM
BASI85A	E	•	•	•		CALL,CEF,DEF,TCH,TEF,TF,TSEF, VER,WCH,WF,XQT
BASI85B	E					CRLSC,CTCR,CTLSC,CTSC,PHCR, PHLSC,PHSC,SCCR, SCLSC
BOLO85	E	•	•	•		Interconnectivity
BOWE85	T					Quality metrics framework containing a large number of quality metrics
CARD85	E					Module Strength

	DISC	HSS	MCC	LOC	AFP	
CAVA85	T					RAB,REN,RFOM
CRAW85	E	•	•	•		
DEMA85	E			•		Number of defects
DRUM85	E			•	•	
FLAH85	E			•	•	
HUIS85	T		•			c(G)
JENS85	E	•	•			Program Band
KAFU85	E	•	•	•		Info,Info-LOC,Invoke,Review, Rev-LOC,Stability, Sta-LOC
KITC85	E			•		
KONS85	E	•				
KUNK85	E			•	•	
LEMO85	T					Structural Complexity
RAMA85	E					RSL metrics
SCHA85	T					MLOC,NMOD
SHEN85	E	•	•			
YAUS85	E					Program Design Stability
CARD86	E			•		IC,LV,MC,MST,MSZ,ST
COTE86	E	•	•	•		Interconnectivity
FENT86	T	•	•			
GAFF86	E			•	•	
GANN86	E					CAM,NGP,NPD,NTPI,PVM
HARR86	E			•		Style
HUFF86	T			•		39 debugging, 9 development & 9 test metrics
KITC86	T		•	•		
KNAF86	T				•	
RAMA86B	T/E	•	•			Weighted metrics
REDI86	E					74 simple code measurements
RODR86	E	•	•	•		
SHAT86	T					Communication complexity
TSAI86	T		•			Complexity polynomial

Key: DISC, discussion (E, empirical; T, theoretical); HSS, Halstead's software science; MCC, McCable's cyclomatic complexity; LOC, number of lines of code; AFP, Albrecht's function points.

Of equal importance is the fact that more and more researchers are producing empirical validations. This is particularly striking if we look at the discussion column for 1985 versus the entries for 1981. This is very encouraging when considering Boehm's statement in [25]: "The software field cannot hope to have its Kepler or its Newton until it has had its army of Tycho Brahes, carefully preparing the well-defined observational data from which a deeper set of scientific insights may be derived."

Although Halstead's software science has been severely criticized [22, 81, 64], it is still further explored today. In the same order of idea, the number of lines of code is still a popular metric. Highly controversial in the past [70], this metric has since been well defined [24, 39]. It is also used more rationally today as its limits are better understood by the community.

Finally, we noted that there is a small number of publications about Albrecht's function points. Although function points are well defined and successfully used in the industry [52, 80], they do not seem to generate much interest in the research community.

3.   Metrics Throughout the Life Cycle

A classification of the bibliography with respect to the various phases of the software life cycle is presented in Table 2. Each row represents one publication. Each column is checked according to the life-cycle phase covered in the corresponding publication. The life-cycle phases are analysis, design, and code. The fourth column is checked if a publication deals with software quality assurance (SQA). Furthermore, the fifth column (labeled "Method") is checked if a publication deals with metrics-related data collection procedures. The last column (labeled "Misc.") is checked if we could not fit a publication in any of the previous categories; i.e., if it did not fit in one of the mentioned phases. These could be general overviews of the field, annotated bibliographies, or maintenance-metrics-related publications.

Table 2. Metrics through the Life Cycle

	Analysis	Design	Code	SQA	Method	Misc.
MCCA76			•			
HALS77			•			
JONE78			•	•		
YINB78		•				
ALBR79	•		•	•		
CURT80		•	•	•	•	•

BASI81A				•	•	
BASI81B		•	•			
BASI81C	•	•	•			
BASI81E	•	•		•	•	
BELA81A		•				
BELA81B		•	•			•
BROW81					•	
CURT81A					•	
CURT81B				•		•
DEMI81					•	
GAFF81			•			
MOHA81		•	•			
SAMM81			•			
SAYW81					•	
SHAW81A					•	
TROY81		•		•		
BESE82			•			
KAFU82			•			
LASS82			•			
TYLE82			•			
WOOD82			•			
ALBR83	•		•			
BASI83A			•			
BASI83B		•	•			
BEHR83	•					
BOWE83	•	•	•	•	•	
CARP83				•	•	
CURT83						•
EVAN83			•			
HALL83		•				
POEL83	•					
ZWAN83	•					
ALBR84	•					
BASI84A	•	•		•		
BASI84B					•	
BEAN84		•				
BOYD84		•	•			
CAVA84	•	•	•	•		
DUNS84						•
HALL84		•				
HENR84		•	•			
KITC84A				•	•	

	1	2	3	4	5	6
PRAT84			•			
REYN84			•			
SZUL84		•	•		•	
YAUS84						•
BASI85A			•	•	•	
BASI85B			•			
BOLO85			•			
BOWE85	•	•	•	•	•	
CARD85		•	•			
CAVA85	•	•	•	•		
CRAW85			•	•		
DEMA85				•		•
DRUM85	•					
FLAH85			•		•	
HUIS88			•			
JENS85			•			
KAFU85		•	•			
KONS85			•			
KUNK85	•	•	•	•		
LEMO85		•				
MADH85			•			
RAMA85	•	•				
SCHA85						•
SHEN85				•		
SNEE85				•	•	
SUNA85				•		
YAUS85		•	•			
CARD86		•	•			
CERI86	•	•	•	•	•	
COTE86			•			
GAFF86	•		•			
GANN86		•	•			
HARR86			•	•		
HUFF86			•	•		
KITC86	•	•	•	•		
KNAF86	•					
LONG86			•			
RAMA86B			•			
REDI86			•	•		
RODR86			•		•	
SHAT86	•	•				
TSAI86	•	•				

We consider that the objective of the analysis phase is to determine *what* must be done, and not *how* it must be done. Publications that deal with this are classified under "Analysis"; publications that deal with how we must realize the system are classified under "Design"; those that study the code itself are under "Code"; and those that deal with software quality assurance all through the life cycle are classified under "SQA."

An excellent discussion of how software metrics can be applied throughout the life cycle can be found in [49] and in the publications of the Rome Air Development Center. DeMarco [49] offers some very interesting analysis and design metrics based on the structured analysis and design techniques. The Rome Air Development Center has studied extensively [27, 35, 112, 120, 28, 36, 37] the role of software metrics in the software quality assurance process throughout the life cycle.

We can observe that, roughly speaking, more than half of the publications deal with code metrics, a quarter of them deal with either design or SQA metrics, and only one-tenth of them deal with either analysis metrics or data collection. What does this mean? First, most research has concentrated on measuring how things are done. As a matter of fact, code metrics and design metrics are all somehow related to either how software is to be constructed or how it has been constructed. We are confident that this area of research will eventually lead to the construction, for software designers and programmers, of tools that will be the equivalent of the micrometer for the mechanical engineer and the voltmeter for the electrical engineer. Pioneering work in this area can be found in [109].

The counterpart of this argument is that little research is actually completed in measuring what is to be done. Systems analysis defines what must be done to develop a system and not how to develop it. Techniques in this phase of the software life cycle are in rapid evolution if we compare them to the techniques applied during coding. Structured analysis [48] and rapid prototyping [110, 92, 98] are two examples of techniques that have been introduced in the past ten years. We anticipate that analysis metrics will be further explored when certain standards have emerged and with the proliferation of automated design tools [82]. However, one methodology-independent metric available at the end of the external design phase is quickly gaining the endorsement of the data processing industry [52, 80]. We already know of many data processing organizations that have implemented function points.

Finally, we would like to stress the need for more research in the area of specific metrics for the maintenance phase of the life cycle, since two-thirds of the cost of a software system is spent on maintenance [123]. Interesting results in this sector are offered in [120, 103, 121].

4.   CODE METRICS

Table 3 classifies the publications that have examined code metrics by programming language. The most studied languauge, as far as Table 3 is concerned, is FORTRAN, followed by COBOL, Assembler, C, Pascal, and finally, PL/1.

That FORTRAN is studied in approximately half the code metrics publications might seem surprising at first; but the majority of code metrics studies are completed on numerical analysis applications. A typical environment is the Software Engineering Laboratory [8].

In a study of 266 data processing projects coordinated by Xerox in 1985 [80], 44% of the projects were programmed in COBOL. It is noteworthy that the small number of publications on software metrics applied to COBOL does not correspond to the actual industry usage of this language. In this same study 16% of the projects were programmed in a fourth-generation language such as Focus; therefore these should also be further explored. This must be emphasized because these languages are more popular.

	ASM	C	COBOL	FOR-TRAN	PAS-CAL	PL/1	Others
ALBR79			•			•	DMS/VS
BAIL81				•			
BASI81A		•		•			
BASI81B				•			
BASI81C	•			•			
BASI81E		•					
GAFF81	•						
KAFU82		•					
LASS82				•			
WOOD82				•			
ALBR83		•				•	
BASI83A				•			
BASI83B							SIMPL-T
BEHR83		•		•		•	Focus, Wang Utilities ...
POEL83		•					EasyTrieve, MARK IV, RPG-II
BASI84A				•			
BOYD84	•						PL/S
HENR84		•					
KITC84A							SDL/S3

Table 3. Code Metrics

SZUL84							Ada[a]
BASI85A				•			
BASI85B				•			
BOLO85				•			
CARD85				•			
CRAW85		•					
DEMA85	•	•	•	•	•	•	Others...
FLAH85	•						PL/S
JENS85					•		
KAFU85				•			
KITC85	•	•	•				ALGOL
KONS85							APL
KUNK85					•	•	A Lot...
MADH85						•	
MIYA85			•				
SHEN85	•				•		PL/S
YAUS85					•		
CARD86	•			•			
CERI86				•			Ada[a]
COTE86					•		
GAFF86	•						HOL
GANN86							Ada[a]
HARR86		•					
KNAF86			•				
LONG86				•			
RAMA86B					•		
REDI86				•			
RODR86					•		
SHAT86							Ada[a]

Ada[a] is a registered trademark of the U.S. Government (Ada Joint Program Office).

Finally, there are Assembler and Pascal. Although Assembler is used, it is less portable than higher-level languages and will remain so. Thus code metrics on assembly language code are highly machine dependent. Pascal is not widely used commercially but is a good testing ground for studying software metrics. It is usually widely available in academic environments and possesses a sound structure, thus making it relatively easy to study new metric concepts, which can then be exported to other languages.

5.   NEW METRICS

Table 4 introduces what we call "new" metrics. As discussed in Section 2, Halstead's software science, McCabe's cyclomatic complexity, lines of code, and Albrecht's function points were considered classic metrics on the basis of the number of studies on them. Far from limiting themselves to these metrics, researchers have developed new ones. The strongest incentive behind this is probably the need for measuring specific things in a given situation and the fact that we don't know what to measure. We found very interesting concepts behind a large number of these new metrics. Table 4 is therefore a list of these new metrics with a brief description and the appropriate bibliographic reference.

These metrics can be classified as being either environment related (E), graph related (G), or information related (I). The environment-related metrics measure properties that depict the process rather than the product, such as the effort metrics. The graph-related metrics are those that are affiliated with the same basis as McCabe's cyclomatic complexity. These metrics mainly measure properties that are depicted on a graph of some sort. This graph can represent the control flow of a program or system, the data flow, etc. [72, 90, 69]. The information-related metrics are those that are affiliated with the basis of Halstead's software science. They basically measure properties associated with the textual representation of a program or system. Their roots can be traced to such things as vocabulary and information content [43, 88, 26].

Table 4. New Metrics

Metric Name	C	Reference	Description
A1	G	YINB78	# of network arcs from level 0 to 1 in structure chart
BALmod	I	BOYD84	# of lines of modified BAL code
BALnew	I	BOYD84	# of lines of new BAL code
BALunch	I	BOYD84	# of lines of unchanged BAL code
c(G)	G	HUIS85	Cyclomatic Complexity + degree of nesting
CALL	I	BASI83A BASI85B	Number of calls in a program
CAM	I	GANN86	Component access metric, refers to non-local data types
CEF	E	BASI85A	Coding effort
Chapin's Q	I	MOHA81	Average frequency of data objects
Clustering Complexity	G	BELA81A	Connectivity of clusters. Based on fan-in and fan-out

Communication Complexity	G	SHAT86	Number of concurrently active rendezvous
Complexity Polynomial	G	TSAI86	Polynomial reduction on the data structure graph
CRLSC	I	BASI85B	Computer runs per line of source code
CTCR	E	BASI85B	Computer time per computer run
CTLSC	I	BASI85B	Computer time per line of source code
CTSC	E	BASI85B	Computer time per software changes
DecS	G	BASI83B	Number of decisions in a program
DEF	E	BASI85A	Design effort
Direct Local Flow	I	KAFU82	Information flow passing thru module hierarchy in system
DL	I	BASI81B	Developed lines of code
DSM	IG	YAUS84	Design stability measure
ECE	E	BASI84A	Error correction effort
Entropy	I	MOHA81 CURT80	Measure of system disorder
ERMO	I	BASI84B	Number of error corrections per module
FFIN	G	YINB78	Fan-in of a module in structured chart
FFOT	G	YINB78	Fan-out of a module in structured chart
Global Flow	I	KAUF82	Information flow passing thru global data structures
HOLmod	I	BOYD84	# of lines of modified HOL code
HOLnew	I	BOYD84	# of lines of new HOL code
HOLunch	I	BOYD84	# of lines of unchanged HOL code
IC	G	CARD86	Invocation Class
Indirect Flow	I	KAFU82	Information flow passing thru shared data structures
INFO	I	KAFU85	Information flow complexity
INFO-LOC	I	KAFU85	INFO adjusted with lines of code
Interconnection Complexity	G	KAFU82	Fan-in and fan-out of each module
Interconnectivity	I	BOLO85 COTE86	Measure of statement interconnectivity in a program
INVOKE	G	KAFU85	Module invocation complexity
L	G	YINB78	Level of a module in structured chart
LSM	IG	YAUS84	Logical stability measure
LV	I	CARD86	Location of variables
M	IG	BASI81B	Number of modules
MC	G	CARD86	Module Class
McClure's Complexity	I	MOHA81	Program readability

MLOC	I	SCHA85	Number of modified lines of code in a routine
Modmod	I	BOYD84	# of modified modules
Module Strength	I	CARD85	Number of "function types" of modules (i.e., I/O, logic, ...)
MST	IG	CARD86	Module strength
MSZ	I	CARD86	Module size
mu	G	PRAT84	Complexity measure based on sequence, decisions and loops
NGP	I	GANN86	Number of generic packages
NI	G	YINB78	# of modules from level 0 to 1 in structure chart
NL	I	BASI81B	New lines of code
NM	I	BASI81B BOYD84	Number of new modules
NMOD	I	SCHA85	Number of changed modules per change request
NPD	I	GANN86	Number of packages declared
NTPI	I	GANN86	Number of times a package is instantiated
Number of defects	I	DEMA85	Number of failed tests
Path	G	BEAN84	Sum of the legnth of path of each connection
PHCR	E	BASI85B	Programmer hours per computer run
PHLSC	IE	BASI85B	Programmer hours per line of source code
PHSC	E	BASI85B	Programmer hours per software change
Program BAND	G	JENS85	Average nesting level in control flow graph of a program
Program Design Stability	I	YAUS85	Number of assumptions made by modules on parm. and data
PVM	IG	GANN86	Package visibility metric
RAM	I	CAVA85	Reliability assessment benchmark based on production failures
REN	I	CAVA85	Reliability estimation number based on testing failures
REV-LOC	IG	KAFU85	REVIEW adjusted with lines of code
REVIEW	G	KAFU85	Revision complexity
RFOM	I	CAVA85	Reliability figure-of-merit number based on early indicators
RLS metrics	IG	RAMA85	Large number of metrics taken on RSL specifications
S	I	POEL83	Size estimator of system. Based on # of files, flows, ...

SCCR	I	BASI85B	Software changes per computer run
SCLSC	I	BASI85B	Software changes per line of source code
ST	I	CARD86	Software type
STA-LOC	I	KAFU85	STABILITY adjusted with lines of code
STABILITY	I	KAFU85	Estimation of system stability
Stress Point	I	BEAN84	# of connections per parts / avg. # of connections per parts
Structural Complexity	G	LEMO85	Complexity of calling tree of system or program
Style	I	HARR86	Conformance of code to a defined style
SynC	G	BASI83B	Syntactic complexity of program code. Measure of "niceness"
TCH	I	BASI85A	Total changes
TEF	E	BASI85A	Total effort
TF	I	BASI85A	Total faults
TL	I	WOOD82	Time estimator. Based on software science & hierarchy
TSEF	E	BASI85A	Tasting effort
VER	I	BASI85A	# of versions
WCH	I	BASI85A	Weighted changes
Weighted metrics	IG	RAMA86B	Software science weighted by the control structure
WF	I	BASI85A	Weighted faults
X1 to X21	IG	TROY81	21 simple measures taken on structured charts and specs.
XQT	I	BASI85A	# of executable statements
Zipf	I	CURT80	Measure of information content

Key: C, metric class; G, graph related; I, information related; E, environment related.

6. METRIC-BASED SOFTWARE PROCESS MODELS

Table 5 presents publications dealing with metric-based software process macromodels. As usual, each row represents one publication. The "Discussion" column is checked as empirical if the publication contains some empirical validation.

The first thing we noticed is that there are more models than there are publications! This is because some of the publications are actually reviews of many models.

It is very clear from Table 5 that there is a large number of models. Although each of these models has its particular merits, the field of software modeling is still very young. A lot of ideas are still being explored, and software engineers are far from being able to count on a standard well-tested macromodel for cost and/or effort estimation.

This is not to say that these models do not work in practice. In fact, some of them have been applied in large corporations [38, 87]. Unfortunately, they can't usually be applied early in the life cycle with a high degree of certainty.

Table 5. Metric-Based Models

	DISCUSSION	SDC	ARON	TRW	WOLVERTON	DOTY	IBM-FSD	PUTNAM-SLIM	PRICE-S	GRC	PARR	COCOMO	BAILEY-BASILI	BASILI-FREIBR	SOFTCOST	COPMO	ALBRECHT	POEL	JENSEN	BOYDSTON	HUFF
YEAR		65	69	72	74	77	77	78	79	79	80	81	81	81	81	83	83	83	83	84	86
FREI79	T								•												
BOEH80	E	•		•		•	•	•	•								•				
BAIL81	E/T											•	•	•							
BASI81B	E						•														
BASI81C	E							•			•										
BASI81D	T		•		•	•		•		•	•	•									
TAUS81	T														•						
ALBR83	E																•				
POEL83	E																	•			
THEB83	E											•				•					
WARB83	E							•													
BOEH84	T					•	•		•			•	•		•				•		
BOYD84	E																			•	
KITC84B	E							•				•									
KITC85	E							•				•									
MIYA85	E											•									
SCHA85												•									
HUFF86	E/T											•									•
KITC86	T											•									
KNAF86	T																•				

7.   CONCLUSION

As you can easily observe from the preceding sections, there is a wealth of publications on software metrics. Fortunately, certain authors are publishing a synthesis of the field. We will conclude this article by quoting what we believe to be the two most authoritative publications in the field of software metrics and models.

Boehm in [24] explains in detail the COCOMO model and thoroughly discusses software process modeling. Miyazaki and Mori [87] say this about Boehm's book [24]: "*Software Engineering Economics*, in which COCOMO is explained and evaluated, is a milestone contribution in software engineering."

Conte, Dunsmore, and Shen in [39] cover all aspects of software metrics and models in detail. We are convinced that this work will become a classic, and we recommend it highly.

ACKNOWLEDGEMENTS

The authors thank Jean Goulet and Richard St-Denis for their useful comments on this paper. This work has been supported by the NSERC and by Grant 86-EQ-2916 from the FCAR.

BIBLIOGRAPHY

1.   ALBR79, A. J. Albrecht, Measuring application development productivity, *Proc. IBM Applications Development Symp.* pp. 83-92, 1979.
2.   ALBR83, A. J. Albrecht and J. E. Gaffney, Jr., Software function, source lines of code, and development effort prediction: A software science validation, *IEEE Trans. Software Engineering* SE-9:639-647 (1983).
3.   ALBR84, A. J. Albrecht, *AD/M Productivity Measurement and Estimate Validation.* Purchase, NY: IBM Corporate Information Systems and Administration, 1984.
4.   ARTH85, L. J. Arthur, *Measuring Programmer Productivity and Software Quality.* New York: Wiley, 1985.
5.   BAIL81, J. W. Bailey and V. R. Basili, A meta-model for software development resource expenditures, *Proc. 5th Int. Conf. on Software Engineering* pp. 107-116, 1981.
6.   BASI81A, V. R. Basili, Data collection, validation and analysis, in *Software Metrics: An Analysis and Evaluation* (A. Perlis et al., eds.), pp. 143-159. Cambridge, MA: MIT Press, 1981.
7.   BASI81B, V. R. Basili and K. Freburger, Programming measurement and estimation in the software engineering laboratory, *J. Systems and Software* 2:47-57 (1981).
8.   BASI81C, V. R. Basili and J. Beane, Can the Parr curve help with manpower distribution and resource estimation problems? *J. Systems and Software* 2:59-69 (1981).

9. BASI81D, V. R. Basili, Resource models, in *Software Metrics: An Analysis and Evaluation* (A. Perlis et al., eds.), pp. 111-130. Cambridge, MA: MIT Press, 1981.

10. BASI81E, V. R. Basili and D. M. Weiss, Evaluation of a software requirements document by analysis of change data, *Proc. 5th Int. Conf. on Software Engineering* pp. 314-323 (1981).

11. BASI83A, V. R. Basili, R. W. Selby, Jr., and T. Y. Phillips, Metric analysis and data validation across FORTRAN projects, *IEEE Trans. Software Engineering* SE-9:652-663 (1983).

12. BASI83B, V. R. Basili and D. H. Hutchens, An empirical study of a syntactic complexity family, *IEEE Trans. Software Engineering* SE-9:664-672 (1983).

13. BASI84A, V. R. Basili and B. T. Perricone, Software errors and complexity: An empirical investigation, *Commun. ACM* 27:42-52 (1984).

14. BASI84B, V. R. Basili and R. W. Weiss, A methodology for collecting valid software engineering data, *IEEE Trans. Software Engineering* SE-10:728-738 (1984).

15. BASI85A, V. R. Basili and R. W. Selby, Jr., Calculation and use of an environment characteristic software metric set, *Proc. 8th Int. Conf. on Software Engineering* 386-391 (1985).

16. BASI85B, V. R. Basili and C. L. Ramsey, ARROWSMITH-P—A prototype expert system for software engineering management, *Proc. Symp. on Expert Systems in Government* pp. 252-264 (1985).

17. BASI86, V. R. Basili, R. W. Selby, and D. H. Hutchens, Experimentation in software engineering, *IEEE Trans. Software Engineering* SE-12:733-743 (1986).

18. BEAN84, J. N. Beane, N. Giddings, and J. Silverman, Quantifying software design, *Proc. 7th Int. Conf. on Software Engineering* pp. 314-322, 1984.

19. BEHR83, C. A. Behrens, Measuring the productivity of computer systems development activities with function points, *IEEE Trans. Software Engineering* SE-9:648-652 (1983).

20. BELA81A, L. A. Belady and C. J. Evangelisti, System partitioning and its measure, *J. Systems and Software* 2:23-29 (1981).

21. BELA81B, L. A. Belady, Complexity of large systems, in *Software Metrics: An Analysis and Evaluation* (A. Perlis et al., eds.), pp. 225-233. Cambridge, MA: MIT Press, 1981.

22. BESE82, N. Beser, Foundations and experiments in software science, *ACM Performance Evaluation Review* 10:48-72 (1982).

23. BOEH80, B. W. Boehm and R. W. Wolverton, Software cost modeling: Some lessons learned, *J. Systems and Software* 1:195-201 (1980).

24. BOEH81, B. W. Boehm, Software Engineering Economics. Englewood Cliffs, NJ: Prentice-Hall, 1981.

25. BOEH84, B. W. Boehm, Software engineering economics, *IEEE Trans. Software Engineering* SE-10:4-21 (1984).

26. BOLO85, G. A. Boloix, Mesure de la complexité du Logiciel utilisant un modèle d'interconnexions. Ph.D. thesis, Ecole Polytechnique de Montréal, Canada, 1985.

27. BOWE83, T. P. Bowen, J. V. Post, J. Tsai, P. E. Presson, and R. L. Schmidt, *Software Quality Measurement for Distributed Systems*. RADC-TR-83-175 (3 volumes), Rome Air Development Center, Rome, NY, 1983.

28. BOWE85, T. P. Bowen, G. B. Wigle, and J. T. Tsai, *Specifications of Software Quality Attributes*. RADC-TR-85-37 (3 volumes), Rome Air Development Center, Rome, NY, 1985.

29. BOYD84, R. E. Boydston, Programming cost estimate: Is it reasonable? *Proc. 7th Int. Conf. on Software Engineering* pp. 153-159 (1984).

30. BROW81, J. C. Browne and M. Shaw, Toward a scientific basis for software evaluation, in *Software Metrics: An Analysis and Evaluation* (A. Perlis et al., eds.), pp. 19-41. Cambridge, MA: MIT Press, 1981.

31. BROW83, B. R. Brown, H. Herlich, M. D. Emerson, C. L. Williamson, M. V. Greco, and W. Sherman, *Productivity Measurement in Software Engineering*. SSA/STECS/PROD-83/1, U.S. Social Security Administration, Washington, DC, 1983.

32. CARD85, D. N. Card, G. T. Page, and F. E. McGarry, Criteria for software modularization, *Proc. 8th Int. Conf. on Software Engineering* pp. 372-377, 1985.

33. CARD86, D. N. Card, V. E. Church, and W. W. Agresti, An empirical study of software design practices, *IEEE Trans. Software Engineering* SE-12:264-271 (1986).

34. CARP83, C. L. Carpenter, Jr., and G. E. Murine, Applying software quality metrics, *ASQC Quality Congress Trans.*, 373-377 (1983).

35. CAVA84, J. P. Cavano, Software reliability measurement: Prediction, estimation, and assessment, *J. Systems and Software* 4:269-275 (1984).

36. CAVA85, J. P. Cavano, Toward high confidence software, *IEEE Trans. Software Engineering* SE11:1449-1455 (1985).

37. CERI86, D. A. Cerino, Software quality measurement tools and techniques, *Proc. Computer Software and Applications Conf.* pp. 160-167, 1986.

38. COCO85. COCOMO/WICOMO User's Group meeting, Wang Institute of Graduate Studies, May 16-17, *Software Engineering Notes* 10:23 (1985).

39. CONT86, S. D. Conte, H. E. Dunsmore, and V. Y. Shen, *Software Engineering Metrics and Models*. Menlo Park, CA: Benjamin/Cummings, 1986.

40. COOK82, M. L. Cook, Software metrics: An introduction and annotated bibliography, *Software Engineering Notes* 7:41-60 (1982).

41. COTE86, V. Côté, P. Bourque, and S. Oligny, An automated approach for evaluating programs in an academic environment, *Proc. Congr. Canadian Information Processing Soc.* pp. 175-179, 1986.

42. CRAW85, S. G. Crawford, A. A. McIntosh, and D. Pregibon, An analysis of static metrics and faults in C software, *J. Systems and Software* 5:37-48 (1985).

43. CURT80, B. Curtis, In search of software complexity, *Proc. Workshop on Quantitative Models for Reliability, Complexity and Cost* pp. 95-106, 1980.

44. CURT81A, B. Curtis, Experimental evaluation of software characteristics, in *Software Metrics: An Analysis and Evaluation* (A. Perlis et al., eds.), pp. 61-76. Cambridge, MA: MIT Press, 1981.

45. CURT81B, B. Curtis, The measurement of software quality and complexity, in *Software Metrics: An Analysis and Evaluation* (A. Perlis et al., eds.), pp. 225-233. Cambridge, MA: MIT Press, 1981.

46. CURT83, B. Curtis, Software metrics: Guest editor's introduction, *IEEE Trans. Software Engineering* SE9:637-638 (1983).

47. DACS86, Data and Analysis Center for Software, *The DACS Measurement Annotated Bibliography: A Bibliography of Software Measurement Literature*. Rome Air Development Center, Rome, NY, 1986.

48. DEMA78, T. DeMarco, *Structured Analysis and System Specification*. New York: Yourdon Press, 1978.

49. DEMA82, T. DeMarco, *Controlling Software Projects*. New York: Yourdon Press, 1982.

50. DEMA85, T. DeMarco and T. Lister, Programmer performance and the effect of the workplace, *Proc. 8th Int. Conf. on Software Engineering* pp. 268-272, 1985.

51. DEMI81, R. A. DeMillo and R. J. Lipton, Software project forecasting, in *Software Metrics: An Analysis and Evaluation* (A. Perlis et al., eds.), pp. 77-94. Cambridge, MA: MIT Press, 1981.

52. DRUM85, S. Drummond, Measuring applications development performance, *Datamation* 31: 102-108 (1985).

53. DUNS84, H. E. Dunsmore, Software metrics: An overview of an evolving methodology, *Information Processing & Management* 20:183-192 (1984).

54. EVAN83, W. M. Evangelist, Software complexity metric sensitivity to program structuring rules, *J. Systems and Software* 3:231-243 (1983).

55. FENT86, N. E. Fenton and R. W. Whitty, Axiomatic approach to software metrication through program decomposition, *Computer J.* 29:330-339 (1986).

56. FLAH85 M. J. Flaherty, Programming process productivity measurement for System/370, *IBM Systems J.* 24:168-175 (1985).

57. FREI79, F. R. Freiman and R. E. Park, Price software model—Version 3: An overview, *Proc. IEEE-PYNY Workshop on Quantitative Software Models* pp. 32-41, 1979.

58. GAFF81, I.JE. Gaffney, Jr., Software metrics: A key to improved software development management, *Proc. 13th Symp. on the Interface* pp. 211-220, 1981.

59. GAFF86, J. R. Gaffney, Jr., The impact on software development costs using HOL's, *IEEE Trans. Software Engineering* SE-12:496-499 (1986).

60. GANN86, J. D. Gannon, E. E. Katz, and V. R. Basili, Metrics for Ada packages: An initial study, *Commun. ACM* 29:616-623 (1986).

61. HALL83, N. R. Hall and S. Preiser, Dynamic complexity measures for software design, *Proc. IEEE Total Systems Reliability Symp.* pp. 57-66, 1983.

62. HALL84, N. R. Hall and S. Preiser, Combined network complexity measures, *IBM J. Research and Development* 20:15-27 (1984).

63. HALS77, M. H. Halstead, *Operating and Programming Systems: Elements of Software Science.* New York: Elsevier, 1977.

64. HAME85, P. Hamer and G. Frewin, Software metrics: A critical overview, Pergamon Infotech State of the Art Report 13(2) (1985).

65. HARR86, W. Harrison and C. R. Cook, A note on the Berry-Meekings style metric, *Commun. ACM* 29:123-125 (1986).

66. HENR84, S. Henry and D. Kafura, The evaluation of software systems' structure using quantitative software metrics, *Software Practice and Experience* 14:561-573 (1984).

67. HUFF86, K. A. Huff, J. V. Sroka, and D. E. Struble, Quantitative models for managing software development processes, *Software Engineering J.* 1:17-23 (1986).

68. HUIS85, G. Huisheng and M. Schmidt, A complexity measure based on selection and nesting, *SIGMetrics* 13:14-19 (1985).

69. JENS85, H. A. Jensen and K. Vairavan, An experimental study of software metrics for real-time software, *IEEE Trans. Software Engineering* SE-11:231-234 (1985).

70. JONE78, T. C. Jones, Measuring programming quality and productivity, *IBM Systems J.* 17:39-63 (1978).

71. JONE86, T. C. Jones, *Programming Productivity.* New York: McGraw-Hill, 1986.

72. KAFU82, D. Kafura and S. Henry, Software quality based on interconnectivity, *J. Systems and Software* 2:121-131 (1981).

73. KAFU85, D. Kafura and J. Canning, A validation of software metrics using many metrics and two resources, *Proc. 8th Int. Conf. on Software Engineering* pp. 378-385, 1985.

74. KITC84A, B. A. Kitchenham, Program history records: A system of software data collection and analysis, *ICL Tech. J.* 4:103-114 (1984).

75. KITC84B, B. A. Kitchenham and N. R. Taylor, Software cost models, *ICL Tech. J.* 4:73-102 (1984).

76. KITC85, B. A. Kitchenham and N. R. Taylor, Software project development cost estimation, *J. Systems and Software* 5:267-278 (1985).

77. KITC86, B. A. Kitchenham and J. A. McDermid, Software metrics and integrated project support environments, *Software Engineering J.* 1:58-64 (1986).

78. KNAF86, G. I. Knafl and J. Sacks, Software development effort prediction based on function points, *Proc. Computer Software and Applications Conf.* pp. 319-325, 1986.

79. KONS85, A. H. Konstam and D. E. Wood, Software science applied to APL, *IEEE Trans. Software Engineering* SE-11:994-1000 (1985).

80. KUNK85, J. E. Kunkler, *A Cooperative Industry Study—Software Development/Maintenance Productivity.* Rochester, CT: Xerox Corp., 1985.

81. LASS82, J. L. Lassez, D. Van Der Knijff, J. Sheperd, and C. Lassez, A critical examination of software science, *J. Systems and Software* 2:105-112 (1981).

82. LEHN86, S. Lehnert, P. G. Sorenson, and J. P. Tremblay, A survey of computer-aided tools for performing systems analysis and design, *Proc. Congr. Canadian Information Processing Soc.* pp. 109-119, 1986.

83. LEMO85, O. E. Lem, A simple measure of software complexity, *SIGMetrics* 13:33-47 (1985).

84. LONG86, H. D. Longworth, L. M. Ottenstein, and M. R. Smith, The relationship between program complexity and slice complexity, *Proc. Computer Software and Applications Conf.* pp. 383-389, 1986.

85. MADH85, N. Madhavji, Compare: A collusion detector for Pascal, *Techniques et Sciences Informatiques* 4:489-497 (1985).

86. MCCA76, T. J. McCabe, A complexity measure, *IEEE Trans. Software Engineering* 5:308-320 (1976).

87. MIYA85, Y. Miyazaki and K. Mori, COCOMO evaluation and tailoring, *Proc. 8th Int. Conf. on Software Engineering* pp. 292-299, 1985.

88. MOHA81, S. B. Mohanty, Entropy metrics for software design evaluation, *J. Systems and Software* 2:39-46 (1981).

89. POEL83, K. G. Van der Poel and S. R. Schach, A software metric for cost estimation and efficiency measurement in data processing system development, *J. Systems and Software* 3:187-191 (1983).

90. PRAT84, R. E. Prather, An axiomatic theory of software complexity measure, *Computer J.* 27:340-347 (1984).

91. QAI85, *Quality Assurance Manager's Handbook.* Orlando, FL: The Quality Assurance Institute, 1985.

92. RAMA84, C. V. Ramamoorthy, A. Prakash, W. T. Tsai, and Y. Usuda, Software engineering problems and perspectives, *Computer* 17:191-210 (1984).

93. RAMA85, C. V. Ramamoorthy, W.-T. Tsai, T. Yamaura, and A. Bhide, Metrics guided methodology, *Proc. Computer Software and Applications Conf.* pp. 111-120, 1985.

94. RAMA86A, C. V. Ramamoorthy, V. Garg, and A. Prakash, Programming in the large, *IEEE Trans. Software Engineering* SE-12:769-783 (1986).

95. RAMA86B, B. Ramamurthy, and A. Melton, A synthesis of software metrics and the cyclomatic number, *Proc. Computer Software and Applications Conf.* pp. 308-313, 1986.

96. REDI86, K. A. Redish and W. F. Smyth, Program style analysis: A natural by-product of program compilation, *Commun. ACM* 29:126-133 (1986).

97. REYN84, R. G. Reynolds, Metrics to measure the complexity of partial programs, *J. Systems and Software* 4:75-91 (1984).

98. ROBI85, P. N. Robillard, *Le Logiciel: De sa conception à sa maintenance.* Chicoutimi, Canada; Gäétan Morin, 1985.

99. RODR86, V. Rodriguez and W.-T. Tsai, Software metrics interpretation through experimentation, *Proc. Computer Software and Applications Conf.* pp. 368-374, 1986.

100. RUBE68, R. J. Rubey and R. D. Hartwick, Quantitative measurement of program quality, *Proc. ACM Nat. Conf.* pp. 671-677, 1968.

101. SAMM81, J. Sammet, High-level language metrics, in *Software Metrics: An Analysis and Evaluation* (A. Perlis et al., eds.), pp. 131-142. Cambridge, MA: MIT Press, 1981.

102. SAYW81, F. G. Sayward, Design of software experiments, in *Software Metrics: An Analysis and Evaluation* (A. Perlis et al., eds.), pp. 43-59. Cambridge, MA: MIT Press, 1981.

103. SCHA85, H. Schaefer, Metrics for optimal maintenance management, *Proc. Conf. on Software Maintenance* pp. 114-119, 1985.

104. SHAT86, S. M. Shatz, On complexity metrics oriented for distributed programs using Ada tasking, *Proc. Computer Software and Applications Conf.* pp. 247-254, 1986.

105. SHAW81A, M. Shaw, When is "good"' enough? Evaluating and selecting software metrics, in *Software Metrics: An Analysis and Evaluation* (A. Perlis et al., eds.), pp. 251-262. Cambridge, MA: MIT Press, 1981.

106. SHAW81B, M. Shaw, Annotated bibliography on software metrics, in *Software Metrics: An Analysis and Evaluation* (A. Perlis et al., eds.), pp. 263-399. Cambridge, MA: MIT Press, 1981.

107. SHEN85, V. Y. Shen, Yu Tze-Jie, M. Thebault, and L. R. Pausen, Identifying error-prone software—An empirical study, *IEEE Trans. Software Engineering* SE11:317-323 (1985).

108. SHOO83, M. L. Shooman, *Software Engineering Design, Reliability and Management.* New York: McGraw-Hill, 1983.

109. SNEE85, H. M. Sneed and A. Mérey, Automated software quality assurance, *IEEE Trans. Software Engineering* SE-11:909-916 (1985).

110. SOFT82, Special issue on rapid prototyping, *Software Engineering Notes* 7(5) (1982).

111. SUNA85, T. Sunazuka, M. Azuma, and N. Yamagishi, Software quality assessment technology, *Proc. 8th Int. Conf. on Software Engineering* pp. 142-148 (1985).

112. SZUL84, P. A. Szulewski, N. M. Sodano, A. J. Rosner, and J. B. DeWolf, *Automating Software Design Metrics.* RADC-TR-84-27, Rome Air Development Center, Rome, NY, 1984.

113. TAUS81, R. C. Tausworthe, *Deep Space Network Software Cost Estimation Model.* JPL Publication 81-7, NASA Jet Propulsion Laboratory, at Cal. Inst. of Tech., 1981.

114. THEB83, S. M. Thebault, Model evaluation in software metrics research, *Proc. 15th Symp. on the Interface* pp. 277-285, 1983.

115. TROY81, D. A.Troy and S. H. Zweben, Measuring the quality of structured design, *J. Systems and Software* 2:113-120, 1981.

116. TSAI86, W.-T. Tsai, M. A. Lopez, V. Rodriguez, and D. Volovik, An approach to measuring data structure complexity, *Proc. Computer Software and Applications Conf.* pp. 240-246, 1986.

117. TYLE82, T. W. Tyler, Software science—An introduction, *Proc. 9th Australian Computer Conf.* pp. 847-870, 1982.

118. WARB83, R. D. H. Warburton, Managing and predicting the costs of real-time software, *IEEE Trans. Software Engineering* SE-9:562-569 (1983).

119. WOOD82, S. N. Woodfield, V. Y. Shen, and D. H. Dunsmore, A study of several metrics for programming effort, J. Systems and Software 2:97-103, 1981.

120. YAUS84, S. S. Yau, *Methodology for Software Maintenance*. RADC-TR-83-262, Rome Air Development Center, Rome, NY, 1984.

121. YAUS85, S. S. Yau and J. S. Collofello, Design stability measures for software maintenance, *IEEE Trans. Software Engineering* SE-11:849-856 (1985).

122. YINB78, B. H. Yin and J. W. Winchester, The establishment and use of measures to evaluate the quality of software design, *Software Engineering Notes* 3:45-52 (1978).

123. ZELK79, M. V. Zelkowitz, Large-scale software development, in *Principles of Software Engineering*, pp. 1-44. Englewood Cliffs, NJ: Prentice-Hall, 1979.

124. ZWAN83, K. Zwanzig, Estimating and productivity measurement, GUIDE 56:416-440 (1983).

Appendix C.
CASE '92
Standards Coordination Workshop

Minutes from July 6, 1992

Prepared by:
David Sharon, CASE Associates, Inc.
14985 SE 82nd Drive, Clackamas, OR 97015 (503) 656-0986
and
Myer Morron, BNR Europe Ltd.
Concorde Road, Maidenhead, England SL6 4AG
+44 G28 794 594

CASE '92 Standards Coordination Workshop, Appendix A

CASE standard update reports from CASE '92 Standards Coordination Workshop:

IEEE Std 1175

Purpose: To help builders, testers, and users of CASE tools to integrate tools into a family of tools. The standard provides the following:
1. Reference model for tool-to-organization interconnections.
2. Reference model for tool-to-platform interconnections.
3. Standard text language (STL) for information transfer between tools.

Scope: IEEE Std 1175 describes interconnections that must be considered when buying, building, testing, or using software tools. These software tools are special-purpose tools that are developed for use in creating computing systems. These tools include:
1. Computer-aided engineering tools
2. Computer-aided software engineering tools
3. Computer-aided system engineering tools

Status: Approved as trial use standard by the IEEE Standards Board on December 5, 1991.

Immediate Plans: In 1993, after one year of trial use, convert standard to full use.

© 1992 David Sharon and Myer Morron

Future Plans: Extend the STL to include other life cycle phases and tool types after one year of trial use.

Contact: Secretary of the IEEE Standards Board, P.O. Box 1331, 445 Hoes Lane, Piscataway, NJ 08854 (908) 562-3806.

Liaisons With Other Standards: EIA/CDIF and ISO IEC JTC1/SC7/WG11.

ANSI X3H4 — Information Resource Dictionary Standard (IRDS)

Project - 336M

Purpose/Scope: Carry out the development of an information resource dictionary standard and provide a focal point for all standards activities directed in the area of IRDS.

Status: Approved as an American National Standard on October 19, 1988 as ANSI X3.138-1988.

Immediate Plans: In maintenance.

Future Plans: X3H4 is developing a requirements document for IRDS2. This document will serve as the basis for discussion with the ISO IRDS and setting the priorities for standardization.

Project - X3H4.1 570-DT, Reference Model for Information Resource Dictionary Systems

Purpose/Scope: To provide a framework for logical placement of the IRDS in the Information Systems Environment. This framework clarifies the role of the IRDS and illustrates the interfaces to software within this environment. The IRDS Reference Model defines the terms, concepts, components, and service domains of the IRDS and serves as the basis for development and coordination of standards for the IRDS and related efforts.

Status: Current draft is under review in 1992.

Future Plans: This document is expected to affect the ISO IRDS framework and help bring ANSI and ISO closer together on the issues.

Project - X3H4.2 569-D, External Software Interface (IRDS Services Interface)

Purpose/Scope: To define a low-level interface specification to the IRDS database for external tools to exploit the contents of the IRD.

Status: Approved as an American National Standard as X3.185-1992.

Future Plans: This standard will evolve as the key IRDS Services Interface for integrating applications around a common database specification.

Project - X3H4.2 680-D, IRDS Export/Import

Purpose/Scope: To describe the functional file format requirements identified in ANSI X3.138-1988 for interchanging data between IRDSs and a non-standard repository.

Status: Approved as an American National Standard as X3.95-1992.

Future Plans: Future IRDS export/import standards will be developed by EIA/CDIF and processed through the International Standards Organization (ISO) by ANSI X3H4.

Project - X3H4.4 701-DT, Naming Convention Verification

Purpose/Scope: To determine the requirements for a standard to support local naming conventions and name administration for entities described in an IRDS.

Status: Published as a technical report by X3 in 1991.

Future Plans: Initiate a project (896-DT) IRDS administration and control to examine the requirements to support operation and integrity/quality maintenance of an installed IRDS.

Project - X3H4.6 738-DTR, Integration of IRDS Schemas

Purpose/Scope: To develop a technical report to provide an understanding of the issues involved in integrating an IRD schema from an external source into a local IRD schema and to develop guidance for IRDS administration in support of this need.

Status: Target for technical report is 12/92 pending the outcome of Project 819-DT, Model Unification for Data Repositories.

Project - X3H4.2 754-D, IRDS Extensions to Support CASE

Purpose/Scope: To develop an interface to support current and evolving CASE technologies, especially object-oriented tools. This will require extensions to the underlying X3.138 data model to support such concepts as type inheritance, behavior, and type-specific services.

Status: The project is currently referred to as *A Tool Integration System* (ATIS). A specification for the ATIS model has been completed for the ISO IRDS data model.

Immediate Plans: Complete technical report by 6/94.

Project - X3H4.6 819-DT, Model Unification for Data Repositories

Purpose/Scope: To write a technical report specifying an approach by which models developed using one recognized paradigm (source code, database schema DDL, JCL, etc.) may be referenced or used by another modeling paradigm. The report will support the integration of the representation of these models and will specify the requirements for the IRDS conceptual schema and associated services.

Status: A working draft was approved 10/91.

Immediate Plans: Technical report complete 10/92.

Project - X3H4.4 896-DT, IRDS Administration and Control

Purpose/Scope: To define the dimensions and scope of IRDS administration mechanisms as quality assurance and rules management for the information model and the software development process model and identify areas of proposed standardization.

Status: First meeting was held 1/92.

Immediate Plans: Technical report complete 12/93.

X3H4 Liaison Activities

Liaison Activities:
   (1) Database Languages (X3H2)
        Purpose: To maintain awareness of X3H2 dpANS activity and to coordinate on interfaces between DBMS standards and the IRDS standard. There is a dependency, especially from the IRDS Rapporteur Group perspective on the specification of an object-oriented IRDS and the specification of SQL3 as an object-oriented DBMS. It is unclear what the impact of this dependency will be on both X3H2 and X3H4. To coordinate on conceptual schema, schema languages, and model unification aspects of database and repository standards. No formal liaison exists with X3H2.

   (2) SPARC Database Management Systems Study Group (DBSSG)
        Purpose: To maintain awareness of DBSSG activities, to provide the study group with an H4 perspective on database framework and database standards architecture, and to coordinate with the related work on the Unified Data Model project by the Common Data Model Group. No formal liaison exists with DBSSG.

   (3) Vocabulary (X3K5)
        Purpose: To assure understanding of terminology and to prevent invention of new terminology when existing terminology will do. Formal liaison exists with this committee.

   (4) International Advisory Committee
        Purpose: To be aware of international standards activities related to the IRDS. H4 has an International Representative.

   (5) ISO/JTC1/SC21/WG3 (Data Management)
        Purpose: To promote the X3H4-produced documents for standardization within the International Standards Community. Several H4 representatives attend the IRDS Rapporteur Group meetings.

   (6) Data Interchange (X3T2)
        Purpose: The IRDS work on model unification has resulted in work that may contribute to conceptual schema work. To maintain awareness and coordinate activity on conceptual

schema issues for the X3H4 repository technology and the role of the conceptual schema in data interchange. X3H4.6 is working very closely with X3T2 on this issue.

(7) CASE Tool Integration Models (X3H6)
Purpose: X3H4 and X3H6 each recognize the need for very close liaison. Recently at a joint meeting, the two committees agreed that:
> X3H6 will work on models of tool integration, including control integration. X3H4 will work to provide a sufficiently complete set of services so that X3H6 models could be implemented on top of an IRDS.

(8) Object-Information Management (X3H7)
Purpose: The IRDS2 standard will be object-oriented and will assume an object-oriented model exists. It is unclear whether that need is best served by the work of X3H7 or X3H2.

(9) Open Distributed Processing (X3T3)
Purpose: To maintain awareness and coordinate activity on conceptual schema issues for repository technology and the role of the conceptual schema in ODP. No formal liaison exists with X3T3. X3T3 and X3H4 have schedule a joint meeting for December 1992.

(10) Open Systems Interconnection (X3T5)
Purpose: To maintain awareness and coordinate activity on conceptual schema issues for X3H4 repository technology and the role of the conceptual schema in OSI. No formal liaison exists with X3T5.

(11) PDES Dictionary Methodology Committee (PDES/DMC)
Purpose: To maintain awareness of PDES/DMC activities, to provide the DMC with X3H4 perspective of IRDS repository technology standards and IRDS Conceptual Schema with its Normative Language and Defining Language, to coordinate with the related work, SUMM (Semantic Unification Meta Model) project, and to achieve a common semantic for our respective logic based work.

(12) Knowledge Sharing Effort
Purpose: To maintain awareness of Knowledge Sharing Effort activities; to provide the X3H4 perspective of IRDS repository technology, conceptual schema, database framework and database standards; and to coordinate with the related work, KIF (Knowledge Interchange Format) project to achieve a common semantic for our respective logic based work.

(13) EIA/CDIF
Purpose: The EIA/CDIF standards organization is working closely with X3H4. EIA/CDIF will be specifying the interchange form for IRDS content. In addition, it is expected that EIA/CDIF will develop the information model for CASE, and this model will become an IRDS content standard.

(14) U.S. TAG to SC7
Purpose: To support the integrated specification of CASE data models, and to promote their international standardization through both SC7 and SC21.

X3H4 Future Trends

The technology of IRDSs is becoming a critical element within information processing environments. It is becoming the central source of data to support integration and control of information environments. The IRDS Reference Model reflects this role.

The current ANSI X3.185 does not support this integration and control function as well as might be considered desirable. The purpose of the IRDS Service Interface is to specify the software (services) interface which will allow the IRDS to provide the necessary support to this environment. The purpose of the IRDS Extensions to Support CASE is to further enhance this support. The Model Unification project is examining the requirements for a data model unification approach.

The current standard does not support model representation, integration, and translation. The Model Unification project is addressing this issue by providing a logical approach for the IRDS conceptual schema. Since the IRDS is the repository for all enterprise resources and provides management control as well as services, the conceptual schema must support a wide range of requirements and therefore has a scope that includes the more general issue of conceptual schema.

Contact: Jerry Winkler, (703) 425-4558.

NIST ISEE Working Group

Purpose: Provide guidance to Federal agencies in acquiring integrated software development and maintenance environments (ISEEs).

Scope: Identify and stimulate the plans and coordination needed among software industry parties and relevant standard activities for consensus direction on open system ISEEs by doing the following:
1. Identify and explore fundamental issues in ISEEs.
2. Identify the needed set of standards that define a comprehensive interface for integrating software tools.
3. Develop guidelines on interface standards for ISEEs.

Status: Enhance the joint NIST/ECMA Reference Model document for the 2nd edition NIST publication.

Immediate Plans: Complete the revised NIST/ECMA Reference Model and publish it as the 2nd edition of the joint NIST/ECMA Reference Model for Frameworks of Software Engineering Environments Technical Report by the end of December 1993.

Future Plans: Harmonize/share information with other groups developing reference models for Open System Environment.

Contact: William Wong, (301) 975-3341.

ANSI X3H6 — CASE Tool Integration Models

Purpose: To define what a tool must do to interact with the integration models defined by the standard and create a repository-independent specification using a known representation technique and relying heavily on existing standards.

Scope: To define the set of obligations to be met by a software engineering environment to improve the integration of the environment's components.

Status: Three working groups started in 1992 to cover tools, representations, and integration requirements. Two meetings were held 1/92 and 4/92 and X3H6 schema requirements were defined along a coordination understanding between X3H4 and X3H6.

Immediate Plans: Outline object model needs by 7/92, make recommendations on a representation technique by 7/92, define versioning and configuration management models by 10/92 and create a requirements baseline document by 10/92.

Contact: Hal Pierson, (703) 742-7155.

Liaisons: ANSI X3H4, OMG and trying to provide a forum for joint work between the CASE Interoperability Alliance and CASE Communique.

CASE Communique

Purpose: Provide an industry-acceptable standard specification for control integration in CASE framework environments.

Scope: Intertool communications between CASE tools in framework environments that support REQUEST/REPLY and NOTIFICATION message services. Enable the "plug and play" of tools in framework environments which allows environments to be built and maintained with a minimum amount of effort while allowing flexibility of tool choice.

Status: Began work in October 1991 with the first specification completed June 15, 1992. The group is sponsored by Hewlett Packard, IBM, Informix, and Control Data Corp. and includes over 60 member organizations.

Immediate Plans: Update/revise the specifications.

Future Plans: Develop a useful operation specification based on user requirements and validated through actual implementations and submit the specification to ANSI for consideration.

Liaisons: Share information with Object Management Group, ECMA/PCTE, EIA/CDIF and the SunSoft CASE Interoperability Alliance in an attempt to move toward a single standard specification.

Contact: Edie Bailey, (303) 229-6611.

ECMA/TC33 PCTE

Purpose: To standardize a portable common tool environment.

Scope: To develop a public tools interface for repositories and ensure a firm base exists for common schemas to aid in tool portability and integration.

Status: Completed version 1 of ECMA 149 Abstract Specification 12/90, ECMA 158 C Binding 6/91, ECMA 162 Ada Binding 12/91, and Technical Report (TR) 55 Reference Model version 1 12/91.

Immediate Plans: Version 2 for ECMA 149, 158 and 162 12/92, Version 1 C++ Binding in 1993, TR 55 Reference Model Version 3 in 1993 and TR on Reference Model Version 2 12/92.

Future Plans: Move standardization process faster within the ISO JTC1.

Liaisons: Joint meetings with EIA/CDIF and ISO JTC1 SC7 WG11. Information sharing with ISO IRDS, the Object Management Group, DoD PCIS, and NIST ISEE.

Contact: Myer Morron, (+44) 628 794 594, or Dr. Ray Crispin, (+44) 272 799910.

EIA/CDIF — CASE Data Interchange Format

Purpose: To provide a transfer format to enable CASE tools to transfer information between themselves. The format covers both the semantic information and the presentation of that information to the CASE tool user. The CDIF architecture keeps the transfer format and the CASE interchange metamodel distinct so these components can be used by other standards groups.

Scope: To remove the need for custom interfaces between CASE tools and between the tools and repositories by enabling the interchange of all information needed to develop and maintain software systems at any stage in the life cycle.

Status: The CDIF Technical Committee has produced a set of interim standards which are being prototyped and expanded based on feedback from the prototypers and from other standard working groups. The interim standards are:

EIA/IS-81 CDIF — Framework for Modeling and Extensibility (Completed 7/91)
EIA/IS-82 CDIF — Transfer Format Definition (Completed 7/91)
    Part 1: General Rules for CDIF Syntaxes and Encoding
    Part 2: CDIF Transfer Format Syntax
    Part 3: CDIF Transfer Format Encoding
EIA/IS-83 CDIF — Standardized CASE Interchange MetaModel (Completed 7/91)
    Part 1: Semantic Model
    Part 2: Presentation Model

Immediate Plans: Update/revise the interim standards in 1992. Start work in the following subject areas: state/event modeling, real-time extensions to data flow modeling, relational database, program structure specification, user interface (including GUI), and project management.

Future Plans: Enhance the transfer format to meet the needs of repository interchange and support international character sets. Continue standard coordination efforts so CDIF can play a lead role in developing the information model for software engineering.

Liaisons: Joint meetings and coordination have occurred with ANSI X3H4, ANSI X3H6, IEEE Std 1175, and ECMA TC33 PCTE. CDIF participates on the ISO JTC1/SC7 WG11 for developing standard data schema. The CDIF Transfer Format is being considered by ANSI X3H4 as the basis for the IRDS Import/Export and by ECMA TC33 PCTE for the PCTE Import/Export.

Contact: Mike Imber, (+44) 71 636 4213.

U.S. Technical Advisory Group for ISO/IEC JTC1/SC7 — Software Engineering

Purpose: The U.S. Technical Advisory Group (TAG) for ISO/IEC JTC1/SC7 is chartered to determine and present through the IEEE and ANSI, the consensus position of the United States in the area of JTC 1/SC7. The U.S. TAG organizes the delegations attending working group meetings, is the source of the technical contributions and is the balloting body for positions related to work items of JTC 1/SC7.

Scope: Develop guidelines for management techniques and standardization of supporting methods and tools necessary for the development and testing of software.

Working Group 1: Symbols, Charts, and Diagrams

a. To develop standards for symbols, charts, and diagrams representing all appropriate stages of the software life cycle; and
b. To develop standards for symbols, charts, and diagrams in the area of screen-based tools for specification, development, and documentation of software.

Projects:

07.06	Program Flow for Processing Sequential Files in Terms of Record Groups (ISO Standard 6593)
07.07	Single Hit Decision Logic Table (ISO 5806)
07.08	Documentation Symbols and Conventions for Data, Program, and System Flowcharts, Program Network Charts, and System Resource Charts (ISO 5807)
07.16	Computer System Configuration Diagram Symbols and Conventions (ISO 8790)
07.11	Basic Constructs for Programs and Conventions for Their Application (approved new project)
07.19.01	Standard Diagrams for Software Development Methods (approved working draft)
07.19.02	Charting Techniques for Software Development and Maintenance (5-part working draft)
07.--	Conventions for Usage of Symbols and Icons in Software Engineering (proposed new project)

Working Group 2: System and Software Documentation

To develop standards for documentation:

Projects:

07.03.01   User Documentation and Cover Information for Consumer Software Packages (ISO Technical Report 9127)

07.03.02   Guidelines for Documentation of Software (revision of ISO Standard 6592)

07.18   Guidelines for the Management of Software Documentation (ISO TR 9294)

07.--   Management of Information Transfer Between Life Cycle Phase (proposed new project*)

Note: (*) Indicates proposals discussed and agreed to in principle by the U.S. TAGE for introduction as proposed new projects at the forthcoming ISO/IEC JTC 1/SC7 meetings. Majority of new project proposals accepted by SC7 have been originated by the USA based on technical work done in the United States.

Working Group 3: (Completed program of work, disbanded)

Working Group 4: Tools and Environment

Preparation of standards and technical reports for tools and CASE environments.

Projects:

07.25   Evaluation and Selection of CASE Tools (approved new project)

Purpose: To define a consistent approach for selecting CASE tools by identifying user needs.

Scope: To define a consistent approach for selecting CASE tools by identifying user needs.

Status: Working draft reviewed June 1992. Third draft available August 1992.

Plans: Register as committee draft to ISO in January 1994.

Liaison: ISO JTC 1/WG6, IEEE P1209, ECMA/NIST.

Contact: P. Voldner, (416) 581-5619.

07.--   Portable Common Tool Environment (PCTE) ECMA Standard 149 (proposed new project for ISO/IEC JTC 1 standard using fast-track method).

Working Group 5: (Disbanded, June 1992)

Working Group 6: Evaluation and Metrics

Preparation of standards and technical reports related to evaluation and metrics.

Projects:

07.13.01	Software Quality Characteristics (ISO 9126)
07.13.02	Software Quality Subcharacteristics (approved working draft)
07.13.03	Software Quality Management and Rating (approved new project)
07.24	Software Quality Requirements and Testing Directives (approved new project)
07.--	Software Process Improvement (preliminary study recommendation for a proposal for new project)
07.--	Process Improvement Indicators, including productivity and quality metrics (proposed new project*)

Working Group 7: Life Cycle Management

Preparation of standards and technical reports on life cycle management.

Projects:

07.21	Life Cycle Management (approved Committee Draft)
07.26	Guide to Life Cycle Management (approved new project)
07.--	Process Management and Assessment (proposed new project*)
07.--	Standard for each life cycle management phase or process (potential new projects*)

Working Group 8: Integral Life Cycle Process

Preparation of standards and technical reports on integral life cycle processes.

Projects:

07.23	Software Configuration Management (approved new project)
07.27	Integral Life Cycle Processes (approved new project)
07.--	Software Maintenance (proposed new project*)
07.--	System and Software Safety (proposed new project*)
07.--	System and Software Engineering Management Process (proposed new project*)
07.--	Software Verification and Validation Plans (proposed new project*)

Working Group 9: Classification and Mapping

Preparation of standards, technical reports, and guidance on classification, mapping, and standards placement.

Projects:

07.20.03	Mapping and Categorization of Relevant ISO Standards to Reference Model (working draft)
07.22	Categorization of Software (approved new project)
07.--	Placement Guide for SC7 Standards and Work Items (approved internal SC7 project)

Working Group 10: Evaluation and Assessment of Processes (interim)

To prepare a series of standards in the area of evaluation and assessment of processes in software life cycle.

Projects:

07.--   Software Process Assessment (new work item proposal, pending JTC 1 approval)

Working Group 11: Description of Data for Software Engineering

To provide basis for data integration by describing the data necessary to support common software engineering methods. This will form the basis of the IRDS Content Modules for these definitions and of the PCTE Common Data Schemas. A direct tool-to-tool transfer format will be provided.

Projects:

07.--   Description of Data for Software Engineering

Purpose: To provide a standard description of data used in the software engineering life cycle to form the basis of an exchange mechanism/format and the standard repository schemas for both IRDS and PCTE.

Scope: To provide descriptions of data supporting software engineering methods to form the basis of the IRDS Content Modules and PCTE Common Data Schemas.

Status: The working group proposal has been approved by SC7.

Plans: The working group plan is to be presented to JTC1/SC7 at the Plenary in June 1993.

Liaisons: ISO IRDS, STEP, ISO SC7, EIA/CDIF, IEEE Std 1175, ECMA TC33.

Contact: Peter Eirich, (410) 993-5634

Object Management Group (OMG)

OMG was not represented at the July 6, 1992 Standards Coordination Workshop. What follows is a repeat of the OMG report found in Deliverable 4, Summary and Forecast of Tool Integration Standards.

Purpose: The purpose of the OMG is to produce a framework and specifications for commercially available object-oriented environments by providing a reference architecture with terms and definitions upon which all specifications are based.

Scope: The scope of the standard is the development of a set of standard interfaces for interoperable software components which supports modular production of software; encourages reuse of code; allows useful integration across developers, operating systems and hardware; and enhances the long term maintenance of the code.

The objective of the OMG is the development of a standard set of specifications and interfaces to maximize the portability, reusability, and interoperability of software. To accomplish this objective, the OMG is promoting the adoption of object technology focusing in five key areas:

1. A reference model with definitions and terminology
2. APIs independent of operating systems
3. Distributed object management
4. Interfaces to object and standard DBMSs
5. Common services, e.g., security, system management, etc.

Status: Developing with its membership the specification for the Object Request Broker and the Object Data Model.

Future Plans: Developing and implementing a three-year plan and cooperating with ANSI X3 and ISO IEC/JTC1/SC21. The Object Services Request for Information (RFI) evaluation process and subsequent release of the Request for Proposal (RFP) is scheduled for 1992.

Contact: Object Management Group, 492 Old Connecticut Path, Framingham, MA 01701, (503) 820-4300.

Liaisons with Other Standards: ECMA PCTE, CASE Communique, ANSI X3H6

U.S. Navy — PSESWG, Project Support Environment Standards Working Group

Purpose: To support the Navy's acquisition of a modern, cost-effective project support environment (PSE).

Status: Working on a PSE reference model. Have produced a report on PSE technology and selected initial baseline standards from IEEE, ANSI, ECMA, and ISO.

Immediate Plans: Continue work on reference model and produce an initial PSE standard report, October 1992.

Future Plans: Identify all interfaces of potential interest and narrow down the list by assessing available candidates and the payoff to the Navy. Develop a Mil-Std by September 1998.

Contact: Patricia Oberndorf or Carl Schmiedekamp, Naval Air Warfare Center, Aircraft Division, Code 7033, Warminster, PA 18001-5000, (215) 441-2737 or 441-1779.

ISO TC184/SC4 (STEP) — U.S. IGES/PDES Organization

Purpose: Prepare a standard for the description of software as a product, throughout the software life cycle, as an integrated portion of the overall ISO STEP standard for product data exchange.

Scope: Develop an activity model reflecting software development processes, develop EXPRESS models for software concepts, integrated into the overall STEP model architecture and define an electronics-to-software interface model.

Status: Initial work is on the activity model and the electronics-to-software model.

Plans: The models from ISO JTC1/SC7/WG11 will form the basis for corresponding STEP models for software products.

Liaisons: ISO JTC1/SC7/WG11

Contact: Thomas G. Baker, Chairman, Software Products Committee, (206) 234-6234.

IEEE P1209 — Recommended Practice for the Evaluation and Selection of CASE Tools

Purpose: To develop criteria for evaluating software tools aimed at supporting software engineering life cycle processes.

Scope: Software engineering development and maintenance tools, not general purpose tools like word processors. To provide a framework to facilitate comparisons of tools.

Status: Standard is currently being balloted.

Plans: Approval planned for Fall 1993.

Liaisons: ISO/JTC1/SC7 WG4

Contact: Dr. Thomas Vollman, (301) 862-0798

SIGMA Members Association

Purpose: To promote CASE technologies in Japan, open systems for CASE environments and sharing of software assets.

Scope: Data integration through a standard repository and exchange system.

Status: Develop preliminary data and activity models in the software development process.

Plans: Complete preliminary models in 1992, refine and extend the models in 1993 through 1994, and evaluate and recommend CASE standards in 1994.

Liaison: None, but looking for help.

Contact: Mr. Hiroyuki Takabatake or Mr. Masao Toyawa, 81-3-3255-0423.

Appendix D.
Example DID Template

This is one of a complete set of 16 DOD 2167A DIDs provided in machine-readable format on request at no additional charge by Iconix Software Engineering, Inc., as a service to their upgrade service customers.

The document template contained in this appendix is reproduced courtesy of and by permission of Iconix. It is for the Computer Resources Integrated Support Document (CRISD). The CRISD describes all the resources required to support the software being delivered by the project. It describes the required support software, hardware, facilities, personnel, and many other resources. This document is used by system planners to deploy, integrate, and operate the software to be delivered.

The 16 available DID templates are for all of the following required documents:

- Computer Resources Integrated Support Document (CRISD)
- Computer System Operator's Manual (CSOM)
- Firmware Support Manual (FSM)
- Interface Design Document (IDD)
- Interface Requirements Specification (IRS)
- Software Design Document (SDD)
- Software Development Plan (SDP)
- Software Programmer's Manual (SPM)
- Software Product Specification (SPS)
- Software Requirements Specification (SRS)
- System (or Segment) Design Document (SSDD)
- Software Test Description (STD)
- Software Test Plan (STP)
- Software Test Report (STR)
- Software User's Manual (SUM)
- Version Description Document (VDD)

Electronic versions of these templates are also available through Iconix Software Engineering, Inc.

[Document control number and date: Value X of Y (if multi-volume)]

[Rev. indicator: date of Rev.]

**COMPUTER RESOURCES INTEGRATED
SUPPORT DOCUMENT**

FOR THE

[CSCI NAME]

OF

[SYSTEM NAME]

CONTRACT NO. [contract number]

CDRL SEQUENCE NO. [CDRL number]

Prepared for:

[Contracting Agency Name, department code]

Prepared by:

[contractor name and address]

TABLE OF CONTENTS

1. SCOPE

1.1 Identification

This paragraph shall contain the approved identification number, title(s), and abbreviation(s), if applicable, of the system of the CSCI(s) and the system to which this CRISD applies. If the document applies to all CSCIs in the system, this shall be stated.

1.2 System Overview

This paragraph shall briefly state the purpose of the system and the software to which CRISD applies.

1.3 Document Overview

This paragraph shall summarize the purpose and contents of this document.

2. Referenced Documents

This section shall list by document number and title all documents referenced in this document. This section shall also identify the source for all documents not available through normal Government stocking activities.

3. SUPPORT INFORMATION

This section shall be divided into the following paragraphs and subparagraphs to provide the support information.

3.1 Software Support Resources

This paragraph shall be divided into subparagraphs to identify and describe the components of the software engineering and test environments required to support the deliverable software. This paragraph shall identify the interrelationships of the components. A figure can be used to show the interrelationships. The following subparagraphs shall include items necessary to modify the software, perform testing, and copy software for distribution.

3.1.1 Software

This subparagraph shall identify and describe all of the software and associated documentation required to support the deliverable software. Each item of software shall be identified as Government furnished software, commercially available software, deliverable software, or non-deliverable software, as appropriate.

3.1.2 Hardware

This subparagraph shall identify and describe the hardware and the associated documentation necessary to support the deliverable software. Rationale for the selected hardware shall be provided. A figure can be included to show the interrelationship of hardware.

3.1.3 Facilities

This subparagraph shall describe the facilities required to support the deliverable software and shall identify their purpose.

3.1.4 Personnel

This subparagraph shall identify the personnel required to support the deliverable software, including the types of skills, number of personnel, security clearance, and skill level.

3.1.5 Other Resources

This subparagraph shall identify any other resources required for the support environment not discussed above.

3.2 Operations

This paragraph shall be divided into the following subparagraphs to describe the operations necessary to support the deliverable software.

3.2.1 Software Modification

This subparagraph shall describe the procedures necessary to modify deliverable operational and support software. This subparagraph shall also describe (other directly or by reference) the procedure for accommodating revisions to commercially available and reusable computer resources.

3.2.2 Software Integration and Testing

This subparagraph shall describe the procedures necessary to integrate and fully test all software modifications. It shall include procedures to identify portions of changes that need further testing in the operational environment and to establish guidelines for determining, developing, and verifying the amount of testing required.

3.2.3 Software Generation

This subparagraph shall provide the information necessary to facilitate compilations or assemblies of the contractually deliverable software. This subparagraph shall identify, by title, version, etc., all equipment and software required to perform this function and the appropriate manuals or reference documents. This subparagraph shall also contain the necessary instructions for loading, executing, or recording the results of the compilations or assemblies. This subparagraph shall include any optional methods of producing new object code (such as partial translation), producing a new listing, producing a new object program on different media, and loading the new object programs into the target computer system(s). Any known scheduling information or requirements shall also be included.

3.2.4 Simulation

If simulation is necessary to support the deliverable software, this subparagraph shall detail the hardware, software, and procedures necessary for the required simulation. It shall include all modes of simulation available and any limitations imposed by the simulation methods.

3.2.5 Emulation

If emulation is necessary to support the deliverable software, this subparagraph shall detail the hardware, software and procedures necessary for the required emulation. It shall identify all modes of operation that are emulated, the relationships with the simulation modes described above, and any limitations imposed by the emulation.

Computer Resources Integrated Support Document (5)

3.3 Training

This paragraph shall describe the contractor's plans for the training of personnel to manage and implement software of the deliverable software. The schedule, duration, and location for all required training shall be provided, as well as the delineation between classroom training and "hands-on" training. This paragraph shall provide (either directly or by reference) provisions for:

a. Familiarization with the operational software and target computer(s)
b. Familiarization with the support software and host system
c. Equipment maintenance procedures

3.4 Anticipated Areas of Change

This paragraph shall describe the anticipated areas of change to the deliverable software.

4. Transition Planning

This section shall be divided into paragraphs and subparagraphs as appropriate to describe the contractor's plans for transitioning the deliverable software to the support agency. This section shall address the following:

a. Describe the resources necessary to carry out the transition activity and identify the source from which each resource will be provided.

b. Identify the schedules and milestones for conducting the transition activities. These schedules and milestones shall be compatible with the contract master schedule.

c. Describe the procedures for installation and checkout of the deliverable software in the support environment designated by the contracting agency.

5. NOTES

This section shall contain any general information that aids in understanding this document (e.g., background information, glossary). This section shall include an alphabetical listing of all acronyms, abbreviations, and their meanings as used in this document.

APPENDICES

Appendices can be used to provide information published separately for convenience in document maintenance (e.g., charts, classified data). As applicable, each appendix shall be referenced in the main body of the document where the data would normally have been provided. Appendices can be bound as separate documents for ease in handling. Appendices shall be lettered alphabetically (A, B, etc.) and the paragraphs within each appendix be numbered as multiples of 10 (e.g., Appendix A, paragraph 10, 20.1, 10.2, 20, 20.1, 10.2, etc.) Pages within each appendix shall be numbered alpha-numerically as follows: Appendix A pages shall be numbered A-1, A-2, A-3, etc. Appendix B pages shall be numbered B-1, B-2, B-3, etc.

Appendix E.
A Document Quality Model

Assessing the Adequacy of Documentation Through Document Quality Indicators*

James D. Arthur

The Department of Computer Science
Virginia Tech
Blacksburg, VA 240601 [sic]

K. Todd Stevens

Wang Incorporated
Lowell, MA 01851

Abstract: This paper presents case study results of a research effort funded by the Naval Surface Warfare Systems (NSWC) at Dahlgren, Virginia. The investigation focuses on assessing the adequacy of project documentation based on an identified taxonomic structure relating documentation characteristics. Previous research in this area has been limited to the study of isolated characteristics of documentation and English prose, without considering the collective contributions of such characteristics. The research described in this paper takes those characteristics, adds others, and establishes a well-defined approach to assessing the "goodness" of software documentation. The identification of Document Quality Indicators (DQIs) provide the basis for the assessment procedure. DQIs are hierarchically defined in terms of document Qualities, Factors that refine Qualities and Quantifiers that provide for the measurement of Factors.

1.0 Introduction

A recognition of the need to view software costs in the context of a life cycle helped to focus attention on the root problems with early software/hardware systems. Aided by the visibility attributed to software maintenance, computer scientists were able to explain the need for a disciplined development process, controlled through meticulous attention to configuration management and governed by an emerging set of fundamental principles. Among these principles is Concurrent Documentation: the recording of requirements, design, specification and implementation decisions as they occur with the commitment to convey purpose, content and clarity [TAUR77].

The failure to observe the concurrent documentation principle unfortunately is common in all application domains. In particular,

- project documentation is often given a low priority on the deliverable schedule, and subsequently, either

    — arrives *after* significant changes have been made to the deployed system,
    — is developed *after-the-fact,* and/or
    — is developed in an *ad-hoc, unstructured* manner, and

- as maintenance is performed, required documentation changes are incorporated *after* the completion of the maintenance activity, and

*This work supported by the U.S. Navy through the Systems Research Center under Basic Ordering Agreement N60921-83-G-A165 B038

427

even then are often *inadequate* in relation to the magnitude of the system change.

Subsequently, many system changes never appear in life-cycle documents crucial to the support of maintenance activities. As expected, such deficiencies exact a significant price during the maintenance process, and contribute to the familiar claim that more than one-half the total life cycle costs are incurred during the maintenance phase [BOEB76, LIEB78].

The research presented in this paper does not attempt to prescribe another method by which one can guarantee that the principle of concurrent documentation is employed. It does, however, suggest one approach to *evaluating the adequacy of documentation* relative to the system that it purportedly describes.

1.1 Background

Experiencing documentation problems like those mentioned above and seeking to overcome their negative impact on the maintenance effort, a group of software engineers at the Naval Surface Warfare Center (NSWC) in Dahlgren, Virginia has developed the Automated Design Description System (ADDS) [NSWC87] to support the maintenance activity for the AEGIS Combat system software. This group, in response to the need for improved project documentation of software deliverables, has adopted an approach based on *reverse engineering.*

Reverse engineering in the maintenance phase is achieved through the synthesis of documents based on the analysis of existing databases populated by the product (and possibly data collected during the process of) software development. With respect to ADDS the database consists of the AEGIS combat system source code and the Program Performance Specifications (PPSs). In essence, ADDS generates specialized documents based on the structure and relational characteristics of the *extant* AEGIS software.

The documents currently being generated by ADDS are having a significant and beneficial impact on maintenance activities. Nonetheless, methods are still being sought to further enhance the generation process and the

quality of the synthesized documents. In concert with this objective the authors were tasked by NSWC to explore techniques and methods for improving ADDS and its generated products. Intrinsic to such an effort is the investigation of two fundamental questions:

- *What constitutes "adequate" documentation?*
- *How does one "measure" the adequacy [of] documentation?*

Among the several findings coming from an investigation of the above questions, the following are viewed as key:

- the formulation of a general theory of documentation analysis based on the Document Quality Indicator (DQI) concept,
- the development of an Evaluation Taxonomy that relates document Qualities to Factors and document Factors to Quantifiers.

A discussion of how these findings enable one to effectively address and answer the above two fundamental questions is provided below.

2.0 The Evaluation Taxonomy

An investigation of the above two questions has led to the formulation of a general taxonomy for the evaluation of computer documentation. The taxonomy is best described by a tree model whose top-level, intermediate and leaf nodes represent document Qualities, Factors of Qualities, and Quantifiers, respectively. This section presents the taxonomy tree in a top-down fashion, beginning with a discussion of documentation Qualities. The complete taxonomy for document evaluation is given by Figure 4. Because of length restrictions, however, only representative portions of that taxonomy are described. More specifically, this Section provides a detailed description of "Accuracy" and discusses its role in assessing the adequacy of documentation. The identification and development of other documentation characteristics supporting the assessment of documentation adequacy follows a similar path. The authors refer the interested reader to [STEK88] for a more expansive description of the evaluation taxonomy.

2.1 What Constitutes Adequate Documentation?

A preliminary investigation and extensive literature review [ARMY84, AFOT87, COLJ86, HORE86a, HORE86b, MURG86, SNEH85] reveals that the main, high-level Qualities of good documentation can be identified as: *Accuracy, Completeness, Usability,* and *Expandability.* Qualities are the very abstract characteristics of Adequate Documentation, defined as the essential components of adequate documentation. In the taxonomy tree, Qualities are the nodes directly under and most closely tied to the even more abstract notion of Adequate Documentation (see Figure 1). Although abstract, Qualities most closely convey the meaning of Adequate Documentation. When considering what makes documentation good, the most natural Qualities are Accuracy, Completeness, Usability, and Expandability. The following sections provide a brief definition and description for all four of these Qualities.

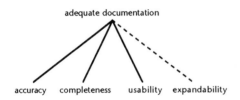

Figure 1. Decomposition into Qualities

Accuracy

The common definition for "accuracy" is the freedom from mistake or error; a synonym is "correctness." Within the context of computer documentation, Accuracy implies that the documentation must correctly reflect the actual state of the system it represents. Relative to documentation quality, *Accuracy* can be defined as: the consistency among the code and all documentation of the code, for all requirements.

Inconsistencies among documents and the instantiated system can be introduced in several ways. For example, errors can be introduced when system requirements are translated into design specifications, or when

the design specifications are being interpreted and implemented as code. Effectively, the requirements can be correct and the code and/or development documentation incorrect. Alternatively, the produce can be modified to correct an execution defect, but the corresponding development and/or requirements documentation might not be updated. As a result, some or all of the development documentation could be incorrect.

Completeness

The standard definition for "completeness" is the possession of all necessary parts, elements, or steps. For the purposes of computer documentation, a set of documentation is complete if all of the required information is present.

With respect to document Completeness, however, the major problem lies in determining what *is* required or needed. To determine what documentation is necessary for a computer system, one must first consider the computer system itself; computer systems vary significantly, so their documentation must necessarily vary. Their differences notwithstanding, standards exist for every type of computer system; these standards define what is required for documentation completeness. Many such standards have already been established [ANSI74, IEE185, POSA84, USDC76]. Hence, incorporating standards into the description, a more precise definition for *Completeness* in the context of document quality is: the existence of all documents required by a set of standards.

Usability

The dictionary definition for "usability" is the capability, convenience, or suitability of being employed. Relative to assessing documentation quality, *Usability* is more appropriately defined as the suitability of the documentation relative to the ease with which one can extract needed information. For example, part of assessing Usability is evaluating the Logical Traceability of the documentation. That is, assessing the ease with which one can (a) locate an item or the presentation of a concept within a set of documents and/or (b) trace an item or the development of concept through different parts of the documentation.

Expandability

A general definition for "expandability" is the ability to increase an object's extent, number, volume, or scope. A synonym is "extensibility." The rationale for including expandability as a desirable Quality is to reflect concepts underlying document maintainability, and in particular, the ease with which the documentation can be added to and modified. In concert with the notion of document maintainability, a more precise definition for *Expandability* is: the capability of the documentation to be modified in reaction to changes in the system. This Quality is assessed through measures reflecting ease of modification.

Because the research effort discussed in the paper considers only pre-defined, static sets of documentation, the partitioning of Expandability into its constituent Factors and Quantifiers has not yet been completed. Nonetheless, Expandability is included here to complete the description of documentation Qualities relative to assessing the adequacy of documentation.

2.2 How Does One Measure Documentation Adequacy?

The first step in assessing the adequacy of documentation entails the identification of desirable Qualities that one wants to measure. The previous discussion enumerates four such qualities. Because of their intangible nature, however, document qualities elude direct measurement. A subsequent search for *measurable surrogates* has led to the synthesis of Document Quality Indicators (DQIs). Intuitively, a DQI is a variable whose value can be determined through the direct analysis of document characteristics and whose evidential relationship to a document quality is undeniable. More precisely, a DQI is defined to be a triple whose elements are

- a Quality (of a document),
- a Factor (refining a Quality), and
- a Quantifier (measuring a Factor).

As one moves from the concept of a document Quality to a Factor and from a Factor to a Quantifier, the ability to directly measure document characteristics increases significantly. Consider for example the document quality:

accuracy. Research results indicate Factors of accuracy to be

- design/requirements traceability, and
- consistency (conceptual and factual).

Consider further the Factor: design/requirements traceability. Again, research results indicate that "top-down/bottom-up equivalence" is a Quantifier of this Factor. Intuitively, top-down/bottom-up equivalence is achieved if all design and requirements specifications appear in the code AND all code functions directly relate to design/requirements specifications. A verbalization of the above DQI is

"accuracy relative to design and requirements traceability as reflected through top-down and bottom-up equivalence."

One measurement of this DQI (and hence, one measure of accuracy) might be based on metrics that employ data derived from a simple checklist or matrix-oriented template.

As the preceding description might suggest, a tree-structured model provides a natural basis for reasoning about documentation adequacy because it most naturally conveys the relationships among the contributors to document quality. Each branch of the tree structure implies a reduction in the level of characteristic abstraction; each path from a Quality node to a Quantifier (leaf) node *uniquely* defines a DQI. Implicit in this tree structure is the recognition that documentation adequacy can be determined through its Qualities, each of which must be assessed through Factors that are measured at the Quantifier level. Based on the identification of Qualities of documentation and reflecting the tree-structured model, the following sections discuss particular Factors refining Qualities and Quantifiers supporting the assessment of those Factors and related Qualities.

2.2.1   Factors of Accuracy

Factors are intermediate characteristics, defined as an essential part which contributes to the production of a result. In the taxonomy tree (see Figure 4), Factors are all of the intermediate characteristics between the extremely abstract Qualities and the measurable Quantifiers. Each is directly derived from one of the Qualities, less abstract, and provide the second of three elements comprising the DQI triple. Figure 2 illustrates all Factors relative to their respective Qualities in the taxonomy. The intent of this section is to discuss several Factors and present how each supports a designated Quality. Again, because of length limitations, the authors have chosen to discuss only Factors of Accuracy.

In general, to demonstrate that documentation exhibits the Quality of Accuracy, one must show that the documentation is consistent with the deployed system. Effectively, all documentation elements, from requirements to high- and low-level design documents, need to be consistent with the code and exhibit consistency among themselves. In order to assess consistency, pertinent information items must be linked in some manner and must be traceable from one documentation element to another. As illustrated in Figure 4 this traceability characteristic, along with two forms of consistency, are the Factors which support an assessment of Accuracy. In the following sub-sections, each Factor of Accuracy is discussed.

Requirements/Design Traceability

Requirements/Design Traceability is viewed as the ability to track individual system requirements and design requirements to/from their corresponding manifestation in the source code. Requirements/Design Traceability provides the means for assessing whether the necessary links exist to evaluate Accuracy. To achieve traceability, the requirements and design decisions must be enumerated as "atoms," with each requirement given as a single, indivisible entity. These atoms can then be traced through code and documentation, and assessed for consistency.

Suppose, for example, that one system requirement states that specifications set forth in Standard 'X1' be met. Among those specifications, one might state: "error messages must be logged in file 'ERROR FILE.' " Not only do the high- and low-level designs might, in fact, group the atoms together in the same general way that the system requirements do, such as by simply saying, "in accordance with Standard 'X1.' " Nonetheless, it is important for the evaluation that the requirements can be atomized because

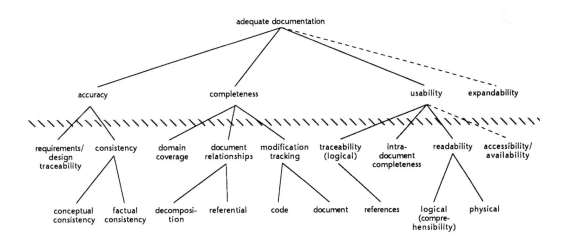

Figure 2. Decomposition to the Factor Level

- the requirements cannot be systematically assessed for consistency, unless the requirements can be treated as atoms, and
- the requirements can break apart at the source code level, in that only some of them are germane to each section of the code.

The manner in which these requirements are actually assessed for traceability is described later in this paper.

Conceptual and Factual Consistency

Consistency is the agreement or harmony demonstrated among separate items. Relative to documentation, it is the agreement or concurrence of all information in the documentation. That is, the same idea must be expressed in a similar fashion or in a way that is not contradictory. Consistency has two facets: Conceptual and Factual. *Conceptual Consistency* means that an idea may be stated in different forms, but the forms must convey the same thought or notion. For example, one expects the physical representation of a stated requirement to change as it moves from a realization rooted in a requirements language, through a design language and finally culminating in an implementation. Nonetheless, the conceptual idea expressed in each of these forms must be consistent. *Factual Consistency* means that statements of value, logical relationships, and definitive structure must remain *invariant* irrespective of their location and repetition within the documentation. Many system requirements, for example, are stated as simple numeric or name facts, e.g., the system must be able to buffer a minimum of 10 requests. The design document would state the same numeric fact, and the code would explicitly reflect that lower bound.

2.2.2 Quantifiers Measuring Factors of Accuracy

By virtue of their direct relationship to Qualities, Factors do support a more tangible basis for assessing documentation adequacy than do Qualities. Nonetheless, as conveyed by the examples given above, Factors of Quality are still missing the "concreteness" necessary to support measurement. Quantifiers, on the other hand, *are* measurable characteristics, and through their direct link to Factors, provide for Factor assessment. In the

taxonomy tree, Quantifiers are at the bottom, i.e., the leaves. Quantifiers occupy the third position in each DQI triple, and in conjunction with related Factors and Qualities, *uniquely* define each DQI. With the addition of the Quantifier level the associated taxonomy tree is complete—the resulting tree structure is precisely as illustrated in Figure 4.

Again, the authors choose to restrict the following discussion to Quantifiers supporting an assessment of Factors related to the Quality of documentation Accuracy, and in particular, Requirements/Design Traceability.

Requirements/Design Traceability: Top-down/Bottom-up Equivalence

Top-down/Bottom-up Equivalence is the equality between specified requirements and those implemented in the system source code. In order to meet a necessary-and-sufficient condition, equality must be assessed through a top-down and a bottom-up evaluation of the documentation and code. The requirements must be "sufficiently" met by the implementation, and all of the code must be "necessary" to meet the requirements, i.e., there is no superfluous code.

The top-down trace checks whether all of the requirements have been "sufficiently" met by the implementation. All of the requirements are enumerated as atoms, so that they can be uniquely identified and associated with separate features which are helping to meet or satisfy them. The separate features are then further divided, thereby dividing the requirements with which they are associated. The bottom-up trace checks whether all of the code modules are actually "necessary" or needed to meet a requirement.

This top-down/bottom-up tracking can best be accomplished by setting up evaluation matrices (see Figures 3a and 3b). The matrix shown in Figure 3a relates requirements to design modules; the matrix in Figure 3b illustrates the relationships that exist between design modules and code modules. In the first matrix (Figure 3a), the requirements are enumerated across the top of the matrix and the design modules along the left side. For each requirement, an "X" is marked for the design module(s) that partially or completely fulfills that requirement. For the second matrix (Figure 3b), the design modules from the first matrix are enumerated across the top and the code modules along the left side. Similar to the first matrix, an "X" is marked for the code module(s) which partially or completely implements each design module.

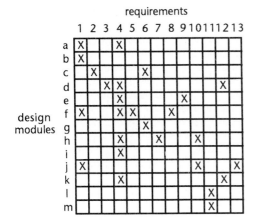

Figure 3a. Requirements/Design Matrix

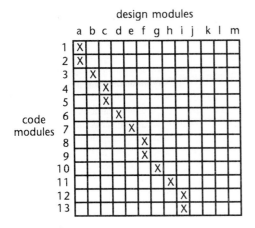

Figure 3b. Design/Code Matrix

Once the matrices are filled in, they are used to check that all of the requirements are met and that all of the code modules are necessary. If a requirement column in the first matrix does not have at least one "X," this is evidence that no design module exists to implement it. Further, the requirements also depend on the design modules being implemented; each design in the second matrix which is not implemented in a code module fails to fulfill requirements. In this manner, the requirements can be checked to determine whether they are all *sufficiently* fulfilled. Next, the rows of the matrices need to be examined. Any row which does not have at least one "X" in it is not needed; it does not help to fulfill a requirement. This examination allows one to determine whether a design module is *necessary* to meet requirements.

The above description of the matrices illustrates how one might check the documentation and code for "sufficiently meeting the requirements" and "necessary to meet the requirements," respectively. Using the one DQI, "accuracy relative to design and requirements traceability as reflected through top-down and bottom-up equivalence," as an example, the above sections outlines the relevance *and* importance of the DQI concept in document analysis.

In summary, Section 2 focuses on documentation characteristics relating to Accuracy and their contribution to the assessment of documentation adequacy. In particular, the presentation describes an evaluation taxonomy based on the identification of (a) documentation Qualities, Factors and Quantifiers, and (b) a set of natural relationships among them. Moreover, each path from the root node of the taxonomy tree to a leaf node uniquely defines a measurable DQI that supports the evaluation process. Through the relationships implied by each DQI triple, Quantifier *values* (provided by metric computations) can be related to specific document Qualities. In turn, the collective measure of the Qualities provide a means for assessing documentation adequacy. Currently, the investigative effort has lead to the identification of

- four (4) major document Qualities,
- thirteen (13) Factors of Qualities, and
- thirty (30) unique Quantifiers, all combining to form
- thirty seven (37) document quality indicators (DQIs).

433

3.0 Concluding Remarks

Motivating the research described in this paper is the recognition that system and project documentation are crucial for high quality software development and maintenance. Implicit in this recognition is that documentation must be accurate, complete and usable. Armed with this realization the authors have initiated a research effort that attempts to identify the crucial components of "adequate" documentation and to establish a meaningful basis for quantitatively measuring the contributions those components from both the individual and collective perspectives.

During the course of this research, a categorization of documentation properties has emerged: Qualities, Factors, and Quantifiers. Based on recognized relationships among Qualities, Factors and Quantifiers, the authors describe an evaluation framework for assessing the extent to which desirable characteristics are present in a document. The framework reflects an undeniable set of linkages among document Qualities, Factors, and Quantifiers. In turn, the assessment process exploits these linkages in the evaluation of DQIs, formally defined as a Quality/Factor/Quantifier triple. Fundamental to the assessment process is a recognition that

- each quantifier is a non-abstract, measurable document characteristic, and that
- Factors provide the bridge relating Quantifier measurements to the evaluation of documentation Qualities.

Although the evaluation taxonomy presented in this report represents a significant step toward assessing document adequacy, it remains only a framework. That framework, however, has been applied "in principle" to a set of maintenance documents generated by ADDS. The results of that assessment are encouraging. The interested reader is referred to [ARTJ88] for a further discussion of those results.

Clearly, the examination and evaluation of project documentation is difficult—many issues still remain unresolved. The following paragraphs outline four future research directions that require investigation before a total process for document analysis can truly be realized.

The Quest for Additional Quantifiers: The first investigative effort involves a reassessment of the evaluation taxonomy focusing on substantiating the current DQIs and the formulation of additional ones. In particular, an emphasis needs to be placed on the identification of additional Quantifiers supporting the assessment of existing Quality/Factor pairs.

Metric Identification and Formulation: A second effort must address the identification and synthesis of metrics to support the computational process underlying document evaluation through DQIs. The findings presented in this report suggests several such metrics. Those metrics, however, are incomplete and primarily reflect the authors' intuition. Like the undeniable relationships on which DQIs are based, the proposed metrics must be succinct, well-defined and reflect a high level of reliability and validity with respect to the DQIs they are measuring. Clearly, such an investigation requires significant experimental studies validated through statistical confirmation.

An Automated Assessment Framework: An investigation is also needed which focuses on the identification of those metrics that can provide an automated framework for DQI assessment. Several of the DQIs identified in the current research suggest metrics that require raw data whose collection is manpower intensive and susceptible to bias. Ideally, one desires metrics whose data elements can be collected through an automated process predicated on objectivity. Recognizing that both subjective and objective metrics do exist and only some of either can be collected automatically, one possible research direction might focus on the identification of a subset of metrics that are (a) amenable to an automated evaluation framework, and (b) whose collective characteristics and evaluation implications represent those of the total set.

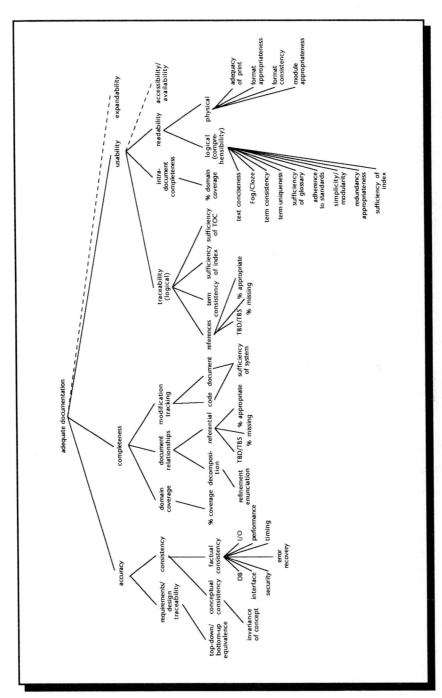

Figure 4. The General Evaluation Taxonomy Tree

A Validation of the Assessment Procedure: Utilizing results from the above three efforts, the authors envision a final research effort aimed at validating the assessment procedure. Such an effort would require a collaborative investigation involving a sponsoring group that has at its disposal several sets of project documentation, knowledgeable people willing to provide an objective assessment of the documents, and an automated process for effecting the assessment process based on DQIs.

In summary, the research findings presented in this report provides a well-defined framework for the evaluation of documentation. The need for methods to evaluate documentation is readily apparent within the maintenance domain. The need becomes even more obvious when one considers assessing the quality of complete software systems through an evaluation of the developmental process as well as the developed product. As indicated above, however, difficult issues must be resolved before the long range goals of this investigative effort can be realized.

The authors would like to acknowledge the contributions of

- Dr. Richard E. Nance, whose initial work on Software Quality Indicators provided a basis for the DQI concepts, and

- Mr. Dave McConnell, Mr. Angel Martinez and Mr. Bob Barthelowe at NSWC (Dahlgren, VA), whose constant feedback had a significant impact in shaping and refining the underlying document characteristic taxonomy.

References

[AFOT87] Department of the Air Force, "Acquisition Management: Software Maintainability—Evaluation Guide," AFOTEC Pamphlet 800-2, Vol. 3, March 1987.

[ANSI74] American National Standards Institute. "American National Standard for Guidelines for the Documentation of Digital Computer Programs," ANS-N413-1974, American Nuclear Society, 1974.

[ARMY84] United States Army, *Software Quality Engineering Handbook,* Computer Systems Command, Ft. Belvoir, VA, August 1984.

[ARTHJ88] Arthur, J. D., R. E. Nance, K. T. Stevens, "Prospects for Automated Documentation Analysis in Support of Software Quality Assurance," Technical Report SRC-88-002, Systems Research Center, Virginia Tech, 1988.

[BOEB76] Boehm, B., "Software Engineering," *IEEE Transactions on Computers,* C25 (December 1976), pp. 1226-1241.

[COLJ86] Collofello, J. S. and S. Bortman, "An Analysis of the Technical Information Necessary to Perform Effective Software Maintenance," *Proc. of the Fifth Annual Phoenix Conference on Computers and Communications,* March 1986, pp. 420-424.

[IEEI85] The Institute of Electrical Engineers. *Guidelines for the Documentation of Software in Industrial Computer Systems,* The Institute of Electrical Engineers, 1985.

[HORE86a] Horowitz, E. and R. C. Williamson. "SODOS: A Software Documentation Support Environment—Its Definition," *IEEE Transactions on Software Engineering,* SE-12, No. 8 (August 1986), pp. 849-859.

[HORE86b] Horowitz, E. and R. C. Williamson. "SODOS: A Software Documentation Support Environment—Its Use," *IEEE Transactions on Software Engineering,* SE-12, No. 11 (November 1986), pp. 1076-1087.

[LIEB78] Lientz, B. "Issues in Software Maintenance," *ACM Computing Surveys,* 15, No. 3 (September 1983), pp. 271-278.

[MURG86]   Murine, G. "Using Software Quality Metrics as a Tool for Independent Verification and Validation," *Proc. of the Fifth Annual Phoenix Conference on Computers and Communications,* March 1986, pp. 433-437.

[NSWC87]   Naval Surface Weapons Center. *Final AEGIS Design Description System (ADDS) User's Manual,* Computer Sciences Corporation, 24 June 1987.

[POSA84]   Poschmann, A. W. *Standards and Procedures for Systems Documentation,* American Management Association, 1984.

[SNEH85]   Sneed, H. M. and A. Merey. "Automated Software Quality Assurance," *IEEE Transactions on Software Engineering,* SE-11, No. 9 (September 1985), pp. 909-916.

[STEK88]   Stevens, K. T., J. D. Arthur and R. E. Nance. "A Taxonomy for the Evaluation of Computer Documentation," Technical Report SRC-88-008, Systems Research Center, Virginia Tech, January 1988.

[TAUR77]   Tausworthe, R. C. *Standardized Development of Computer Software,* Prentice-Hall, 1977.

[USDC76]   U.S. Department of Commerce. "Guidelines for Documentation of Computer Programs and Automated Data Systems," Federal Information Processing Standards Publication 38, 15 February 1976.

*This work supported by the U.S. Navy through the Systems Research Center under Basic Ordering Agreement N60921-83-G-A165 B038

Appendix F.
An Example Project Style Guide
and Checklist

Page Layout

Page size: 8.5 x 11

Margins: Top, 1"; Bottom, 1"; Left, 1"; Right, 1.25"
           Mirror even/odd margins, even/odd headers

Styles:
Body text:	Bookman, 12 pt, left flush
Bullet 1:	Indent: left 0.75; first -0.25
	Tab stops: 0.75; 5.125; 6
Bullet 2:	Indent: left 1.25; first -0.25
Bullet 3:	Indent: left 0.5; first -0.25
Code listing:	Courier, 10 pt
	Indent: first 0.5
Figure Caption:	Avant Garde, 10 pt, italic, centered
Left Footer:	Avant Garde, 10 pt, left flush
Right Footer:	Avant Garde, 10 pt, right flush
Level1head:	Avant Garde, 18 pt, bold, underline
Level2head:	Avant Garde, 14 pt, bold
Level3head:	Avant Garde, 12 pt

Problem Words

accept, except	Use *accept* when you mean to receive something (willingly); to agree with an idea or circumstance, or to say yes. *Except* can be used as a verb or preposition. As a verb, it means to omit or exclude. As a preposition, it means *other than*. Some examples of correct usage:

> Everyone *except* Bruno went to the fair.
>
> He was *excepted* from the service because of poor health.
>
> He was *accepted* into the service regardless of his flat feet.

acronym	Always say what it stands for when you first use it. When forming the plural of an acronym, *do not* add an apostrophe before the *s*. For example:

> A Data Item Description (DID) template accompanies this document.
>
> Many DIDs have templates available.

affect, effect	*Affect*, as a verb, means to influence. The result is an *effect*. *Affect*, as a noun, is best avoided. *Effect*, as a verb, means to *bring about or cause* (such as *effects a cure*). *Effect*, as a noun, is more common and means *result*. (By the way, there is a noun *affect* in psychology, meaning a feeling or emotion.) Some examples are:

> Your performance appraisal will *affect* your earning potential. The *effect* could be devastating.
>
> The amazing special *effects affected* my emotions.

afterward	Not *afterwards*.
all right	Not *alright*.
allow	See *enable*.
ANSI	The acronym for *American National Standards Institute*. An industry standards organization.

apostrophe	Do not add an apostrophe before the final *s* when you pluralize numbers, acronyms, etc., unless you are showing the possessive form of something.

1970's	incorrect
1970s	correct
PC's	incorrect
PCs	correct

appendixes

Not *appendices* (archaic).

application software

Not *applications software*. Applies the system's resources and ability to perform a particular task, such as text processing or database management.

arguable, arguably

Arguably is frequently misused in the popular press, and is one of the best arguments for why you shouldn't pick up and use popular terms unless you are sure of what they mean. *Arguably* means capable of being argued with. How it's used wrong is when people use it to prop up their statements and make them sound more official. Here's an example that one of the authors of this book (Leslie) actually read a few years ago in a *very well known* magazine. The name of the magazine won't be mentioned here to protect the guilty:

> "Harrison Ford is *arguably* one of the best young actors to arrive on the scene in recent years."

Well, we're not certain what the writer really meant here but, since the rest of the article was so flattering, we'll assume they meant this as a compliment. We'll assume that they meant to say that Harrison Ford is *inarguably* one of the best young actors to arrive on the scene. We suppose that the writer thought that adding *arguably* as a qualifier would add force to his opinion. Instead, it came out as kind of a slap. What they *really* said was that it could be argued with that he's one of the best actors to arrive on the scene. Well, if you can't say something nice ...

articles

Do not use in references to specific keys when you are showing the key name in all caps ("press CONTROL," *not* "press the CONTROL key"). Always use articles when referring to disks and other nouns: *the disk, a file.*

ASCII	The acronym for *American Standard Code for Information Interchange.*
as, like	*As* is a conjunction and should be used to introduce clauses. *Like* is a preposition and requires an object. It is also correct to use *like* as a conjunction if it is followed by a word that could be regarded as a simile.
assembly language (n.), *assembly-language* (adj.)	Not *assembler language.*
assure	See *ensure, assure, insure.*
auto-repeat	Note hyphenation.
backspace (n., v., and adj.)	One word.
BACKSPACE key	Use *DELETE* if you are documenting Macintosh software.
backup (n., adj.)	Do not hyphenate when used as a verb or predicate adjective:
	You must back up the system daily.
	Daily, you should do a backup.
backward	Not *backwards.*
BASIC	A computer language. Acronym for *Beginners All-purpose Symbolic Instruction Code.* No apostrophe when forming plural.
baud	Not necessarily the same as *bits per second.* Know the difference.
because	Preferred to *since* when expressing a cause-and-effect relationship.
bitmap	Refers to correspondence between bits in memory and dots on the display. See also *dot matrix, raster.*
black-and-white (adj.)	Note hyphenation. Do not hyphenate when used as a verb or predicate adjective:
	The dog was black and white.
	It was a black-and-white movie.

boldface	Use for computer jargon, tags in boxes, glossary terms, figures and tables, sometimes for lead-in to paragraphs. See also *italics*.
Boolean logic	Note capitalization. Named after George Boole.
boot	Use *start up* or *invoke*.
both, each	Use *both* when you mean two together. Use *each* when you mean each one separately.
braces	Not *curly brackets*. *Curly brackets* might be used to define *braces* when the term is first used.
built-in (adj.)	Note hyphenation. When used in a callout, caption, or title, do not capitalize *in*: i.e., Built-in.
built-in disk drive	Use instead of *internal disk drive*.
callouts	Capitalize same as titles and captions. Use a period at the end of all callouts for a figure if any of the callouts are complete sentences or long phrases. See also *capitalization*.
can, may	Use *can* to express ability, power, and so on. Use *may* to express permission. Use *might* to express possibility.
cancel	Unconditional, permanent halt that carries connotation of undoing something. Can use *cancel* instead of *halt* to avoid awkwardness. See also *halt, suspend, stop*.
canceling, canceled	Not *cancelling, cancelled*.
capital, capitol	The word *capital* applies to letters. The word *capitol* means a center of government.
capitalization	Use the following rules when capitalizing titles, captions, and callouts:

- Always capitalize the first and last word.

- Usually capitalize the second word in hyphenated compounds: *High-Resolution Graphics,* not *High-resolution Graphics.* Exception: *Built-in Disk Drive.*

- Capitalize prepositions of four letters or more: *About, With, From, Between.*

- Don't capitalize coordinating conjunctions: *and, but, or, for, nor, yet, so;* or articles: *a, an,* and *the.*

- Don't capitalize *to* in infinitives.

captions Capitalize same as titles and callouts. Use a period at the end of a figure or table title when more information follows the title. See *capitalization.*

caret Use to describe this character: ^. Not *circumflex.*

catalog Preferred to *directory,* except in Pascal references.

central processor Meaningful only in contrast with *peripheral processor.* Never *the unit* or *CPU.*

chapter Capitalize in specific references: *Chapter 8, Chapters 4 and 5.*

circumflex Don't use to describe this character: ^. Use *caret.*

clichés Avoid the following clichés:

> *Enclosed please find* … (Use *Here is* … or *I have enclosed* …)
>
> *Pursuant to our conversation* … (Use *After our conversation,* …)
>
> *Please be advised that* … (Eliminate the phrase entirely.)
>
> *… at your earliest convenience* … (Give a specific deadline.)
>
> *As per your letter* … (Use *Regarding your letter* …)
>
> *If we can be of further assistance, please do not hesitate to contact us* … (Use *I'd like to help. My number is* …)

COBOL Notice capitalization.

colon Use a colon before a list, enumeration, or illustration. Capitalize the first word after the colon if the material after the colon can stand alone as a complete sentence.

command	Something you type to make something happen immediately. See also *instruction, statement*.
command names	Use initial caps for names of application program commands, but do not capitalize *command:* the Find command, the Execute command (not eXecute command), the Save command, the Verify command. See also *key word*.
commas	Insert a comma before the conjunction at the end of a series separated by commas.

        Incorrect: The paper was red, blue, purple and green.

        Correct: The paper was red, blue, purple, and green.

communications	Acceptable to use plural, especially when referring to a system.
computer	The physical thing (what's inside and part of the case, including the keyboard). See also *system*.
computer voice	A special monospaced font used only for: what is seen on the display, program listings, and what users key in. Zeros in computer voice should have slashes (virgules). Use backslashes to indicate this in manuscripts. See also *keycaps*.

consensus, consense, consensed

    Consensus is a real word meaning *to reach agreement* or *general opinion*. However, it is often misspelled and misused. The phrase "consensus of opinion" has been so widely used that it is hackneyed and trite. It's also redundant, since *opinion* is implied in the meaning of the word *consensus. Consense* is not a real word at all, no matter how often you hear people using it. *Consensed* as the past tense of *consense* is not a real word either. This is one of those words that is becoming popular through frequent use. However, it is not yet commonly used enough to avoid being laughed at. Instead, use *reach* (or *reached*) *consensus* or *reached an agreement* or *agreed*.

connector	*Be more specific.*

    plug   connector with prongs or pins
    socket connector with holes
    slot   long, skinny holes on main board
    jack   small, round one-pin socket

	Never use *male* or *female* in reference to types of connectors.
console, CRT	Don't use when you mean *video monitor*.
constant	Sequence of characters that stands for a particular, unchangeable value.
control-character (adj.)	Note hyphenation. Do not hyphenate when used as a verb or predicate adjective: Press the control character.
controlled and controlling	Not *controled* or *controling*.
coprocessor	Not hyphenated.
copy-protected (adj.)	Note hyphenation. Do not hyphenate when used as a verb or predicate adjective: The disk is copy protected.
CP/M	*Control Program for Microcomputers*. An operating system.
CPU	Use *central processor*.
curly brackets	Use *braces*.
cutout	One word. A hole in the back panel of the computer. Also used to describe the oval hole in diskettes (but not the write-enable notch.
dashes	When used to indicate "long" dashes in manuscript, use two hyphens with no spaces around them.
data, datum	*Data* is a plural noun, which must take a plural verb; i.e., the data are on the disk. *Datum* is the singular form. Try to avoid in favor of *information*.
database	One word.
data file	Two words.
data-flow diagram	Note hyphenation.
default	Try to avoid the verb and noun. It is less objectionable when used as an adjective. Explain carefully with first use.

desktop (adj.)	One word.
device name	Two words. See also *filename, volume name.*
different from	Not *different than.*
differently than	Not *different than* or *differently from.*
diskette	Use *diskette* to denote a floppy and *disk* to denote a fixed disk.
disk drive	Good generic term for referring to drives.
diskette names	Usually follow what the label says and italicize. Do not use quotation marks or capitalize *diskette*. Continue to use all caps for diskettes that do not have new labels, which are uppercase and lowercase.
Disk Operating System	Capitalized in specific references to *DOS*. Lowercase in generic references.
display	What appears on the screen.
display device	Device connected to the computer for displaying text or graphics. More specific: *video monitor* or *television set.*
display screen or *the screen*	Where text or graphics appear.
DOS-formatted (adj.)	Note hyphenation.
dot matrix	An array of dots. Usually refers to a method of forming characters on a printer or display device. See also *bitmap, raster.*
drive	Use *disk drive* except in passages where it becomes cumbersome.
due to, due to the fact that	Use *because of* and *because.*
EBCDIC	Acronym for *Extended Binary-Coded-Decimal Interchange Code.*
effect, affect	*Affect,* as a verb, means to influence. *Affect,* as a noun, is best avoided. *Effect,* as a verb, is rarely used and means *to cause* (such as *effects a cure*). *Effect,* as a noun, is more common and means *result.*

e.g.	Use *for example.*
electromagnetic interference	Note spelling. Also known as *EMI.* Don't use acronym without explaining what it stands for.
embed	Not *imbed.*
enable, permit, allow	*Enable* means to "make capable." *Permit* means something you need to have permission to do. *Allow* also means something you need to have permission to do. Do not use permit or allow when you really mean enable. For example, the software does not *allow* you to create graphics, it *enables* you to create graphics.
ensure, assure, insure	Use *ensure* to mean guarantee; use *assure* to mean reassure or comfort; use *insure* when you are referring to the purchase of insurance for something or someone.
extensible, extendible	Both of these words are commonly used in technical writing. However, there are slight shades of difference in meaning between the two. *Extensible* means "capable of being extended or protruded." *Extendible* means "capable of being extended." The shade of difference is in the *protruded* part of *extensible.* You should use *extensible* when you are discussing lumps, bumps, extrusions, protrusions, pregnancy, and so on, when something juts out or protrudes. You should use *extendible* when you are discussing something that can be extended, like a project schedule. Even though some schedules have lumps, bumps, and protrusions, the thought is slightly nauseating. (Besides, it is easier to just say "the capabilities can be easily extended" or some such.)
figures	When your documents include figures and tables (except for marketing literature): Always refer to a figure or table before you insert one. They should not just "appear." Give every figure and table a number. Give every figure and table a title.
filename	One word.
flammable, inflammable	You'd thing that if *flammable* meant that something could be burned, *inflammable* would mean that it couldn't be burned. Not so. They both mean the same thing. Why have both? Who knows. They're both okay. However, for whatever reason, you probably wouldn't want to say he has a *flammable* temper.

FORTRAN	The acronym for <u>FO</u>rmula <u>TRAN</u>slation. Note capitalization.
he, she	Try not to use gender-specific pronouns. If you must, then give equal time to both genders. "She bought the tool from him." If you need to say *he or she,* it's becoming more and more acceptable to say *s/he.* The virgule (slash) equals *and/or.* The *he* is fully contained within the term and both are given equal time.
hex	Use *hexadecimal* for the first reference. *Hex* is acceptable for subsequent references.
highlighted, inverted	*Highlighted* is acceptable in this sense: The default value is *highlighted.* However, use *displayed in inverse* instead of *inverted.*
high-resolution (adj.)	Note hyphenation. Do not hyphenate when used as a verb or predicate adjective.
hyphenation	The general rule for hyphenation is that when two words modify a noun as a unit and not as two individual modifiers, a hyphen joins those two words. Follow this rule when:

- One of the words is a past or present participle (free-moving graphics, DOS-formatted disk).

- Confusion might result if the hyphen were omitted (read-only memory, machine-language program, rigid-disk drive).

- The two modifiers are a number or single letter and a noun (80-column text card, D-shaped connector).

Notable exception: *word processing* is never hyphenated.

Also, do not hyphenate two words when one is *very* or an adverb that ends in *ly:* newly completed bridge, very good time. See specific compound in style sheet.

identifier	Sequence of characters that can be used as the name of something and is constructed according to definite rules. An identifier that refers to a variable is the *name* of the variable. One that refers to a statement in a program is a *label.*
i.e.	Use *that is.*

IEEE	Acronym for *Institute of Electrical and Electronics Engineers*. An industry standards organization.
imbed	The preferred spelling is *embed*.
indexes	Not *indices* (archaic).
information	Better than *data*.
in order to	Wordy; rarely necessary. Better to just say *to*.
input (n., adj.)	Never use as a verb. Use *enter* or *type*.
instruction	Part of a machine-language or assembly-language program that is executed directly by the processor. See also *command, statement*.
insure	See *ensure, assure, insure*.
internal disk drive	Use *built-in disk drive*.
interrupt	A running program can be interrupted only at the hardware level (for example, by pressing an interrupt switch).
irregardless	This is not a real word and makes people sound really stupid when they say it. After all, would you say *disregardless*?
ISO	Acronym for *International Standards Organization*. An industry standards group.
italics	Use for explicit references to other manuals or chapters, words as words, letters as letters, phrases as phrases, and emphasis. Italics also should be used after *stands for, labeled to,* etc., to avoid problems with punctuation and quotation marks. For example: INIT, which stands for *initialize,* is used ... See the column in the directory labeled *EOF* ... See also *quotation marks*.
its, it's, its'	Use *its* when you mean *belonging to* (possessive); use *it's* when you mean *it is;* do not use *its'* since there is no such word.

-ize
This suffix has created hundreds of standard words such as pasteurize, dramatize, and sterilize. Unfortunately, many weird terms have also resulted, such as *powerize* and *productize* (which we use, but we show it in quotation marks to indicate that it hasn't quite reached real-word status yet).

jacket
The black cover that holds a flexible disk.

keycaps
Used for function keys (ESC, ESCAPE, DELETE, CONTROL, SHIFT, RETURN, ENTER, etc.) and for single keys in combination keystrokes (when joined by a hyphen). Some customer's prefer small caps (ESC, ESCAPE, DELETE, CONTROL, SHIFT, RETURN, ENTER, etc.)

keys
Use all uppercase letters for labels. Use keycaps for function keys when typeset. In combination keystrokes, hyphens signify that the keys should be pressed simultaneously:

CONTROL-SHIFT-N (all three keys pressed simultaneously)

ESC N (not pressed simultaneously)

Use *type* for those keys representing printable characters. Use *press* for nonprinting keys as well as buttons on hand controls and combination keystrokes.

Use keycaps for each key in simultaneous keystrokes—even single characters. The word *key* is unnecessary in manuals using keycaps.

keystroke
One word.

keyword
A word that identifies a particular type of statement or command, such as IF or CATALOG. Follow the capitalization conventions of the programming language.

label
See *identifier*.

labeled
Note spelling.

less, fewer
Fewer is used with individual items; *less* with quantity or bulk: Fewer hedgehogs require less food.

life cycle	Two words.
like, as	See *as, like.*
medium, media, medias	*Medium* is the singular form. The plurals are *mediums* and *media*. *Media* is the more common (and generally preferred) plural form. *Medias* is not a real word.
nauseous, nauseated	*Nauseous* means "*causing* sickness." *Nauseated* means "*feeling* sickness." If you said (as most people do) "I feel *nauseous*," you'd be saying. "I feel like I make people sick." Think about it.
numbers	Spell out the numbers one through ten. Use numerals for anything over ten. However, do not spell out numbers in dates, percentages, or units of measure (including the ages of people). Also, do not mix spelled-out numbers and numerals in the same sentence:

> *Incorrect:* Of the 33 people at the party, five left early.

> *Correct:* Of the 33 people at the party, 5 left early.

O.K.	We prefer the *okay* spelling.
pathname	One word.
pre-defined	Note hyphenation.
productize	Since this hasn't quite reached real-word status yet, if you *must* use this word, enclose it in quotation marks to show that you are being unique and original.
quotation marks	Not *quote marks*. You usually use quotation marks to show things that are actually quoted.
raise	*Raise* is something someone does; *rise* does it by itself.
semicolon	Use a semicolon when a comma isn't enough and a period is too much. Capitalize the first word after the semicolon if the material after the semicolon can stand alone as a complete sentence.
slash	See *virgule.*

spaces	If you are using right-justified text, use only one space between sentences. If you are using a ragged right margin, you can use either one or two spaces (your choice).

that, which

There is a difference, and this is a tough one. *That* refers to persons, animals, or things; *which* only applies to animals and things; *who* and *whom* only apply to persons. We're only going to address *that* and *which* here because these are the two with which most people have a problem.

You can usually determine which of these pronouns to use by the nature of the clauses that introduce them. *That is used* in restrictive clauses. *Which, who, and whom are used in introducing nonrestrictiv*e (not-defining) clauses: "This man, *who* pays his bills promptly, is liked by everyone." *That* usually denotes a specific object (that book, that man, that choice); *which* usually denotes a choice of something (*which one is it, of which, to which, from which, with which*). This gets very confusing. However, we offer here what we hope is a simple example of how to determine which to use:

"She was wearing the perfume *that* drives me crazy."

This example is a restrictive clause. It's talking about a specific perfume that drives him crazy.

"She was wearing the perfume, which drives me crazy."

This example is a nonrestrictive clause. Notice the comma before the word *which*? The comma makes it nonrestrictive. It also changes the meaning of the sentence. This time it means that it is the fact of her wearing the perfume that drives him crazy and not the perfume itself. See the difference?

So, the next time you aren't sure whether to use *that* or *which*, put a comma in front of the word *which*. If it changes your intended meaning, then *that* is probably the word you want (unless you mean *of which, to which,* or some such). Nine times out of ten, in a normally structured sentence, you will have been using *which* when you should have been using *that*.

UNIX

Note capitalization.

virgule	Also called a *slash*. *Virgule* is actually the proper name for the slash unless you are using the slash as part of a command to the computer. The virgule represents *and/or*. Do not use virgules to separate word pairs like *input/output*. If you mean *input and/or output*, then write it out that way. Otherwise, use hyphens, like *input-output, checkin-checkout*, etc.
voice	Use the active voice whenever possible. For example:

> *Passive:* The document should be checked for typos.

> *Active:* Check the document for typos.

> *Passive:* This component is intended to be used for the development of production applications.

> *Active:* You can develop production applications using this component.

wait for, wait on	You can *wait for* someone patiently or impatiently, in the car or in front of the house, at the elevator or on the roof. You can *wait for* them wherever you want. However, you do not *wait on* them anywhere unless you are serving them something. For example, "I will *wait for* you in the car," is correct if you mean you are waiting for someone, and you'll be in the car. If you say, though, "I'll *wait on* you in the car," then you will be bringing someone food, or beverages, or some other substance while they wait *for you!*

> *Example:* I will wait for Table Three.

> *Interpretation:* I am waiting for the slob at Table Three to hurry up because I want his table.

> *Example:* I will wait on Table Three.

> *Interpretation:* I will be bringing food to the slob seated at Table Three.

Example Project Checklist

Chapter Checklist	P.	1	2	3	4	5	6	7	8
Have you specified the next chapter?									
Have you changed 2 spaces to 1?									
Have you spell checked all, including headers?									
Have you completed all index entries?									
Have you compared it to the style guide?									
Have all TOC entries been made, including in the chapter header?									

Glossary

4GL	The acronym for *fourth-generation language*.
ANSI	The acronym for *American National Standards Institute*.
ASCII	The acronym for *American Standard Code for Information Interchange*.
Associative memory	Recognizing in the present problem familiar features of other problems we have solved long ago.
Bang metric	Invented by Tom DeMarco, *Bang* is also a function metric. It is a "measure of the true function to be delivered as perceived by the user. ... Bang is ... an implementation-independent indication of system size." He goes on: "The size of the specification model is a direct measure of Bang." The specification model is composed of a function network, data dictionary, object diagrams, and state diagrams. These are made up of twelve primitives, such as functions, data elements existing at various places in the model, objects, relationships, states, and state transitions. All of these are counted, weighted, and combined to produce the bang value of the system to be built [DeMarco 1982].
Bang per buck (BPB)	The ratio of the bang and the sum of dollars spent so far and those expected to be spent in developing the system. [**Author's note:** We include in the ratio the notion of "dollars spent so far" because, by the time one is in a position to compute Bang, one has produced a specification model, which is very costly, almost impossible to do well, and is at least halfway through the development of the system using the Waterfall.]

Call graph metric

This is a measure of the complexity of the intermodule relationships that exist in a modular, hierarchical program. There are two measure here: (1) the average number of modules per level and (2) the average number of calls to other modules per module. We find that *call graphs*, otherwise known as *call trees*, are the most frequently used complexity measure of engineering programs.

There are two important issues here. First, modules should communicate only with those modules immediately above them, which are the *calling routines*, or those modules below them, which are the *called routines*. If a module at the top of the tree calls a module at the bottom of the tree, something is usually wrong with the decomposition.

Second (and this is another curious idea), in a well modularized program, the number of modules in any level will be about *seven* times the number of modules in the previous level.

We believe that the goodness of the number *seven*, used in the *cyclomatic* and *call graph* measures, has to do with short-term memory in human beings and the idea that we can hold only about seven things in there without greatly increasing the difficulty of remembering them. If there are more than seven, then the program or module appears more complex to us.

COBOL

The acronym for *COmmon Business Oriented Language*, which is a programming language commonly used for business applications.

Code aggregates

Functional chunks of program code that make for convenient reuse and measuring.

Complexity measures

These metrics have to do with complexity of software perceived by a human being trying to write, read, or change it. One assumes that machines aren't affected by complexity, yet. The types we run across most frequently are the cyclomatic measure and the call tree graph; however one may infer complexity from Halstead's Program purity.

Computing science

"Concerned with the interplay between mechanized and human symbol manipulation usually referred to as computing and programming respectively." Definition by Edsger Dijkstra in On the Cruelty of Really Teaching Computer Science," Communications of the ACM, December 1989, Vol. 32, No. 12, pp.1398-1414.

Correctness

The extent to which a program satisfies its specifications (which is called verification) and fulfills the user's mission objectives (which is called validation). "Did we build the system right? Did we build the right system?" One of the characteristics of good software.

Critical path chart

A chart that defines the shortest path through a network of tasks in the time domain.

Crock pot effect

When formerly fashionable kitchen appliances, such as the crock pot, are pushed further and further back on the counter top until they eventually become merely storage spaces for food or truly useful tools.

Customer satisfaction

The degree of acceptance of our product or service by our customer. Satisfaction is measured in money, especially in repeat sales and sales resulting from referrals and testimonials.

Cycle time

The time it takes a process to cycle once through some process.

Cyclomatic Measure

Named by Tom McCabe who invented it, the Cyclomatic Measure is a measure of the number of paths through a module caused by exercising each decision point: the more paths, the more complex the module. A figure of *seven* here is about as complex as one can easily handle. See Figures G-1 and G-2. They both show complex code, but which code would you rather maintain?

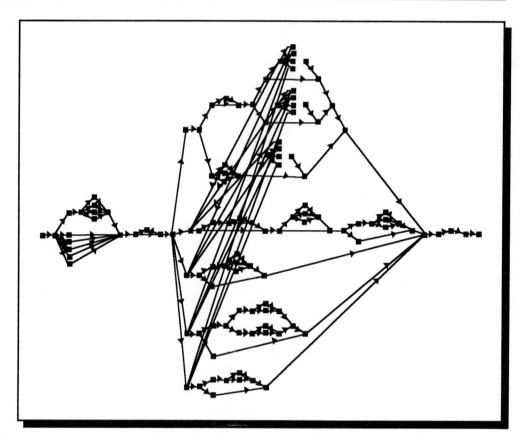

*Figure G-1. Extremely Complex Graph with a Measure Exceeding 50 Lines of Code
(Taken from Verilog's literature on Logiscope)*

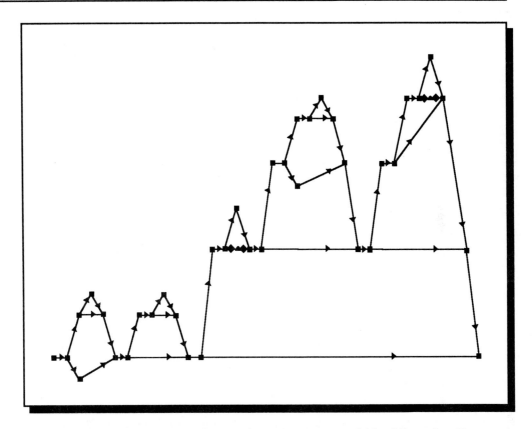

Figure G-2. A Graph with a Cyclomatic Measure of 12 of Complex, Yet Understandable Code (Taken from Verilog's literature on Logiscope)

Defects	Imperfections in software that decrease customer satisfaction. These could be caused by an imperfect expression of requirements or by an imperfect set of requirements.
Defects per cycle time	A measure of customer satisfaction, it measures the *badness* of the software after it is released. It also measures the defects that are passed from one process to another and from various suppliers to their customers in the software development and maintenance life cycles.

Deliverables	The products of a project that are usually defined before the project starts. They are composed of plans, schedules, other Gantt charts and, sometimes, even the actual product itself. They are frequently called *intermediary products*. Sometimes they are wampum,* virtually hanging from project managers' belts.
Dichotomy	A division into two usually contradictory parts or opinions; schism. A lack of agreement or correspondence; discrepancy. [The Tormont Webster's Illustrated Encyclopedic Dictionary.]
DRM	The acronym for *data resource management.*
Efficiency	The amount of computing resources and code required by a program to perform a function. There are several types of efficiencies: execution, storage, and data. These all have to do with conserving the machine's resources of time and space. One of the characteristics of good software.
Flexibility	The effort required to modify an operational program. One of the characteristics of good software.
FORTRAN	The acronym for *FOrmula TRANslation*, which is a programming language commonly used for engineering and scientific applications.
Function points	Function points are a size metric invented by Allen Albrecht at IBM in the early seventies. He perceived that, properly weighted, the inputs to an application, the outputs from the application, inquiries by users, the data files to be updated, and interfaces to other applications should represent the common concerns of the users and, therefore, the functionality of the application. Function points are based on the assumption that there is a simple mapping of each input to one or very few internal processes and to an output.

---

* They act as *wampum* when people *think* something has intrinsic value when, in fact, it does not. Wampum only has value if someone is willing to accept it in trade.

Gantt chart	A chart that displays the progress of a set of tasks, especially those of a work breakdown. The tasks are listed on the left-hand side of the chart and time progresses toward the right. When the steps of a task are completed, they are entered on the chart. (See also the definitions for *milestones* and *deliverables*.)
GIBIS	Acronym for *Group Issue-Based Information System*, a groupware product from the Microelectronics and Computer Consortium in Austin, Texas. GIBIS is a hypermedia, networked, database information system that allows discussions over an extended period and various locations.

Halstead's Software Science Measures

In contrast to the Bang Metric, which measures data going into and coming out of a module, Halstead's measure measures the process inside a module. Halstead uses the number of distinct operators and operands, *n1* and *n2*, and the total number of occurrences of each, *N1* and *N2*, to construct his metrics. He combines these in several ways to measure various aspects of the code:

Vocabulary, $n = n1 + n2$

Program (module) length, $N = N1 + N2$

Program Size, $n_i = n1 \log_2 n1 + n2 \log_2 n2$

Program Volume, $V = N \log_2 n$

Halstead goes on to use n1, n2, N1, N2 to construct measures for what he calls the *implementation level, difficulty, intelligent content* (by which he means the *information content*), *mental effort, estimated number of errors, programming time, program purity*, and *language level* using various elements already calculated [Halstead 1977]. We haven't found these metrics used much, although there are software tools that measure them. Logiscope, for instance, gives many of his measure.

463

Hand tools	Tools that are held in the hand and powered by the person using them.
IEEE	Acronym for *Institute of Electrical and Electronics Engineers.* An industry standards organization.
"Ilities"	Characteristics of good software, which we refer to as *ilities* because so many of them end in *ility*; for example, reliability, usability, etc.
Inch-pebbles	Small steps on Gantt charts.
Integrity	The extent to which access to software or data by unauthorized people can be controlled, and to which the software is protected from viruses. The former is very important in banking and DoD stuff; the latter in networks, especially PC networks such as bulletin boards and commercial network services. One of the characteristics of good software.
Interoperability	The effort required to couple one system with another. This may occur at many levels, but it is usually accomplished through intermediate files. One of the characteristics of good software.
ISO	Acronym for *International Standards Organization.* An industry standards group.
Level of effort	An activity, such as software maintenance or incremental software development, that is funded in such a way that the time is fixed (for example, one year of resources), but the goals are variable (although frequently known in advance). Progress often occurs serendipitously and opportunistically.
LOC	The acronym for *lines of code.*
Machine tools	Non-portable, stationary power tools.

Milestones	Small triangles entered on Gantt charts to show when a step of a task has been completed. Sometimes folks call small steps inch-pebbles.
Modularity	The characteristic of good software where code that performs a single function in a program is enclosed in a program unit such as a subroutine, function, or paragraph. In FORTRAN, a module is usually a subroutine that can communicate with other subroutines through global data or arguments passed to it by the calling routine when the called routine was invoked. For COBOL, modules are usually paragraphs that can communicate with all the other paragraphs of the program through the global data in the Data Division.
Modules	A good approximation of the intention of function points in engineering programs is the number of modules or subroutines in the program. The reason why modules work is that each module tends to add an increment of information to the solution; perhaps not as directly as in business software, but increments of the solution nevertheless.
	If the software is made up of loosely coupled, functionally cohesive modules, so much the better. But, if not, then some coefficient ought to be applied to account for the unnecessary complexity that occurs as a result of tightly coupled modules that aren't cohesive.
	Module counts are also very useful in environments where code reuse is being measured because such code is mostly offered as modules or code fragments that can be treated as modules.
	And, module counts are useful in maintenance where you want to locate those naughty modules where (the folklore tells us) 80% of the maintenance effort is made.
Portability	The effort required to transfer a program from one hardware configuration or software system environment to another. One of the characteristics of good software.

465

Power tools	Hand tools that have an additional source of power, such as an electric motor or compressed air. Also called power-driven hand tools or portable power tools.
Product size	The measure of our product or service by determining the space the product occupies, or dimensions or magnitude of the product or service. Product size measure include the code aggregates, such as modules count, various lines of code measures, and, of course, some of Halstead's measures.
Program	1. A large objective designed to meet some socially desirable goal. Programs are usually created by bureaucrats to implement some political mandate. 2. A series of instructions executed by a computer.
Program Evaluation and Review Techniques (PERT) Chart	A technique for creating a project plan that rates legs of a task network according to expectations, usually optimistic, realistic, or pessimistic.
Project	A specifically defined task, usually within the larger context of a *program* (definition 1). It is set up to reach a single main objective, whether the objective is a product, a place, or an advance in technology. The goal is fixed. Time varies around it. The effort to create a computer program is frequently called a *project*.
Proletarians	Common people.
Rat-killing	The effort required to locate and fix an error in an operational program. One of the characteristics of good software.
Re-engineering	Re-engineering evolved from restructuring. It means decomposing large routines, and removing patches and dead code. It includes: identifying the essential data structures; reporting where each COMMON block occurs, checking that each block has the same structure in every routine in which it appears, and checking where elements of each block are used and set; identifying redundant code, adding improved layout features, reducing the complexity of the

code, and creating a call tree and context diagrams; reformatting the code to make it more readable.

Reliability	The extent to which a program can be expected to perform its intended function with the precision the user requires and when the user needs it. One of the characteristics of good software.
Restructuring	Reorganizing the procedural logic of a computer program so that it conforms to the rules of structured programming.
Reusability	The extent to which a program can be used in other applications. This also includes parts of programs such as, say, a set of nifty character string manipulation routines in FORTRAN and a set of all the date routines you could ever want in COBOL. One of the characteristics of good software.
Reverse engineering	The process of producing the intermediate products of forward engineering. Reverse engineering contains restructuring and re-engineering, but attempts to go further. It hopes to recover the functional specifications or even the user requirements from the code.
Self-descriptiveness	The quality of software to reveal its makeup easily to anyone who reads it. There are two types of self-descriptiveness: the effectiveness and quantity of comments, and the self-descriptiveness of the implementation language.
Smile metric	A wicked cousin of customer satisfaction, the smile metric purports to measure customer satisfaction by interviewing customers and getting testimonials from them that are favorable to our product or service. There are many ways to produce smiles, but only a few ways of producing good software.
Software engineering	"A term coined in 1967 by the Study Group on Computer Science of the NATO Science Committee to imply the need for software manufacture based on the types of theoretical

foundations and practical disciplines traditional in established branches of engineering. Software engineering is concerned with the development and implementation of large-scale software systems on production-model computers. Encompasses a broad range of topics related to the controlled design and development of high-quality computer software, including programming methodology (structured programming, ego-less programming, software quality assurance, programming productivity aids) and management of software projects (structured walkthroughs, chief programmer teams, program support library, HIPO Technique)." [Webster's New World Dictionary of Computer Terms 1988.]

STRUCTURED STUFF   Structured stuff elevated to a level of importance requiring capitalization and reverential tones.

Structured Stuff   Structured analysis, design, and programming together with the Waterfall model.

Testability   The effort required to test a program to ensure it performs its intended function; the more effort the better. One of the characteristics of good software.

Time metrics   Depending on how you are organized, time is a fixed or variable amount. As a fixed amount, it is usually measured in fiscal years. When it is variable, it measures the length of important events in the life of software. Shorter events such as the following, are measured in familiar time units regardless of organization:

Time to Make (TTM)—The time required to make something; in this case, to develop and test software.

Mean Time Between Failure (MTBF)—"A measure of the reliability of a computer system equal to the average operating time between failures as calculated on a statistical basis from known failure rates of various components of the system." [McGraw-Hill Dictionary of Scientific and Technical Terms 1989, p.1163]

Time to Repair (TTR)—A maintenance function, TTR is the time required to find and fix bugs in software.

Time to Port (TTP)—Another maintenance function, TTP is the time required to move software to a new platform and test it there. When one is estimating TTP, it is one of the most surprising metrics around. It is almost always being seriously underestimated or overestimated.

Time to Change (TTC)—Yet another maintenance function, TTC is the time required to make changes and enhancements in software after it is in production or after it has been released. Some folks want to make the process of enhancing software part of the original project or, subsequently, into new projects created for the purpose of making changes. Because of overhead expenses, making projects out of enhancements increases the total cost of the software.

Tool
A tool is an implement or device used directly upon a piece of material to shape it into a desired form [Encyclopædia Britannica, Macropædia, Knowledge in Depth, Vol. 28, p.712, Tools].

Usability
The effort required to learn, operate, prepare the input to, and interpret the output of a program; the less effort, the better. One of the characteristics of good software.

Various measures of lines of code
The various measures of lines of code are some of the simplest and cheapest size measures. These come in several flavors:

LOC	lines of code
KLOC	thousands of lines of code
SLOC	source lines of code
DeSLOC	delivered SLOC

ELOC	executable lines of code
KELOC	thousands of executable lines of code

and, our choice,

ALOC	all lines of code, including JCL, commentary, test data, and even users' guides.

Bibliography

American Programmer, Vol. 2, No. 4. New York, New York: American Programmer, Inc., Children's Computer Company, Ltd., April 1989.

Appleton, D.S. "Very Large Projects." *Datamation,* Vol. 32, No. 2. Cahners Publishing Company, January 1986.

Beer, Eisenstat, and Spector. "Why Change Programs Don't Produce Change." *Harvard Business Review*, November-December 1990.

Blakeslee, T.R. *The Right Brain.* Garden City, New York: Anchor Press/Doubleday, 1980.

Blakeslee, T.R. *The Right Brain.* New York: Anchor Press/Doubleday, 1980.

Boehm, B. *Software Engineering Economics.* Englewood Cliffs, New Jersey: Prentice-Hall, Inc., 1981.

Bork, Judge Robert. Bellevue, Washington, October 1992.

Brooks, Frederick P. *The Mythical Man Month, Essays on Software Engineering.* Reading, Massachusetts: Addison-Wesley Publishing Company, 1982.

Calvin, W.H., Ph.D and G.A. Ojemann, M.D. *Inside the Brain.* New York: Mentor Books, from the New American Library, 1980.

Card, D.N., McGarry, F.E., and Page G.T. "Evaluating Software Engineering Technologies." *IEEE Transactions on Software Engineering,* Vol. SE-13, No. 7, July 1987.

"CASE Symposium for Aerospace, Defense and Engineering Proceedings." Andover, Massachusetts: Digital Consulting, Inc., 1988.

Coad, Peter and Edward Yourdon. *Object-Oriented Analysis.* Englewood Cliffs, New Jersey: Yourdon Press, 1991.

Compton's Encyclopedia, Online Edition, © 1991. Britannica Software, Inc., downloaded from America Online, July, 1991.

Conklin, J. and M. Bergman. "gIBIS[sic]: A Tool For All Reasons." *MCC Technical Report,* Number STP-252-88. Austin, Texas: Microelectronics and Computer Technology Corporation, 1988.

Corbeil, Jean-Claude. *Visual Dictionary.* New York, Oxford: Facts On File Publications, 1986.

Côté, V., P. Bourque, S. Oligny, and N. Rivard. "Software Metrics: An Overview of Recent Results." *The Journal of Systems and Software,* 8. Elsevier Science Publishing Co., Inc., 1988.

Cox, Brad J. *Object Oriented Programming, An Evolutionary Approach.* Reading, Massachusetts: Addison-Wesley Publishing Company, 1987.

Deaton, M. "Improving Software Documentation Accuracy with Writer and Editor Partnerships." Redmond, Washington: Microsoft Corporation (© 1990 IEEE, CH2888-6/90/0000-0013).

DeGrace, P.G. and L.H. Stahl. *Wicked Problems, Righteous Solutions: A Catalogue of Modern Software Engineering Paradigms.* Englewood Cliffs, New Jersey: Prentice-Hall, Inc., 1990.

DeMarco, Tom. *Controlling Software Projects, Measurement and Estimation.* New York, New York: Yourdon Press, 1982.

Dieli, M. "Usability Evaluation: Involving Writers in the Problem Definition Process." Redmond, Washington: Microsoft Corporation (© 1989 IEEE, 89CH2786-2/89-85229).

Dijkstra, E. "On the Cruelty of Really Teaching Computer Science." *Communications of the ACM,* Volume 32, Number 12, December 1989.

Durant, W. *The Story of Civilization: Cæsar and Christ.* New York, New York: Simon & Schuster, 1966.

Edey, M.A. *The Missing Link.* New York, New York: Time-Life Books, 1972.

Encyclopædia Britannica. Chicago, Illinois: Encyclopædia Britannica, Inc., 1986.

Entsminger, Gary. *The Tao of Objects, A Beginner's Guide to Object-Oriented Programming.* Redwood City, California: M&T Books, 1990.

Feinstein, Debra. "My Life as a Document." Reprinted from *Benchmark,* a quarterly magazine for Xerox customers, Spring 1988.

Feinstein, Debra. "The Secret Life of Organizations." *Benchmark,* a quarterly magazine for Xerox customers, Winter 1989.

Feynman, Richard P. *What Do You Care What Other People Think?* New York, New York: W.W. Norton Company, Inc., 1988.

Frederick, P., Jr. *The Mythical Man-Month.* Reading, Massachusetts: Addison-Wesley Publishing Company, 1982.

"Function Point Analysis." East Amherst, New York: Productivity Management Group.

Grady, R.B. *Practical Software Metrics for Project Management and Process Improvement.* Englewood Cliffs, New Jersey: Prentice-Hall, Inc., 1992.

Grady, R.B., and D.L. Caswell. *Software Metrics: Establishing a Company-Wide Program.* Englewood Cliffs, New Jersey: Prentice-Hall, Inc., 1987.

Grindley, K. "Cutting Through the CASE Hype." A joint report by Price Waterhouse and Datamation, *Datamation,* April 1, 1989.

Grolier's Academic American Encyclopedia, Online Edition, © 1992. Grolier Electronic Publishing, downloaded from CompuServe, July, 1991.

Guindon, Raymonde. "The Process of Knowledge Discovery in Systems Design." *MCC Technical Report Number STP-166-89,* Microelectronic and Computer Technology Corporation, April 13, 1989.

Halstead, Maurice H. *Elements of Software Science.* New York, New York: The Computer Science Library, 1977.

Humphrey, Watts S. "CASE Planning and the Software Process." Technical Report CMU/SEI-89-TR-26, ESD-TR-89-34. Pittsburgh, Pennsylvania: Software Engineering Institute, Carnegie Mellon University, May 1989.

Humphrey, Watts S. "Characterizing the Software Process: A Maturity Framework." Technical Report CMU/SEI-87-TR-11, ESD-TR-87-112. Pittsburgh, Pennsylvania: Software Engineering Institute, Carnegie Mellon University, June 1987.

Jones, T.C. *System Development*, 1989.

Kidder, Tracey. *The Soul of a New Machine*. Avon Books, 1982.

Knuth, D. *The Art of Computer Programming*. 3 vols. Second Edition. Reading, Massachusetts: Addison-Wesley Publishing Company, 1973.

Knuth, D. *The Art of Computer Programming*. Second Edition. Vols. 1, 2, and 3. Reading, Massachusetts: Addison-Wesley Publishing Company, 1973.

Lammers, S. *Programmers at Work*. Microsoft Press, 1986.

Ledgard, H. and M. Marcotty, *The Programming Language Landscape*. Chicago, Palo Alto, Toronto, Henley-on-Thames, Sydney: Science Research Associates, Inc., 1981.

Manley, Dr. John. "Large-Scale Systems: DoD, NASA, and Industry." *Computer-Aided Software Engineering Symposium for Aerospace, Defense, and Engineering, Proceedings*, Andover, Massachusetts: Digital Consulting Incorporated, Summer 1988.

Martin, J. and C. McClure. *Diagramming Techniques for Analysts and Programmers*. Englewood Cliffs, New Jersey: Prentice-Hall, Inc., 1985.

Martin, J. *Application Development Without Programmers*. Englewood Cliffs, New Jersey: Prentice-Hall, Inc., 1982.

Martin, J. "James Martin Productivity Series." *Computer-Aided Software Engineering (CASE)*. Volume 6. Marblehead, Massachusetts: James Martin Report, Inc.

Masaaki Imai. *Kaizen, The Key to Japan's Competitive Success*. New York, New York: Random House Business Division, 1986.

McCall, J.A. and M.T. Matsumoto. "Software Quality Metrics—Enhancements—Final Report." U.S. Air Force Systems Command, Rome Air Development Center, Griffiss Air Force Base, Rome, New York, 1979.

McGraw-Hill Dictionary of Scientific and Technical Terms. Fourth Edition. Sybil B. Parker, Editor in Chief. New York, New York: McGraw-Hill Book Company, 1989.

Mensa Bulletin, July/August 1991.

Merlyn, V. *The CASE Experience.* CASE Tutorial, Bellevue, Washington: CASE Research Corporation, 1989.

Norman, D.A. *The Psychology of Everyday Things,* 1988.

Ozick, D.N. "How to Make Program Printouts Easier to Read." Unpublished paper (© 1990).

Palmer, J. "Playing with Stella." *American Programmer,* Vol. 3, No. 9, September 1990.

Parikh, G. and N. Zvegintzov. *Tutorial on Software Maintenance.* Los Angeles, California: IEEE Computer Society, 1983.

Pearson, Andrall E. "Corporate Redemption and the Seven Deadly Sins." *Harvard Business Review,* May-June 1992.

Phister, N.M., Jr. *Data Processing Technology and Economics.* Bedford, Massachusetts: Digital Press, Digital Equipment Corporation, 1979.

Posner, G.P. "Nation's Mathematicians Guilty of Innumeracy." *Skeptical Inquirer,* Vol. 15, No. 4, Summer 1991.

"Production Oriented Management Stifles Innovation." *EDN Magazine,* February 3, 1992.

Reader's Digest History of Man: The Last Two Million Years. Pleasantville, New York: Reader's Digest Association, Inc., 1973.

Ready, M. "Fog—and How to Fight It." *Excellence Etc!,* the Monthly Evergreen Training Center Magazine, Vol. 1, Issue 6, Holiday Edition (1991). Marana, Arizona: Evergreen Air Center.

Rickert, N.W. "The Parable of Two Programmers." Department of Mathematics, Statistics, and Computer Science, University of Chicago at Illinois, from *ACM SIGSOFT Software Engineering Notes*, Vol. 10, No. 1, January 1985.

Rose, M. *The Open Book, A Practical Perspective on OSI.* Englewood Cliffs, New Jersey: Prentice-Hall, Inc., 1990.

Schaffer, R.H. and H.A. Thomsom. "Successful Change Programs Begin with Results." *Harvard Business Review*, January-February 1992.

Schneiderman, B. "Control Flow and Data Structure Documentation: Two Experiments." *Communications of the ACM*, Volume 25, No. 1, January 1982.

Sharon, D. and M. Morron. "CASE '92 Standards Coordination Workshop," Minutes from July 6, 1992 meeting.

Shere, K. *Software Engineering Management.* Englewood Cliffs, New Jersey: Prentice-Hall, 1988.

Shrock, G.L. "Summer Computer Simulation Conference Proceedings," Vol. 1. San Diego, California: Cubic Corp., 1983.

Slivinski, J. "Paradigm Revisited: The Documentation Odyssey of Microsoft Excel." Redmond, Washington: Microsoft Corporation (© 1988 IEEE, 88CH2646-8/88/0000-0015).

Smith, D. and J. Dietrich. "An Overview of Neural Networks." *Engineering and Science*, California Institute of Technology , Summer 1990.

Stahl, D.M. "Simplified English." *DynAir Flight Line,* Vol. III, Issue 4, July 1992.

"System Engineering Management Guide." 1986. Washington, D.C.: Government Printing Office, Stock No. 008-020-01099-5.

Taylor, David A., Ph.D. *Object-Oriented Technology: A Manager's Guide.* Reading, Massachusetts: Addison-Wesley Publishing Company, 1990.

Tsichritzis, D.C. and O.M. Nierstrasz. "Fitting Round Objects Into Square Databases." *ECOOP '88, European Conference on Object-Oriented Programming.* Oslo, Norway: Springer-Verlag, August 1988. Berlin, Heidelberg, New York, London, Paris, Tokyo.

Vick, C.R. and C.V. Ramamoorthy. *Handbook of Software Engineering.* Van Nostrand Reinhold Electrical/Computer Science and Engineering Series. New York: Van Nostrand Reinhold Company, 1986.

Webster's New World Dictionary of Computer Terms. Third Edition. New York, New York: Simon & Schuster, Inc., 1988. Distributed by Prentice-Hall Trade.

Webster's New World Dictionary of the American Language. Second College Edition, David B. Guralnik, Editor-in-Chief. Cleveland, Ohio: William Collins Publishers, Inc., 1979.

Weiner, Philip P., Editor-in-Chief. *Dictionary of the History of Ideas.* Vol. IV. New York, New York: Charles Scribners Sons.

Wexelblat, R.L., ed. "History of Programming Languages." The Backus article. New York, New York: Academic Press, 1978.

Wirfs-Brock, Rebecca, et al. *Designing Object-Oriented Software.* Englewood Cliffs, New Jersey: Prentice-Hall, Inc., 1990.

Zvegintzov, N. "Software Maintenance Technology Reference Guide." *Software Maintenance News, Inc.,* Los Altos, California.

Index

References are to page numbers. Pages numbers shown in **_bold italics_** indicate illustrations. The titles of illustrations, articles, and books are shown in _italics_. Illustrations are listed under the heading "Illustrations," alphabetically arranged by abbreviated titles. Please refer to the Contents for a complete listing of all illustrations, and to the Bibliography for a complete, descriptive listing of the works of all indexed authors.

E

J

K

"Keep 'em running and change 'em" (one of three basic requirements for software) 69, 71–72, 74
KELOC (thousands of executable lines of code) 306
Kidder 1982 355
KLOC (thousands of lines of code) 306
Knuth, D.
   The Art of Computer Programming (1973) 173, 185

L

Lammers, S.
   Programmers at Work (1986) 150
Language 167
   COBOL vs. FORTRAN 284–286
Language processors 30
   and their relation to CASE 27
Language skills 166
Language standards 338
Language-sensitive language editors 359
Leakey, L.S.B. 2
Leakey, Mary 2
Learning process 197, *199*
Ledgard H. and M. Marcotty
   The Programming Language Landscape (1981) 272, 276
Left-brain specialization 167
Level of effort, defined 464
Levels of abstraction *164*
Levels of effort 312, 321–322, 348
   for Greeks 323
   for Romans 323
   organizations 322
Levels of the software process 345–346
   Defined Process 345, 351
   Initial Process 345, 350
   Managed Process 346, 351
   Optimized Process 346
   Repeatable Process 345, 351
Liebniz's Dream 160
Lines of code (LOC), various measures 469
      See also LOC.
Lines of code as a metric 305

P

The Olduvai Imperative

Tsichritzis, D.C and O.M. Nierstrasz
   Fitting Round Objects Into Square Databases (1988)   191
Turf issues, defined   41
Twelve-ball problem   171, 176–178
Typefaces in documentation   252–253
Types of development   280–282
Types of operations   270–273

U

Upper CASE tools   30
Usability   93–95, 358
   communicativeness   94
      of user input interfaces   94
      of user output interfaces   94, 95
   defined   469
   one of the 11 "ilities" of good software   75
   one of the qualities of good documentation   232
   operability   95
   training   93
Usability of documentation   251
User involvement   361
User requirements   230
User's documents characteristics of good ones   238
User's guides   230

V

VAF, computing   309
Validation   80, 127
Verbose terms   235
Verification   80, 127
Verification stage of creative process   181
Vestigial code   72
Vick, C.R. and C.V. Ramamoorthy
   Handbook of Software Engineering (1986)   193
Violin makers   262
Visualization   167, 181
vos Savant, Marilyn   178

W

Waterfall model   35, 42
    and its relation to CASE   31
    Initiation phase   39
    problems inherent in   211
Weinberg-Schulman experiment   311
Wet code   182, 184
Wexelblat, R.L., ed.
    History of Programming Languages (1978)   274
White space, in documentation   252
Wicked problems   152, 205
Windowing standards   338
Wirfs-Brock, R. et al.
    Designing Object-Oriented Software (1990)   192
Wordiness   235
Work Breakdown Structures (WBSs)   47
Workers' skill emphasis   297–301
Writing, different types   255
Written language   167

Z

Zinjanthropus   2
Zvegintzov, N.
    Software Maintenance Technology Reference Guide   30